Down in the Holler

A Gallery of OZARK Folk Speech

Vance Randolph & George P. Wilson

University of Oklahoma Press : Norman and London

ISBN: 0–8061–1535–1

Copyright © 1953 by the University of Oklahoma Press, Norman, Publishing Division of the University. All rights reserved. Manufactured in the U.S.A. First edition, 1953; second printing, 1979; third printing, 1986.

4   5   6   7   8   9   10   11   12   13   14   15   16   17   18   19   20   21

To H. L. Mencken

Preface

THE PRESENT WORK began with a series of fifteen articles which I contributed to *Dialect Notes* and *American Speech* during the period of 1926–36. Several papers, as indicated in the bibliography, were written with the help of Miss Anna A. Ingleman, Miss Patti Sankee, and Miss Nancy Clemens. Some of the same material was printed in my book *The Ozarks,* published by the Vanguard Press in 1931. Since 1936 I have made many radical changes, corrected many errors of my own, and added a lot of hitherto unpublished data. I have rewritten the whole thing and divided it more or less arbitrarily into chapters. The chapter headings should not be taken too seriously, and they are not mutually exclusive. Except for some historical references in Chapter IV, I have tried to confine myself to a descriptive study of the Ozark speech. My purpose is to write down what I have heard the Ozark hillman say, how he said it, and what he meant by it.

Many persons have helped in the collection of material, but it is impossible to mention them all. A special word of appreciation is due Mrs. Isabel France, Mountainburg, Ark.; Mr. Lewis Kelley, Cyclone, Mo.; Mrs. Mary Elizabeth Mahnkey, Kirbyville, Mo.; Mrs. May Kennedy McCord, Springfield, Mo.; Mrs. Mabel E. Mueller, Rolla, Mo.; Miss Rose O'Neill, Day, Mo.; Mrs. Mary Wardlaw Randolph, Pineville, Mo.; Mr. Clyde Sharp, Pack, Mo.; Mrs. Lillian Short, Galena, Mo.; Mr. Fred Starr, Greenland, Ark.; Mrs. Olga Trail, Farmington, Ark.; Mr. John Turner White, Jefferson City, Mo., and Mr. Charles Morrow Wilson, Fayetteville, Ark.

George Lyman Kittredge, Harvard University, read parts of the manuscript and offered valuable suggestions. So did Louise Pound, University of Nebraska, and Robert L. Morris, University of Arkansas. I am grateful to E. H. Criswell, University of Tulsa, for assistance with some pronunciations in Chapter IX. Mary Celestia Parler, University of Arkansas, went through the entire manuscript and eliminated many errors and obscurities, especially in Chapters II and III. Without Miss Parler's encouragement the book would not have been written. For help in identifying animals and plants, the vernacular names of which appear in Chapters V, VII, and IX, I owe thanks to I. T. Bode, director of the Missouri Conservation Commission; Joe Hogan, supervisor of the Arkansas Game and Fish Commission; W. E. Maneval, University of Missouri; William H. Elder, University of Missouri; and Dwight M. Moore, University of Arkansas. I wish to acknowledge my indebtedness to these people, but I have not always followed their advice. They are not, of course, responsible for any inaccuracies that may remain in the text.

My collaborator, George P. Wilson, editor of the *Publication of the American Dialect Society,* has done a vast amount of editing and annotating, and provided many illustrative quotations. The book is the product of two authors, Professor Wilson and me. But since I did the collecting over a period of many years, without any foreknowledge of this collaboration, the material is inextricably entangled with personal reminiscence and anecdote. We have decided, therefore, to retain the first person singular pronoun throughout.

VANCE RANDOLPH

Eureka Springs, Arkansas

Contents

Down in the Holler

A Gallery of Ozark Folk Speech

1 Introduction

A GREAT DEAL has been written about the people who live in the Ozark Mountains of southern Missouri, northern Arkansas, and eastern Oklahoma. These backwoodsmen were, until recently, the most deliberately unprogressive white people in the United States. The descendants of pioneers from the Southern Appalachians, their way of life changed very little during the whole span of the nineteenth century. They lived in a lost world, where primitive customs and usages persisted right down into the age of industrial civilization.

Within my own memory there were unregimented families in the Ozarks who lived by hunting and fishing, raising a few mast-fed hogs, growing a little corn, and distilling moonshine whiskey. There were hill-folk who denned in log cabins with dirt floors and no windows; men who slept on cord beds and killed deer with muzzle-loading rifles; women who used spinning wheels and wove cloth on homemade looms; minstrels who sang English ballads brought over by the seventeenth-century colonists; old settlers who believed in witchcraft and all sorts of medieval superstitions; storytellers who could neither read nor write, but who spoke the most interesting English in America.

I first visited the Ozark country in 1899 and have been more or less identified with the region ever since. For many years I spent my holidays and vacations in the Ozarks. Since 1920 I have lived here practically all the time, sometimes in the villages and sometimes in the wildest and most isolated hollers. Avoiding the prosperous people of the Ozark towns, I tried to become intimately acquainted with the old-time hillfolk. I learned to chew tobacco, and became a deputy sheriff, and gathered local items for the newspapers. By marriage and otherwise I associated myself with several old backwoods families. I traveled about on horseback, in a covered wagon, in a rattletrap Ford. I consorted with hunters and moonshiners and berry-pickers and yarb-doctors and patch farmers. These people were the best talkers I have ever known. Their speech was musical and soothing, full of strange, meaningful words and phrases. It was very different from anything I had heard in Kansas, where I was born, or in Massachusetts, where I went to school.

The people in these hills, as Raymond Weeks points out, "have inherited a feeling for superior English. They know that it is more expressive to say *I done it* and *I ain't said nothin'* than to say flabbily and ineffectually *I did it* and *I haven't said anything.*"[1] The backwoods humorist has a great store of ancient sayings that seem always fresh and appropriate. Even though hundreds of his turns of speech are inherited, the hillman employs them with a fitness that lends the appearance of originality. He has a feeling for the vivid phrase, whether in the form of an old proverb or a spontaneous creation.

"Even the stranger within our gates," said President Walter Williams of the University of Missouri, "when he hears the Missouri dialect as it was before the old-maid dictionary-makers robbed it of much of its distinctive charm, marvels at its surpassing beauty. He may not be able at first to understand it, any more than he understands classical music, but he will rave over its delightsomeness."[2]

The solid citizens of the Ozark towns scoffed at President Williams' admission that the local speech might be difficult for outsiders to understand. These fellows feel, of course, that they speak the standard American English, and that it is the "furriners" who are afflicted with brogues and dialects. But anybody who is familiar with the American language as it is used elsewhere can see that President Williams told the truth. How many Yankees would know that *durgen* means uncouth, or that *grub hyson* is sassafras tea, or that *woodscolt* is the polite name for an illegitimate child, or that *ramp* means garlic? Ask a tourist from Chicago to define such nouns as *mommix, blue-john, jillikens, cooter,* and *whickerbill.* How many would recognize *grandmaw* as a verb meaning to steal timber? Few city people know that an Ozark *scorpion* is a harmless lizard, or that *tomfuller* means hominy. How many are familiar with the adjective *reverend* in the sense of undiluted, particularly as applied to whiskey?[3]

The stranger's inability to understand the Ozark speech has furnished

---

[1] *The Hound-Tuner of Callaway* (New York, 1927), 208.

[2] *Missouri Magazine,* December, 1928, p. 7.

[3] *American Speech,* Vol. V (1929), 19–20. Cf. Nancy Clemens, Kansas City *Star,* August 21, 1938.

the material for many hillbilly stories. Some of those credited to Opie Read and Governor Jeff Davis of Arkansas and Senator Champ Clark of Missouri have never been committed to print, but they will not soon be forgotten. And the ridge-runners around Springfield, Missouri, will long remember Ray Garris, who came down from Milwaukee to investigate "this *ary* and *nary* business" in 1934. The fact that Mr. Garris bought a few drinks for his informants rated a two-column headline in the local paper: "MR. GARRIS SPENDS $194 TO HEAR OZARKS DIALECT."[4]

It is true that the dialect of today is a weak, watered thing as compared with that of thirty years ago. The saltiest of the old-timers are dead now, and no man will hear again the rich folk-speech which so impressed me in my youth. But the Ozark dialect is far from extinct, even in these degenerate days.[5] One finds splendid scraps and tatters of it everywhere, even among educated hillfolk. Sleek young men at our whistle-stop colleges, proud possessors of dinner jackets and fraternity pins, still use words and phrases unintelligible to the ordinary American from beyond the hilltops.[6] It was one of these second-growth hillbillies who announced some years ago that there is no Ozark dialect, the whole thing being "made up" by novelists from the city.[7] "What does the man mean?" demanded Rose Wilder Lane, of Mansfield, Missouri. "It is as astounding as though he had said there are no Ozark hills. Has he never *heard* the Ozark speech? Or has he never heard any other? Of course there is an Ozark dialect; one of the richest, most picturesque, most interesting that exists in the United States."[8]

Many city people believe that the Ozark dialect was invented by hillbilly comedians such as Will Rogers, Bob Burns, the Weaver Brothers, and the radio comics known as Lum and Abner. Charles H. Driscoll, a New York columnist who had visited the hill country, once assured his readers that Will Rogers' dialect was "almost pure Ozark," adding that in Arkansas and Oklahoma "many thousands of people speak that way all the time and *think nothing of it!*"[9] I clipped this out of Driscoll's column and showed it to a college professor in Massachusetts. The professor said that a newspaperman couldn't be expected to know much about linguistics, and that

[4] Springfield, Mo., *Leader & Press*, February 2, 1934.
[5] Cf. Stanley Vestal, *Saturday Review of Literature*, December 26, 1931.
[6] Cf. Virginia Carter, "University of Missouri Slang," *American Speech*, Vol. VI (1931), 203–206.
[7] Quoted by Charles Phelps Cushing, New York *Evening World*, May 28, 1928.
[8] Springfield, Mo., *Leader*, June 7, 1928.
[9] Syndicated column, November 7, 1943.

5

Rogers' speech was "a theatrical convention comparable to that of the blackface minstrels, not intended to represent any actual dialect." I heard Will Rogers many times. My neighbors heard him too, and they noticed nothing strange about his speech. We thought he talked pretty much like the rest of us.

My interest in recording the Ozark speech stems from five scholarly papers by Joseph W. Carr, a professor at the University of Arkansas. These studies appeared in *Dialect Notes* between 1904 and 1909, and I read them about 1915. It was not until 1920 that I began to carry scraps of newsprint in my pocket and write down words and phrases which I heard in conversation with my neighbors. The material was later typed on cards and placed in a filing cabinet. I kept this up for thirty years, and at one time had cards enough to fill a steamer trunk. This method of collecting has its drawbacks, particularly in the matter of pronunciation. When the hillman says *where* it usually sounds like *whar,* but often it's more like *whur* or *whirr.* And sometimes, as Charlie May Simon points out,[10] it may be something between *whar* and *whirr,* a sound which cannot be set down in ordinary English letters. For a while I tried to record pronunciations in the International Phonetic Alphabet, but, not being trained in phonetics, I never felt at ease with these characters and soon gave up the attempt.

At one time it occurred to me that dialect could best be collected on phonograph records. I used a portable electric recorder in gathering Ozark folksongs, and the nine hundred recordings which I deposited in the Library of Congress preserve the hillman's pronunciation accurately enough, so far as the words of his songs are concerned. This method works very well with rhymes, riddles, set speeches, or anything that is deliberately memorized to be sung or recited. It is easy to record the speech of educated people by having them read a trick script like *Arthur the Rat* into your microphone. But this can't be done in the Ozarks, because so many of our best talkers are illiterate. And such a procedure seems limited to the study of pronunciation, anyhow. Many other items, such as grammatical peculiarities, familiar words in unusual meanings, euphemisms, picturesque comparisons, and the like, are not easily collected by the folksong method. This material must be picked up in casual conversation, and it is not practicable to have a dictaphone always at your elbow. Gold is where you find it, and the stuff generally turns up unexpectedly. I got some of my best dialect while camping with deer hunters on the ridges, or playing poker in the villages, or easing a johnboat through a riffle, or dancing with some farmer's daughter at a crossroads kitchen-sweat.

6

Introduction

Mark Twain once declared that he wrote seven distinct Missouri dialects, and discussed them *seriatim* in an "explanatory note" prefixed to *Huckleberry Finn*. Mark Twain was spoofing,[11] but many writers have used the word dialect quite seriously with reference to English as it is spoken in the Ozark country. I follow their example for the sake of brevity, but have no quarrel with learned folk who contend that there are no dialects in the United States.[12] I am not concerned with distinctions between true dialect and other forms of substandard speech, nor with any of the scholarly disputations about such matters.

I have read everything available on the Ozark dialect, including word lists and papers by Raymond Weeks, D. S. Crumb, Rupert Taylor, Jay L. B. Taylor, Charles Morrow Wilson, Allen Walker Read, and several others. Much of this material is reviewed in the fourth edition of H. L. Mencken's *The American Language,* published in 1936, and the two *Supplements* of 1945 and 1948. All of the titles which have appeared to date are listed in the bibliography at the end of the present study. There is much unpublished material,[13] some of which may never be printed,[14] and the collection of Ozark words and phrases still goes on. Otto Ernest Rayburn, of Eureka Springs, Arkansas, showed me a large file of backwoods expressions which have not appeared in his books and magazine articles. Professor W. Cabell Greet[15] and his disciples at Columbia University made speech records from many parts of the United States, and there are some Ozark recordings in the collection. The University of Arkansas has eighty-odd reels of tape recordings, collected since 1949 by Merlin Mitchell and Irene Carlisle; much of this material is from northern Arkansas.[16] E. H.

[10] *Straw in the Sun* (New York, 1945), 218.

[11] William Clark Breckenridge (*American Local Dialects,* 9) writes: "This statement must not be taken seriously; it is merely a sample of Mark Twain's humor."

[12] *American Speech,* Vol. IV (1929), 203. For a definition of dialect, see George P. Wilson, *Publication of the American Dialect Society,* No. 11 (1949), 38.

[13] Cf. the study of place-names at the University of Missouri by Professor Robert L. Ramsay and his students; note especially the typescript theses of Margaret Bell, Mayme Hamlett, Eugenia Harrison, Anna O'Brien, Cora Ann Pottenger, and Gertrude Zimmer.

[14] E.g., many recordings of "unprintable" speech from Missouri and Arkansas in the Folklore Archive, library of Congress. Cf. also such manuscripts as "Preeminent Sons of Bitches of Boone County, Missouri," cited by W. A. Dorrance in *We're From Missouri,* 31.

[15] *American Speech,* Vol. V (1930), 333–58.

[16] Wesley A. Davis, *Ozark Folklore* (Fayetteville, Ark.), Vol. I (January, 1951), 12–13.

Criswell[17] mentions a surveyor who has set down 2,500 Ozark terms from McDonald County, Missouri, also a schoolteacher who has been working with the Ozark dialect in Dade County, Missouri, for more than a quarter of a century.

My own studies of the Ozark dialect end with the publication of this volume. The manuscript is full of pleasant memories for me, because the persons who supplied the material were my friends and neighbors. Reading one of these old-time sayings, I recall who said it, and when, and under what circumstances. There was a lot of interesting conversation around Pineville, Missouri, and Sallisaw, Oklahoma, back in the nineteen twenties. A garland of lusty sayings came to me from the possum hunters of Scott and Polk counties, in Arkansas. The village of Galena, Missouri, was full of splendid talkers in the nineteen thirties and early nineteen forties. I remember some fascinating people near Tar River, Oklahoma, and many who lived in and about Fayetteville, Arkansas. Numerous colorful items were picked up at the old House of Lords, a kind of tavern in Joplin, Missouri. It was a long time ago, but I shall never forget one cold night at Hot Springs, Arkansas, when I got out of bed to write down a bit of backwoods hyperbole heard earlier in the evening. And how we laughed about it then, and later! I had a pretty good time, collecting the material for this book.

[17] *Publication of the American Dialect Society*, No. 9 (1948), 65–66.

2 Ozark Pronunciation

THE OZARKER does not drawl like a Southern lowlander or whine like a radio hillbilly, but there is no denying that he lingers over certain accented syllables. Some of the Ozark vowels, says Robert L. Morris of the University of Arkansas, "have a plaintive quality which at times becomes like oaths or tears."[1] Rose Wilder Lane of Missouri refers to "that inimitable cadence that makes the simplest remark as musical as though it were sung."[2] Remembering the Ozark dialect of the early nineteen hundreds, Rose O'Neill spoke of its "sedative" quality. "Our neighbors' speech was like a song," she told me, "a recurrence of gentle, old-time refrains. We never tired of it."

A distinguished foreigner once declared that "the Ozark dialect has only two vowel sounds, and they are used interchangeably." This is not true, of course. But the Ozarker does shift his vowels about in a manner disconcerting to Americans from the Northern and Eastern states.

The *a* in care, share, and scare is pronounced like long *e*, as if the words were spelled *keer, sheer,* and *skeer.* When a backwoods preacher uses the word apparently, he nearly always says *appeerently.* Scarce is usually *skeerce,* although one hears *skurce* occasionally, and even *skace*[3] has been reported from McDonald County, Missouri. Albert Pike long ago wrote: "Hair, bear, stair, et id omne genus, are pronounced *har, bar, star,* etc."[4] Chair is generally *cheer,*[5] but sometimes it sounds like *churr.* The verb dare is usually *dar,* and spare is nearly always *spar.*

In some parts of Arkansas one hears a very long *a* in have, which almost rhymes with *stave.* Usually, however, the vowel is nearer to short *e,*

[1] *University Review* (Kansas City, Mo.), Winter, 1936, p. 125.
[2] Springfield, Mo., *Leader,* July 3, 1928.
[3] *Dialect Notes,* Vol. V (1923), 221.
[4] "Life in Arkansas," *American Monthly Magazine,* Vol. I (March, 1836), 302.
[5] Marguerite Lyon, *Take to the Hills* (Indianapolis, 1941), 147.

so that the word sounds like *hev*. Calf often rhymes with *safe*, while the plural calves sounds exactly like *caves*. The name Ralph is frequently pronounced in the English fashion; consequently the dialect writers spell it *Rafe*. Instead of hasn't and haven't the hillman frequently says *hain't*, which rhymes with paint. Can't usually sounds like *cain't*, and past is often pronounced *paste*.

Most hillfolk say *wrop* when they mean to wrap, and pamper sounds like *pomper*. When tramp and stamp are used substantively, the *a* is flat, but the corresponding verbs are nearly always *tromp* and *stomp*. The vowel sound in catch and gather is generally short *e*, so that the words are best spelled *ketch* and *gether*. The verb scalp is nearly always *skelp* among the old-timers, and some hillfolk pronounce the noun scalp to rhyme with *help*, also.

The short *a* in lack sounds pretty much like long *i*, as Joseph W. Carr long ago reported from Fayetteville, Arkansas.[6] The word is regularly pronounced *like* in southwest Missouri and is often so spelled in the country newspapers: "Reece Woolridge *liked* only a few months of having his high school work completed."[7]

In such words as any and many, the *a* sounds like short *i*. One rarely hears almanac and tabernacle correctly pronounced in the Ozarks; they may well be written *almanick* and *tabernickel*.

Calm and balmy are regularly pronounced *cam* and *bammy*. Palm, both noun and verb, generally rhymes with *ham*. The word gargle is usually *gaggle*, with the *a* as in hat. Sometimes one hears star pronounced *stair*, and the adjective starry often rhymes with *hairy*. The noun bar is correctly sounded, but the adjective barred is generally *bared;* a boy who was thrown into jail at Batesville, Arkansas, told me that the windows of the jail-house were *bared all round*. A woman near West Plains, Missouri, described a dried-apple pie as *cross-bared*, meaning that there were several narrow bars of crust across the top of it. The verb parboil is very often pronounced *pare-bile*.

Rather nearly always sounds like *ruther*, and far is usually pronounced *fur*. What generally rhymes with *butt*. Most hillfolk say *wawsh* for wash, but one often hears *woish* and sometimes *woirsh*.

Old settlers say that skating was always *skeeting* in the eighteen sixties and seventies.[8] The verb drain rhymes with green. James is still pronounced

---

[6] *Dialect Notes*, Vol. III (1905), 86.

[7] Pineville, Mo., *Democrat*, January 1, 1932.

[8] B. W. Rice, *Arcadian Life* (Caddo Gap, Ark., March, 1936), 3.

Jeems by some of the old-timers, particularly when they refer to the James River; Uncle Jack Short, Galena, Missouri, tells me that in the eighteen seventies the old folks called it the *Jim* River.

The preterite of eat is usually *et*, and naked is generally *neckid*. Hame-string is nearly always pronounced *hem-string*, with a short *e*. The nape of the neck frequently rhymes with *cap*. Sometimes a long *a* sounds like short *i*; grated bread, made of soft corn rubbed on a metal grater, is called *gritted* bread.

A final unstressed *a* is often pronounced *y*, particularly in proper names: Clara sounds like *Clary*, Laura is generally *Laury*, Ida sounds like *Idy*, and so on. Ursula is shortened to Sula, pronounced *Sooly*. The name Noah is pronounced *No-ey*, just as Jonah is nearly always *Joney*.

Robert Lee Meyers[9] has noted this in the names of certain Missouri villages: Bona, Stella, Saint Martha, Iantha, Neola, and Arcola. The town of Galena, Missouri, is often called *Galeny*, sometimes *Galener*. The word alfalfa is pronounced *alfalfy*, extra is nearly always *extry*, and soda is invariably *sody*. Cholera is usually pronounced *cholery*, and is often so spelled in the country newspapers. Mamma is pronounced *mommy* or *mammy;* papa sounds like *poppy* or *pappy*.

Something of the sort is true of words ending in *ia*, such as pneumonia and malaria, which are nearly always pronounced *pneumony* and *malary*. Amelia sounds like *Meely*, Delia is often *Deely*.

The word idea is generally pronounced *idy*, as, "I ain't got no *idy* where Hank is at." But sometimes, at the end of a sentence or where some special emphasis is required, it sounds like *idee*, with a strong accent on the second syllable.

Near Waldron, Arkansas, I heard of a sawmill operator named Canada, though everybody called him *Kennedy*. But when an Ozarker wishes to speak elegantly, he avoids these final *y* sounds, so that a man whose name really is Kennedy finds himself addressed as *Canada* or *Kennedah*. A girl named Dorothy is called *Dorotha*, spaghetti becomes *spaghetta*, macaroni is often *macarona*, taxi is turned into *taxa*. I know a woman in Galena, Missouri, who always says *remedah* when she means remedy, and another female at Pineville, Missouri, used to deliver patriotic lectures about "our *countrah*," meaning country. There is a soft-spoken butcher in Carroll County, Arkansas, who pronounces salami as if it were spelled *salamah*.

May Kennedy McCord, of Springfield, Missouri, says that the names

9 "Place-Names in the Southwest Counties of Missouri," Master's thesis, University of Missouri, 1930, pp. 43–44.

Emma, Stella, and Ella are often pronounced *Emmer, Steller,* and *Eller* in Stone County, Missouri. In Galena, Missouri, lives a woman whose given name is spelled Drilla, but everybody pronounces it *Driller.* Mrs. Mary Elizabeth Mahnkey, Kirbyville, Missouri, told me that a girl named Rosella was always called *Roseller* in her neighborhood, and that Beulah was sometimes pronounced *Bewler.* The name Drusilla often sounds like *Drusiller,* and I knew the parents of a girl named Marcella who always spoke of her as *Marceller.*

Seneca is the common name of a medicinal herb (*Polygala senaga*), but the plant is sometimes called *senicker* in southwest Missouri. Often, however, it is *senicky,* and I have seen it spelled *senicy* or *cinacy* in the local papers.[10]

Arkansas is always *Arkansaw,* never made to rhyme with *dances.*[11] In March, 1881, the state legislature affirmed that the name "should be pronounced in three syllables, with the final *s* silent, the *a* in each syllable with the Italian sound, and the accent on the first and last syllables." John Gould Fletcher, born in Little Rock, minced no words about this: "However midwesterners may think the name of Arkansas should be pronounced, to the natives it has always been sounded in only one way, as *Arkansaw.*"[12] Despite all this, Northerners persist in mispronouncing the word. Sally Walker Stockard wrote: "I know of an Arkansas teacher in Massachusetts who was asked by the directors to teach her geography class to pronounce Arkansas to rhyme with Kansas, and not to rhyme with Choctaw and Chickasaw."[13] As recently as the late nineteen twenties I met a college professor in New York who called the state *Ah-kin-siss,* with a strong accent on the second syllable.[14]

Certain nouns ending in *a* are pronounced as if the terminal vowel were long *o.* As Rose Wilder Lane points out,[15] the word cupola, meaning a sort of steeple, is pronounced *kewpalo,* with a strong accent on the first syllable. Quota is always *quoto* in the Ozarks. Scrofula is regularly *scrofulo,* and is often spelled that way in the country newspapers. There is even a

[10] Springfield, Mo., *Leader & Press,* December 10, 1946.

[11] For a full account of the controversy about this pronunciation, with unexpurgated texts of the famous "Change the Name of Arkansas" speech, see James R. Masterson's *Tall Tales of Arkansaw,* 180–85, 352–55. Also Allen Walker Read, *American Speech,* Vol. VIII (1933), 42–43, 46.

[12] *Arkansas* (Chapel Hill, 1947), *vii.*

[13] *History of Lawrence, Jackson, Independence, and Stone Counties, Arkansas* (Little Rock, 1904), 186.

[14] Cf. my *Ozark Anthology* (Caldwell, Idaho, 1940), 5.

[15] *Old Home Town* (New York, 1935), 3.

verb form: "Them Taylor kids is all *scrofuloed* something terrible." Fistula is another member of this group; I have before me a country weekly[16] in which one J. Q. Gardner advertises his ability to "Cure *Fistulo* in Horses or Mules." Occasionally this shift to a final *o* affects proper names: a girl named Sarah is usually called *Sary*, but sometimes her name is pronounced *Saro*, with the *o* very long. The town of Alpena, Arkansas, is often called *Alpeny*, but some of the real old-timers say *Alpeno* very distinctly.

The verb rear is nearly always pronounced *rare* or *rar*. The adjective clear is sometimes *clair*, often *clar*. Yellow is pronounced *yaller*, and celery sounds pretty much like *salary*. The *e* in Eva is nearly always short, and the surname Edens is pronounced *Eddens*.

There are hill people in McDonald County, Missouri, who call a centipede a *santy fay*,[17] exactly as they pronounce the name of the Santa Fe railroad.

The flower known as a peony elsewhere is very often a *piney* in the Ozarks. This is a good old-time pronunciation, but some elegant upstarts prefer to say *pe-o-ny*, accenting the second syllable.[18]

Certain is pronounced *sartin* in some sections of the hill country. Concern sounds like *consarn*, merchant like *marchant*, and mercy is often pronounced *marcy*. Sometimes one hears an old man say *clark* when he means clerk. Service-berries are always *sarvis-berries* or *sarvises*. Search very often rhymes with *arch*, and herb generally sounds like *yarb*. The noun circumstance is pronounced *sarcumstance*. Nervous is frequently *narvous* or *narvish*. The fine gravel which is heaped up about lead-mines in the Joplin, Missouri, district is correctly known as chert, but the local people always call it *chat*, to rhyme with *hat*.

Wrestle is always *wrastle*, and mesh is often pronounced *mash*. Egg and leg sound pretty much like *aig* and *laig*. Keg is generally *kaig*, but occasionally one hears *kagg*.

The verb bleat, in the back hills, is usually pronounced so as to rhyme with *hate*.

The word Nebraska, among the old settlers, nearly always sounds like *Newbraska* or *Newbrasky;* I have heard it so pronounced by people who were born and raised in Nebraska, but migrated to the Ozarks in the eighteen nineties.

A long *e* sound is used in such words as pert and perch, which are pro-

---

16 Crane, Mo., *Chronicle*, January 11, 1940.
17 Cf. *Dialect Notes*, Vol. V (1923), 219.
18 *Dialect Notes*, Vol. III (1906), 150.

nounced *peert* and *peerch*. Lever is generally *leever*, and deaf is nearly always *deef*. Eleanor Risley told me that the old folks near Mena, Arkansas, say *eend* when they mean end, but this pronunciation is rare among the hillfolk of my acquaintance.

Octave Thanet reported that country people in Lawrence County, Arkansas, pronounce been "in the old way, as it is spelled," to sound like *bean*,[19] but I seldom hear this nowadays; my neighbors say *ben* or *bin*. Joseph W. Carr listed *ben* as the common pronunciation of been in northwest Arkansas.[20] Professor Morris, of the University of Arkansas, says that "been never rimes with seen, but is *bin* or *ben*, the latter form being favored."[21]

The short *e* in kettle, chest, and get is regularly pronounced like short *i*; *kittle, chist*, and *git* are almost universal in the backwoods. Steady nearly always sounds like *stiddy*, bedstead is invariably *bedstid*. As Raymond L. Weeks long ago observed, men is usually pronounced *min*, with the singularly distinct short *i* sound also heard in the *ing* endings.[22] The name Evans is generally *Ivvens*, and Evansville, Arkansas, is nearly always called *Ivvensville*.

In the Ozark cities and towns, a man whose given name is Cecil calls it *Ceecil*. But in the backwoods they pronounce the *e* short, just as the English do. The family name Reynolds is nearly always *Runnels*, to rhyme with funnels.

Most hillfolk pronounce sleek so that it sounds like *slick*. The noun creek, oddly enough, is pronounced correctly; the old-time Ozarker doesn't say *crick*, as country folk elsewhere often do.[23] Clink O'Neill of Taney County, Missouri, tells me that the progressive young folk in his neighborhood have recently adopted *crick* as the proper pronunciation, since they hear it used by tourists from such centers of culture as St. Louis and Kansas City.[24] Elsie Bates of Hollister, Missouri, says that the old-timers make creek rhyme with *seek*, but that schoolmarms from the North are teaching the children to say *crick*.

Either is usually given a long *e* sound, but neither frequently rhymes with *mother*. Alice Curtice Moyer-Wing tells of a woman in the Ozarks who ended a long speech with: "It ain't that I'm a angel, *nuther*."[25]

The possessive their is either pronounced correctly or made to rhyme

[19] *Journal of American Folklore*, Vol. V (1892), 121.

[20] *Dialect Notes*, Vol. III (1906), 126.

[21] *University Review* (Kansas City, Mo.), Winter, 1936, p. 125.

[22] *Dialect Notes*, Vol. I (1892), 240. Cf. *Oklahoma, a Guide to the Sooner State*, 121.

14

with *fur*, but there is very often *thar*. Even the official state guidebook admits that some people in Newton County, Arkansas, say *thar* for there.[26] In some combinations the *th* is elided, so that *them there* sounds like *them 'ar*. Many old-timers pronounce here as if it were spelled *hyar;* others make it sound more like *hyur*, to rhyme with *burr*. I have known educated hillmen, who pronounce here quite correctly in conversation, to fall back on the old dialect when calling dogs: "*Hyar*, Tige! *Hyar*, Bulger!" Where is generally pronounced *whur*, but in some cases, notably the question "Where at?" it carries a very broad *a* sound, almost rhyming with *car*. Pear is pronounced *purr*, sometimes *par*. Terrible is usually *turrible*. Errand generally sounds like *urrant*.

Dulcimer is very often *dulcimore* in the back hills, with the long *o* pronounced very distinctly.[27]

Terrapin is generally pronounced *tarpin*, and is often spelled *tarpin*[28] or *tarripin*[29] in the Ozark newspapers. Mrs. C. P. Mahnkey, of Kirbyville, Missouri, writes me that "a tortoise, in the old days, was always called a *tarpon*," and that's her own spelling.

Fire, tire, iron, wire, and hire have a single-vowel sound like that of the *a* in far. One of my neighbors at Pineville, Missouri, published a verse in which she rhymed tired with lard, and that's exactly the way she and her people always pronounced it. The family name Myers sounds pretty much like *Marrs*, and Byers is pronounced *Barrs*. The noun life, as used by country folk in the Ozarks, sounds like the New England pronunciation of *laugh*, and is perhaps best spelled *lahf*. Squire is pronounced *square*, sometimes *squar*. My wife and I were convulsed when one of our neighbors, a prim Methodist lady, shouted out something about what fine luck she was having with her *arse;* she meant iris, a flowering plant in her dooryard.

The words might and fight, in many sections of the hill country, are pronounced to rhyme with *out*. Oblige generally sounds like *obleege*. The noun whip is pronounced correctly, but the verb is somewhere between *whup* and *whoop*. Mrs. Isabel Spradley, of Van Buren, Arkansas, tells me that some old-timers in her neighborhood pronounce wish as if it were spelled *woosh*.

[23] Joseph W. Carr and Rupert Taylor, *Dialect Notes*, Vol. III (1907), 221.
[24] Cf. *Dialect Notes*, Vol. I (1892), 238.
[25] St. Louis *Post-Dispatch*, May 5, 1918.
[26] *Arkansas, A Guide to the State* (New York, 1941), 297.
[27] Cf. my *Ozark Folksongs* (Mo. Hist. Soc., 1946–50, 4 vols.), I, 36.
[28] Springfield, Mo., *Leader & Press*, June 23, 1946.
[29] Springfield, Mo., *News & Leader*, November 8, 1936.

Many of the old folks pronounce the *i* in April very long, and I have seen the word spelled *Aprile* on old tombstones in both Missouri and Arkansas. The noun reptile has a long *i* too, and no marked accent on either syllable.

Lilac, meaning not a color but a flowering shrub, generally sounds like *laylock*.

In such words as little, itch, and inch the *i* usually sounds like *ee*, while hitch, bitch, stitch, rich and pitch are correctly pronounced. Fish is pronounced *feesh* in McDonald County, Missouri.[30] One hears *feesh* occasionally in other sections of the Ozarks, but it is not common nowadays. Mary Elizabeth Mahnkey, Kirbyville, Missouri, tells me that some of her old neighbors say *deesh* when they mean dish.

Stint and risky are pronounced *stent* and *resky,* while the verb hinder usually sounds like *hender*. Since is often pronounced *sense*. Lid is generally *led,* particularly in the combination *skillet-an'-led,* which means Dutch oven. Spirit and pith fall into the same category; the Ozarker generally says *sperrit* and *peth*.

Many old-time singers and preachers pronounce a final *y* with a long *i* sound. Not in ordinary conversation, but in songs, sermons, and serious public speeches goodly becomes *good-lye,* stately becomes *state-lye,* quickly becomes *quick-lye* and so on. Geraldine Parker, California, Missouri, told me that she had heard windy pronounced *wind-eye*. Nancy Clemens, Springfield, Missouri, heard sweetly pronounced that way in an old hymn with the line "*sweet-lye* rest and murmur not." Mrs. W. A. Patton, Jane, Missouri, reported an old song:

> *It grieves me most to think that I must die,*
> *To think that I must go to a long* eterni-tye.[31]

There is a similar rhyme in "The Death of a Romish Lady" as sung by Mr. J. M. Peacock, Rocky Comfort, Missouri, in which speedily is pronounced with a long *i* ending:

> *To the place of torment they brought her* speedi-lye,
> *With lifted hands to heaven she then agreed to die.*

A schoolmarm in Sulphur Springs, Arkansas, once explained to me that

[30] *Dialect Notes,* Vol. V (1923), 209.
[31] Cf. my *Ozark Folksongs,* IV, 41.

16

this is comparable to the old poetic pronunciation which makes "the Winter wind" rhyme with kind, blind, behind and so forth.

The noun hole is correctly pronounced, but whole generally sounds like *hull*. The short *o* of the noun crop is lost when the word is pronounced *crap*. The verb drop is usually *drap* and rhymes with *trap*. A lawyer in St. Louis had graduated from an eastern university and spoke citified English, but in a moment of excitement he shouted, "*Drap* that gun!" thus reverting to the pronunciation of his youth in the Ozarks. The noun drop is sometimes pronounced *drap* too, but much less frequently than the verb; I have heard the distinction made in a single sentence, when a woman said, "You just *drap* one drop of that medicine in a gourdful of water."

"Did you ever notice," asks May Kennedy McCord, "that the old Ozarkers call their worries their *wearies*? A sweeter word, isn't it? Someway a gentler word, not so harassed."[32] Robert L. Morris reports that one of his students at the University of Arkansas wrote: "He told her to stop *wearying* about it."[33] On the other hand, many people in southern Missouri, especially preachers and radio announcers, pronounce weary as if it were spelled *worry*, or sometimes *wary*.

In the word cover the vowel sound is very close to short *i*, and the writers of dialect fiction sometimes spell it *ḳivver*. Mattock sounds like *mattiḳ*, but hollyhock is usually pronounced *hollyhawḳ*.

All the old-timers pronounce hog as if it were spelled *hawg*. Dog is nearly always *dawg*, even among the younger generation, and God is very often *Gawd*.

Many people in rural Arkansas pronounce comrade as *cumrad*. This is a traditional pronunciation, still common in accepted British usage.

The final *o* in potato is generally pronounced *er*, so that the word sounds like *potater;* sometimes the first *o* is affected too, so that *pertater* is not uncommon. The same principle applies in words like tomato and tobacco, which are pronounced *termater* and *terbacḳer*. Sometimes the first syllable is omitted, so that *'tater, 'mater* and *'bacḳer* are good Ozark nouns.

The sound represented by *ow* at the end of a word is often *er*, so that hollow, bellow, fellow, wallow, swallow, widow, and window sound like *holler, beller, feller, waller, swaller, widder,* and *winder*. Shadow is often pronounced *shadder*. The nouns marrow, harrow, and sparrow are usually *marr', harr',* and *sparr',* although a gentle *er* ending is sometimes heard even here.

32 Springfield, Mo., *News*, June 9, 1942.
33 *American Speech*, Vol. XXIII (1948), 305.

The adjective narrow is generally pronounced *narr'* or *narrer,* but in certain combinations the form *narry* is not unknown—*narry-minded, narry-hipped, narry-gauge,* and so forth. Barrow, meaning a castrated pig, is usually *barr'* or *barrer,* sometimes *barry.* Minnow is pronounced *minner,* sometimes *minny.* Shallow is generally *shaller,* but occasionally *shally.* Borrow is nearly always *borry.* The family name McCullough, common in southwest Missouri, is often pronounced *McCully.*

A judge in Greene County, Missouri, used to "warn the prosecuting attorney to beware of *urr,* and avoid causing the case to be reversed."[34] This pronunciation of error is still very common in the Ozarks. On the other hand, at least a score of times I have heard backwoods orators say *errow* or *urr-o* when they obviously meant error, pronouncing the long *o* sound very distinctly. Only a few days ago I heard a prominent physician, in a radio speech, use the word terror repeatedly, and every time he pronounced it *turr.*

Yonder is usually pronounced *yander,* to rhyme with gander. May Kennedy McCord says that she has often heard old-timers start it off with an aspirate, so that the word sounds like *hyander.* D. S. Crumb long ago reported *hyander* from southeastern Missouri.[35] Sometimes an *s* sound is added, and the local-color novelists spell it *yanders.* In backwoods song and recitation the word is frequently *yandress* or *yandro.* It is capitalized as a proper name, as "at the foot of *Yandro* Mountain" in manuscript copies of old ballads. According to Carl Sandburg there really is a mountain called Yandro, somewhere in North Carolina.[36]

One of the most striking and outlandish pronunciations, still common in the back hills, is that of onion—the old-timers make it sound like *ing-urn* or *ing-ern.* Jay L. B. Taylor included *ingern* in a word-list from McDonald County, Missouri.[37] Patricia Lockridge reports *ingern* as popular in the Missouri Ozarks generally.[38] I have met men and women in Newton County, Arkansas, who had apparently never heard onion pronounced in the ordinary Middle Western fashion, and didn't know that the tourists meant *ing-urns* when they asked for onions. A lady in Galena, Missouri, told me that little children in her neighborhood use the word *ing-urn,* but that the adults say onion. "There must be something about *ing-urn,*" she said thoughtfully, "that makes it easier for children to pronounce."

[34] Springfield, Mo., *Leader & Press,* September 16, 1936.
[35] *Dialect Notes,* Vol. II (1903), 337.
[36] *American Songbag* (New York, 1927), 3.
[37] *Dialect Notes,* Vol. V (1923), 211.
[38] *Publication of the American Dialect Society,* No. 2 (1944), 57.

Ozark Pronunciation

The word on is usually pronounced as *awn*, but the last syllable of upon often rhymes with *gun*.

Cocklebur is nearly always *cucklebur* in the Ozarks.[39] When cocklebur appeared in Spider Rowland's column in the *Arkansas Gazette*, several readers pointed out the error, one explaining that "the word is cucklebur." Spider accepted the correction. "But don't go putting it on my back," he said. "I wrote it *cucklebur*, not having any earthly idea that there is any other way to spell it. Then one of these grade-school graduates changed it to cocklebur just because the dictionary spells it that way."[40]

The name Jordan, rather common in the hill country, is generally pronounced *Jerdan* or *Jurden*.

Two and too are pronounced in a more or less orthodox fashion, but to sometimes sounds like *ter*. This *ter* pronunciation is still heard, even among educated Ozarkers, but it is nowhere so common as the hillbilly novelists would have us believe.

Hungry is often pronounced *hongry* or *hawngry*. Brush is generally *bresh*, such sounds like *sich* or *sech*, and shut is nearly always *shet*. Judge is pronounced *jedge*. *Poppet*, the backwoods term for doll, is doubtless a variant of puppet. The verb duck is sometimes pronounced with a vowel sound like that of goose, as "I seen that feller *dook* in behind the barn." Hurricane is often pronounced *harrycane*. In such words as until, unhandy, and unhook the *u* sounds like short *o*, so that these terms are pronounced *ontil*, *onhandy*, and *onhook*.

The hillman always calls a female sheep a *yo*,[41] pronounced to rhyme with *woe*.

Sure and surely generally sound like *shore* and *shorely*. Your is pronounced *yore*, and poor is nearly always *pore*. Pure is usually *pyore* or *puore*.

Gum, meaning the flesh about the teeth, is often pronounced *goom*, and cud sounds like *cood*;[42] these words rhyme with *boom* and *snood*. Touch is usually *tetch*, sometimes *totch*.

The verb put sounds exactly like the golfer's term *putt*, and rhymes with the Ozark pronunciation of *soot*.

Many of the old settlers say *cowcumber* instead of cucumber. I have

[39] *Dialect Notes*, Vol. II (1903), 310.

[40] *Arkansas Gazette*, Little Rock, Ark., December 26, 1948.

[41] Cf. Carr and Taylor, *Dialect Notes*, Vol. III (1909), 406. In his *Pronouncing Dictionary* of 1790, John Walker condemns this vulgar pronunciation of ewe, but it is now common among sheepmen in both England and America.

[42] *Dialect Notes*, Vol. V (1923), 204.

heard a hillman refer to a twisted picture frame as *skewed*, but he pronounced it so as to rhyme with *cowed* or *loud*.

Routine is regularly sounded like *rotine*, with the *o* very long.

The Ozarker pronounces new almost in the English fashion; he never says *noo*,[43] as many people do in other parts of the United States.

The hillman sometimes says *ye* instead of you, in both singular and plural. It is pronounced with the long *e* sound, to rhyme with *he*. "The distinction between you and ye is elusive," says Professor Morris, of the University of Arkansas. "It seems that if the vowels preceding are heavily accented and if emphasis is desired, the form ye is used. But I should hesitate to set this as a rule."[44] One sometimes hears both forms in a single short sentence; a woman in Stone County, Missouri, signifies her emphatic agreement by crying "You bet ye!" The Ozarker's "Lookee thar!" is evidently "Look ye," and his "Harkee now!" must have been "Hark ye" originally. *Thankee* or *thanky* are not uncommon. Even the "Howdy!" which is the universal backwoods greeting, is from some phrase containing *ye* or *you*.

Sauce, saucy, gaunt, and jaundice are pronounced *sass, sassy, gant*, and *janders*. Professor F. M. Goodhue, Mena, Arkansas, tells me that saucer is not quite *sasser* in his neighborhood; he thinks it is nearer *saiser* or *say-ser*. I have heard *sassage* for sausage occasionally. The vowel sound in aunt is generally flat *a*, but some of the older people lengthen the *a* until aunt can hardly be distinguished from ain't. The same is true of haunt, which is a noun meaning ghost; the common pronunciation is *hant* to rhyme with the Midwestern can't, but not infrequently one hears it pronounced with a long *a* sound, almost like *hain't*.

The *au* in audacious is sounded like the *ow* in plow. And the *ou* of snout is pronounced so that the word rhymes with *shoot*.

In such words as spoil, soil, hoist, poison, oil, boil, roil, and join the *oi* has the sound of long *i*, so the words may be spelled *spile, sile, h'ist, pizen, ile, bile, rile*, and *jine*. Mary Elizabeth Mahnkey quotes a rhyme she learned from her mother in Taney County, Missouri:

> *After breakfast, work and toil,*
> *After dinner, set a while,*
> *After supper, walk a mile.*

At C. V. Wheat's tomato cannery near Aurora, Missouri, in 1935, the

---

[43] Charles Morrow Wilson, St. Louis *Post-Dispatch,* June 9, 1930.
[44] *University Review* (Kansas City, Mo.), Winter, 1936, p. 125.

boiler bucket was painted red and labelled BOILER to keep it separate from other buckets. Some workman corrected the spelling to BILER. Informed that was not quite right, Tom McKinley changed it to BILAR. Later on somebody else made it BILOR, and so it remained for the season.[45] Note that all three of these backwoods orthographers were agreed about the *i* in the first syllable.

Broil nearly always sounds like *brile*. A man in Eureka Springs, Arkansas, was speaking of the peculiar habits of tourists from Chicago. "They pull off most of their clothes," said he, "an' then go right out in the *brilin'* hot sun!"

This confusion of *oi* with *i* sometimes works the other way round; the literate hillman who wishes to speak elegantly says boil when he means bile, as in the sentence: "Boil is a yellow fluid secreted by the liver."

A kind of dynamite used in blowing stumps and building roads is known as giant powder. The word giant, as pronounced by the "furrin" road-builders, sounds pretty much like the Ozark pronunciation of *joint*. Thus it is that the country correspondents, wishing to be very correct, frequently spell it *joint powder* in their newspaper stories.[46] I have seen a letter from a woman in Christian County, Missouri, in which her common-law husband was described as "a regular *joint*, six feet four in his sock feet."

James Sharp, an Ozark "messiah" who gained a great deal of newspaper publicity under the name "Adam God" and served a prison sentence for murder, once threatened to catch a certain detective out in the woods, "butcher him like a hog, an' fry the tenderloin for supper." When I interviewed Sharp at Joplin, Missouri, in 1935, he repeated this threat, pronouncing tenderloin very distinctly as *tenderline*.

Fritz Williams, who runs a newspaper in West Plains, Missouri, told me of a man who demanded a *harr-pint* at the hardware store, when he wanted a harrow point. The adverb pointedly is usually pronounced *p'intedly*, sometimes shortened to *p'int'ly*.

The verb coil, meaning to subside, perhaps to quail, is invariably pronounced *quile*, as "Jim he *quiled* right down soon as he seen the sheriff a-comin'." Sometimes this word seems to mean quell: "It'll take a whole army to *quile* them Starbuck boys, if they git on the rampage!" The noun is usually pronounced in the same fashion. A farmer drove his Ford into a repair shop at Ava, Missouri, saying that he wanted "the *pints of the quiles*

[45] Springfield, Mo., *Leader & Press*, November 14, 1935.
[46] *American Speech*, Vol. VIII (1933), 50.

filed," meaning the points of the coils. Occasionally one hears the noun coil pronounced *quall,* so as to rhyme with *squall.*

The noun ointment is sometimes given three distinct syllables: *i-ent-ment,* with a long *i* and a secondary accent on *ent.*

Among consonants, the letter *t* is always bobbing up in unexpected places. Vermin is invariably *varmint,* sudden is generally *suddint,* wish sounds like *wisht,* and trough is pronounced *trawft.* A final *t* is frequently heard in virgin, sermon, and orphan. Isabel France, of Mountainburg, Arkansas, tells me that cousin is often pronounced *cousint.* The same superfluous *t* is sounded at the end of certain other words, such as once, close, dose, across, skiff, cliff, and chance. Carr and Taylor report a terminal *t* sound on the adjective *safe* in northwest Arkansas.[47] The adjective trifling, which means indolent, is often pronounced with a final *t* sound. Mrs. Rowland Thomas, of Morrilton, Arkansas, spells it *triflant.* "Throughout my childhood," she writes, "it was a familiar Southern word, the superlative for lazy or shiftless. Everyone knew there was a class of *triflant* people."[48]

There is some confusion between *t* and *d.* Many illiterate hillfolk say *terrectly* or *terreckly* when they mean directly, presently. A *t* is used as the final consonant in salad, ballad, errand, scared, hold, and killed, so that these words are pronounced *sallet, ballet, urrant, skeert, holt,* and *kilt.* The title Reverend, often used without the preacher's name, even in direct address, is usually pronounced *Reverent.* Diamond is nearly always *diamant.* The verb beaddle, which means to confuse, generally sounds like *beattle.* Partner is always *pardner,* and in some sections the family name Stuart or Stewart is regularly pronounced *Steward.* In further a *d* sound is often used instead of the voiced *th,* so that the word rhymes with *murder.*

The *t* sound in brittle is frequently pronounced like *k,* and anyone who listens to the backwoods preachers will sooner or later hear some reference to the "*brickle* thread of life." The snapping-turtle is sometimes called a *turkle.* Walnut often sounds like *warnuck* or *warnick,* and vomit is pronounced *vomick.*[49] The little green heron (*Butorides virescens*) is known as a shite-poke in many parts of the United States, but in the Ozarks it is nearly always a *shike-poke.*

The hillman pronounces height with a *th* instead of a *t* sound, and some old-timers give it a very long *a* for a vowel, so that the word rhymes with *wraith.*

[47] *Dialect Notes,* Vol. III (1907), 235.
[48] *Arkansas Gazette,* December 3, 1950.
[49] Joseph W. Carr, *Dialect Notes,* Vol. III (1906), 163.

In some words a medial *th* sounds like *t*, so that the hillman says *panter* or *painter* rather than panther. The *th* of girth is often pronounced as *t*, and I have seen the noun *saddle-girt* in several country newspapers.

The *f* sound in after is sometimes not pronounced, so that the word sounds like *atter*. The hillman sometimes pronounces the *t* in often, but it is silent in such words as crept, slept, kept, and wept. I know a woman who grew up in the backwoods, but now teaches English in a Missouri college; she still says a *track* of land, instead of a *tract*. The noun mast, which means acorns, is often pronounced without the *t*, and is sometimes spelled *mass* in the village newspapers.

P sounds like *b* in the word Baptist, which is regularly pronounced *Babtist* in the hill country. A superfluous *b* is sometimes pronounced in family and chimney, which sound like *fambly* and *chimbly*. Heavy, water-soaked firewood is often described as *sobby*, a word which literate hillfolk regard as a mispronunciation of soggy.

There is some confusion of *b* and *v*, particularly in the nouns marble and marvel. A cavern near Notch, Missouri, is called Marvel Cave by its present owners, but the natives insist that Marble Cave is the older and better name. Goodspeed, writing in the early eighteen nineties, describes this place at some length as *Marble* Cave.[50] Children in the Ozarks play with "store-boughten *marvels*," which are cheap marbles of the sort called *potteries* in Kansas and Nebraska. A man at Searcy, Arkansas, complained that "them 'taters ain't no bigger than *marvels*," and he surely meant marbles.

I have heard a few old people say *billify* when they meant vilify; Colonel Charley Short, of Galena, Missouri, uses this pronunciation humorously, and says that it was common in Stone County when he was a boy.

Jay L. B. Taylor reports that culvert is pronounced *culbert* in McDonald County, Missouri.[51]

There is at least one word in which *v* sounds like *d*. Mary Elizabeth Mahnkey, of Kirbyville, Missouri, wrote me that some of the old-timers, including her own husband, pronounce covey as if it were spelled *cuddy*, in referring to "a *cuddy* of quails."

The initial *d* of dubious is pronounced *j*, so that the word may be spelled *juberous*, and means jealous or suspicious as well as doubtful. Dew very often sounds like *jew*, and I have heard educated Britishers pronounce

---

[50] *Goodspeed's History of the Ozark Region* (Chicago, 1894), 26.
[51] *Dialect Notes*, Vol. V (1923), 205.

it the same way. Something of the sort is true of tedious and idiot, which are usually pronounced *teejus* and *eejit*. There's also the word immediate, which sounds pretty much like *imeejit*.

The *d* sound is generally omitted in handle, candle, and the like, but corner is sometimes pronounced *cornder*.

Some persons in the hill country pronounce inning as if it were spelled *inding* or *indin'*. Several professional ballplayers have affected the intrusive *d* in this word; among them was the famous "Pea Ridge" Day, a native of Benton County, Arkansas, who pitched for the Kansas City Blues in the early nineteen thirties.

The word mile, especially when used as a plural, is sometimes pronounced *mild*.[52] I have been told that pioneers in the lead-mining district near Joplin, Missouri, often referred to a mine as a *mind*. Scholar, according to some oldsters in southwest Missouri, should be pronounced *scholard*. There are backwoods preachers in Arkansas who pronounce soul to rhyme with *cold,* and I have seen it written *sould* in manuscript copies of old hymns and in memory-books which dated back to Civil War times. Many Ozark people say *brand* when they mean bran; I have heard educated hillfolk pronounce this final *d* very distinctly, even when reading aloud from the label on a box of B-R-A-N breakfast food. The proprietor of a lunch counter at Caddo Gap, Arkansas, always spelled the word *brand* on his bill-of-fare. Otto Ernest Rayburn, Eureka Springs, Arkansas, tells me that some of the old-timers sound a *d* at the end of the noun school, as "I went to *schoold* myself, more'n four years, right here in Carroll County."

The intrusive *h* is not common, but many Ozarkers say *overhalls* when they mean overalls.[53] The noun welt is often pronounced *whelt* or *whelp*.[54] A girl I know in Greene County, Missouri, has a master's degree in English, but she still complains of the big *whelps* which result when mosquitoes bite her legs.

As Crumb long ago observed in southeastern Missouri, the pronoun it is pronounced *hit* only at the beginning of a sentence or clause, or when some unusual emphasis is required.[55] Carr and Taylor found the same usage in northwest Arkansas.[56] Charles Morrow Wilson says that *"hit*

---

[52] Cf. *Dialect Notes,* Vol. V (1923), 214.
[53] Cf. Carr and Taylor, *Dialect Notes,* Vol. III (1907), 207.
[54] Bryan and Rose, *Pioneer Families of Missouri* (St. Louis, 1876), 77.
[55] *Dialect Notes,* Vol. II (1903), 316.
[56] *Dialect Notes,* Vol. III (1907), 232.

and *it* may follow one another in the same sentence or even in an identical clause, as the delicacies of a primitive euphony may require."[57] Rose Wilder Lane points out that "the Ozark people do not actually say *hit*. The added aspirate is really the soft Arabic *h*, which transliterators usually indicate by an apostrophe. I think no method of conveying that lightly breathed sound exists in English print."[58] Sometimes, but not often, I have found the word spelled *hit* in old letters and diaries. For a further discussion of this matter, with references to the literature, see V. C. Allison's paper "On the Ozark Pronunciation of *It*."[59]

The hillman sometimes uses an *n* sound instead of a medial *ng*, as when length and strength are pronounced *lenth* and *strenth*.

In ordinary talk such participial and gerundial forms as running, jumping, fighting, and the like end with an *n* sound instead of an *ng*. The final syllable is pronounced *in'* with the short *i* very distinct, never turned into the blurred or neutral vowel so common in the Middle West. The Ozarker says sleepin'—never *sleep'n'*, *sleepen*, or *sleepun*. Nothing is pronounced *nothin'*, and something often sounds like *somethin'*, but I have never heard an Ozark hillman say *anythin'* for anything.

The hillman who wishes to speak with particular elegance is careful to pronounce all these final *ng's* very distinctly. Not content with this, he often uses a terminal *ng* where *n* is indicated. Mary Elizabeth Mahnkey mentions an old woman who always called her saddle horse *Morging*, though the name was obviously Morgan.[60] Mrs. Mahnkey used to run a little store at Mincy, Missouri, and observed that when the folks sent a list of things to be purchased they frequently wrote *aspering* instead of aspirin, though the word is printed in large letters on every package.

A little stream which flows through Springfield, Missouri, is known as Jordan Creek. The ordinary Ozark pronunciation is *Jerdan* or *Jurden*, but some "fine-haired" citizens call it *Jurding*. People who wish to be very correct fall into a similar confusion in the case of Joplin, the chief city of southwest Missouri. Robert R. Witten says the town got its name from Joplin Creek, and the creek was named for Harris G. Joplin, a Methodist minister who settled there in the early days.[61] Even the newspapers have discussed this question, some contending that the town was named for a

---

[57] *Virginia Quarterly Review*, Vol. VI (April, 1930), 243.

[58] New York *Evening World*, June 5, 1928.

[59] *American Speech*, Vol. IV (1929), 205–206.

[60] Springfield, Mo., *Press*, May 7, 1933.

[61] *Pioneer Methodism in Missouri* (Springfield, Mo., 1906), 14.

Reverend *Jopling.*[62] Dolph Shaner repeats the story that the preacher's name was originally *Jopling.*[63] "This was confirmed," he writes, "by Ezra Smith of Neosho, a descendant of one branch of Joplins."

I once knew a jimson-weed preacher in Benton County, Arkansas, who always shouted *brethering* when he meant brethren and pronounced heaven as if it were spelled *heving*. In 1917, at Camp Pike, Arkansas, I heard *capting* for captain almost daily. Chicken is sometimes pronounced *chicking*. An old friend from Dutch Mills, Arkansas, always said *muzzling* when he meant muslin. The word certain is generally *sartin* in the backwoods, but I have heard an Arkansas legislator, in a public address, pronounce it *sarting*. We had some neighbors at Searcy, Arkansas, who always said *sunning-law* rather than son-in-law. A stately lady near Cotter, Arkansas, spoke at great length about the *herrings* she had seen on White River; it was some time before I realized that she meant herons, the birds which most Ozarkers mistakenly call cranes. *Mounting* for mountain is not uncommon, and I have several times heard the Boston Mountains of Arkansas designated as the *Bosting Mountings,* a pronunciation quoted in many newspapers.[64] A physician at Pineville, Missouri, told me that he had often heard indigestion pronounced *indigesting* by his up-the-creek patients.

I have often heard unknown pronounced *unknow-en,* in three distinct syllables, and occasionally it comes through clearly as *unknowing*. My neighbor's wife once remarked: "When I was young I used to slip out of a night, *unbeknow-en* to Paw an' Maw." But when this woman wishes to speak elegantly she pronounces the word *unbeknowing,* and always writes it that way.

In some clans and families the syllable *ing* is pronounced so that it rhymes with *rang*. Mrs. C. P. Mahnkey, Mincy, Missouri, once remarked that some of her neighbors pronounce earrings exactly like *year rangs*. I have heard a fiddler refer to the *strangs* of his instrument, and a child speak of extracting the *stang* of a honeybee from her forearm. The noun sanger ordinarily means a digger of "sang" or ginseng roots, but at backwoods singin' conventions it is applied to vocalists, and one hears of bass *sangers,* tenor *sangers,* and so on. Once a little girl told me of a *sangin'* teakettle somebody had purchased in Neosho, Missouri. One of my neighbors in Taney County was *langerin'* with an incurable disease. The pro-

[62] Springfield, Mo., *News,* April 20, 1936.
[63] *The Story of Joplin* (New York, 1948), 15.
[64] Cf. Kansas City *Star,* November 30, 1934.

26

nunciation of *ing* indicated in this paragraph cannot be called common anywhere in the Ozarks, but it is still heard, usually among elderly people in the remote settlements. Some thoughtful old-timers have told me that the *ang* pronunciation was formerly much more common than it is today. This item seems to have escaped most of the fiction-writers, but Charlie May Simon reports a woman near Little Rock as saying *thang* when she meant thing.[65] And Amos Harlin has one of his Howell County, Missouri, characters use *sprang* for spring, *sanglin's* for singlings, and *Sprangfield* for Springfield.[66]

Something of the sort occurs in words like think and pink, which are sometimes given an *a* sound, so that they rhyme with *spank*. But this is not so noticeable as the vowel change in ring, sting, thing, sing, and linger.

The noun resin is usually pronounced *rosum* or *rozzum*. The *n* in ransack sometimes sounds like *m*, as in the sentence: "I been *ramsackin'* the whole place for that there knife." Bantam, meaning small, is often pronounced *banta* or *banty*. The *en* of golden is frequently given a *y* sound, as when my neighbor spoke of "a purty gal with *goldy* hair." An *n* is often used in trickle and trickling, so that one hears "livin' water *a-trinklin'* over the rocks."

Walter Williams remarks that *"r* has small place in the Missouri dialect," and quotes Missourians who say *do'* for door, *flo'* for floor, and *wah* for war.[67] I have heard little of this in the Ozarks. As Professor Morris says, "the letter *r* is pronounced, but not emphasized."[68] The hillman sounds the final *r*, despite the fiction-writers who would make him say *suh* when he means sir.

The medial *r* is silent in such words as nurse, curse, burst, and parcel, which sound like *nuss, cuss, bust,* and *passel*. Some hillfolk pronounce carry very much like the last syllable of de*cay*. There are people in Stone County, Missouri, who say *th'ob* when they mean throb, but this pronunciation is not really common anywhere. The verb throw, however, is nearly always *th'ow* in the backwoods sections of both Missouri and Arkansas. I once knew a girl in Hot Springs, Arkansas, who pronounced foreign parts as if it were spelled *fern pots*, but her speech had probably been corrupted by association with tourists from the Deep South. Most hillfolk sound the *r* in parts, although they do not dwell upon it.

[65] *Scribner's Magazine,* May, 1933, p. 312.
[66] *For Here Is My Fortune* (New York, 1946), 47, 237.
[67] *Missouri Magazine,* December, 1928, p. 7.
[68] University Review (Kansas City, Mo.), Winter, 1936, p. 125.

Metathesis of medial *r* appears in several words, producing such mis-pronunciations as *interduce, childern, hunderd, aggervate, pertect, afeerd,* and so on.

In some isolated sections one hears people saying *brent* very distinctly, when they obviously mean burnt.

Heathen is nearly always pronounced *heathern,* and the intrusive *r* is heard in many other words. Constant sounds like *cornstant,* and caution is sometimes pronounced *cortion.* There are some elderly folk who say *murch* for much, and even *urs* for us, but this usage is not common now-adays. Many people who spell their name Lincoln pronounce it *Linkern* or *Linkhorn.* The little town of Lincoln, in Washington County, Ar-kansas, is still called *Linkern* by many of the old-timers. The verb wash frequently sounds like *worsh* or *woirsh.* Hogue quotes an old Ozark song in which lodging is spelled *largin'.*[69]

Rose O'Neill hears an *r* sound in woman as pronounced in Taney County, Missouri, and thinks it should be spelled *worman.*[70] Lucile Morris also reported *worman* from Taney and Christian counties, Missouri.[71] Isabel France, of Mountainburg, Arkansas, spells the word *wermun.*[72] May Kennedy McCord,[73] of Springfield, Missouri, and Eleanor Risley,[74] of Mena, Arkansas, place the *r* in the second syllable, and prefer to spell it *womern,* meaning woman and not women. The singular form *womarn* is common among my neighbors in Carroll County, Arkansas, but I don't think I ever heard an *r* in the plural.

The late "Pretty Boy" Floyd, of Sallisaw, Oklahoma, sometimes used an *r* sound in going; when he said "I'm a-goin'," it sounded like "I'm a-gorn." Jay L. B. Taylor reports *gorn* for going as current in McDonald County, Missouri.[75] Some hillfolk use an *r* in pup, which sounds like *purp.* A poached egg is generally a *porched* egg. Solder, both the noun and verb, is often pronounced *sorder.* Occasionally one hears an *r* in fuss, so that it rhymes with *purse.*

The word ague is generally pronounced *ager.* Sometimes one hears *banjer* for banjo, and a few old people shout *hallelujer* instead of hallelujah.

[69] *Back Yonder* (New York, 1932), 87.
[70] Kansas City *Star,* November 19, 1939.
[71] *Bald Knobbers* (Caldwell, Idaho, 1939), 17, 18.
[72] *Arkansas Gazette,* March 4, 1951.
[73] Springfield, Mo., *News & Leader,* November 10, 1935.
[74] *Atlantic Monthly,* May, 1931, p. 630; *An Abandoned Orchard* (Boston, 1932), 111.
[75] *Dialect Notes,* Vol. V (1923), 208.

Ought to, in the sense of should, is usually *orter*. Sort of, which means rather or tolerably, is pronounced *sorter*. Kind of, which also means rather, often sounds like *kinder*: "This here meat's *kinder* tough, ain't it?" Sometimes an Ozarker who wishes to be very correct pronounces it *kindly*. A woman from Blue Eye, Missouri, once remarked, "Buster looks *kindly* scratched up, like he'd been a-fightin' a circle-saw."

The noun flail is often turned into *frail*. Charles Cummins refers to "the grain *frail*, which is now out of date."[76] *Frail* is a verb, too, as Charles Morrow Wilson points out.[77] One of my neighbors near Pineville, Missouri, threatened to "*frail* them kids till they cain't stand up." James West tells of a farmer in Hickory County, Missouri, who "*frailed* out his wheat."[78] Jesse Lewis Russell says that in Carroll County, Arkansas, he and his brothers walked to school, and "Father would go along ahead of us with a club to *frail* the dew off the bushes to keep us from getting wet."[79] *Frair* is a rare form of flail or *frail*, which I have heard a few times in Barry County, Missouri; I have never seen it written and have heard it only as the verb.

The terminal *s, se,* or *ce* is sometimes pronounced like *sh*. Licorice is nearly always *lickerish,* and rehearse is often *reharsh*. Taylor says that cornice is pronounced *cornish* in McDonald County, Missouri.[80] Nervous often sounds like *narvish*. The verb rinse, however, is pronounced *rench,* and wince is nearly always *winch*. The noun blemish, oddly enough, is usually pronounced *blemage,* which almost rhymes with damage. Many old-timers say *rubbage* when they mean rubbish.

More than fifty years ago Missourians were wrangling about the pronunciation of the word Missouri. "Nobody says *Miss-sou-ry* but puritans and softheads," wrote a prominent newspaperman. "The correct pronunciation is *Mizzoura*. The people who affect *Miss-sou-ry* are of the same tribe that say *crick* when they mean creek, *rud* for road, and *noo* for new."[81] Frederick Simpich, another distinguished Missourian, declares that "*Mizzoura* it was first spelled and *Mizzoura* it is still pronounced by its two and a half million native sons."[82] Walter Williams, sometime president of the

---

[76] Springfield, Mo., *Press*, August 9, 1933.
[77] *Backwoods America*, 19.
[78] *Plainville, U. S. A.* (New York, 1945), 11.
[79] *Behind These Ozark Hills* (New York, 1947), 60. Cf. *Dialect Notes*, Vol. III (1907), 222; *American Speech*, Vol. V (1929), 18.
[80] *Dialect Notes*, Vol. V (1923), 204.
[81] Columbia, Mo., *Herald*, February 9, 1894.
[82] *National Geographic*, April, 1923, p. 460.

University of Missouri, always insisted that the name is *Miz-zou-rah* or *Miz-zou-ry,* "never *Mis-sou-ri* to any genuine Missourian. The hissing sound of *s* does not appear in the name of Missouri."[83] Homer Croy says that "it's pronounced *Miz-zou-rah,* never Missouri. I was more than twenty years old before I heard it called anything but *Miz-zou-rah.*"[84] There are those who disagree, however. I have often heard Dewey Short, a Methodist minister several times elected to Congress from Missouri, pronounce it *Miss-soo-ry,* with a hissing *ss* sound. Short was a native of Stone County, the descendant of pioneer settlers.[85]

The name Casey, in the backwoods, is very often made to rhyme with *crazy.* The Kissee family, who gave their name to the village of Kissee Mills, Missouri, pronounce it *Kah-see* or *Kah-zee,* with a strong accent on the last syllable. Another common Ozark family name is spelled Kissire, but is pronounced *Kah-zarr,* the second syllable carrying the accent.

In ordinary conversation the Ozarker pronounces Miss and Mrs. very much alike. When a hillman wishes to speak very formally at a wedding, funeral, or other ceremony, he pronounces Mrs. distinctly as *Mistress.* In England and Scotland, *Mistress* was once the correct title for both single and married ladies. Most people who try to write the Ozark dialect spell Mrs. either *Miss* or *Miz.* One reporter referred to a married woman as *Mis.*—period and all.[86] Burton Rascoe, who was brought up in Oklahoma, writes me: "Most Southerners that I know say *Miz* for Mrs., which is just as correct, I think, as the *Missis* which Northerners say. If the Ozark people pronounce Miss and Mrs. exactly alike, that is probably peculiar to them." In my own writing I refer to an unmarried woman as Miss and a married woman as *Mis',* but there is really little difference in the Ozarker's pronunciation of the two titles. I know that there are many who dispute this, but I have heard a lot of Ozark talk, and my ear does not distinguish Miss from Mrs., as the ordinary hillman pronounces the words.

Most hillfolk pronounce tusk, muskrat and muskmelon as if they were spelled *tush, mushrat,* and *mushmelon.*[87] Ask, asks, and asked all sound like *ast* in many a hillman's speech, although the forms *ax, axes,* and *axed* are also heard on occasion.

[83] *Missouri Magazine,* December, 1928, p. 7.

[84] *Corn Country* (New York, 1947), 314.

[85] For a fully documented discussion see Allen Walker Read's "Pronunciation of the Word Missouri," *American Speech,* Vol. VIII (1933), 22–36. Cf. University of Missouri *Bulletin,* Vol. LII (January, 1951), 16.

[86] Alice Curtice Moyer-Wing, St. Louis *Post-Dispatch,* January 13, 1918.

[87] Cf. Carr and Taylor, *Dialect Notes,* Vol. III (1909), 400.

Charles Arnold thinks that *pitcher* for picture is "false dialect, indicating a pronunciation that does not exist in the Ozarks."[88] Nevertheless, my neighbors in southwestern Missouri certainly do pronounce picture, and pitcher exactly alike. Taylor reports that picture is pronounced *pi'ture* in McDonald County, Missouri.[89]

Figure, both noun and verb, is pronounced *figger,* just as it is in England. In several other words a final *ure* sounds pretty much like *er*. Nature, tincture, rupture, pasture, and scripture are pronounced *nater, tincter, rupter, paster,* and *scripter*. The word mixture, however, nearly always sounds like *mixtry.*

An intrusive *w* sound is generally heard in singletree, which is pronounced *swingletree*. Till is often pronounced *tell,* and sometimes *twell*. Singe sounds like *swinge,* and the verb sag is usually pronounced *swag.*[90] Shrivel is nearly always *swivel,* and there is an adjective form as well: "Don't leave them apples out on the gallery, or they'll git *swivelly*." Sometimes one hears shrink pronounced *swink,* and shrunk sounds like *swunk.*

Several times, in Stone County, Missouri, I have heard *drindle* for dwindle: "Our family is just *a-drindlin'* away to nothin', all dead now but me an' Susie."

The omission of *w* is common. In backward and awkward the *w* is not pronounced, so that the words sound like *back'ard* and *awk'ard*. The same is true of inward, and especially the noun inwards, meaning entrails, which is always pronounced *innards*. The names Edward and Edwards sound like *Ed'ard* and *Ed'ards*. The *w* is generally omitted from always, so that most dialect writers spell it *allus.*

The *wh* sound is frequently lost in somewhere, and an *s* added, so that the word sounds exactly like summers: "I ain't seen Bill; reckon he must have strayed off *summers.*"[91]

May Kennedy McCord, of Springfield, Missouri, tells me that some old people omit the *y* sound in yearn, so that the word sounds like *earn* or *urn*. "I got kind of lonesome, an' just *urned* to see somebody. Didn't keer much who it was."

Walter Williams reports that many Missourians say *gyurl* for girl, *gyarter* for garter, and *kyernal* for colonel.[92] The mayor of Springfield,

[88] "The Missouri Ozarks as a Field for Regionalism," Master's thesis, University of Missouri, 1925, pp. 137–38.

[89] *Dialect Notes,* Vol. V (1923), 217.

[90] *American Speech,* Vol. VIII (1933), 52.

[91] Cf. Carr and Taylor, *Dialect Notes,* Vol. III (1909), 404.

[92] *Missouri Magazine,* December, 1928, pp. 7, 25.

Missouri, spells his name Carr, but the old-timers pronounce it *Kyarr*. An old lady near Galena, Missouri, upset a dinner party by suddenly declaring that she smelled *kyarn*, which is the old pronunciation of carrion. I am writing this page in Carroll County, Arkansas, but the early settlers and many of their descendants call the place *Kyarl* county. Some hillfolk say *gyar* for gar, *gyarden* for garden, and *kyard* for card.

Earth is often pronounced *yearth*, and ear sounds pretty much like *year*. Champ Clark, famous Missouri politician, once threatened publicly to cut a heckler's throat "from *year* to *year*."[93] Many Ozarkers rhyme hearth with *worth*, and one often hears something like *hyearth*. Charles Cummins, of Springfield, Missouri, always held that the pioneers pronounced heart as if it were spelled *hyeart*.[94] My neighbor's name is Herbert, and everybody calls him Herb, pronouncing it just as people do in Iowa or Illinois; but when the same persons refer to herb as a medicinal plant they say *yarb* or *yurb*. One often hears a *y* sound in villain, and I have seen it spelled *villyan* in old letters and manuscripts.

Despite his tendency to linger over accented vowels, the hillman frequently lops off sounds and syllables at a great rate, and it is difficult to record his speech without considerable use of the apostrophe. Eternal becomes *'tarnal*, comfortable sounds like *cum'terble*, bedstead is reduced to *'stid*, tarantula is shortened to *trant'ler*, and tolerable is pronounced *tol'able*. Persuade is cut down to *'swade*, and nearly always used with on: "I didn't want to git married nohow, but Lizzie she *'swaded* on me all evenin', an' so finally I done it." Rose O'Neill, of Taney County, Missouri, says that the noun literary, which means a meeting at which "pieces" are spoken and papers read, is pronounced *lit'ry* by the oldest residents. Ordinary is often cut to *ord'n'ry;* this contraction must not be confused with *ornery* or *onnery*, which is a different word and generally means lazy. Venison is pronounced *ven'zen* in the Ozarks, as it is in England. I have heard old men say *sigh* when they meant scythe, and *lay*[95] when they meant lathe. Lennis L. Broadfoot quotes a chair-maker in Eminence, Missouri, who refers to his lathe as "this ol' turnin' *lay*."[96] Many hillfolk pronounce mayor so that it sounds like *mare*. The adjective barren is generally pronounced *barn*, and when a backwoodsman uses the noun *barns* he doesn't mean farm buildings, but unproductive flat lands. I shall not soon forget the *Butler Barns* and the *Hale Barns*, near Blue Eye, Missouri.

[93] Opie Read, *I Remember* (New York, 1930), 283.
[94] Springfield, Mo., *Leader & Press*, September 19, 1936.
[95] *American Speech*, Vol. VIII (1933), 50.

In other cases the Ozarker uses extra syllables. A final *m* after *l* is sometimes stretched into a distinct syllable, so that elm and film are pronounced *ellum* and *fillum*. Combs reports *rellum* as a dissyllabic pronunciation of realm prevalant in some parts of Arkansas.[97]

Backwoods preachers usually pronounce Pharaoh in three syllables as *Pha-ry-o;* one of our neighbors, who pondered much upon Biblical prophecy, was much impressed by the cicadas that holler *Pha-ry-o! Pha-ry-o!* all day long in the summer time. Most country preachers use five syllables in Armageddon, which makes it sound like *Army-gideon*.

The town of Poplar Bluff, Missouri, is persistently called *Popular* Bluff by radio announcers and the like, and the name is often spelled that way in the newspapers.

A lady in Branson, Missouri, was shocked by my phonograph records of bawdy folk songs. "Them songs is too brash for my taste," she said. "I don't sing nothin' but *modesty* songs myself." A man in Eureka Springs, Arkansas, remarked of a ribald modern ditty that "there's a lot of *vulgary* words in it."

The noun mushroom often sounds like *mush-y-room;* this trisyllabic pronunciation is very common in Reynolds County, Missouri.[98] Burglar is frequently pronounced *bur-gu-lar* by radio announcers in the Ozark towns. Nuisance is generally pronounced in three distinct syllables as *nu-i-sance,* with a strong accent on the first syllable.

There are many people in Missouri and Arkansas who persist in using *superstitious* when they mean suspicious.

In a hospital at Fayetteville, Arkansas, I heard many patients say *arthuritis* in speaking of their stiffened and painful joints. In Missouri I knew a physician, an M.D. from a recognized medical school, who wrote arthritis correctly but always pronounced it *arthuritis* just as his backwoods patients did.

Scarecrow is often pronounced *scare-y-crow* in southwest Missouri, and the word is sometimes spelled *scareycrow* in the country papers.[99]

Mischievous sounds like *mis-chee-vi-ous,* the second syllable being accented. Grievous is often *gree-vi-ous,* grievance is pronounced *gree-vi-ance*. A radio announcer at Springfield, Missouri, crying up the advantages of asbestos roofing, always pronounced it in five syllables as *as-a-bes-ti-us*.

[96] *Pioneers of the Ozarks* (Caldwell, Idaho, 1944), 140.
[97] *Dialect Notes*, Vol. V (1919), 36.
[98] Cf. D. S. Crumb, *Dialect Notes*, Vol. II (1903), 322.
[99] Springfield, Mo., *News & Leader*, March 26, 1939.

Most hillfolk are content with four, so that the word sounds like *as-bes-ti-us.*

Tarpaulin is nearly always *tar-po-le-on* in four distinct syllables, accent on the second.[100] I once heard an Arkansas politician say, in a public address, that he "slept right out on the prairie, with sagebrush for a blanket, an' Heaven's blue canopy for a *tar-po-le-on.*"

Possessives ending in *ts* sometimes take an additional syllable. I shall never forget a hired man who signaled every mishap or exasperation with the cry: "Oh, for *Christ-es* sake!"

Some verbs in *ts* or *tes* carry a spare syllable. A storekeeper at Calico Rock, Arkansas, once told me: "Them blue overalls *last-es* better'n the brown uns." There was a girl in Taney County, Missouri, who said: "My feet git sore whenever'n it *frost-es.*" One of our neighbors at Pineville, Missouri, was a jealous old woman who told her daughter: "Your Paw he *trust-es* them people, but *I* sure don't trust 'em." A little boy in Stone County, Missouri, couldn't buy a toy pistol, because "the feller says they *cost-es* forty-five cents." One often hears such expressions as "them fellers *rest-es* under a tree," or "them logs *drift-es* down the river," or "turkeys always *roost-es* in the big cedars." A lady who runs a boardinghouse in Galena, Missouri, observed that "Doc makes a terrible face, every time he *tast-es* them cabbage." And a pretty girl in Eureka Springs, Arkansas, told me that tin water buckets were no good, because "they *rust-es* out too fast."

Many hillmen say *ailded* for ailed, *hurted* for hurt, *drownded* for drowned, *attackted* for attacked, and *foalded* for foaled. A boy who is repulsed or dismissed by his sweetheart is said to be sacked, and the word is often pronounced *sackted.*

A tool or implement which has been used for a season is never second-hand, but always *second-handed.*

Certain monosyllabic adjectives—striped, streaked, forked, and so on—are often pronounced in two syllables. Sometimes such words are made trisyllabic by the addition of *y,* so that striped becomes *stripedy,* streaked becomes *streakedy,* and speckled is turned into *speckledy.* I have heard *grizzledy* used several times, where most Americans would say *grizzled.* And once, in Hot Springs, Arkansas, I heard a lady describe a new hair-do as *frizzledy.*

There are several family names which seem to be pronounced in as many syllables as possible. Members of the Ransom family, for example, generally call themselves *Ran-se-om.* A lady named Forbes, in Wayne

[100] Crumb, *Dialect Notes,* Vol. II (1903), 333; Carr and Taylor, *Dialect Notes,* Vol. III (1907), 237.

County, Missouri, always pronounces her name in two syllables, so that it sounds like *For-bus.*

Nearly all of the old-timers pronounce mountainous as *moun-tay-nous,* with the accent on the second syllable. Some of them make four syllables of it—*moun-tay-ne-ous.* This form is more pleasing to the Ozark ear than the pronunciation favored by the dictionary-makers. A backwoods preacher or politician with a sonorous voice can do mighty well with *moun-tay-ne-ous.* Discussing the late war in Italy, an old gentleman said to me, "This here Italy must be a *tre-men-ji-ous moun-tay-ne-ous* country!"

In the matter of accent the Ozark dialect does not differ greatly from that of Southern speech in general. The hillman pronounces Tennessee as the Indians did, with a strong accent on the first syllable.[101] He usually places a heavy stress on the first syllable of guitar, parole, police, insane, engineer, insurance, harangue, event, relapse, repeat, and cigar, and generally has a "stronger" vowel in the stressed syllable.

In the word character the Ozarker nearly always accents the second syllable. Marion Bennett, who represents the Sixth Missouri District in *Congress,* pronounces spectacle so that it sounds like *speck-TACK-el.* Many Ozark speakers, radio announcers, and the like, pronounce obstacle in the same strange fashion. Signature is accented on the second syllable, with the *a* long; housewives used to save the *sig-NAY-tures* off'n Arbuckle's Coffee, since prizes were offered for these signatures by the coffee salesmen. I once knew a high school principal in Missouri who said he "figured on writin' an *ar-TICK-el*" for a St. Louis newspaper.

The verb aggravate, which means only irritate, is accented on the last syllable: "Bill was just a-talkin' to *aggervate* them fellers." In genuine the final syllable is stressed, and pronounced exactly like wine. Brogan, meaning a rough shoe with a metal fastener, is regularly pronounced with the *a* very flat, and a strong accent on the last syllable.

Such words as settlement, government, commandment, pulpit, infidel, libel, docile, and hostile are often accented on the final syllable. But sometimes these terms are pronounced in a singularly flat, toneless manner, without noticeable stress on any syllable. Backwoods orators are fond of the word havoc, which they pronounce in this strange unaccented fashion, so that it somehow almost rhymes with *hemlock.*

Several educated hillmen have read this chapter in manuscript, and they didn't like it. "Everything you say is true," a small-town lawyer said,

101 Crumb, *Dialect Notes,* Vol. II (1903), 333.

"if each sentence is considered by itself. But when you string these items together, the over-all picture is false and misleading."

"What do you mean, false and misleading?" I asked.

"Well, suppose some possum hunter talks for two hours and mispronounces ten words. You record the mispronunciations accurately enough, but never mention the words that were pronounced correctly. The goddamn' Yankees who buy your book will think that the fellow only spoke ten words, and mispronounced every one of 'em!"

It seems to me that such local criticism is interesting, and maybe significant. Therefore I set it down here as part of the record.

3 Backwoods Grammar

THE MOST conspicuous differences between the Ozark dialect and the folk-speech of the United States in general are matters of vocabulary and pronunciation, but certain other peculiarities are not altogether devoid of interest. One thing that impresses casual "furriners" is the hillman's confusion in the tense forms of the verbs. Sometimes he shows a perverse preference for the weak conjugation, rejoicing in such uncouth preterites as blowed, ketched, drawed, weeped, seed, knowed, sweared, drinked, and throwed. In other cases there is a transfer of affection from the weak conjugation to the strong, which gives such preterites as *clumb* for climbed, *div* for dived, *drug* for dragged, *het* for heated, *snuck* for sneaked, and *skun* for skinned.

The preterite of swoop is sometimes *swope;* a woman in Stone County, Missouri, said that "a hawk *swope* down twice" to catch one of her chickens.

I have frequently heard *scrope* used as a past tense of scrape, even by graduates of the village high schools.

John Turner White, who lived near Springfield, Missouri, in the eighteen sixties, told me that his family "always used *eat* for the past as well as the present tense," but that most of their neighbors used *et* for the past tense of eat, just as the English do.

I have heard *fotch* only as the preterite and past participle of fetch. But the old-timers tell me that fifty or sixty years ago it was used in other tenses. Rufe Scott, of Galena, Missouri, remembers that his father used to say: "*Fotch* me that ax."

Mrs. Lillian Short, of Stone County, Missouri, told me about an old man who watched glumly when the soldiers marched away in 1917. "I fit in Linkhorn's war," he said, "but the folks never *wove* me goodbye." That story is still told in the Short family.

In the same category is the tale of a woman who lost her startin' of yeast. She tried to borrow from a neighbor, but the neighbor wouldn't lend. "It looks like she could have *spore* me a little," the woman said later.

The people who repeat these tales realize that *wove* and *spore* are not correct; that's why they tell the stories. I do not believe that *wove* for waved and *spore* for spared were ever really common in the Ozarks.

Mrs. C. P. Mahnkey, of Mincy, Missouri, says that she has occasionally heard *ruck* as the preterite of rake. A loaded hay wagon was driven into the barn to avoid a sudden shower, and a woman feared that her son had been *ruck off* by a low-hanging door.

The preterite and past participle of heat are nearly always *het,* but in the infinitive one sometimes hears *hotten*: "Nellie will *hotten* up the coffee whilst we're a-ketchin' the horses."

Shore is sometimes heard as the past participle of shear, as in the sentence: "Me an' Bob have *shore* ten sheep since dinner time." The preterite is usually *shirred,* which rhymes with bird.

In some sections the preterite of touch sounds like *totch* or *toch.* Jeff Davis, governor of Arkansas from 1901 to 1907, once pardoned a convicted murderer; in explaining his action to the press, he said that somebody asked the convict's little daughter if her father had killed his alleged victim. "No, he never *toch* him," the girl answered. "This reply *toch* me to the quick," said Governor Davis, "so I *toch* my hand to a pen and wrote a pardon for that father. I believe also that I *toch* the heart of that convict, his wife and child."[1]

Sometimes one hears *retch* as the past participle and preterite of reach. Jay L. B. Taylor reports *retch* as meaning reached in McDonald County, Missouri.[2]

The strong participial *n* is sometimes used instead of *ed,* as when the hillman uses *pourn* for poured. A guest in my house at Pineville, Missouri, once said: "I want my coffee *pourn* out in the sasser."

The word *holden* means held; auctions are sometimes advertised "to be cried and *holden*" on a certain date.

Charles Cummins says that the old-timers used *wored* as the preterite of wear, as "Where's them gallusses you *wored* yesterday?"[3] I have myself heard *wored* as an adjective meaning worn, but am not sure that I ever heard the preterite.

The past tense of ail is very often *ailded.* Mary Elizabeth Mahnkey, of

[1] F. W. Allsopp, *Folklore of Romantic Arkansas* (New York, 1931), II, 330.
[2] *Dialect Notes,* Vol. V (1923), 218.
[3] Springfield, Mo., *Press,* March 9, 1930.

Taney County, Missouri, has heard ailment used as a verb: "My man was turrible sick, an' Doc couldn't tell what *ailmented* him."

The hillman frequently says "I *wisht*" instead of "I wish." Raymond L. Weeks reported this from Kansas City, Missouri, as *wished,* but he recognized it as "a true present tense," not the preterite.[4] A man in jail at Pineville, Missouri, said to me: "I ain't contented here. I *wisht* I was back home." Perhaps it's merely a contraction of *wish that.*[5]

A schoolmarm at Farmington, Arkansas, told me that her pupils "insisted on saying *sont* or *sahnt* instead of sent." I have heard this occasionally, in both Missouri and Arkansas. It seems to be passive; I don't remember anybody who *sont* anything, but have known several men to be *sont for* or *sont after,* meaning summoned.

At a Holy Roller meeting near Harrison, Arkansas, a woman fell to the floor unconscious. "She was throwed by the Power," as her friends put it. I asked whether they had picked her up off the floor. "Not by no means," answered one of the preachers. "We just left her a-layin' where Jesus *flang* her." The preterite was pronounced to rhyme with rang.

The past participles of take and write are very often substituted for the preterite forms, so that the sentences "I *taken* a drink" and "she *written* a letter" are perfectly good Ozark speech.[6] The substitution works the other way round, too, the preterite being used in place of the past participle. The hillman says "she has *wrote* a letter" and "I have *tuck* a drink."

The past tense of take is regularly *taken* as shown above, except in certain idioms: "Jim he *tuck* up with a no-good woman" or "Paw he *tuck* down with pneumonia fever" or "Jennie she *tuck* out for the kitchen."[7] A woman at Galena, Missouri, noticed some dried mud on my bedroom floor. "Them rugs orter be *tuck out an' shuck*," she said.

There are other verbs in which the past participle serves conspicuously as a preterite. Rose Wilder Lane uses *chosen* as the past tense of choose,[8] as, "She *chosen* Dave." Rose O'Neill, of Day, Missouri, reports her neighbor as saying "I *ridden* over an' holp Jim cut wood." Occasionally one hears *given,* sometimes reduced to *gi'n,* used instead of the preterite gave. Some hillfolk prefer *guv,* both as preterite and past participle. Ambrose Bierce found that people in the vicinity of Sedalia, Missouri, say *guv out* when

[4] *Dialect Notes,* Vol. I (1892), 242.
[5] *Dialect Notes,* Vol. V (1926), 404.
[6] Cf. Marguerite Lyon, *Fresh from the Hills,* 136.
[7] Cf. Carr and Taylor, *Dialect Notes,* Vol. III (1907), 219.
[8] *Country Gentleman,* May, 1931, p. 92.

they mean exhausted, powerless.[9] The substitution of *seen* for saw is common, and one sometimes hears a strange combination of the two: "I ain't *sawn* the preacher this mornin'." The weak preterite *seed* is still very common in some sections.

In general, the tendency is to break down all distinction between preterites and past participles in irregular verbs, and when the two forms differ they are often used interchangeably. This trend is illustrated in the principal parts of the following verbs:

PRESENT	PRETERITE	PAST PARTICIPLE
bear	beared	beared
break	broke	broke
bring	brung	brung
climb	clim, clum	clim, clum
creep	crope	crope
dive	div, dove	div, dove
do	done	done
dream	dremp, drempt	dremp, drempt
drink	drinked	drinked
drive	driv, druv	driv, druv
fetch	fotch	fotch
hear	heerd, heern	heerd, heern
heat	het	het
heave	hove	hove
help	holp, holpen	holp, holpen
pick	puck	puck
rake	ruck	ruck
ride	rid, ridden	rid
reap	rept	rept
rise	riz	riz
set	sot	sot
shake	shuck	shuck
squeal	squole	squole
squeeze	squoze[10]	squoze
swell	swole	swole
swim	swum	swum
throw	throwed	throwed
wink	wunk	wunk
wring	wrang	wrang

The hillman sometimes uses the present tense instead of the preterite, as: "The old man *come* home last night," or "What went with the dime I *give* you last Sunday?" One seldom hears the preterite *ran* in the Ozarks; it's nearly always *run*. Backwoods gamblers sometimes say "I *win* four dollars last night" rather than "I won four dollars last night."

Occasionally I have heard the present *swap* made to serve as a past participle. I don't believe a hillman would say "I swap" when he meant "I swapped." But sometimes he does say "You've been *swap* off bad," which means "you've been cheated or fooled or deceived."

The hillman rarely uses, in the first person, the *s* ending of the third singular present. In recording past exploits he doesn't say "I *runs*" for "I ran," "I *goes*" for "I went," "I *fights*" for "I fought." The most conspicuous exception to this rule is the verb say; the Ozarker nearly always uses "I *says*" when he means "I said."

One seldom hears *were* with the second person. The morning after I narrowly escaped drowning, a neighbor asked jovially: "You *wasn't* scared, *was* you?" Subjunctive forms have little part in the Ozark speech. One hears "If I *was* you" rather than "If I were you." I have heard old men say "If I *war* to go," but they also say "If we *was* to go," and "He *war* turrible drunk last night." The fact is that the word *was* is rather common in all persons and numbers.

The Ozarker usually says "I did plow" or "I done plowed" rather than the simple preterite "I plowed."[11] The negative "I never did see" is regularly used instead of the less emphatic "I never saw." Doesn't is very seldom heard, don't being almost invariably substituted.

There are several odd combinations of tense forms with done, as in the sentences "Lee Gifford's done dead," and "the chores done been done," and "she's done went to Bentonville." It seems to me that the word done is used only when the action is complete.[12] The writers of dialect often say "he's done goin'," but I have never heard a real Ozarker use this expression, although "he's done gone" is common. When a hillman says "I done done it," he means "I have finished doing it." When he says "It's done done," he means "it is already done, completely finished."

Ain't does duty for am not, is not, and are not. Has not and have not are sometimes rendered *hain't*, although the unaspirated *ain't* is quite cor-

[9] *Collected Works* (New York and Washington, 1912), XI, 370.
[10] Cf. Carr, *Dialect Notes*, Vol. III (1906), 158.
[11] Octave Thanet, *Journal of American Folklore*, Vol. V (1892), 121.
[12] *American Speech*, Vol. III (1927), 3.

rect even here. *Hain't* for am not is reported from McDonald County, Missouri,[13] but it is not common among the hillfolk of my acquaintance.

Will is invariably substituted for shall, even in the imperative, but the negative form *shan't* is heard occasionally.

The auxiliary should is sometimes used in indirect discourse to indicate a certain degree of doubt. "They do say Jim Burwell should have set his barn afire, to git the insurance money" means that Jim probably *did* set the barn afire.[14] In the sentence "I hear that Mabel should have been a-runnin' after Lucy's man," the *should* stands between the speaker and a direct accusation of misconduct, like the word alleged as used by old-fashioned journalists.

May is rarely used except in the combination maybe, and here it has lost its verbal significance and means no more than possibly or perhaps. Octave Thanet thinks that *mebbe* as used in Arkansas "is probably a contraction of *mayhap* rather than of *maybe*."[15] This doesn't make sense to me, but I set it down here for what it may be worth.

Sometimes might is used with could, rather in the sense of perhaps.[16] "I *might could* ketch a possum tonight, over on East Mountain," said a man in Eureka Springs, Arkansas. And a girl in Cassville, Missouri, remarked to her hostess, "I *might could* dry them dishes for ye."

The hillman generally prefers the future progressive form to the simple future tense; he doesn't say "I'll come over to your place," but rather "I'll be a-comin' over to your place."

Some verbs which are transitive in ordinary American speech are often intransitive in the Ozarks. "I don't want my boy *usin'* round no whore-house!" shouted an irate farmer in Joplin, Missouri. When my neighbor said that his corn was *a-hurtin'*, he meant that the crop was being damaged by dry weather. Crying up a certain brand of whiskey, a bootlegger said "It sure does *drink* easy." Of a love-sick girl in Crane, Missouri, someone remarked: "She's still *a-torturin'* 'bout that fool Connor boy." A gentleman in Taney County, Missouri, told me that "these here seedticks *harbors* in the crabgrass." Booth Campbell, of Cane Hill, Arkansas, once remarked to me, "I didn't *educate* when I was young; didn't see no use in it." Mr. Campbell meant that as a boy he refused to attend the local academy. Near Pineville, Missouri, I shot several small groundhogs, and my hostess spoke enthusiastically: "Them young-uns'll *fry* wonderful!"

---

[13] *Dialect Notes,* Vol. V (1923), 198.
[14] Cf. *Dialect Notes,* Vol. V (1923), 220.
[15] *Journal of American Folklore,* Vol. V (1892), 121.

The verb *holler* is often used in the transitive sense of call or summon. A boy stopped in front of our house at five in the morning, yelling "Jim! Jim!" at the top of his lungs. Jim was our hired man. I asked the boy what was the matter, and he answered, "Jim told me to *holler him up* at five o'clock. We're goin' a-fishin'." In the same way, the boy might have *hollered him out* of the house. If a man were riding along the road, people who lived near by could *holler him in*—into the cabin, that is. When I had business with my neighbor across the river, I had only to *holler him over,* that is, call him from his own cabin to ours.

Reckon and hope are used in some peculiar expressions. *"Reckon how* hot it is" means "I wonder how hot it is." *"Reckon what* time it is" means "I wonder what time it is." Two similar items, *"Reckon who* he is?" and *"Reckon how old* he is?" are reported from McDonald County, Missouri.[17]

When a hillman says "I just *hope how* long the frost holds off," he means "I hope it doesn't frost for some time." The sentence "I *hope how* big it is" means "I hope it is big." A mountain woman says to a parting guest "I *hope how* soon you'll be comin' back," meaning "I hope you'll come back soon."[18] Having called at a backwoods cabin to ask about a sick child's condition, I said: "Well, I reckon Sally will get well pretty soon." The mother answered me: "Lord, I *hope how soon* she will!" meaning "I hope she gets well soon."

In the free fashion of Shakespeare, the backwoodsman does not hesitate to turn a noun or an adjective into a verb. When one says "they done *churched* old Mis' Blackmar for card-playin'," he means that she was deprived of her membership in the church. "Don't *fault* my least young-un" means "don't blame my smallest child." One of my friends "figgered on *vealin'* two calves," adding that they would *"meat* the whole family a month, easy." Another man remarked boastingly that he could cut sufficient grass in one day to *hay* the cow all winter. "Bill just *ideals* that red-headed Heflin gal" means that he thinks very highly of her. A notorious outlaw was surrounded by officers in the woods, but managed to *eel out* somehow and escaped. The noun aunt, pronounced *ain't,* is often used as a verb; in Galena, Missouri, a woman was asked "How many time you been *aunted?"* which means "How many nieces and nephews have you?" Of a wealthy family it was said "they don't *neighbor* much with pore folks." A woman complained that her husband wouldn't work, except as a musician: "He's

[16] *Dialect Notes,* Vol. III (1905), 87.
[17] *Dialect Notes,* Vol. V (1923), 218.
[18] Cf. H. L. Mencken, *American Language: Supplement II,* 234.

just *a-pleasurin'* himself, fiddlin' for them dances." In Taney County, Missouri, I heard that the authorities were *jay-peein'* a friend of mine; this meant that he was being tried before a J.P., Justice of the Peace. A young girl in Pineville, Missouri, refused an elderly suitor, though he had given her some expensive presents. "Why, his whiskers is plumb white," she said scornfully. "I wouldn't *bed* with him, if he was to put candy on the trees!" A woman in Taney County, Missouri, said, "I never was one to *tea* my children," meaning that she did not treat their childish ailments with herbs, but preferred to summon a physician. The noun *hippin'*, which means diaper, becomes a transitive verb in the sentence: "Nancy, go *hippin'* that there baby."

Many good verbs are made from commonplace adjectives. Sultry is converted into a verb meaning to smother or suffocate: "I mighty nigh *sultered* down in that there holler." To *green* a man means to tease or ridicule him. "Let me *weak* that coffee for ye," said a mountain hostess, pouring milk into my cup. Much is a verb meaning to praise excessively, usually applied to the treatment of children. When one of our neighbors suddenly became insane people said, "It must have been losin' his money that *crazied* the old feller."

Such odd verbal combinations as *house-clean, horse-race,* and *hay-rake* are not uncommon. "I sure do love to *squirrel-hunt*," remarked a prominent Arkansas lawyer. *Rabbit-hunt, fox-hunt, deer-hunt* and *turkey-hunt* are common. Even *bee-hunt*, meaning to line bees and thus locate bee-trees, is often heard in the backwoods. A boy at Sallisaw, Oklahoma, showed me a new rifle; "Let's go out and *target-practice* a while," he suggested. Near Cyclone, Missouri, the chief occupation is hacking out railroad ties and hauling them to market; asked how the natives make a living, my guide answered, "Some *tie-hacks* an' some *tie-hauls.*" A young woman in Fort Smith, Arkansas, said, "I've *school-taught* three year now, an' it's beginnin' to taste of the keg." Near Pineville, Missouri, I asked a boy to cut the grass about the cottage. "Do you-uns aim to *lawn-mow* the whole place?" he asked. By lawn-mow he meant to cut grass with the lawnmower, rather than with the scythe or reap-hook. "If I had eddication," another Missourian remarked, "I could *bookkeep* or somethin' like that." At Cape Fair, Missouri, an old man said to me, "I *freight-hauled* for the merchants in the early days." A neighbor of ours, contemplating legal action against a man who had injured her, said, "I'm a-goin' to *law-sue* that feller." A radio announcer at Springfield, Missouri, used to advise: "Folks, whenever you *grocery-shop*, don't forget Raymey's Market!"

A lady at Pineville, Missouri, had no patience with jokes and jokers. "I love a fool," she said to a village smart-alec, "but you *over-suit* me." She did not refer to his lack of intelligence, but to his liking for practical jokes.

"They say Bill favors his Paw, but I think he *out-favors* him." This means literally that Bill looks more like his Paw than his Paw does; in other words, the father's features and characteristics are exaggerated in the son.

There is a tendency to coin verbs ending in *fy* and *ify*: *argufy* instead of argue, *speechify* instead of orate, and so on. One of Rose O'Neill's neighbors near Walnut Shade, Missouri, boasted that he could *clockify*, meaning that he knew how to repair clocks.

The hillman likes adjectives ending in *ified*. *Dressified* means particular about clothing, *fitified* means subject to fits, *citified* means urban, having the airs and manners of the city. A little boy from Massachusetts spent a summer in the Ozarks, and the local people were amused by his "*Yankee-fied* ways." A *prettyfied* woman is one provided with good clothes, a permanent wave, cosmetics, and the like. The word *holyfied*, in some of the backwoods Protestant cults, means sanctified, "possessed of the Holy Spirit." I have heard a schoolmarm speak of term papers as being *rectified* when she meant corrected, and the word *rightify* is sometimes used in the same meaning. *Jokeyfied* means habitually jocular or even clownish, sometimes in the sense of feebleminded. *Airified* means conceited, and applies to one who "puts on airs." A man in Taney County, Missouri, remarked that his mother "sure was *workified;* we couldn't git her off'n the plow till she was pretty near eighty." Uncle Jack Short, of Galena, Missouri, once remarked, "I ain't been very *eatified* the last few days," meaning that his appetite was poor. Speaking of the prospects of rain, a woman said to me, "It sure don't look very *rainified* this evenin'." Mrs. C. P. Mahnkey, of Kirbyville, Missouri, referred to a mixture of burnt whiskey and bacon grease, used as a remedy for bellyache, as "a *witchified* potion." When a man says that he's *hurtified,* he refers to a general lameness or soreness rather than a sharply localized pain. There is an old song with the line: "Madam, I have a very fine house, just newly *erectified*," meaning erected, built.[19] Cal Tinney is reported as saying that his army discharge papers had finally *mister-fied* him, made him a civilian, that is.[20] Tinney was born in Pontotoc County, Oklahoma, and spent much time in the hill country.

There are some strange verbs ending in *n* or *en*. When one of our

[19] See my *Ozark Folksongs*, III, 53.
[20] *Saturday Review of Literature*, June 22, 1946, p. 46.

neighbors said, "That there medicine sure did *pearten* Elmer right up," she meant that it made him feel better, more lively. *Quieten* means to subside: "We'll have to wait till things kind of *quieten* down an' blow over." The preterite and past participle are *quietened*. *Belongen* is a form of belong, as in the sentence, "Them dogs *belongen* to Ab Landers." The old verb *enlargen* means to enlarge or expand; Wayman Hogue makes an Arkansas politician denounce his opponent who wants to *"enlargen* the free schools."[21]

With a taste for emphatic speech, the Ozarker is fond of attaching the intensive prefix *be* to certain participles. *Beaddled* or *beattled* means confused, addled, bewildered. *Bedaubed* and *begaumed* mean smeared, more or less covered with a liquid or semi-liquid. A man who is muddy, or stuck in the mud, is *bemired*. To describe a man as *benastied* means that he is bedaubed with some unpleasant substance, such as vomit or dung.[22] A woman at Pineville, Missouri, told me that her husband had "done got drunk and plumb *benastied* himself."

Many nouns concerning time and space use the singular form for both singular and plural. One often hears such phrases as *seven year back, twenty rod off, six foot high,* and the like. On the highway north of Neosho, Missouri, there used to be a large sign: JOPLIN, SEVEN MILE FROM HERE. Most natives use mile as indicated above, but some of the old-timers pronounce the plural as *mild*.

Such quantity words as bushel, pound, dozen, head, cord, rick, pair, and so on seldom have any plural form, never when preceded by a numeral. This is true of many animal names, like coon, skunk, mink, otter, possum, fawn, wolf, fox, bear, and panther. Also the names of certain fishes, such as goggle-eye, skipjack, pumpkinseed, and so on. Tom Shiras, veteran newspaperman of Mountain Home, Arkansas, always used to say "these gar."

When my old neighbor at Pineville, Missouri, said, "Them is the illest *bee* I ever seen," he referred to an entire colony, thousands of individual bees. By ill he meant irritable, easily moved to anger.

Some nouns which pass for singular elsewhere are treated as plurals in the Ozarks. Molasses is one of these, as in the sentence, "How many molasses have you got?" Arch T. Hollenbeck, newspaperman at West Plains, Missouri, discussed this matter at some length: "Being myself a native 'lasses lapper I easily lapse into the local way of using the plural

---

[21] *Back Yonder,* 116.
[22] *Dialect Notes,* Vol. VI (1928), 63.

those molasses, as it doesn't seem right to call 'em *it* or *that*. The real Ozarker usually calls 'em sorghum, anyhow. He takes a thin case knife and mixes soft butter with 'em and spreads 'em on his cornbread good and thick."[23]

Manerva Carolyn Shepherd, of Osceola, Missouri, remembers an old song about molasses:

> *How they got so thick with flies,*
> *They resembled raisin pies.*[24]

Jay L. B. Taylor says that sorghum is called *sogrums* in McDonald County, Missouri, and is "always used as if plural in form."[25] In some sections it appears that sogrums means either the cane in the field or the syrup made from the cane. I have heard people in Taney County, Missouri, say, "Pass me them *sogrums*" when they wanted "long sweetenin' " to put on their pancakes.

Cheese is another plural noun; the hillman always speaks of *them cheese*. Yet the common phrase "hit an' crackers"[26] means "cheese and crackers," comparable perhaps to "ham and" or "coffee and" as used elsewhere. Logically it should be *"them* an' crackers," but I have never heard it so. Edson and Fairchild reported the Tennessee mountaineers using *chee* as a singular form of cheese, but this seems to be unknown in the Ozarks.[27]

A few times I have heard *ho* used as the singular of hose, meaning stocking. A gentleman at Camp Pike, Arkansas, said thoughtfully that "a good slick *ho* sure does purty up a gal's leg," using *purty up* in the sense of beautify. I have seen a letter from a storekeeper at Cabool, Missouri, in which he describes a certain brand of wartime nylons as "a beautiful *ho.*" In Katrina Johnson's novel *Evening Street*[28] one woman says to another: "There's a hole in your *hoe,*" but that's the only time I have ever seen the word in print. Ethel Strainchamps, Springfield, Missouri, says that *"hoe,* as the singular of hose, is used by men's clothing salesmen everywhere," but I have been unable to confirm this.

The word hose, in the sense of garden hose or fire hose, is nearly

---

[23] West Plains, Mo., *Journal,* October 24, 1931.
[24] *Ozark Guide* (Eureka Springs, Ark., October-December, 1944), 71.
[25] *Dialect Notes,* Vol. V (1923), 221.
[26] Amos Harlin, *For Here Is My Fortune,* 233.
[27] *Dialect Notes,* Vol. I (1896), 376.
[28] New York, 1947, p. 80.

always plural: "Fetch me them hose. They're layin out in the yard." In McDonald County, Missouri, a man remarked that "It didn't take the boys long to put out the fire, but they was pretty all night a-windin' up *them Goddam hose."*

Many hillfolk use fertilize as a noun, meaning commercial fertilizer; it seems to be a plural, as one often hears *these fertilize* or *them fertilize.* Sometimes a singular form *fertili* is used. Leonard Parker, farm agent in Stone County, Missouri, in the early nineteen forties, spoke often in favor of "choosin' the right *fertili,* an' then stickin' to it." If he had said *fertilize,* Parker would doubtless have advised stickin' to them.

Cabbage is always plural, too. An ordinary hillman says "pass me them cabbage," but an educated mountain girl who wishes to be very elegant may say "those cabbage." A fiddle tune popular at the country dances is called "Bile *Them* Cabbage Down."

Sauerkraut is generally plural also, and bulk sausage is always referred to as *them* in backwoods talk. W. H. Strong, an Ozarker who moved into town and wrote for the outdoor magazines, complained of his "futile efforts to obtain *sausage like these* in the city."[29]

Spinach is generally plural, perhaps because the Ozarker pronounces it *spinage,* and thus the last syllable connects the word with cabbage and sausage. Occasionally one hears *these lettuce* and sometimes *them salad.*

Gunpowder is singular, so is blasting powder, and so is face powder, but baking powder is generally used as a plural form: "Put in a spoonful o' them *bakin'-powders."*

The noun license is always used as if it were a plural: *them license, these here license,* and so on. A young farmer led his sweetheart into the courthouse at Forsyth, Missouri, and said, "We want to git *some license,"* meaning a marriage license. I don't think I ever heard a native Ozarker say *a license.* Frequently he dodges the issue by omitting the article,[30] as when an amateur veterinarian insisted that "a feller don't *need license* to doctor his own critters." A village boy complained about the poor fishing in the Cowskin River at Noel, Missouri, saying, "I paid a dollar an' a half *for license,* an' didn't even skin a minner!" A high school student in Stone County, Missouri, developed a morbid interest in surgery. 'I wish to God I was a doctor," he said. "A doctor can cut an' slash, an' *have license* to do it!"

The article is often omitted before mortgage, too: "Tom figures maybe

[29] *Midwest Sportsman* (Kansas City, Mo.), January, 1929, p. 15.
[30] Cf. George Clinton Arthur, *Backwoodsmen* (Boston, 1940), 79.

48

I'll starve out this winter, so he can *git mortgage* on my farm." Education is used in the same way; no old-timer would say *an* education. Insurance, census, and bounty are generally plural, and the same is often true of the noun cost. Judge John Turner White, of the Missouri Supreme Court, told me that many old-timers still refer to court costs as *them cost*.

Some people call oatmeal breakfast food *them porridge*. A young matron told me that she "had to bake *biscuit* three times a day." Her husband wouldn't eat cornbread, she said, "but he sure does go for *them biscuit*."

A barber at Pineville, Missouri, remarked that "it sure is a job to shave *them beard* of old man Jeffers; *they're* tough as bailin'-wire." Rose O'Neill, of Taney County, Missouri, quotes a local girl who cried, "I just love *them sandy mustache* Tommy's got!"

The sheriff at Southwest City, Missouri, told reporters, "I seen *both of them corpse* a-layin' in the road." A lady near Marshall, Arkansas, sang an old song with the line: "Lay down *them clay cold corpse*"—meaning one body. I have heard another old ballad about "those pale corpse."[31]

The radio announcers in Springfield, Missouri, nearly always say lens instead of lenses; they seem to feel that *lens* must be a plural. Cracked corn is called corn-chops and referred to as *them chops*. And a girl in a "beauty shoppe" at Crane, Missouri, spoke seriously of *"them* cuticle."

A newspaper editor in Benton County, Arkansas, once told me: "I aim to print the news, *all of 'em,* no matter whose ox is gored." This usage is good inheritance, I think. News was originally plural, after the Old French *nouveles,* "new things." Many early writers, including Shakespeare,[32] used it as a plural.

The names of certain diseases—chickenpox, smallpox, paralysis, flux, diarrhea—are generally plural. A teacher in southwest Missouri "caught the smallpox an' brought *'em* home." A man in Branson, Missouri, remarked, *"These goddamn' rheumatism* is a-gittin' worse every day."

Ooze, meaning a thick paste of herbs or bark, is nearly always plural: "Slippery-ellum ooze is mighty good, if you can get *'em.*" I heard a doctor in Joplin, Missouri, use pulse in the same way: "Couldn't count his pulse at all, *they were* runnin' so fast."

The noun brush is apparently plural, meaning bushes; "out in them brush" means "among the bushes," while "one of them brush" is a bush or a shrub. On James River, in Missouri, an old man said, "Jim's field is rougher'n mine, but there ain't so *many brush* in it."

[31] Cf. my *Ozark Folksongs,* I, 138.
[32] *Othello,* Act I, scene 3, lines 1–2.

49

Mrs. C. P. Mahnkey, of Taney County, Missouri, tells me that her neighbor was talking of a new variety of oats. *"They're* a small, white oat,"* he said, "an' we sure did cut a lot of *'em."*

A storekeeper at Big Flat, Arkansas, showed me a pair of cotton trousers with the remark, *"Them* sure is a fine pant."

Charley Hiatt, of Galena, Missouri, brought some rotted manure in a wheelbarrow for the flower beds. "Where do you want *these* rich dirt?" he asked.

One often hears the noun gravels, but the singular form gravel is rare. A lady in Washington County, Arkansas, told me of the time a saddle mare "shied when she come to the creek, an' throwed Sally Byrd right down in them gravels." This same woman spoke of *gravel roads,* but I never heard her use gravel as a noun. Even when a pebble got into her shoe, she called it "one of them pesky river-gravels."

I once spent nearly an hour trying to maneuver a man near Hollister, Missouri, into pronouncing the word tomato, but he always avoided the singular by saying "one of them 'maters" or "one of them termaters."[33] I have heard *ter-ma-ter-ses* used near Mena, Arkansas, but do not think the four-syllable plural is common anywhere in the Ozarks.

Near Dutch Mills, Arkansas, a man named Sharp told me of killing a very large wildcat. "It was what they call a link," he said. This man was familiar with the word *lynx,* but evidently regarded it as a plural.[34] Elsewhere in the Ozarks I have heard link-cat used as a synonym for catamount, which means a lynx or a big bobcat.

Otto Ernest Rayburn remarks that "perhaps the folk of the backhills say *gentlemens* for gentlemen, but you do not hear them refer to the male of the species as *gents."*[35] I have noticed that many Ozarkers who speak comparatively correct English, people who would never say gentlemens, do use *fishermens* as the plural of fisherman. Elbert Short, of Crane, Missouri, once referred to *footmens,* as distinguished from *horsebackers.*

A redhorse is a fish, a kind of sucker, and the hillman uses it as both singular and plural: "I ketched a big redhorse" or "I ketched two big redhorse." But sometimes he shortens the word to horse, and in this case the plural takes an *s,* as "I ketched five big *horses* this evenin'."

The noun offals, meaning something discarded, is common, but I have not heard the singular form offal. "We feed the pigs on offals from

---

[33] *American Speech,* Vol. III (1927), 10.
[34] Cf. Mencken, *American Language: Supplement II,* 239.
[35] *Roadside Chats* (Beebe, Ark., 1939), 21.

the hotel" is good Ozark English. The word is pronounced without any noticeable stress on either syllable. It is sometimes used figuratively. When my neighbor said of a local girl, "She's one of Jim Blake's offals," he meant that she was the discarded mistress of Mr. Blake. In this meaning one often hears the noun *offcasts*, which is regularly preferred to castoffs. This term also is plural, and the lady would be called "one of them offcasts" rather than simply an offcast.

A few nouns like post, nest, desk, waist, wrist, beast, and vest add another syllable in the plural, so that they sound like *postes, nestes, deskes, waistes, beastes*, and *vestes*. Moffat reports that in the Tennessee mountains the word fist requires two added syllables, the plural being *fisteses*,[36] but the Ozarker is content with *fistes*. The plural of guest is sometimes *guestes*, and ghosts is often pronounced *ghostes*. A lady in Taney County, Missouri, said, "Pass me one of them *toastes*," meaning a slice of toasted bread. I remember an outraged innkeeper denouncing a traveling salesman who "et four *breakfastes* just 'cause it was his birthday an' he didn't have to pay nothin'."

A hillbilly musician on a radio station in Missouri used to refer to the *requestes* he had received for certain fiddle tunes and songs. The word locust, meaning cicada, takes a similar plural; neighbor told me that "them trees was full of *locustes*, an' every one a-hollerin' fit to bust his guts." I once knew a blacksmith in Arkansas who referred to his bellows as *them bellerses*, and Dr. O. St. John, of Pineville, Missouri, says that this plural was formerly common in southwest Missouri.

The word folk is not heard in the backwoods, but both *folks* and *folkses* are common and seem to be interchangeable. Leaving a group of five or six friends, a hillman says, "Well, *folkses*, I'll be a-seein' you-uns tomorrow." Folks is sometimes used to designate a member of the speaker's own kind or community, so that "he's *folks*" means "he's all right."

Some of the most impressive backwoods nouns are converted verbs, as in the sentence: "Did you-uns hear the *give-out* at the church-house?" *Give-out* means announcement. "We was up late every night last week," sighed a waitress at the City Hotel in Noel, Missouri. "Yes," answered another, "an' there was some mighty early *git-ups*, too." My wife found an old woman in tears, and asked what was the matter. "There ain't nothin' the matter," said the old lady; "I just got to thinkin' about the *bygones*, when my man was alive an' we lived on Sweet Greasy!" A boy from Joplin, Missouri, came to ask for a job; he had a "plumb good

[36] *Journal of American Folklore*, Vol. IV (1891), 315.

recommend" in his former employer's "own *handwrite."* The woman at Aurora, Missouri, who complained that she "didn't git no *invite"* meant that she had received no invitation.

Occasionally one finds an adverb doing duty as a noun. A boy in Stone County, Missouri, where I was a deputy sheriff, said, "If I had my *rathers,* I wouldn't be a-settin' in this here jail-house." Rathers may be translated preferences, and is often pronounced *ruthers* or *druthers.* When Elviry Weaver, of Springfield, Missouri, used "if I had my *druthers"* in a movie entitled "Swing Your Lady," people all over America wrote in to ask what it meant.[87]

Adjectives are sometimes made into nouns, as in the sentence: "Them Pea Ridge folks is all *hatefuls;* don't have nothin' to do with 'em." Also in the answer: "Well, if they come down here a-lookin' for trouble, they'll sure git a *lavish* of it!"

The hillman has a weakness for more or less redundant combinations such as tooth-dentist, hound-dog, doe-deer, jay-bird, brant-goose, moth-miller, flesh-meat, ham-meat, show-actor, boar-hog, cash-money, grave-hole, navel-hole, pasture-field, sheep-shepherd, rain-shower, cook-kitchen, oak-acorn, acorn-mast, witch-woman, widder-woman, widder-man, boss-man, preacher-man, spice-clove, buzzard-bird, hymn-song, chamber-room, puddle-pond, doll-poppet, brush-thicket, bosom-breast, stand-table, eye-oculist, chimney-flue, grape-vinyard, fruit-orchard, bottle-flask, milk-dairy, hog-lard, pulpit-desk, cot-bed, biscuit-bread, play-toys, and meadow-field.

A fork-turn is the division of a road. In telling me how to get to a place called Garber, Missouri, an old man said, "When you come to the first *fork-turn,* take the left-hand *prong."*

Rose O'Neill, Day, Missouri, has adopted the Ozark term *neighbor-woman,* and uses it in her ordinary correspondence, though without the hyphen. One occasionally hears *lie-tale,* meaning a serious falsehood intended to deceive, as contrasted to a humorous tale or *windy.* The term *pot-vessels* means all the metal pots, kettles, stewers, and heavy pans used in cooking.

Another of these redundant combinations is *rim-edge,* as "We was a-livin' on the *rim-edge* of poverty in them days."

Although tourists often burst out laughing at our use of church-house and similar compounds, the Ozarker uses them with distinguishing meaning. When he says church-house, he means the actual building, the church edifice. No hillman, however unlettered, would speak of "joining the

[87] Cf. the "Beverly Hills" column in *Liberty,* March 5, 1938.

church-house." I am not sure that church-house is any worse than school-house and courthouse, which are used in many parts of the United States. Anyhow, I have seen church house on the printed stationery of the Reverend John Haynes Holmes, an educated fellow who lives in New York.

The word *jail-house,* common in the Ozarks and elsewhere, likewise refers to a building made with hands.

For many years I thought that horse in horse-jockey was redundant, like tooth in tooth-dentist. But in 1945 I heard a dog-breeder and wolf-hunter at Crane, Missouri, referred to as a *dog-jockey.*

City people often think that choppin' in choppin'-ax is redundant, not knowing that it distinguishes the ordinary double-bitted ax from the pole-ax and the broad-ax.

A grubbin'-hoe is very different from the ordinary garden hoe with which tourists are familiar; the latter is generally called a *goose-neck* in the Ozarks.

When a hillman says "that's mighty fine drinkin'-whiskey," he means that it is mild and pleasant to the taste; it may be very inferior stuff, diluted with water and sweetened with molasses. "It drinks mighty easy" doesn't mean that it's of good quality.

The old-timer applies the name rifle-gun to the weapon which most people call a rifle nowadays; he means to distinguish it from a smoothbore, a gun which is *not* rifled. Modern smoothbores are used only as shotguns, and are so designated, but smoothbore guns adapted for a single ball were formerly common and may still be seen occasionally in the Ozarks.

Elviry Weaver, of Springfield, Missouri, used to lay 'em in the aisles by saying *posey-flowers* when she meant bouquet. O. O. McIntyre, of Plattsburg, Missouri, and Bentonville, Arkansas, frequently used *shoe-cobbler.* A headline in a Little Rock newspaper refers to "a gatherer of *bee honey.*"[38] Judge John Turner White, of the Missouri Supreme Court, used to say *picket-guard* when he meant sentinel; he showed me his manuscript autobiography which contained several references to "an old-fashioned *carpetbag satchel.*" A Forest Ranger in Arkansas found the term *new beginner* in his official instructions from the federal government.[39] The Ozark papers are full of similar expressions, and once I found an editorial writer who described a local celebrity as a *poet-woman.*[40]

The terms menfolks and womenfolks, boy-children and gal-children

[38] *Arkansas Democrat,* October 20, 1938.
[39] *Field Program,* U. S. Forest Service, May, 1909, p. 26.
[40] Springfield, Mo., *News & Leader,* November 10, 1935.

are common. Sometimes one hears *man-person, woman-person,* and even *gal-person.* Near Jane, Missouri, an old gentleman was defending the thesis that physicians are of no use in obstetrical cases. "An' it ain't right nohow," he added, "for a *man-person* to be thar when a woman's a-havin' a baby." In some sections the hillfolk use *young person* to mean a young girl, and a male is never so designated unless the speaker wishes to be very insulting. I have heard the term *lady-folks,* but only a few times, and I am not sure just what is meant by it.

The hillman seldom says grocer or jeweler, but nearly always *grocery-man* and *jewelryman.* A village newspaper carries an advertisement: T. D. SPENCER, *Jewelryman.*[41] I have heard radio announcers in Missouri and Arkansas refer to bakers as *bakerymen.* The editor of a newspaper at Springfield, Missouri, uses *factoryman* to designate the manager of a big arms and munitions factory.[42] A locomotive engineer is often an *engineer-man,*[43] while a hoister in a lead mine is a *h'isterman.* One seldom hears the word juror in the Ozarks, but *juryman* is common. In some isolated sections the term gambler is used by the young folks only; the old-timers still say *gamblin'-man.* Even *hunterman,* meaning hunter, is sometimes printed in the Ozark newspapers.[44] Isabel France, in her newspaper column, writes *bankerman* when she means banker.[45]

People going to or from a religious meeting are often called *meetin'ers.* "It must have been about eleven o'clock," said a witness in a murder trial, "because I heard the *meetin'ers* go by just about that time." In Galena, Missouri, a lady spoke of the boys who caroused in the streets as "them *Halloweeners.*" I once heard the Christians who attended a baptising on Bear Creek, in Taney County, Missouri, referred to as *babtizin'ers;* this meant the whole crowd, not merely those who were baptised or the preachers who did the baptising. The members of a wedding party are regularly called *weddin'ers;* one of my neighbors remarked, "I heerd the *weddin'ers* a-whoopin' an' a-hollerin' 'long about sun-up."

County and state health officers, or any persons who concern themselves with sanitation and the like, are called *healthers,* even in the newspapers.[46] Members of local draft boards are known as *drafters.* At a meet-

[41] Gentry, Ark., *Journal-Advance,* July 22, 1943.
[42] Springfield, Mo., *Leader & Press,* August 11, 1945.
[43] *Dialect Notes,* Vol. III (1905), 78.
[44] Springfield, Mo., *Press,* November 18, 1931; December 11, 1931.
[45] *Arkansas Gazette,* Little Rock, January 9, 1949.
[46] Springfield, Mo., *Leader & Press,* December 3, 1941; October 31, 1942.

ing of teachers, principals, and superintendents I once heard the whole company referred to as "them *schoolers.*"

There are several other agent nouns in *er*. A *carter* is one who drives a cart; a *horsebacker*,[47] one who rides a horse; a *footbacker*, always used jokingly, means a pedestrian; a *gossiper* is one who gossips; a *musicker* or *musicianer* is a musician; a *sawmiller* is a man who runs a sawmill; a *steamboater*, one who pilots a steamboat. Tourists are still called *touristers* in the back hills. *Residenter* means resident, but is applied only to the early settlers; I knew many *old residenters,* but never heard of a *new residenter.*

The Ozarker has a fondness for nouns ending in *ment*. Some of these are survivals of earlier English; others are evidently recent creations. A man at Forsyth, Missouri, felt that he was being persecuted by the local peace officers, and said to the sheriff: "I'll take no more of your *abusements!*" The words *botherment* and *botheration* mean nuisance, and *worryment* is often used with the same significance. The hillman says *foolishment* rather than foolishness or folly, and feels that *frightment* is a stronger noun than fear or fright. *Nursement* means milk, as when a baby "throws up his *nursement,*" but perhaps it's only a corruption of nourishment. Toys or playthings are often called *playments,* sometimes *playpretties.* The noun *scatterment* means a scattering or dispersal or *scatteration.*[48] My old neighbors used *tanglement* with reference to a thicket or briar-patch, but sometimes it is employed figuratively to mean any sort of confusion. A two-headed calf which was exhibited in our village was called a *wonderment,* and this term may be applied to any curious, odd, or surprising object.

The Ozarker handles his personal pronouns with some disregard for the case distinctions, using the objective forms where the nominatives are indicated, as "it sure is *me,*" and "*us* fellers cain't git out of this here jail-house." A member of the Missouri legislature told me of the days "when *me* an' *her* was a-sparkin'," and often used such expressions as "*him* an' his woman they fit scandalous." Any attempt to speak with special elegance seems to reverse this condition, and we find the nominative substituted for the objective form in such sentences as "that feller done kissed all of *we* girls," or "she seen *he* an' *I* a-comin' down the road" or "the old church-house is good enough for *I* an' Abner."

The absolute form of the possessive is often marked by a final *n* instead of *s*. Thus we have *yourn, hisn, hern, ourn,* and *theirn* in common

[47] *American Speech,* Vol. VIII (1933), 50.
[48] *Dialect Notes,* Vol. III (1909), 403.

though not exclusive use. The *n* doubtless represents an old termination preserved in analogy with mine and thine.

Double-barreled pronouns such as *we-all, you-all* and *they-all* are common in the Ozarks, as in many parts of the South. "You-all is not a corruption," said Walter Williams,[49] "but the best of English from the King James version of the Bible. When the Missourian went to meetin' he heard the apostolic benediction, 'The grace of our Lord Jesus Christ be with *you all*.'" President Williams used you-all in the plural only, and never wrote you-all's save as a plural possessive. Taylor reports *you-alls* and *we-alls* without the apostrophe from McDonald County, Missouri,[50] but his distinction between *you-all* and *you-alls,* and between *we-all* and *we-alls,* is not clear to me. Personally, I have heard the terminal *s* only in the possessive case.

In standard English *you-all* may be either singular or plural, according to the *Oxford Dictionary;* Professor Robert L. Ramsay, of the University of Missouri, says that the *Oxford Dictionary* "seems mistaken in this."[51] Most Missourians and Arkansawyers who write about such matters agree with Ramsay. Carr lists *you-all* only as a plural in northwest Arkansas.[52] Crumb thinks that you-all is never used as a singular in southeastern Missouri, "although often appearing thus in dialect fiction."[53] Wayman Hogue says that "there is not a man, woman or child in the whole state of Arkansas who uses the word *you-all* in addressing the second person singular."[54]

Well, I have certainly heard *you-all* used with reference to one person, in both Missouri and Arkansas.[55] In many cases, of course, *you-all* may be addressed to one person without being a true singular; when one gentleman says to another, "*You-all* come over to my house," the compound pronoun often means *you-and-your-wife-and-your-children*. But when I win a pot in a poker game, and the dealer pushes the chips toward me with the remark "*You-all* take the money, Vance," he is surely speaking to me, and nobody else. And when my neighbor and I are hunting, just the two of us in a vast wilderness, and he cries out "Why don't *you-all* shoot?" then it seems to me that *you-all* is used in the second person singu-

---

[49] *Missouri Magazine,* December, 1928, p. 7.
[50] *Dialect Notes,* Vol. V (1923), 198, 224, 225.
[51] *A Mark Twain Lexicon* (Columbia, Mo., 1938), cxi.
[52] *Dialect Notes,* Vol. II (1904), 422.
[53] *Dialect Notes,* Vol. II (1903), 337.
[54] *Back Yonder,* 218.
[55] Cf. *American Speech,* Vol. III (1927), 5.

lar. Also I prefer to believe that certain intimate communications, whispered in my ear by a native of Arkansas, were intended for and addressed to me exclusively. Granting this assumption, the lady certainly used *you-all* in the singular. One sometimes hears backwoods preachers hailing the Deity as *you-all,* but the speaker's intent may be obscured by some theological consideration with which I am not familiar; perhaps such prayers are addressed to the Blessed Trinity rather than to Jehovah. Estelle Rees Morrison says positively that she has heard *you-all* as a singular, in Missouri and elsewhere.[56] Burton Rascoe, in reviewing one of my books, discusses the Ozark dialect at some length, and prints letters concerning *you-all* and *you-uns* from his correspondents.[57] See H. L. Mencken for an amusing and fully documented account of the controversy about *you-all.*[58]

May Kennedy McCord tells me that the hillfolk she knows never say *we-uns,* although *you-uns* is very common. Mary Elizabeth Mahnkey says that *"we-uns* is rarely heard" in her neighborhood, although *you-uns* is in daily use. I have heard *we-uns,* both nominative and possessive, in many parts of Missouri and Arkansas. I do not believe that it is really common anywhere nowadays, but I still hear *you-uns* every day, even among educated people in the Ozark towns. Wayman Hogue observes that the Ozark hillfolk "generally say *you'ens* for the plural of you, instead of you-all as so many think."[59] Hogue does not say whether *you'ens* ever functions as a singular, but Charles Morrow Wilson makes a character in his novel[60] use it in addressing one person. Carr and Taylor, at the University of Arkansas, recorded *you-uns* only as a plural.[61] I do not recall having heard *you-uns* in the singular.

Occasionally one hears an odd combination of *you-uns* with *all.* An old gentleman in Stone County, Missouri, used to shout, "How are *you-uns* all?" He was talking on the phone to his son in a distant city, but presumably meant to inquire about his daughter-in-law and grandchildren as well.

Sometimes the plural possessive *you-uns'* is pronounced in three syllables as *you-uns-es.* The phrase "at *you-uns-es'* house" means "at the house belonging to you and your family." A man near Crane, Missouri, addressing two little boys, said: "I seen *yournses'* cows in the corn," but I

[56] *American Speech,* Vol. IV (1928), 54–55.
[57] New York *Sun,* October 30, 1921; November 5, 1931; November 21, 1931.
[58] *American Language: Supplement II,* 375–80.
[59] Kansas City *Journal-Post,* March 1, 1931.
[60] *Acres of Sky* (New York, 1930), 118.
[61] *Dialect Notes,* Vol. III (1909), 238.

believe this is the only time I ever heard *you-uns'* with an *r* sound in it. The form *yous,* reported by Crumb from southeastern Missouri,[62] is not common in the Ozarks. When it is used, I think it is always plural.

The related pronoun *us-uns,* although rare, is not altogether unknown to the hill people.[63] Elizabeth Seifert, in a Missouri story entitled "Hillbilly Doctor,"[64] uses both *us-uns* and *us-all.* The form *us-uns* or *us'ns* is sometimes quoted in court testimony and news items in the Ozark newspapers.[65]

The Ozark farmer is so closely identified with his land that he actually refers to it as *me.* One often hears a hillman say that a certain fence or spring is *on me,* meaning that it is located on his land. A neighbor once told me that the new highway "busted old man Price right square in two," and I heard that a recent flood had "throwed gravel all over the Widder Scroggins." I once asked a farmer near Bentonville, Arkansas, how far a certain cavern was from his farm. He answered: "Why, it's right *at me,*" meaning that it was outside, but very near, the boundary line of his property.

The relative pronouns are used much as they are elsewhere in the South, but *whose* is not common, and *whom* is never heard in the Ozarks at all. *That* is very generally substituted for *whom,* and *what* is often used in place of *that,* as "them's the kind of gals *what* I like." Often it is linked with *but* and made to serve as *that* in still another sense: "I don't know *but what* I better be a-gittin' on home." Several times I have heard *as* used as a relative: "The gal *as* I danced with, she was a humdinger!"

The hyphenated pronouns *who-all* and *what-all* are common, particularly in interrogative sentences like *"Who-all* was at the frolic?" and *"What-all* did them folks have to eat?" The possessive form of who-all is frequently heard: *"Who-all's* is this here choppin'-ax?"

Ever-what is equivalent to whatever. "Just tell me *ever-what* you want done, an' I'll tend to it." After a disastrous fire one of my neighbors remarked: "Well, *ever-what* was in that there shanty is done burnt up."

Ever-who is not uncommon. *"Ever-who* wants to fight, let him stand up an' say so like a man!" At a dancing contest the manager announced: "We always give the prize to *ever-who* is the best dancer, even if they *ain't* no kin to the judges." The possessive form is sometimes heard, as, "Them fellers stole *ever-who's* horse come down the road."

[62] *Dialect Notes,* Vol. II (1903), 337.
[63] *American Speech,* Vol. III (1927), 6.
[64] *Redbook,* May, 1940, pp. 131–64.

Ever-which is not often heard, but a man once showed me half-a-dozen stock saddles hanging in a barn. *"Ever-which* of them saddles you want, just holler an' it's yourn," said he.

The demonstrative pronouns this and that often become *this here* and *that there.* The plural form *these here* is common, but I never heard *those there*—the hillman says *them there* instead. Two other common demonstratives are best spelled *this'n* and *that'n,* contractions of this one and that one. The word *it* or *hit* is sometimes used almost as a demonstrative; looking first at my rifle and then at his own, a hillman once said: "How'd you swap *hit* for *hit?*"[66]

Sometimes the Ozark pronoun agrees with its antecedant in number, but frequently it does not. *"Anybody'd* be gravelled to see *their* woman a-talkin' to that feller" is good Ozark English. So is a sentence like *"each* gal better git *their* own basket." In the intensive forms the mountain man says *hisself* rather than himself, and frequently adds emphasis by interpolating *own*—"he done it *his own self."*

Such tautological sentences as "the feud it went on" and "the man he fell down" and "the gal she begun to holler" illustrate what might be called a tonic use of the pronoun, which is very common in the Ozark speech.

Many writers represent the Ozarker as omitting both definite and indefinite articles on every possible occasion, but I have not found it so. The hillman may say "I hope Old Scratch ketches that boy!" instead of "I hope *the* Old Scratch ketches him," but that is because Old Scratch is regarded as a proper name, like Satan. He may fail to put *the* or *a* before a few nouns such as license, bounty, and mortgage which are generally treated as plurals, but there is no such general omission of limiting adjectives as Rose Wilder Lane,[67] Louise Platt Hauck,[68] and others would have us believe.

Ary and *nary,* derived from e'er a and ne'er a, are heard frequently. "Lizzie," shouted a girl in our kitchen, "you got *ary* fresh egg handy?" And Lizzie answered "No, we didn't git ary-un today." A storekeeper once put my small purchases into a very large paper bag, and remarked apologetically "I ain't got *nary* little poke."[69] The form *not ary* is sometimes used instead of *nary,* but the latter seems more emphatic. Still more forcible is the double negative *"not nary* one of them fellers is worth killin'."

[65] Springfield, Mo., *Leader & Press,* May 3, 1940.
[66] *American Speech,* Vol. III (1927), 7.
[67] *Cindy, a Romance of the Ozarks* (New York, 1928), 41, 121 ff.
[68] *Wild Grape* (Philadelphia, 1931), 232.
[69] Cf. Charles Morrow Wilson, *Virginia Quarterly Review,* Vol. VI (1930), 247.

In the comparison of adjectives the hillman is likely to overwork the *er* and *est* terminations; *beautifuler* and *perfectest* are not uncommon, and sometimes *badder* is heard. May Kennedy McCord used to tell a story about a boy and girl walking in the moonlight, when they saw a bush covered with spiderwebs. The boy threw a stone at it, and when the stone passed through the webs without effect, they were sure it was a ghost. The couple broke and ran, as fast as they could. As the boy said later, "The furder we run, the *fearder* we got."

Sometimes the hillman fancies both the prefix *more* and the *er* ending, so we hear *more better, more harder, more higher,* and the like. *Nearder* and *nighder,* meaning nearer, are still common in the back hills, and even *more nighder* is not unknown. Seeing a horseman approaching, I asked my neighbor, "Ain't that one of the Lauderdale boys?" He looked long and carefully at the rider. "No," he answered, "it comes *more nighder* to a Yancey." A radio announcer at Hot Springs, Arkansas, used to say *more gayer.* Double superlatives such as *most meanest, most dirtiest, most jealousest,* and even *most almightiest God* are encountered occasionally. Sometimes one hears *only* intensified by the superlative suffix: "Betty is the *onliest* gal I ever figgered on marryin'."[70]

The comparative form of *far* is sometimes used in an odd fashion. In the sentence "two mile was *all the further* he could run," *all the further* means *as far as.* A few other words—high, fast, hard, long, and the like— are employed in the same manner. Carr and Taylor noted this usage in the country about Fayetteville, Arkansas.[71]

When participles are used attributively, they are compared like any other adjectives: "Lucy is a *lovin'er* gal as Fanny, but Mary is the *lovin'est* gal I ever seen." Superlatives of this type are very numerous, such as *fightin'est, dancin'est, shootin'est, askin'est, cryin'est, insultin'est,* and so on. In the sentence "Jim was the *beatin'est* feller I ever seen," the word *beatin'est* means extraordinary or astonishing. A lady in McDonald County, Missouri, had outlived four husbands, and I once heard her described as "the *marryin'est* woman that ever wore a dress." A headline on the sports page of a Little Rock newspaper says that a certain baseball player is "the *winningest* pitcher in America."[72]

The hillman seems to feel that an extra syllable strengthens almost any superlative. He often uses *worsest* for worst, *mainest* for main, *ripestest*

[70] *Dialect Notes,* Vol. III (1906), 149; *ibid.,* Vol. V (1923), 216.

[71] *Dialect Notes,* Vol. III (1907), 392.

[72] *Arkansas Gazette,* Little Rock, Ark., December 13, 1950.

for ripest. A radio announcer at KGBX, Springfield, Missouri, in 1944, regularly said *fartherest* when he meant farther.[73] Many hillfolk say *leastest* for least, meaning smallest. *Bestest* is sometimes used for best, as "them is the *bestest* boots I could buy," but I have heard it applied to plural nouns only. The horse which comes in last, or the candidate who receives the smallest number of votes, is the *hindest*—never the hindmost. Uncle Jack Short, of Galena, Missouri, usually says *freckledy* when he means freckled, and sometimes brings out a four-syllabled superlative, as "he was the *frecklediest* boy you ever saw." *Goddamndest* is very common, and occasionally one hears *God-damndedest!* "Ain't this the *by-goddest* weather you even seen?" asked a mail-carrier in Polk County, Arkansas. A neighbor complained that his daughter had "married up with the *idlesomest* loafer in the whole damn' township." A minister of the gospel in Baxter County, Arkansas, once said to me: "That's the *crowdedest* church-house I ever preached in." The weekly newspaper at Forsyth, Missouri, announced editorially that 1940 was "the *cucumberest* year ever known,"[74] meaning that the local gardeners had produced a very large quantity of cucumbers. Somebody once said that the Ozark region has no folklore, and Otto Ernest Rayburn, Eureka Springs, Arkansas, rebuked him in the local idiom: "Why, it's the *folklorinest* country you ever heard tell of!" he wrote.[75]

Compound adjectives like snake-bit, fire-burnt, lightnin'-struck, and briar-scratched are very common. A *horse-throwed* neighbor of mine rolled down the mountain and died in a tangle of *wind-blowed* trees. I have worn *moth-et* britches and have seen *wolf-killed* sheep in my own pasture. An acquaintance of ours was described as "a pore lonesome *wife-left* feller," and a Missouri newspaper referred to a local man as *wife-tamed*.[76] "If I was to turn that baby loose," said a woman near Pineville, Missouri, "it would be *hog-et* afore sundown." A lady in northwest Arkansas asked a schoolmarm to excuse her son from classes "on account he's been a-trappin' an' he got *polecat-stunk* yesterday." The editor of a county-seat newspaper in Missouri told me of a man who was "*car-hit* an' hurt so bad he damn' near died." A newspaper gravely reports that the wife of George Q. Fenn was *wasp-stung* on the way to Marble Falls, Arkansas.[77]

Occasionally in a compound adjective one finds a past participle where most Americans would use the present participle. Thus *good-tasted* means

[73] Cf. *furtherest, American Speech*, Vol. VIII (1933), 49.
[74] *Taney County Republican*, August 22, 1940.
[75] *Arcadian Life* (Caddo Gap, Ark., October, 1940), 7.
[76] Springfield, Mo., *News & Leader*, March 5, 1939.
[77] Gentry, Ark., *Journal-Advance*, August 9, 1945.

"having a pleasant taste or flavor." Rufe Scott, of Galena, Missouri, heard his father say, "That's as *good-tasted* a fish as I ever et."

There are many compound superlatives, such as *loud-cussin'est, hell-raisin'est, fish-ketchin'est, vote-gettin'est,* and *rabbit-killin'est.* A man once told me, "Katy is the most *out-doin'est* woman that ever lived," and I think he meant that she was surprisingly vigorous or energetic. One of my friends was badly cut in a knife fight and required many stitches to repair his injuries; of the physician who did the work he remarked, "Doc Holton is the *stitch-takin'est* feller I ever met up with." A boatman who prepared meals for tourists on a float-trip was described as "the *pancake-cookin'est* feller on the creek." A man who sold out several times and moved to Oklahoma, invariably returning a few months later, was referred to as "the *back-comin'est* feller in this country." An editorial in a Little Rock newspaper points out that the United States is "the *statistics-keepingest* nation on the face of the earth."[78] A certain state senator in southwest Missouri was described as "the *potguttedest* candidate that ever crawled up on a stump." A mountain man remarked to me that his children were maturing very rapidly, adding, "I believe Lolly is the *growed-uppest* one of the lot." Such superlatives as *sleepy-headedest* and *high-powerdest* are familiar to everybody in the back hills.

In some sections it appears that everything, good and bad, is described as *tore-downdest.* Taylor reports *torn downdest* as a superlative in McDonald County, Missouri, but does not define the term.[79] I once asked an old gentleman in Little Rock, Arkansas, for a definition. He pondered awhile and replied: "Well, *tore-downdest* is just like *God-awfullest.* When you come right down to it, them words don't mean much of anything!"

There are many odd adjectives ending in *y* or *ey. Blackguardy* means suggestive, obscene; a bawdy ballad is described as "one of them dirty, *blackguardy* songs." *Gladey,* which rhymes with shady, means rocky or barren, as in the sentence: "We got lots of pasture, but there's some *gladey* spots in it." When a hillman says that a road is *ledgey,* he means that it's full of ledges, and your car bumps along as if you were driving down a flight of steps. *Resty* means lazy, *hystericky* means flighty or hysterical, *muckledy* means dun-colored. A *visity* woman is inclined to go a-visiting on the slightest provocation. *Withey* generally means wiry, tough, like a hickory withe. "Tommy ain't big, but he's the *withiest* feller I ever seen." *Yieldy* is synonymous with fertile or productive, and one of my neighbors

[78] *Arkansas Gazette,* Little Rock, Ark., January 23, 1949.
[79] *Dialect Notes,* Vol. V (1923), 223.

remarked, "Our west bottom never was very *yieldy,* an' in a dry year it ain't no good at all."

Sometimes a noun is regularly used as an adjective: "There's too many *fool* laws in the settlement." The word master is a common adjective: "My boy is the *masterest* fiddler in this town." A man told me that "Bill tried to educate for a doctor, but he warn't *thoughted* enough"; in other words, he didn't have the brains. Some hillfolk, however, use *thoughted* to mean considerate, thoughtful of the welfare or the feelings of others. The adjective *unthoughted* is rare, but the adverbial form *unthoughtedly* is the common term for carelessly or heedlessly.

Occasionally an adverb serves as an adjective, as "Maw's mighty *porely* this evenin'." B. A. Botkin mentions a *"grandly* barbecue" in Oklahoma.[80] Meeting an old man in the road near Tar River, just across the Oklahoma line, I asked, "How are you today?" He answered, "Oh, just *moderately.*"

Often several adjectives of similar meaning are strung together: "He's just a common, ordinary, every-day feller," or "I seen a little, small, puny-lookin' bear a-settin' under a bush."

Worse is often used to mean more, as in the sentence: "Hit's *worse'n* three mile to the settlement." The word better, oddly enough, is used in exactly the same sense; substitute *better* for *worse* in the above sentence, and the meaning is not changed at all.

The use of adjective forms instead of adverbs is almost universal—"I ketched her *easy,*" and "she hollered *turrible,*" and "he was hurt quite *bad.*" I have known many village schoolmarms, even school principals and superintendents, who used such expressions and taught them to their pupils.

The double negative, as "I never done nothin'," is the rule rather than the exception. Often the word *nohow* is added for greater emphasis, and we have a triple negative. Even the quadruple form "I ain't never done nothin' nohow" is not uncommon. Occasionally one hears the quintuple, as "I ain't never done no dirt of no kind to nobody!" Such a sentence as "I don't want but one" is used and defended even by educated Ozarkers. When a hillman wishes to deny all knowledge of a subject he says "I never heard tell of it." Sometimes he uses the double negative form "I never heard no tell of it," which means exactly the same thing.

Backwoods folk are fond of scrambling negative implications, particularly with the word *surprised.* Speaking of the village drunkard, a physi-

[80] *American Play-Party Song* (Lincoln, Neb., 1937), 108.

cian told me: "I wouldn't be surprised if Andy don't quit drinkin'," meaning that he thought Andy's reformation was possible. In the same way, "I wouldn't be surprised if you ain't right" really means "I'm inclined to think you are right." In Stone County, Missouri, a county official asked, "Don't reckon them two'll git married, do ye?" And the second courthouse rat replied: "Well, I wouldn't be surprised if they didn't." In Eureka Springs, Arkansas, a farmer was describing in detail the symptoms of his sick hogs. "It looks like cholery to me," he concluded. "Yes," answered an amateur vet who had listened attentively, "I wouldn't be surprised an that ain't what it is." This quite seriously, with no attempt to be humorous. Note the use of *an* with the early English meaning of *if*.

Two hillmen were waiting in an old car for a third, who had agreed to help plant corn for an invalid widow-woman. "Jim said he'd be here," grumbled one fellow, "but I'm afeered he ain't goin' to make it." The other man squinted at the sun. "No, I reckon not," said he. "Jim's got so he *never makes it every time.*"

Mighty is a very popular adverb in the back hills, and one hears mighty good, mighty bad, mighty hot, mighty cold, and so on all over the place. Sometimes the word is used rather oddly, as, "Them children are *mighty* in my way!"

Very is generally used with a negative. The hillman often says "he ain't very tall," but rarely "he is very tall." When the word occurs in a positive statement it seems rather weak; a man who says he is "feelin' very well" means that he is only tolerably well, or "fair to middlin'."

Jay L. B. Taylor says that the adverb plumb means completely, and may be used to modify any adjective.[81] It certainly does mean completely or quite in such sentences as "Dave is *plumb* wore out" and "I ain't *plumb* sure what we better do." But in other cases it seems to mean only very, as, "He'll git here *plumb soon* in the mornin'," very early, that is.

Whenever often means simply when. "*Whenever* I was a boy," said one of my neighbors, "the womenfolks stayed home an' tended to their own business." Often a final *n* is added so that the word sounds like *whenever'n*. One often hears *ever-when* in the same meaning: "*Ever-when* you go a-foolin' with my gal, you're liable to git hurt!" Sometimes the *n* sound is heard in this form, too, as when my neighbor said to his wife, "I'll go to work *ever'n-when* I git ready, an' nary a minute sooner!"[82]

Ever-how is not uncommon, and apparently means however. "That feller's money, *ever-how* much it was, is done gone now."

[81] *Dialect Notes*, Vol. V (1923), 217.

Since ever is sometimes used where most Americans would say *ever since*. Rose Wilder Lane begins a sentence with: "Since ever they was boys . . . ."[83]

Everly means always, or at least usually: "It's *everly* been Pap's way to holler a little, when he gits to drinkin'."

In ordinary midwestern American speech, any more means any longer, and is used with the negative only: "Mary doesn't live here *any more*" implies that Mary did live here in the not-too-distant past. In the Ozarks any more seems to mean merely now or at present, and is not confined to negative expressions.[84] A realtor at Crane, Missouri, said to me, "I can git you a good bottom farm *any more,* for thirty dollars an acre."

Leastways is common among the old-timers, and means no more than at least. "Them bass'll be a-bitin' afore sundown," a guide remarked when we were fishing in the Cowskin River without success. I made no answer, but must have looked incredulous. *"Leastways* that's what Lem Hatfield says," the guide added uneasily.

After is combined with certain verbs in a peculiar fashion. A boy who resembles his father is said to *"take after* his Paw." At the same time, a child may be *named after* his uncle or his grandfather. An old Missouri newspaper carried an editorial plug for a new musical composition: "We recommend it as a beautiful piece to *waltz after*, and easily executed."[85] A woman in Farmington, Arkansas, told me, "Lon Jordan is the best fiddler I ever *danced after*." A prominent woman in southwest Missouri told reporters that she "liked to *read after* Wright," meaning that she enjoyed Harold Bell Wright's novels. And a gentleman at Hot Springs, Arkansas, told me that a local damsel was "the best cook you ever *et after*."[86] When a boy says "I *study after* Professor Baines," he means that Mr. Baines is his teacher. A woman remarked that her son *"hankered after* yaller-yams," meaning that he had a craving for sweet potatoes.

The use of up to intensify the meaning of a verb is very common.[87] Not only does the hillman *meet up* with travelers and *rick up* firewood, but he *ketches up* livestock, *shoots up* revenuers, *loves up* his sweetheart, *knocks up* his wife, and *'fesses up* his sins. Such combinations as *lay up, dry up, tutor up,* and *gaum up* are heard everywhere in the hill country. One of

[82] *American Speech,* Vol. VIII (1933), 49.
[83] *Country Gentleman,* May, 1931, p. 7.
[84] Cf. Harold Wentworth, *American Dialect Dictionary* 24–25.
[85] *Daily Missouri Republican,* St. Louis, July 13, 1850.
[86] *Dialect Notes,* Vol. V (1926), 399.
[87] Cf. Carr, *Dialect Notes,* Vol. III (1905), 99.

my neighbors, after a quarrel with his wife, rushed into the tavern and shouted: "Give me a gallon o' whiskey! I'm fixin' to *raise up* hell!" It always seemed to me that *raise up hell* is a much stronger expression than the plain *raise hell* so common elsewhere.

In the Middle West generally, if a boy came late to a party, the others would say, "We gave you up long ago," meaning that they had assumed he was not coming. But in the Ozarks people say out instead of up. When a speaker failed to appear at a political meeting in a Missouri village, we "just *give him out a-comin'*," and invited a local preacher to speak instead. The hillfolk often use *give up* to mean recognize or acknowledge, as "Jim Burke was *give up* to be the best auctioneer in the county."

Out is used with left to mean depart; sometimes it means to depart furtively, or even to flee headlong. I once went with our sheriff to arrest a man at a roadhouse. "Billy was here all evenin'," said the bartender in answer to the officer's question, "but he *left out* just before sundown."

When the hillman says that a fellow *lit out* he means that the man ran off, or left at high speed. *Took out* sometimes implies a hasty or unexpected departure; but often "he'll *take out*" means only that he'll withdraw from a contest of some kind.

In McDonald County, Missouri, according to Taylor, the hillfolk use *break out* as a verb meaning to break or train an animal.[88]

Went with, in the Ozarks, often means became of, or happened to. A man who searched everywhere for his chisel said: "I just cain't figger out what *went with* it." He did not mean that the tool had been stolen, merely that it was mislaid or lost.

Instead of saying that a man is dead, the Ozarker often says that he has *died off*. When I returned to Stone County, Missouri, after several years' absence and asked for an old friend, a loafer said, "Oh, he *died off* last winter."

Light down means to alight, sometimes only to pause or halt. When a man comes along the road, he is greeted with *"Light down, an' set a spell,"* or *"Light down, an' rest your saddle,"* no matter whether he's riding a horse or not. One of our neighbors remarked that a flock of wild geese had *done lit down* in a near-by field.

Put at is used rather oddly sometimes. A friend said, "The boys *put at* me to run for sheriff," meaning "they tried to persuade me to run."

Put-in is sometimes used as a noun. "It ain't none of my *put-in*" means "it's none of my business." But to say "Lucy is goin' to *put in*" means that she's going to file or apply for a divorce.

A kind of repetition or redundancy in the use of adverbs or conjunctions is very noticeable sometimes. Once I heard a stranger, vainly trying to buy liquor in a dry village on Sunday, cry out in his exasperation, "You-uns act *like as if* I was a Goddamn' preacher!" And a woman who lived opposite us near Hot Springs, Arkansas, used to summon her small son by yelling, "You come *here thar*, Isham, afore I git the hickory!"

Sometimes a number of redundant adverbs or other words are strung together for emphasis, as, "I *most generally always* rocks them dogs off'n the place," or *"finally at last* I got tired of talkin' to them fellers." Just the other day a man told me that he had made seven dollars *over an' above* his expenses. One of my neighbors was *bound an' determined* to tell us about great deeds done in his *day an' time,* and prefaced his wildest stories with *surely an' undoubtedly.* One hears such combinations or repetitions as "It's *still yet a-rainin'* " and "there won't be no sunshine *yet awhile."*

Another strange combination is *candidly an' black-actually,* an expression which W. O. Cralle thinks may have originated in the Ozarks.[89] Charles Morrow Wilson, of Fayetteville, Arkansas, reports *really and back-actually,*[90] *candid and back-actually,*[91] and *candidly and back-actually,*[92] but the hillfolk that I know always say *candidly an' black-actually,* pronouncing the *black* very plainly[93]

The preposition in is sometimes employed rather oddly, as "Jim he hid *in back of* the woodlot." *In back of* means only behind. The sentence "Jim he hid *out"* implies a longer period of concealment; men often *hide out* from the law for months and even years.

Sometimes a number of prepositions are used in series, as "Ab he lives *in under* a bluff, *away back up on* Sugar Creek" or *"away over yonder somewheres down by* Shell Knob." A gentleman in Pineville, Missouri, was telling me where he lived. "To git to my house," said he, "you just cut *across through in back* of Carnell's store." The prize example of this sort of thing came from Benton County, Arkansas, where I was told of some wild exploit which took place *"way over yonder back in there round about* Bear Holler."

The preposition *anent* means near, beside, or even against, in such a sentence as "Will's hat was a-layin' in the weeds, down *anent* the smoke-

[88] *Dialect Notes,* Vol. V (1923), 202.
[89] Springfield, Mo., *Leader,* October 29, 1933.
[90] *The Rabble Rouser* (Toronto, 1936), 287.
[91] *Backwoods America,* 70.
[92] St. Louis *Post-Dispatch,* June 9, 1930.
[93] *American Speech,* Vol. IV (1928), 116.

house." Sometimes it appears that *fernent* and *fernenst* carry the same meaning as *anent*, but generally fernenst means opposite, across from, or *even with*. Fritz Williams, who runs a newspaper at West Plains, Missouri, told me of interviewing a murderer in the local hoosegow. When she asked where the shooting took place, the prisoner answered *"fernenst* the depot,"* meaning across the street from the railroad station.[94]

At is nearly always substituted for to in such sentences as "Just listen *at* the old fool a-hollerin'." The intensive use of at in "Where do you live at?" is very common. A teacher once told a pupil that the above sentence was not correct, and the boy spoke up promptly: "I mean, where*abouts* do you live at?"

To is often used instead of at, as when a man cried, "Them Jeffers boys all jumped on me *to* once," meaning suddenly or simultaneously, or both. When I stopped before a moonshiner's house, intending to *holler him out,* a small boy said, "Pappy, he ain't *to* home."

Another amusing use of to was illustrated by a lady in Howell County, Missouri, who cried out, "I believe *to* my soul I'm a-goin' to be sick *to* my stomach!"

Near to means nearly or almost, and is generally shortened to *near't*, as in the sentence: "That feller purty *near't* killed Lance Bledso."

To is used with an infinitive after have or had, as, "Bob had three shots *to die* on him last week" or "I'll have them gals *to put* dinner on the table." As in early English, the preposition for seems to go with the infinitive: "I come down here *for to* get some coffee." Compare a passage in the King James Bible: "What went ye out for to see?"[95]

In most parts of the United States one would say that an undersized child is small *for* his age, but in the Ozarks I have often heard "That boy is small *to* his age, ain't he?"

On frequently replaces of, as "He's the biggest fool I ever heerd tell *on*." Something of the sort occurs in out of and off of when the hillman says, "Aunt Mary run *out'n* the house an' drug Ike *off'n* his horse." A boy in our village declared, "I'm goin' to marry that gal *spite'n* the whole Howard family an' all the connection!"

Of is preferred to with in "I don't know what's the matter of him," and is used superfluously in such statements as "I don't remember of it."

The combination but though is very common, in such expressions as

[94] Cf. *Dialect Notes,* Vol. V (1926), 398, 400. Also May Kennedy McCord, Springfield, Mo., *News,* January 24, 1937.
[95] Luke 7:25.

"I ain't scarcely able to ride, *but though* I will," where the ordinary Midwesterner would be content with but.

As frequently appears in the place of than: "I'd sooner sleep in the pasture an' pick corn out of horse-droppin's, *as* to teach school for a livin'." An old woman in Polk county, Arkansas, was forever saying, "Well, better late *as* never."

A peculiar negative form is sometimes used for the sake of emphasis. "I wonder if he don't!" really means "He certainly does!"

There is a trick of omitting apparently essential words. One often hears a hillman say, "I ain't been over there for the longest!"[96] meaning he hasn't been there for a long time. In a sentence like "Lizzie run right out an' told *each an' every,*" the final word one is understood but not expressed. *Indeed an' in-double-deed* is an old phrase used when great emphasis is desired; it is sometimes abbreviated, as in the sentence: *"Indeed an' double,* I won't go a step!"

Sometimes the hillman adds emphasis by inserting appropriate profanity not only between the words of a forceful statement, but between the syllables of the words. Combs reported the same sort of thing from the Southern Appalachians.[97] Rose O'Neill, of Day, Missouri, tells an old story with the line: "I'll have you under-*God-damn*-stand that I'm the super-*by-Jesus*-intendent of this place, an' I won't be dic-*hellfire*-tated to by nobody!"

[96] *Dialect Notes,* Vol. V (1926), 401.
[97] *Proceedings* of the Modern Language Association, Vol. XLVI (1931), 1322.

4 Survivals of Early English

People from the cities are often struck with certain archaic words and phrases used by the hillfolk, and a great deal has been written about the Elizabethan character of the Ozark dialect. Enthusiasts have talked a little wildly about "Shakespeare's America" and "our contemporary ancestors" and "seedbeds of Anglo-Saxonism." British tourists have told reporters that the Ozarkers speak English rather than American.[1] "The early Missourian," says President Williams of the University of Missouri, "brought his English speech from the south of England, the speech of Cambridge and Oxford and Stratford-on-Avon. Expressions which seem odd to the over-cultured may be and often are survivals of English used three centuries ago."[2]

Many persons in Missouri and Arkansas have expressed similar convictions. "It is my opinion," writes Otto Ernest Rayburn, "that the natives of the Ozark region have been able to retain, through isolation from other races, the purest of the King's English. Any student will discover in the Ozark speech words from the Elizabethan period, the age of Shakespeare and Ben Jonson." Rayburn quotes from Celia Ray, of the Springfield, Missouri, *News,* the story of an Ozark boy who went to college and was required to write a thesis on "Vagabonds of the Elizabethan Period." In reading for this paper, he found that many of the "quaint" words and expressions of the Elizabethans had been familiar to him since childhood, although students from other parts of the country had never heard them.[3] Charles Morrow Wilson, Fayetteville, Arkansas, declares that "the speech current in the Ozark backwoods is a very old English,"[4] and traces many

[1] Cf. Charles J. Finger, *Adventures under Sapphire Skies* (New York, 1931), 22–24, 46–47, 125.
[2] *Missouri Magazine,* December, 1928, pp. 7, 25.
[3] *Ozark Life* (Kingston, Ark., August, 1930), 11, 13.
[4] St. Louis *Post-Dispatch,* June 9, 1930.

expressions back to Elizabethan times. W. O. Cralle, Springfield, Missouri, says that "the Ozark dialect would be more easily understandable to Shakespeare than to the English professor of today."[5] Nancy Clemens uses the word *Chaucerian* to describe the Ozark speech,[6] and Jay L. B. Taylor of Joplin, Missouri, apparently agrees with her.[7] "I wonder," muses Clyde Brion Davis, "if Miss Clemens isn't stretching it a smidgen to say Ozark accents are Chaucerian. Wouldn't Elizabethan be enough?"[8]

Thomas Hart Benton is a native of Neosho, Missouri, and knows the Ozark dialect better than most of the people who talk so solemnly about it. Benton says that romantic writers have placed too much emphasis upon archaisms and survivals. "The Ozark people do use a lot of Elizabethan expressions," he told me in 1940, "but the general effect is not Elizabethan, because their speech is mixed with modern slang and wisecracks. A hillman will use one of these old English phrases, and then put something like *okie-doke* on the end of it." I string along with Benton so far as the general effect is concerned. But there's no denying that many of the differences between the Ozark dialect and the common folk-speech of other rural areas are survivals of older English usage.

It is not difficult to see how this condition has come about. Nearly all of the Englishmen who settled the American colonies came over in the first half of the seventeenth century. Sir John Seely tells us that the emigration from England to America was negligible for fully one hundred years after the Long Parliament of 1640,[9] and Richard Hildreth says that more colonists were leaving America at this time than were coming to the colonies from England.[10] There was comparatively little communication between England and America; it required nearly four months to cross the Atlantic, and the voyage was an expensive and disagreeable venture at best. The condition of the colonies was not favorable to literary development, and not many English books of the period found their way to our shores. "The Harvard College Library in 1723," says Bliss Perry, "had nothing of Addison, Steele, Bolingbroke, Dryden, Pope, and Swift, and had only recently obtained copies of Milton and Shakespeare."[11]

Therefore, although the English language in England changed rather

[5] Springfield, Mo., *Leader,* October 29, 1933.
[6] *Esquire,* April, 1937, p. 126.
[7] *Missouri Magazine,* February, 1938, p. 10.
[8] *Saturday Review of Literature,* June 22, 1940, p. 15.
[9] *The Expansion of England* (2nd. ed., London, 1895), 84.
[10] *History of the United States* (New York, 1856–60), I, 267.
[11] *The American Spirit in Literature* (New Haven, 1918), 61.

rapidly during the eighteenth century, few of these changes affected the speech of the American colonies. Even at the time of the Revolution the average American spoke the English which the settlers brought over in the seventeenth century, although many of their words and phrases were already obsolete or provincial in England. James Russell Lowell doubtless exaggerated when he said that the American colonists spoke the English of Shakespeare,[12] but it is true that they were familiar with much of Shakespeare's vocabulary and that many of their idioms and grammatical irregularities were Elizabethan. As early as 1792, Jeremy Belknap pointed out that many so-called Americanisms were but survivals of old or provincial English.[13]

Since that time, of course, the language has changed on both sides of the water; Americans on the eastern coast long imitated the current speech of England, and the country at large is always more or less influenced by the language of New York and Boston. At present, because of our increasing literacy and our large floating population, there is little difference between the English spoken in New York and that spoken in Chicago, Dallas, Salt Lake City, and Los Angeles. The radio and the talkies have played an important part in the elimination of local dialects.

There are several isolated places in the United States, however, in which the national folk-speech has made small progress. In the Southern Appalachians—the mountains of Tennessee, Kentucky, West Virginia, and the Carolinas—one finds the descendants of the early colonists, and until recently they had few contacts with modern civilization. Many of the dialectal peculiarities of the southern mountain folk were common to all the American colonies in the early eighteenth century,[14] and some of their most striking words and phrases are survivals of still older usages in England. "In remote parts of the United States," says Mencken, "there are still direct and almost pure-blooded descendants of the seventeenth-century colonists. Go among them, and you will hear more words from the Shakespearian vocabulary, still alive and in common service, than anywhere else in the world, and more of the loose and brilliant syntax of that time, and more of its gypsy phrases."[15] The Ozark hillfolk are the descendants of certain adventurous souls who left the Appalachians more than a cen-

---

[12] Preface to the *Biglow Papers.*

[13] *History of New Hampshire* (Boston, 1792), III, 4–6.

[14] George Philip Krapp, *The English Language in America* (New York, 1925), II, 35–36.

[15] *The American Language* (2nd ed., New York, 1921), 69.

[16] *Canterbury Tales,* 15,151; *ibid.,* 2,863.

tury ago. They have been, until very recently, even more isolated than their Appalachian relatives. It is not surprising, then, that the Ozark speech is full of archaisms.

Our common word *varmint,* for example, is derived from vermin, and preserves an older British pronunciation still standard in such English words as derby and clerk and even in the American pronunciation of sergeant. Surely the hillman's pronunciation of wrestle—he makes it sound like *wrastle*—has much in common with Chaucer's *wrastelying* and *wrastleth.*[16]

The word dare is generally *dar* in the Ozarks, and rhymes exactly with *par* as pronounced by golfers in the Middle West. The pronunciation was long standard in England, and the word is spelled *dar* in Chaucer.[17]

Scared is usually *skeered* or *scairt* in the Ozark country, both very old English forms.

Are is often pronounced *air* in northwestern Arkansas; compare the rhymes in "The Author's Resolution," a seventeenth-century lyric by George Withers, which begins:

> *Shall I wasting in despaire*
> *Dye, because a woman's fair?*
> *Or make pale my cheeks with care,*
> *Because another's rosy are?*

Catch is almost invariably pronounced *ketch,* and is spelled *ketche* by Chaucer,[18] while even the Ozark preterite *kotch* or *kotched* was used long ago in England and is still heard occasionally in the Cockney dialect.

Shakespeare's line about Mab who *"plats the manes of horses"*[19] is still good English in the Ozarks, although the ordinary American usage is plait, with a long *a* sound. The King James Bible spells the word *plat,*[20] just as the Ozarker would.

The preterite of eat is usually *et* in the Ozarks, a pronunciation still common among educated Englishmen, which is defended by the *Oxford Dictionary* and nearly all of the better dictionaries except *Webster's,* which gives the pronunciation as *āt* and adds, "in England usually *ĕt.*" The *Dictionary of Modern English Usage* says, "The past is spelt ate and pro-

---

[17] *Canterbury Tales,* 13,713.
[18] *Troilus and Criseyde,* III, 75.
[19] *Romeo and Juliet,* Act I, scene 5, line 89.
[20] Matt. 27:29.

nounced *ĕt* (wrongly *āt*)." In the Ozarks the past participle of eat is often pronounced *ĕt,* exactly like the preterite. This is true not only in Missouri and Arkansas, but also in eastern Oklahoma, according to the official guide-book issued by the University of Oklahoma Press.[21] I don't think I ever heard a real old-time Ozarker use the word *eaten.* The form *et* as a parti-ciple has been good English since 1300, and was used by Shakespeare, Fletcher, Fuller, Evelyn, Marvell, Purchas, Arbuthnot, Pope, Malmesbury, Peter Pindar, Dr. Johnson, Prior, Coleridge, Jane Austen, Dickens, Tenny-son, Thackeray, and a host of other writers.

Chew, both noun and verb, is always *chaw* to the Ozarker, just as it was to Pepys[22] and Spenser,[23] a form almost universal in England in the seventeenth century, and still common in several English country dialects.

Dr. Samuel Johnson pronounced the preterite of hear with a long *e* sound, as did many Englishman of his day.[24] Noah Webster always con-tended that heard was pronounced *heerd* until the beginning of the American Revolution, and argued that deaf should rhyme with leaf, just as it does today in Westmoreland, Cumberland, and some other parts of England.[25] Both *heerd* and *deef* are still very common pronunciations in the Ozark country.

Even the Ozark pronunciation of pert—we always call it *peert*—is descended from an older standard English pronunciation. Poor is in-variably *pore* in the hill country, as it was in seventeenth-century England. *Slick* for sleek was used by Beaumont and Fletcher[26] exactly as it is in the Ozarks today. Our pronunciation of yet has a certain ancient respectability too—didn't Chaucer write *"yit* sang the larke"?[27] The use of *ben* instead of been was once common in New England, and was justified by James Russell Lowell in the following passage: *"Ben* has the authority of Sack-ville, Gammer Gurton, Chapman, Dryden, and many more, although *bin* seems to have been the more common form."[28]

The equivalent form of might is very often pronounced to rhyme with *out,* at least by the older generation of Ozarkers, and this is a very old English form. Shakespeare spells it *mought,*[29] and *mote* is common in

---

[21] *Oklahoma, a Guide to the Sooner State,* 121.
[22] *Diary,* June 7, 1665.
[23] *Faërie Queene,* 2, 4, 30.
[24] Boswell's *Johnson* (1777), III, 369.
[25] Schele De Vere, *Americanisms* (New York, 1872), 462.
[26] *Knight of the Burning Pestle,* Act II, scene 1.
[27] *Canterbury Tales,* 2,214.
[28] Preface to the *Biglow Papers.*

Spenser.[30] Pegge mentions *mought* as a Londonism, and ironically defends it in the following passage: "The word is allowed by Bailey in his dictionary [Scott's edition] and by Dr. Johnson, to have been formerly used for the modern word *might;* though they both observe that *mought* is now grown obsolete. Chaucer and other writers of an early date use it repeatedly. Dr. Wallace speaking of might voluntarily adds 'olim mought,' though he does not give us any further part of its history. It is clear, however, that our word *might* is merely a delicate pronunciation for female lips, or introduced by foppish refinement under the foolish French appellation of *bon ton* instead of *mought,* which has stronger claims to regular formation."[31]

The *oi* in such words as boil and join is usually given the long *i* sound, so that the words are pronounced *bile* and *jine.* According to John S. Kenyon, "Shakespeare has only *byle.*"[32] And the Authorized Version gives: "Satan smote Job with sore *biles.*"[33] Pope rhymed join with both mine and design.[34] Addison rhymed joined with find, and even Dr. Johnson said: "Bile is generally spelt boil, though I think less properly." I once heard a Missouri schoolmarm laugh at an old woman who put a long *i* sound into royal, but this pronunciation was once quite respectable in England. The same vowel substitution occurs in point, and both *p'int* and *disapp'int* are survivals of a good old English pronunciation. The common verb roil, pronounced *rile,* by which the Ozarker means to stir up anger, was once in general use, but it has long been obsolete in England.[35] Poison is still pronounced in the ancient fashion, as in Oliver Goldsmith's rhyme:

> "*. . . and may this bit be my poison,*
> *A prettier dinner I never set eyes on.*"[36]

The hillman always gives a long *i* sound to joist, too, and even the *Century Dictionary* admits that *jist* is etymologically correct and was formerly good usage, derived from the Middle English *giste.*

Cover is still pronounced *kivver* in the Ozarks, another pronunciation

[29] *3 Henry VI,* Act V, scene 2, line 45.
[30] *Faërie Queene,* 3, 2, 22; 3, 3, 7.
[31] *Anecdotes of the English Language* (1814), 113.
[32] *American Pronunciation* (Ann Arbor, Mich., 1943), sec. 340.
[33] Job 2:7.
[34] *Essay on Criticism, II,* lines 347–48.
[35] Schele De Vere, *Americanisms,* 334.
[36] *The Haunch of Venison,* 1,776.

which is merely old English preserved, being met with frequently in the earlier dramatists, and still heard in the Cockney dialect.

Shakespeare rhymed venture with enter on at least one occasion,[87] and Noah Webster denounced the "affectation" of inserting a *y* sound before the *u* in such words as gradual and nature.[88] The Ozark natives pronounce gradual in something like the modern fashion, but they stand firm with Shakespeare and Noah Webster in regard to venture and nature.

Our present adjective touchy is always *tetchy* in the hill country,[89] and was evidently so pronounced in Elizabethan England, as in Shakespeare's "tetchy and wayward was thy infancy"[40] and "he's as tetchy to be woo'd."[41] Schele De Vere quotes Ray to the effect that tetchy is a North Country word.[42] *Totch* or *totched* as the preterite of touch is common in the Ozarks, and Isaac Walton generally spelled it *totcht*.[43]

Shut is usually pronounced *shet* by elderly folk in the Ozarks. Schele De Vere says that shet was once common in New England and that this pronunciation was warmly defended by James Russell Lowell, who quoted Golden's *Ovid* in its behalf, and said that "Brampton Gurden wrote *shet* in a letter to Governor Winthrop. Our ancestors brought this pronunciation with them from the Old Country, and have not wantonly debased their mother-tongue."[44] And there is no denying that Chaucer spelled the word *schette*.[45]

Cucumber was spelled and pronounced *cowcumber* up to the beginning of the eighteenth century, according to the *Britannica*. It persisted much longer in the popular speech, even in England. Lord Frederick Hamilton says that his aunts, "English noblewomen of the highest rank and breeding," always pronounced yellow as *yaller* and cucumber as *cowcumber* in the eighteen seventies.[46] These pronunciations are still quite common in the Ozarks.

Sparrowgrass or *spar'grass* is the universal Ozark pronunciation of asparagus. Webster lists this as a "corruption," but it must be a pretty old

[87] *Venus and Adonis*, 628.
[88] *Elementary Spelling Book*, ed. of 1829.
[89] Cf. *Publication of the American Dialect Society*, No. 11 (1949), 46.
[40] *Richard III*, Act IV, scene 4, line 168.
[41] *Troilus and Cressida*, Act I, scene 1, line 101.
[42] *Americanisms*, 558.
[43] *Life of Donne*, 41.
[44] *Americanisms*, 541.
[45] *Canterbury Tales*, 14,496.
[46] *My Yesterdays* (Garden City, N. Y., 1931); quoted in the *Saturday Evening Post*, November 28, 1931, p. 329.

one. Dean Swift used the word just as the Ozark hillman does today.[47]

Shoot is often made to serve as a noun. A deer-hunter in Searcy County, Arkansas, said, "I heerd two *shoots* back yonder."[48] Shakespeare used shoot to mean shot, exactly as the Ozark people do.[49]

The omission of certain consonants in Southern pronunciation is said to date from the reign of Charles II. This monarch lived in France and married a Frenchwoman, and his court was strongly under the French influence. He objected to such inharmonious contractions as *willn't, wolln't, wasn't* and *weren't,* and set the fashion of using the more euphonious *won't* and *wan't.* The Ozarker of today often uses weren't without any regard to distinctions of number and person, but he pronounces it *warn't,* giving *er* the sound of *ar,* which most Englishmen still preserve in such words as derby and clerk.

Some of the old-timers say *atter* instead of after, and this was formerly common both in England and in the New England states. Schele De Vere observed long ago that *"atter* for after is a corruption which the New Englander inherited from his Puritan ancestors."[50]

The hillman usually prefers the *n* sound to that of *ng* in length and strength. Well, *lenth* is found in *Cursor Mundi*[51] and *strenth* in Barbour's *Brus,*[52] both poems of the fourteenth century. It is said that Sir Thomas Elyot, who was Henry VIII's ambassador to the court of Charles V, always wrote *strenth* instead of *strength.*

The use of a final *n* instead of *ng* in present participles, a pronunciation almost universal in the Ozarks, is still common among educated Englishmen, and was well known to the Elizabethans. Queen Elizabeth herself was a scholarly woman; yet in a letter to James VI of Scotland she spelled beseeching without the *g.*

The Ozarker nearly always uses an *l* sound instead of the *n* in chimney, so that it sounds like *chimley* or *chimbly.* This is evidently an old pronunciation; Sir Walter Scott refers to "a kirk with a *chimley* in it."[53]

In the Ozarks the pronoun it retains the original English *h* sometimes; *hit* is still heard, just as it was before Shakespeare's day.[54]

[47] Boswell's *Johnson,* II, 268.
[48] *Dialect Notes,* Vol. V (1926), 403.
[49] *Love's Labour Lost,* Act IV, scene 1, line 10; *Lucreece,* 579.
[50] *Americanisms,* 580.
[51] Göttingen version, 1, 1642.
[52] I, 524.
[53] *Rob Roy,* I, 120.
[54] *American Speech,* Vol. IV (1929), 205–206.

The typical Ozarker does not soften his *r's* as much as the writers of dialect fiction would have us believe. In such words as sir and horse, for example, the *r* is sounded more distinctly than in the Southwest. The noun girl, however, is always *gal* or *gel*, and it is pronounced the same way in some parts of England today.

A handkerchief is usually a *hankercher* in the back hills, and was spelled *hankercher* by Shakespeare[55] and by Pepys.[56] As Schele De Vere says, "There can be no doubt that the word was, in the seventeenth century, written by good authors exactly as it was pronounced, and thus imported from England into Virginia,"[57] whence it has since been carried into the Ozark country.

My neighbors sometimes pronounce ask as if it were spelled *axe*. It really was spelled *axe* in Chaucer,[58] and was good English for at least two centuries after Chaucer's death. *Axe* certainly has the warrant of great antiquity and noble patronage, but after Elizabeth's time it was definitely abandoned by the court, although the common people continued to use it and brought it to America. *Axe* is still common in the Cockney and Norfolk dialects. As late as 1869 we find an anonymous Englishman contending that "for purposes of lyrical poetry and musical composition *axed* would be a vast improvement upon the harsh sound *asked*, which no vocalist can pronounce without a painful gasp."[59]

The *sk* sound in such words as muskrat, muskmelon and tusk is generally softened to *sh*. Edward Eggleston observed that many early American hunters and trappers pronounced muskrat as if it were spelled *mush-rat*, and mentions one "early Virginian naturalist" who spelled the word without a *k*.[60] Shakespeare refers to the crooked *tushes* of a boar.[61]

Where most Americans would say anyway, the Ozark hillman uses the adverbial genitive *anyways*, a usage roundly condemned by many of the grammar books. But the *Book of Common Prayer*, published in England about 1560, has: "All those who are *anyways* afflicted . . . in mind, body, or estate."

The use of *t* for *d* in words like ballad and salad is common. A dish of pokeweed leaves is always a *poke-sallet* in the back hills, which recalls

[55] *All's Well That Ends Well*, Act V, scene 3, line 322.
[56] *Diary*, Sept. 2, 1667.
[57] *Americanisms*, 485.
[58] *Canterbury Tales*, 1,349, 3,195, 12,354.
[59] *Blackwood's Magazine*, October, 1869, p. 261.
[60] *Century Magazine*, April, 1894, p. 852.
[61] *Venus and Adonis*, 624.

78

the Shakespearian character who "eats cow-dung for *sallets,*" also the line "I can eat grass, or pick a sallet."[62]

The hillman often pronounces a *t* before the word other, just as Ben Jonson did.[63]

The *w* in such words as forward, backward, awkward, and so on is generally silent in the Ozark speech, and it appears that the same thing was common in seventeenth-century England. Pepys describes one of his friends as *awkerd,*[64] and the expression "an *awkerd* and frightful manner" was used in Boston early in the eighteenth century.[65]

The Ozarker has a tendency to omit prefixes on occasion, and many writers find it difficult to record his clipped speech without an excessive use of the apostrophe. In the same way Shakespeare uses *'cide* when he means decide, and such contractions as *'bove, 'cause, 'stonished, 'tend,* and the like are very common in his writings.[66] The same is true of a host of other English authors; Ben Jonson in particular used *'less* for unless,[67] exactly as the Ozark backwoodsman does today.

The peculiar tense forms of the Ozarker's verbs often amuse the tourists from such centers of culture as Tulsa and Kansas City. Many of these verb forms are archaic. The hillman usually says *rid* instead of rode, but didn't George Washington write "I *rid* to Muddy Hole plantation,"[68] and isn't the same preterite found in many of the best English writers of the eighteenth century and earlier? The poet Pope was especially fond of *rid* as the past tense of ride.[69] Professor Krapp tells us that most educated Bostonians, in 1704, said *rid* instead of rode, *see* instead of saw, *riz* instead of rose, and *come* instead of came.[70] *Rid, see, riz,* and *come* are still very common preterites in the Ozark country.

Many more of the Ozark preterites are found in Shakespeare, and the sentence "Three times today I *holp* him to his horse"[71] might have been spoken yesterday by any one of my neighbors in southwest Missouri, where *holp* is still the past tense of help. Both the preterite *holp* and the participle

[62] *King Lear,* Act III, scene 4, line 137; *2 Henry VI,* Act IV, scene 10, line 9.
[63] *Cynthia's Revels,* Act IV, scene 1; Act V, scene 1.
[64] *Diary,* July 15, 1665.
[65] Sarah Kemble Knight, *Journal,* 1704–1705.
[66] *Sonnet XLVI,* 9; *Macbeth,* Act III, scene 5, line 31; *ibid.,* Act III, scene 6, line 21; *Venus and Adonis,* 825; *Hamlet,* Act IV, scene 3, line 47.
[67] *Sad Shepherd,* Act III, scene 1.
[68] *Diary,* June 19, 1771.
[69] *Dunciad,* III, 51–52.
[70] *The English Language in America,* II, 257.
[71] *2 Henry VI,* Act V, scene 3, line 8.

holpen are old English forms, found in many early writers. *Holpen*, at least, is common in the King James version of the Bible.[72] Even as late as 1815 Daniel Sandiford gave *crope* as the past tense of creep, and *clang* as a correct preterite of cling—all this in a grammar book for use in schools.[73] *Crope* is common in the Ozark speech, and *clang* is not unknown.

The Ozarker has a tendency to use weak verbs rather than strong ones, and such forms as beared, ketched, drinked, throwed, and so on are heard on every hand. The same preference for the weak conjugation is found in many early English writers: Chaucer uses *growed;*[74] Wyclif, *costed;*[75] Caxton, *hurted;*[76] Shakespeare, *shaked, becomed, blowed;*[77] and Milton, *catched.*[78]

The early American colonists generally used *catched* for caught,[79] and the Ozarker pronounces it *ketched*. Fetch and even *fotch*—the latter a very old participle—are still used by the hillfolk rather than bring or brought. *Afeared* is an old preterite and past participle of the verb fear, which has been superseded by the modern form afraid, from the obsolete verb affray. Chaucer spelled it *aferd,*[80] and Shakespeare used *affeared* many times. The hillman usually says *attackted* instead of attacked, and Schele De Vere tells us that this is a very old form, still used by illiterate people in England.[81]

The use of the preterite instead of the past participle is another illustration of the hillman's linguistic kinship with the Elizabethans. "I have *mistook* your passion," "thou hast *fell*," "where have I *took* them up," and "you have *swam*" are examples of this sort of thing in Shakespeare.[82]

The Ozark verb does not always agree with its subject in number, but the same disagreement is found in the Elizabethans and many other early writers. Spenser refers to people "whose names *is* hard to read,"[83] and Shakespeare used such sentences as "here *comes* the townsmen," "his tears

---

[72] Psalms 83: 8 and 36; Luke 1:54; Dan. 11:34.

[73] *Elements of English Grammar*, 2nd ed., p. 28.

[74] *Canterbury Tales*, 6,341.

[75] *Office of Curates*, chap. 25.

[76] *Sons of Aymon*, III, 78.

[77] *The Tempest*, Act II, scene 1, line 319; *Cymbeline*, Act V, scene 5, line 406; *Henry V*, Act III, scene 2, line 98.

[78] *Paradise Lost*, X, 542.

[79] Washington's *Diary*, May 9, 1765.

[80] *Canterbury Tales*, Prologue, 628.

[81] *Americanisms*, 436.

[82] *Julius Caesar*, Act 1, scene 2, line 48; *King Lear*, Act IV, scene 6, line 54; *Julius Caesar*, Act 11, scene 1, line 50; *As You Like It*, Act IV, scene 1, line 38.

[83] *Faërie Queene*, III, xii, 25.

runs down his beard," and "my old bones aches."[84] Unhappily, some editors have "corrected" Shakespeare's grammar.

I have observed elsewhere that "I did plow" or "I done plowed" are regularly preferred to the simpler form "I plowed."[85] Octave Thanet long ago pointed out that a similar preference is evidenced in Pepys' *Diary* and other works of that period.[86]

The purposive *for* before an infinitive is characteristic of the Ozark syntax today, but the same thing is found in many early English writers. Shakespeare says: "Let your highness lay a more noble thought upon mine honor, than *for* to think that I would leave it here," and also "forbid the sea *for* to obey the moon."[87] In Chaucer, too, we find "the holy blisful martir *for* to seek" and "well loved he *for* to drink strong wyn."[88] In the Authorized Version of the Bible we read: "What went ye out . . . *for* to see?"[89]

I have often been struck by the hillman's talk of time *passing over his head,* an expression that does not fit the mouth of an ordinary Middle Westerner. Any one of my old neighbors in McDonald County, Missouri, or Benton County, Arkansas, might have said, "That was the pleasantest day that ever passed over my head in my life." But the sentence was written by Daniel Defoe,[90] who lived in England in the seventeenth century.

Ask a hillman to do you a favor, and he often replies, "I don't *care* to do it," meaning that he has no objection. Care in this sense is found in many sixteenth- and seventeenth-century writings, and the *English Dialect Dictionary* lists it as still common in the Scottish dialect.

When an Ozarker threatens to *feather into* somebody, he means that he is about to shoot this person, or at least to attack him with serious intent. This has been traced back to the days of the longbow in England, when to *feather into* a man was to shoot him with such force that the feather at the butt of the arrow was buried in his body.[91] The meaning of this expression has apparently been weakened within my own memory;

---

[84] *2 Henry VI*, Act II, scene 1, line 68; *The Tempest,* Act V, scene 1, line 16; *ibid.,* Act III, scene 2, line 2.

[85] *American Speech,* Vol. III (1927), 3.

[86] *Journal of American Folklore,* Vol. V (1892), 121.

[87] *All's Well That Ends Well,* Act V, scene 3, line 181; *A Winter's Tale,* Act I, scene 2, line 427.

[88] *Canterbury Tales,* 17; *ibid.,* 637.

[89] Luke 7:24.

[90] *Moll Flanders,* 340.

[91] *Dialect Notes,* Vol. V (1926), 399.

I never heard it used save in reference to physical combat, usually with lethal weapons. But Brewster reports *feather in* as current in Columbia, Missouri, where it means only "to do something vigorously."[92]

I once asked Ed Wall, an aged beekeeper of Pineville, Missouri, to tell me about the various methods of swarm-control, which are pretty difficult for an amateur. "Well," he said dubiously, "set down, an' I'll *riddle it to ye* the best I can." May Kennedy McCord, of Springfield, Missouri, once told me of an old woman who said to her: "Come out to my house an' *riddle me* how to make a calico dress." This use of riddle in the sense of interpret or explain must be very old. Compare a stanza from the traditional ballad of "Lord Thomas and Fair Annet":

> *Come riddle us, riddle us, father dear,*
> *Yea both of us into ane;*
> *Whether sall I marry Fair Annie,*
> *Or bring the brown bride home.*[93]

In many parts of the Ozark country I have heard *ween* as a verb, meaning to show signs of fear or even panic. "Hank he talks mighty big, but he'll mostly *ween* when the fightin' begins."[94] For a long time I thought this must be a form of *weaken*. But George P. Wilson tells me that "a number of English lexical works list *ween* in English dialect as meaning to whine, to whimper." So it seems that *ween*, as used in the Ozarks today, is just another survival of an earlier English speech.

Hearn, an old adjective-participle of hear, was once common in England, and more recently in the United States, being quoted by James Russel Lowell[95] and others. Schele De Vere remarks that it was used by a servant at the funeral of John Randolph of Virginia in 1833.[96]

The Ozarker who remarks that a certain man and woman are *talkin'* means that they are contemplating matrimony, and the word is used in a similar sense by Shakespeare.[97]

---

[92] *American Speech*, Vol. XVI (1941), 22.

[93] This ballad was a common broadside in the time of Charles II and was included in the Pepys collection of 1700, also in Percy's *Reliques*, about 1765. Cf. Francis James Child's *English and Scottish Popular Ballads* (Boston and New York, 1883–98, 5 vols.), No. 73.

[94] *Dialect Notes*, Vol. V (1926), 404.

[95] *Biglow Papers*, II, 161.

[96] *Americanisms*, 486.

[97] *King Lear*, Act IV, scene 5, line 30.

Tole, to entice, is a rather unusual word in most sections of the United States, but is very commonly used in the Ozarks. It is found in many old English writers, as witness the following passage from Fletcher:

> *Or voices calling in the dead of night*
> *To make me follow, and so tole me on*
> *Through mire and standing pool to find my ruin.*[98]

The verb use means to frequent or loiter, and when it is said that "the sheriff's been *a-usin'* round Durgenville" the hillman understands the significance of the remark at once. The same usage is found in Spenser[99] and in Fletcher's lines:

> *I will give thee for thy food*
> *No fish that useth in the mud.*[100]

Gaum, to soil, was once common in England but is now obsolete or provincial, according to Webster. It is still used in the Ozarks.

When my neighbor said of some perfume, "It sure *stinks* beautiful," he was using good Elizabethan English; *stink* was formerly used with reference to any odor, pleasant or unpleasant. Ælfric, the Anglo-Saxon grammarian, used *stink* in the same noncommittal sense.

Mend the fire means to keep adding fuel, as "Bill he had to set up an' mend the fire all night." The sentence "I *mend the fyre* and bleiket me about" dates back to the fifteenth century.[101]

Misdoubt, meaning to suspect or distrust, is a typical Ozark "barbarism," according to the village schoolmarms. It was used by Shakespeare,[102] however, who also wrote *mind* in the sense of intend,[103] exactly as the hillman employs the word today.

A friend of mine often says *conceit* when he means imagine: "Jim Lawton *conceited* he could git rich a-raisin' strawberries." This is common in sixteenth- and seventeenth-century English.[104]

Contrary is still used as a verb in the Ozarks, meaning to contradict

[98] *Faithful Shepherdess,* Act I, scene 1.
[99] *Epithalamium,* 4, 3.
[100] *Faithful Shepherdess,* Act III, scene 1.
[101] *Testament of Cresseid* (c. 1480), 36.
[102] *Merry Wives of Windsor,* Act II, scene 11, line 192.
[103] *3 Henry VI,* Act IV, scene 1, lines 8 and 106.
[104] Cf. John Aubrey (1626–97), sketch of Walter Rumsey.

or antagonize, and it seems to have carried the same significance in Chaucer's day.[105] Chaucer also used the adjective *contrarious*,[106] which is a common word in southwest Missouri.

Disremember, meaning to forget, is not much used nowadays in England or in most parts of the United States, but it is still current in the Ozarks.[107]

Look is used rather oddly as a transitive verb, meaning to examine, to inspect. A careful housewife says, "I don't trust nobody but Mabel to *look my greens* for me," meaning that Mabel makes certain that the salad is clean, with no bugs or dirt in it. A woman in Stone County, Missouri, never learned to read, but she bought expensive reading-glasses so as to *look the baby's head for boogers,* which means lice. An Arkansas soldier told me that "the Colonel comes down an' *looks the barracks* about once a week." When a man says, "I done *looked the paper,*" he means that he has read every word in it. Pepys recalls for posterity the time he asked his wife to "*look my shirt*, for I have itched mightily these six or seven days. She finds that I am lousy."[108]

When a hillman says that somebody has *bored* him, he means that he has been ridiculed, not at all what the word signifies to the ordinary American from beyond the mountains. The Ozarker is much nearer to Beaumont and Fletcher, who used *bored* in the sense of insulted or imposed upon.[109]

The Ozark hillman often says *argufy* instead of argue, and the schoolmarms laugh at him for it, but Schele De Vere says that argufy was formerly quite respectable in England, and proves it by quotations from Halliwell and from O'Flanagan, the biographer of the Lord Chancellors of Ireland.[110]

Reckon, as used in the Ozarks, is not heard in England today except in some northern dialects, but it was once very good English, and is found in the King James Bible.[111]

The hillman often says *ramping* when he means raging; this word occurs in Shakespeare,[112] and is evidently connected with the adjective rampant, which is still in fairly common use.

[105] *Canterbury Tales*, 6,626, 9,371.
[106] *Good Women*, 1,360.
[107] *American Speech*, Vol. V (1930), 425.
[108] *Diary*, January 23, 1669.
[109] *Spanish Curate*, Act IV, scene 5.
[110] *Americanisms*, 434.
[111] Rom. 6:11; 8:18.
[112] *1 Henry IV*, Act III, scene 1, line 152.

The Ozarker's use of *ruinate* for ruin seems fantastic to the casual tourist, but it is employed by Shakespeare[113] and Spenser.[114]

The word host is still a verb in the hill country, meaning to furnish lodgings or to entertain guests, just as it is used by Shakespeare.[115] Spenser, too, has a passage to the effect that "Malbecco will no straunge Knights host,"[116] and there are many similar passages in other early authors.

The Ozarker often says *buss* when he means kiss, recalling Shakespeare's "and buss thee as thy wife,"[117] also his use of buss as a noun: "Thou dost give me flattering busses."[118] Spenser employs the same word on occasion, generally spelling it *busse*.[119]

Only the other day one of my neighbors remarked that he *admired* a flood which had ruined his crops, meaning that it astonished or surprised him. The superior summer colonist smiles at this, but Shakespeare[120] and Milton[121] used the word in exactly the same sense, and Pepys said that Charles II "is so fond of the Duke of Monmouth that everybody *admires* it," that is, wonders at it.[122] Admiration, usually shortened to *miration,* still means wonderment or surprise in the Ozarks. A Little Rock newspaper, in an editorial, observed that: "Some *miration* is being made over the fact that the $34,599,756 that Arkansas received from the federal government was the state's largest single source of income for the 1949–50 revenue year."[123]

The causative use of wonder was good English in the eighteenth century. "She has a sedateness that wonders me still more," wrote Madame D'Arblay,[124] and such a sentence as "Hit sure does wonder me how Elmer lost them two dollars" is still heard in the Ozark country.

When the hillman butchers a hog or a steer, he uses some old names to designate its innards. The spleen, for example, is always called the melt.[125] The word melt means courage, too, or rather recklessness. An old

[113] Sonnet X, 7; *Lucrece,* 944.
[114] *Faërie Queene,* III, viii, 28.
[115] *Comedy of Errors,* Act I, scene 2, line 9.
[116] *Faërie Queene,* III, ix, 1.
[117] *King John,* Act III, scene 4, line 35.
[118] *2 Henry IV,* Act II, scene 4, line 291.
[119] *Faërie Queene,* III, x, 46.
[120] *The Tempest,* Act V, scene 1, line 154.
[121] *Paradise Lost,* II, 677.
[122] *Diary,* Feb. 22, 1664.
[123] *Arkansas Gazette,* Little Rock, Ark., June 20, 1950.
[124] *Journal,* Oct. 25, 1788.
[125] *Dialect Notes,* Vol. V (1926), 401.

man in our neighborhood was talking about his son's quarrel with some village boys, who were always "layin' for him" after school. "They better let Tommy alone," said the father darkly. "Tommy's a-packin' a big knife, an' he's got the *melt* to use it, too." The word melt for spleen, in this meaning, seemed odd to me at the time. But Shakespeare used spleen to signify daring or impetuosity, as "hare-brained Hotspur, governed by a *spleen*."[126] Thinking about this, I asked the old man if he had ever heard of Shakespeare. "There's a whole mess of Shakespeares lives up around Hollister, but me an' Tommy never had no truck with 'em," he answered. I thought the old gentleman was spoofing me and dropped the whole subject for the time being. But later on I learned that he was quite serious; there really are some people named Shakespeare in Taney County, Missouri, not far from the town the old man mentioned.

In ordinary conversation the Ozarker addresses a married woman as *Miz* or *Mis'*, but in formal speeches, such as funeral sermons, he pronounces the word *Mistress* very distinctly, as the Elizabethans did. A backwoods preacher always referred to his wife as "my mistress"; he was horrified and incredulous when I told him that, to many Americans, the use of this word meant that there was no legal marriage between them.

The hillfolk still call a sermon a *preachment,* and the same term is found in Shakespeare.[127] *Pinnywinkle,* the Ozark word for water-snail, seems to be identical with the Anglo-Saxon *pinewinkle,* according to Webster.

A bag or sack is regularly called a poke in the hill country. Chaucer quotes an old proverb about "pigges in a poke"[128]—an expression still current in both England and America, although the noun *poke* is seldom heard in ordinary talk save in the backwoods regions of the South. Shakespeare tells of someone who "drew a dial from his poke."[129]

The hillman's use of *tourister* for tourist, *gossiper* for gossip, and *musicker* or *musicianer* for musician seems a bit odd at first, but *er* was once a commoner suffix for agent nouns than it is at present. That similar terms were common in America in pioneer days is evidenced by the novels of Fenimore Cooper and others. Shakespeare used *moraler, justicer, sworder,* and the like.[130] The Earl of Oxford who lived in the time of Shakespeare wrote *mediciner* where we would use doctor or physician.[131]

---

[126] *1 Henry IV,* Act V, scene 2, lines 16–19.
[127] *3 Henry VI,* Act I, scene 4, line 72.
[128] *Canterbury Tales,* 4,276.
[129] *As You Like It,* Act II, scene 7, line 20.

86

The disyllabic plurals ending in *es* so common in the Ozarks—*nestes, postes, deskes,* and the like—are survivals, too, which were still heard in nineteenth-century England. *Folkses* is probably a later formation on the same model.

The Ozarker's use of the singular form as a plural in such words as rod, cord, pound, foot, mile, and so forth was also common among early English writers. Many such plurals were employed by Roger Ascham, a great scholar who served as tutor to Queen Elizabeth herself. Shakespeare wrote "he would have walked ten mile afoot to see me" and "this boy will carry a letter twenty mile."[132] John Evelyn, in his *Diary,* described a tree of "more than two foote diameter, which serves to nestle and pearch all sorts of birds."

The proprietor of the City Hotel, Noel, Missouri, was telling his guests about a big fish that had been taken from the Cowskin River just below the village. "I tell you, *gentle-people,* I never seen such a catfish!" said he. I have heard this elsewhere in the Ozarks, but it isn't common nowadays. Chaucer and Shakespeare used the plural substantive—*gentils* and *gentles* —to mean men and women, even in direct address.

The word bait, meaning a meal, is well known in the hill country. Pepys used it in this sense when he wrote: "We got a small bait at Leather-head."[133]

The noun budget still means a package or bundle in Arkansas, just as it formerly did in England. Even today the Chancellor of the Exchequer, in making his report to Parliament, is said to "open his budget" —that is, his briefcase.

The hillman uses *bum* and *bummy* to mean buttocks,[134] and Logan Clendening reports that *bummy* is common in Virginia also.[135] Bum is heard in Warwickshire slang to this day, and Shakespeare used it with the same meaning.[136] Dr. Clendening quotes an old English jingle:

> *When to the age of forty they come,*
> *Men run to belly and women to bum.*

130 *Othello,* Act II, scene 3, line 301; *King Lear,* Act IV, scene 2, line 79; 2 *Henry VI,* Act IV, scene 1, line 135.

131 B. M. Ward, *Seventeenth Earl of Oxford* (London, 1928), 89.

132 *Much Ado About Nothing,* Act II, scene 3, line 17; *Merry Wives of Windsor,* Act III, scene 2, line 23.

133 *Diary,* April 30, 1661.

134 *American Speech,* Vol. XI (1936), 314.

135 *The Human Body* (New York, 1927), 187.

136 *A Midsummer Night's Dream,* Act II, scene 1, line 53.

The word generation, in the Ozarks, means a large number of individuals; W. A. Bradley points out that this usage is Elizabethan.[137] The King James Bible, printed in 1611, makes Jesus refer to "a generation of vipers," meaning a crowd, a large number.[138]

In the gales is the Ozark term for "in a good humor"; the word *gale* is an old English term denoting a state of pleasant excitement or hilarity.[139]

Fraction still means a quarrel or fight, just as it did in Shakespeare's day.[140]

Funk, meaning a disagreeable odor, was common in the seventeenth and early eighteenth centuries, according to the *New English Dictionary,* but Webster says it is obsolete. The word is still used in the Ozarks.[141] Speaking of some stale milk, a woman near Branson, Missouri, told me: "It ain't sour, but it's got a feeble *funky* scent."

Heap is used by Chaucer in exactly the Ozark manner when he mentions "the wisdom of an heep of learned men."[142]

The word *nation* means simply a large amount and is used in the true Ozark fashion by Sterne in the sentence: "And what a nation of herbs he had procured to mollify her humours!"[143]

A necklace is sometimes called "a pair of beads" in the back hills; this seemed strange to me until I found Chaucer's reference to the *paire of bedes* worn by the Prioresse.[144]

Spenser used the noun *needments,*[145] which means necessities and is frequently heard in northwest Arkansas to this day.

A *shift of clothes* means a change of clothes, and has no special reference to shirts. "He ain't got shiftin' clothes" means that he has only the garments he is wearing. The expression is recorded in the *Oxford Dictionary* as early as 1570. Hakluyt used it: "Hee that had five or six shifts of apparel had scarce one drie thread to his backe."[146]

"There's a *sleight* to this here giggin' fish," said one of my neighbors

[137] *Harper's Magazine,* August, 1915, p. 437.

[138] Matt. 12:34; 23:33; Luke 3:7.

[139] *American Speech,* Vol. V (1929), 18.

[140] *Timon of Athens,* Act II, scene 2, line 220; *Troilus and Cressida,* Act II, scene 3, line 107.

[141] Cf. Wentworth, *American Dialect Dictionary,* 237–38.

[142] *Canterbury Tales,* Prologue, 575.

[143] *Tristram Shandy,* ccxxii.

[144] *Canterbury Tales,* Prologue, 159.

[145] *Faërie Queene,* I, 1, 6.

[146] *Voyages,* III, 83.

at Pineville, Missouri. He meant some special sort of knack or skill; Chaucer used the word several times in this sense, and so did many of the Elizabethan writers.

When Rose O'Neill died in 1944, one of her Missouri neighbors said, "She was a *prince,* if there ever was one!" This seemed rather odd to me at the time. But Elizabeth was called a prince, both before and after she became queen, according to the *Oxford English Dictionary.*

Shakespeare uses the word *race* in its original meaning of root: "Nutmegs seven, and a race or two of ginger."[147] Very few Americans know the word in this meaning today, but "a *race* of ginger" is still perfectly intelligible to the Ozark housewife.

Weddin'ers, meaning the guests at a wedding party or an infare celebration in the Ozarks, is an old English term, found in John Stagg's poems in the Cumberland dialect.[148] *Zany* is another unusual word that one hears frequently in the backwoods; it means clown or buffoon just as it did in Shakespeare's time.[149]

The sentence "Is she as tall as me?" is a good illustration of the Ozarker's confusion of pronoun case forms, but it was written by Shakespeare.[150] Other examples of this confusion are common in Shakespeare's plays: "And yet no man like he doth grieve my heart," "there's none but thee and I," "between you and I," and "you know my father hath no child but I."[151]

You-uns and *we-uns,* according to Schele De Vere, are merely extensions of vulgarisms once common to many English dialects, and which still survive in Berkshire and elsewhere.[152]

Such possessive forms as *ourn, yourn, hisn, hern,* and *theirn* are almost universal in the Ozarks; they were formed in Middle English times on the old model of mine and thine, and were once common in England, even among the educated. In John Purvey's revision of the Wycliffe Bible, which appeared shortly after 1380, we find such sentences as "restore to hir alle things that ben *hern*"[153] and "some of *ourn* went in to the grave."[154] Dr. Otto Jesperson gives the following old English rhyme:

---

147 *A Winter's Tale,* Act IV, scene 3, line 50.

148 *Dialect Notes,* Vol. V (1926), 404.

149 *Love's Labour Lost,* Act V, scene 2, line 463.

150 *Antony and Cleopatra,* Act III, scene 3, line 14.

151 *Romeo and Juliet,* Act III, scene 5, line 84; *2 Henry VI,* Act I, scene 2, line 69; *Merchant of Venice,* Act III, scene 2, line 32; *As You Like It,* Act I, scene 2, line 18.

152 *Americanisms,* 569.

153 II Kings 7:6.

154 Luke 24:24.

He that prigs what isn't his'n,
When he's cotched, is sent to prison.
She that prigs what isn't hern,
At the threadmill takes a turn.[155]

The word which most dialect writers render *ary* is simply the Ozark pronunciation of *e'er a,* as in Shakespeare's "has the old man e'er a son?"[156] in the same way *nary* is a corruption of *ne'er a,* and Sir Walter Scott makes an English landlord say: "They are all gentlemen, though they ha' *narra* shirt to their back."[157] The sentence "an old trot with *ne'er a* tooth in her head" is Shakespeare's,[158] but it might have been spoken by any one of my Ozark neighbors yesterday. The only difference is a matter of pronunciation; the hillman turns the *a* into *y,* just as he does the final *a* in soda, extra, alfalfa, and the like.

One of the Ozarker's most striking peculiarities of speech has to do with the comparison of adjectives; he has a weakness for such double comparatives and superlatives as *worser, more colder* and *most best.* Shakespeare's works are full of such forms—*worser, more hotter, more larger, more better, more braver, most unkindest,* and *most worst.*[159]

The hillman's use of *er* and *est* endings where *more* and *most* are customary, can be paralleled in many early English writers. In *Piers Plowman,* for example, we find *merveillousest,*[160] while Chaucer did not hesitate to write *rewfullest,*[161] and Spenser used *beautifullest* and *joyfullest.*[162] Shakespeare's works are full of these forms: *horrider, perfecter, certainer, violentest, lyingest,* and *perfectest.*[163]

The word *least,* meaning smallest, is very common in our neighborhood; it is still correct in England, but is rarely heard among educated

155 *Modern English Grammar* (Heidelburg, 1909), II, 403.
156 *A Winter's Tale,* Act IV, scene 4, line 810.
157 *Rob Roy,* I, iv, 5.
158 *Taming of the Shrew,* Act I, scene 2, line 80.
159 *Passionate Pilgrim,* II, 3; *All's Well That Ends Well,* Act IV, scene 5, line 42; *Antony and Cleopatra,* Act III, scene 6, line 76; *The Tempest,* Act I, scene 2, line 19; *ibid.,* Act I, scene 2, line 49; *Julius Caesar,* Act III, scene 2, line 187; *Coriolanus,* Act IV, scene 6, line 73.
160 B. VIII, 68.
161 *Canterbury Tales,* 2,888.
162 *Epithalamium,* VI, 4; *ibid.,* VII, 7.
163 *Cymbeline,* Act IV, scene 2, line 331; *Coriolanus,* Act II, scene 1, line 91; *Much Ado About Nothing,* Act V, scene 3, line 62; *Coriolanus,* Act IV, scene 6, line 73; *Taming of the Shrew,* Act I, scene 2, line 25; *Macbeth,* Act I, scene 5, line 2.

Americans. Least occurs frequently in Shakespeare[164] and other Elizabethan writers.

To say that an Ozarker is *clever* means only that he is generous and accommodating, and has no reference to intelligence. Lounsbury regards clever in this sense as an Americanism,[165] but Mencken places it among the "survivals from the English of the seventeenth century, long since obsolete or merely provincial in England."[166] Schele De Vere says that clever still means honest and respectable in Norfolk, and is used with reference to affability and courtesy in some parts of southern Wales.[167] Professor A. S. Hill of Harvard, writing in 1892, observed that *"clever* in the sense of goodnatured which it bore fifty years ago would be understood by few persons under twenty-five who were brought up in Boston or New York."[168]

The hillman's term *dauncy,* which means particular or fastidious about food, is derived from *daunch,* a word common in fifteenth-century England.[169]

When one of our neighbors described his mother-in-law as "a pore *hippoed* critter," I was at a total loss, and there was nothing for it but to ask what *hippoed* means. He explained that the woman suffered from some imaginary ailment, brought on by "readin' of them fool doctor-books." This word is evidently pretty old; Gilbert Milligan Tucker says that "hypochondria was vulgarly called the hypo" in England about 1711,[170] and probably much earlier.[171]

The word *misling,* which the hillman uses with reference to cool and foggy weather, is found as early as 1438. In Coverdale's version of the Bible we read, "There fel a *myslinge* shower, like a dew."[172]

Mencken says that the adverb plumb, as in *"plumb crazy,"* is an archaism;[173] the *Concise Oxford Dictionary,* however, lists it as American slang.

Sorry means poor or inferior in the Ozark dialect, as in Shakespeare's

---

[164] *Macbeth,* Act III, scene 4, line 28.
[165] *Harper's Magazine,* September, 1913, p. 590.
[166] *The American Language,* 2nd ed., 68.
[167] *Americanisms,* 455.
[168] *Foundations of Rhetoric* (New York, 1892), 29.
[169] Horace Kephart, *Our Southern Highlanders* (New York, 1913), 289.
[170] *American English* (New York, 1921), 245.
[171] *Dialect Notes,* Vol. V (1926), 400.
[172] Isa. 18:4.
[173] *American Language,* 2nd ed., 94.

"a sorry breakfast"[174] and John Evelyn's "sorry beds."[175] It appears that the word is not etymologically related to sorrow at all, but was originally *sorey,* meaning covered with sores.

The hillman's adjective *resty,* meaning indolent, is another Shakespearian survival.[176]

The multiple negative, almost universal in the Ozark dialect, is also common in the old English writers. Spenser uses it in "Good sir, let not my rudeness be no breach,"[177] and Chaucer in "I wol not you contrarien in no wise."[178] The triple and even the quadruple negative are common in Chaucer: "Ne never wol I be no love ne wif," and "he never yet no vileinye ne sayde in all his lyf, unto no maner wight."[179] Beaumont and Fletcher used the double negative freely,[180] and numerous examples are found in the works of Shakespeare and other Elizabethan writers.

The old adverb *whilst,* so common in Shakespeare's writings,[181] is seldom heard in most parts of the United States. But elderly people in the Ozarks still say *whilst* instead of while, just as they do in England to this day.

The hillfolk often say soon when they mean early, as, "I aim to git a soon start in the mornin'." This usage is found in many English writers, including Shakespeare,[182] but is not now regarded as the best usage either in England or America.

Fernent, meaning beside or against or opposite, is seldom heard in the more progressive parts of America, but is still used in the Ozarks. Kephart says that it is common in Scotland,[183] and Schele De Vere reports it from the south of Ireland.[184] A variant form occurs in the old British ballad of "The Cruel Mother":

> *She howkit a grave* forenent *the sun,*
> *An there she buried her twa babes in.*

[174] *2 Henry VI,* Act I, scene 4, line 79.
[175] *Diary,* Jan. 29, 1652.
[176] Sonnet C, 9; *Cymbeline,* Act III, scene 6, line 34.
[177] *Faërie Queene,* III, x, 25.
[178] *Canterbury Tales,* 11,017.
[179] *Canterbury Tales,* 2,308; *ibid.,* 70.
[180] *Spanish Curate,* Act IV, scene 5.
[181] Sonnet 85, 5; *Merry Wives of Windsor,* Act I, scene 1, line 186.
[182] *Antony and Cleopatra,* Act III, scene 4, line 27.
[183] *Our Southern Highlanders,* 280.
[184] *Americanisms,* 475.

The use of right in the sense of very is not common nowadays in most parts of the United States, except in a few set phrases such as "Right Reverend," but it is heard every day in the Ozark country. The use of right as an intensive is regarded as archaic in England, according to the *Oxford English Dictionary*. Many examples of its use are found in Shakespeare, who refers to "a right good husband" and says "right glad I am he was not at this fray."[185] Many comparatively recent English writers cling to this word, as when Carlyle wrote a friend about a new book: "You will get right good reading out of it."[186]

The mountain people frequently say *afore* instead of before, just as Spenser[187] and his contemporaries did. Shakespeare often uses such sentences as "I shall be there afore you" and "if he have never drunk wine afore," while his "Afore God!"[188] rings through the Ozarks to this day. The use of *afore* is no longer correct in England, but it persisted down to comparatively recent times in the New England states, and was warmly defended by James Russell Lowell and others.

Shakespeare and other Elizabethans used the prefix *un* in many cases where modern usage calls for *in* or *im*, producing such words as *unpossible*, *unperfect*, and *unconstant*.[189] All three of these words, and others of the same type, are heard in the Ozark country today.

"This here sugar-liquor ain't no good," said one of my neighbors at Pineville, Missouri, denouncing the synthetic "bourbon" sold in Kansas City. "You cain't make whiskey *withouten* corn." This is an old form of the preposition used by many early writers. Laurence Minot, about 1350, wrote a ballad praising King Edward II with the line: "And grante him joy *withouten* strife."

Many other words and phrases, denounced as "bad English" by the schoolmasters, are of similar ancient lineage. Not every expression in this study has been "run down" in dictionaries and source books. A specialist in these matters could doubtless identify hundreds of such items, as Combs[190]

---

[185] *Henry VIII*, Act IV, scene 2, line 146; *Romeo and Juliet*, Act I, scene 1, line 124.

[186] *New Letters*, I, 178.

[187] *Faërie Queene*, III, iv, 47.

[188] *King Lear*, Act I, scene 5, line 5; *The Tempest*, Act II, scene 2, line 78; *Richard II*, Act II, scene 2, line 1.

[189] *Richard II*, Act II, scene 2, line 126; Sonnet XXIII, 1; *Taming of the Shrew*, Act IV, scene 2, line 14.

[190] "Old, Early and Elizabethan English in the Southern Mountains," *Dialect Notes*, Vol. IV (1916), 283–97.

and others have done in the Appalachians. In the present work the intention is merely to show enough of the earlier usages to arouse interest in this aspect of the Ozark speech and stimulate further research on the part of the inquisitive.

5 Taboos and Euphemisms

FOR MANY YEARS I have been diverted by the extraordinary nature of the Ozarker's conversational taboos, his verbal reactions to sexual and skatalogical topics. Sex is seldom mentioned save in ribaldry, and is therefore excluded from all polite discourse between men and women. Moreover, this taboo is extended to include many words which have no obvious connection with sex, and which are used quite freely in more enlightened sections of the United States.

The adjective brash is defined by Webster as "hasty, impetuous, or brittle," but in the Ozarks it means vulgar or obscene. Many hillfolk will not allow their children to associate with the tourists, because the "fur-riners'" conversation is too *brash*.

In general, it may be said that the names of male animals must not be mentioned when ladies are present; such words as bull, boar, ram, jack, and stallion are taboo.

It was only a few years ago that two women in Scott County, Arkansas, raised a great clamor for the arrest of a stranger who had insulted them by mentioning a bull calf in their presence. Even such words as bullfrog, bull fiddle, bullhead, and bullsnake must be used with caution. A preacher at Pineville, Missouri, once told his flock that Pharoah's daughter found the infant Moses in the *flags*— he didn't like to say bullrushes.[1] Some of my neighbors were much offended by a harmless story about "Ferdinand the Bull" in a Sunday School paper,[2] and refused to allow their children to read this publication thereafter.

Bull Creek is one of the best fishing streams in southwest Missouri, but I have known several native guides who hesitate to use the name in talking with respectable women—not counting tourists, of course. There

[1] *Dialect Notes*, Vol. VI (1928), 58.
[2] *The Highway*, Christian Board of Publication, St. Louis, Mo., July 27, 1941.

was one preacher who insisted on calling the stream Critter Creek, and I have seen letters from a woman in Forsyth, Missouri, who always referred to it as B. Creek. In Searcy County, Arkansas, there is a place called Bull Bottom, but nice old ladies still flinch on hearing it mentioned. The same is true, in some degree, of Bull Mountain and Bull Shoals.

In one backwoods district the polite name for bull is *surly*.[3] I heard some school children using this term, and asked an unusually intelligent schoolmarm what it meant. "That's our name for male animal," she told me. "We're kind of old-fashioned down here, you know. We couldn't come right out an' say *top-cow* like you-all do up North."[4]

It appears that these strange notions about the names of male animals have affected "furriners" who do not ordinarily speak English. Professor Ward Dorrance, of the University of Missouri, who studied the language of an old French settlement near Potosi, Missouri, reports that "the Missouri Creoles, so free in speech at times, at other times observe the taboos of their fellow hillmen of English speech. *Boule*, for instance, is thought more delicate than *taureau*."[5]

Schele De Vere says that many Southerners use ox, male-cow, or even gentleman-cow instead of bull,[6] but the Ozarkers usually say *male, cow-critter, brute*, or *cow-brute*. Charles J. Finger, Fayetteville, Arkansas, told me that when he put up a sign "Registered Jersey Bull Service," a local preacher erased the word *bull* and amended the sign to read "Registered Jersey *Mail* Service."

It is generally supposed that these euphemisms are no longer used by educated Americans, but *male-cow* appeared in a scientific journal as late as 1917.[7]

A stallion is sometimes called a *stable-horse* and occasionally a *stone-horse*, the latter term being considered unfit for respectable feminine ears. Such words as stud and stud-horse are quite out of the question. A farmer on the witness stand at Galena, Missouri, refused to use any of these objectionable terms when questioned about a runaway stallion. "Judge," said he, "it was the kind of horse that hadn't orter been a-runnin' loose in the woods!" A man rode by our cottage on a great stallion one evening, and a little girl from the city cried out, "My goodness, what kind of a horse

[3] Cf. Wentworth, *American Dialect Dictionary*, 613.

[4] *American Speech*, Vol. V (1929), 20.

[5] *Survival of French in the Old District of Sainte Genevieve* (Columbia, Mo., 1935), 62.

[6] *Americanisms*, 488.

[7] *Journal of the American Medical Association*, November 17, 1917, p. 24.

is that?" Some country children giggled at this question, but an old woman answered, "That's what we call a *ridin'-critter,* honey."

A backwoods boy admonished a friend of mine, who had been talking about sheep in the presence of some village women. "Don't say *ram,*" said he; "it sounds so nasty." A man named Freeland, who used to publish a weekly newspaper at Forsyth, Missouri, was severely criticised as late as 1940 because he "printed *ram* right out in the paper!"

Some writers think that *buck,* designating a male goat or deer, is not considered objectionable,[8] but I cannot altogether agree with them. Buck as meaning a male Indian is all right, but *buck nigger* should not be used in the presence of ladies. The word *buck-naked* is avoided in polite conversation, although *bare-naked, mother-naked, body-naked, start-naked,* and *stark-naked* are not offensive. It is strange that Buck is quite admissible as a man's given name, and in this meaning may be pronounced freely anywhere, by men and women alike. The same is true of such compound substantives as buckshot, buckbrush, buck-ague, and buckskin. As the name of a male animal, *buck* is bad, but less offensive than *ram.* In a village newspaper Charlie Williams advertised a "fine yearling *buck sheep*" for sale.[9]

A small boy in southwest Missouri was severely punished because he used the expression "to raise Ned." The word *ned* means bacon in the Ozarks, and I could see nothing bad in what the boy had said. Later on the father told me that *ned* is a very nasty word synonymous with boar,[10] and that no son of his should use such language when girls were present. It appears that pioneer farmers farther west regarded *ned* as a general term for swine; soldiers were called *neds* also, because they fed largely upon pork.[11]

Stag, meaning a gentleman who appears at a social function unaccompanied by a lady, is a new word brought into the country by tourists; the natives regard it as vulgar.[12] It is less objectionable than *boar,* however; I have heard hillmen say *stag hog* in order to avoid the term boar. The professional hog-buyers use the word stag in a technical sense; they tell me it means a male not castrated until he was two or three years old.[13]

[8] *Dialect Notes,* Vol. V (1923), 214.

[9] Crane, Mo., *Chronicle,* September 30, 1943.

[10] *American Speech,* Vol. XI (1936), 316. Cf. G. C. Arthur (*Backwoodsmen* [Boston, 1940], 18, 58), who says that bacon used to be called *boar* in Phelps County, Missouri.

[11] Stanley Vestal, *Mountain Men* (Boston, 1937), 192.

[12] *Dialect Notes,* Vol. VI (1928), 60.

[13] *American Speech,* Vol. X (1935), 272.

The words horse, mare, donkey, and jenny are used in the best Ozark society, but there's something a little suggestive about a hybrid. Rose Wilder Lane, of Mansfield, Missouri, wrote me that "any reference to a *mule,* you know, is slightly indelicate, and to be avoided in the presence of ladies."

Cow, sow, doe, and ewe are used freely enough, but bitch is taboo, since this term is often applied to loose women. Whore-bitch is a common backwoods word for prostitute. Burton Rascoe, who was raised in Oklahoma, wrote me: *"Bitch* is taboo where I come from, too, because bitch means a prostitute. In the mind of a Southerner I think son-of-a-bitch doesn't mean son of a female dog, but son of a whore. I know that as a lad I never thought of *bitch* being a dog."

Many hillfolk use the inelegant *slut* as a euphemism for bitch. Others prefer *gyp,* a term borrowed from the foxhunters. When a resident of Barry County, Missouri, missed his female foxhound, he advertised in the weekly paper:

> Lost or Stolen. White jip with lemon spots, 2 yrs. old. Last seen at Stallions school house. Liberal reward for any information. S. F. Reser, Shell Knob, Mo.[14]

To call a hill woman a *heifer* is to call her a meddlesome gossip, and a *sow* is simply a slatternly housekeeper; neither term has any particular sexual or moral significance. They aren't "fightin' words."

The harmless word sow is sometimes used to designate other female animals; a *sow dog* is a slut, a *sow coon* a female raccoon, and so on. I once heard a man from central Arkansas refer to a colored girl as a "sow nigger" in order to avoid the word *wench,* which is sometimes regarded as vulgar. The male and female redhorse, when they ascend the creeks to spawn, are always known as *sows* and *boars.* One of our neighbors held up a string of these fish to show some women. "I got seven big sows," said he, "an' four of *them others."*

Dam in the sense of female animal is offensive to many hillfolk. A typist in the County Recorder's office at Pineville, Missouri, once refused to copy the phrase "also the increase of the above-described dams." She said that such language should not be set down in the official records of McDonald County. The lawyer who drew up the paper consented to use *females* instead of *dams,* and the stenographer thought this word was all right.

[14] Galena, Mo., *News-Oracle,* January 5, 1951.

98

The male fowl is often called a *crower* in the hill country, since cock is quite out of the question.[15] Crumb reports *chicken-cock* from southeastern Missouri, but it is rare in the Ozarks. Country schoolmarms were horrified by a fable entitled "The Chicken-Cock and the Fox" in an old schoolbook.[16] J. S. Farmer defines *crower* as "a prudish euphemism for cock," and adds that this is not the only instance in which the Americans "fall from the frying-pan of squeamishness into the fire of indelicate suggestiveness."[17] The word rooster is also used as a substitute for cock, and Farmer characterizes this term as "the product of an absurd mock-modesty." Joseph Nelson, writing of the wilderness near Blue Eye, on the Missouri-Arkansas border, says that "some people even refuse the term *rooster* in mixed company. They say *chicken,* or *he-chicken.*"[18]

I have heard mature, dignified hillmen speak of animals as *the he* and *the she.* I have heard the principal of a highschool say *girl-birds* and *boy-birds* in a public address. I once met an old gentleman near Day, Missouri, who described a male cardinal as a *billy redbird,* in order to avoid saying cock or rooster or male before a group of strange women. I have seen grown men, when ladies were present, blush and stammer at the mention of such commonplace bits of hardware as *stop-cocks* or *pet-cocks.*[19] I have heard a United States deputy marshal avoid describing a gun as cocked by some clumsy circumlocution, such as "she's ready to shoot." When a hillman says "I *roostered* my old hog-leg" he means that he cocked his revolver. A woman near Hot Springs, Arkansas, testified that her husband "pulled back both roosters," meaning that he cocked both hammers of a shotgun. Charles Fenton Noland tells of an Arkansas boy who "lost the *rooster* off the lock of his gun."[20]

The word peacock is bad, since it is supposed to suggest micturition as well as the genitals. Even cockeyed, cocksure, cocky, cocker spaniel, and coxcomb are considered in doubtful taste, and many natives shy at such surnames as Cox, Leacock, Hicock, Hitchcock, and the like. Modest hillfolk pronounce cocklebur as if it were spelled *cucklebur,* with the *u* very short.

A veteran schoolmaster near Fayetteville, Arkansas, told me how upset people were when they found the word cock in the old *Blueback*

[15] *Dialect Notes,* Vol. II (1903), 309.
[16] *McGuffey's Fifth Reader* (1885), 70.
[17] *Americanisms Old and New,* (London, 1889), 186.
[18] *Backwoods Teacher,* 134.
[19] *Dialect Notes,* Vol. VI (1928), 59.
[20] *Spirit of the Times,* November 1, 1856, p. 40.

Speller; it was explained on the same page that "the *cock* crows in the morning," but the word was shocking nevertheless. Once through some mistake cock was called out in a public spelling-bee; the children blushed and snickered, and the patrons of the school denounced the teacher. Many parents removed this "dirty word" from their children's books; some teachers scratched it out of all the books on the first day of school.

The editor of a newspaper in southwest Missouri was scandalized to see the noun cock-fight in a national magazine; he remarked to me that "it looks like they would have said *rooster-fight,* anyhow."

Woodcock is the Ozark name for the pileated woodpecker, but refined hillfolk invariably say *woodhen* in polite conversation. Some people even speak of *male woodhens,* and a lady at Noel, Missouri, told me of a *rooster woodhen* whose loud rapping awoke her nearly every morning. Unfortunately the term pecker is almost as objectionable as cock; a resident of Scott county, Arkansas, tells me that ultra-refined people in his neighborhood often say *woodchuck* or *sapsucker* instead of woodpecker or peckerwood. Professor Carr found *woodchuck* used in this sense at the University of Arkansas; he thinks it is "an onomatopoeic word; the woodpecker goes *chuck! chuck!*"[21]

In several parts of the Ozark region I have heard a term for penis, which sounds like *jemson* or *jemmison.* This is a real old-time word, and few of the younger people seem to be familiar with it. Uncle Jack Short, Galena, Missouri, told me that in the eighteen seventies, when he was a boy, *jemmison* was the common term, used by everybody. It has been suggested that this derives somehow from jimson or Jimson weed (*Datura stramonium*), a plant which is said to carry some esoteric sexual significance.

The innocent verb prick is carefully avoided, because the substantive has a sexual connotation; one does not prick up one's ears in the Ozarks, and a real lady was never known to prick her finger with a needle.

The noun root designates the male organ and must be used cautiously in decorous conversation. In Stone County, Missouri, the boys used to sing a vulgar ditty with the lines:

> *The gals up Railey Creek they are full grown,*
> *They'll jump on a root like a dog on a bone.*

The mention of a variation of backgammon known as acey-deucey would shock any backwoods group, because *ducey,* pronounced to rhyme

[21] *Dialect Notes,* Vol. III (1906), 164.

with Lucy, is a very common word for penis.[22] The noun *dinger* means penis, too, but I don't think it is as old, or as widely used, as the other names here listed. *Dood,* which rhymes with rude, also designates the male organ and must be avoided in general conversation. In Barry County, Missouri, one often hears *doodle* used in the same meaning.

Another old-time word for penis sounds like *ying-yang,* accent on the first syllable. Weldon Stone mentions *ying-yang* in his Ozark novel,[23] which is the only time I ever saw the word in print.

When a man was being tried for rape at Granby, Missouri, several witnesses used *long tool* and *hoe-handle* when they meant penis. Quizzed about this later, they said that these euphemisms enabled them to avoid offending some respectable women in the courtroom.

Goober and goober-pea are names for peanut, but are not favored by the ultra-refined because they also designate the male genitals. Some people use *goober-grabber* to mean a lowlander as distinguished from a mountain man.[24] The oldest newspaper in Arkansas assured its readers that *goober-grabber* means merely a stingy person, a penny-pincher.[25] But there are many settlements in Arkansas and Missouri where *goober-grabber* has nothing to do with peanuts or penuriousness; it means a wanton, lascivious woman. I have known several old ladies who always called peanuts *pinders,* a word of Gullah origin[26] which carries no double meaning.

Another doubtful word is the proper name Peter. It is so universally regarded as a name for the male "family organ" that it never quite loses this significance. Very strait-laced old-timers seldom named a boy Peter. I recall an evangelist from the North who shouted something about the church being founded upon Peter, and he was puzzled by the flushed cheeks of the young women and the ill-suppressed amusement of the ungodly. Another preacher, a real Ozark circuit rider, after talking about Peter's denial of Christ, suddenly shouted, "How many *Peters* air they here?" There was no laughter or snickering; the congregation was simply flabbergasted, and the poor preacher almost collapsed when he realized what he had said. This happened in Pineville, Missouri, more than forty years ago, but it is still remembered and commented upon whenever this preacher's name is mentioned.

Petered out means simply exhausted, and has no particular connection

[22] *Dialect Notes,* Vol. V (1927), 474.
[23] *Devil Take a Whittler,* (New York, 1948), 9.
[24] *American Speech,* Vol. XI (1936), 315.
[25] *Arkansas Gazette,* Little Rock, Ark., May 3, 1942.
[26] Lorenzo D. Turner, *Africanisms in the Gullah Dialect* (Chicago, 1949), 199.

with sex, but I have often noticed that a hillman stumbles and hesitates over the phrase in the presence of strangers, especially women. He feels that it is just a trifle off color, not quite the thing to say "right out before folks."

Saltpeter is a bad word, too. An old man was telling the schoolmarm how to pickle pork. "You put in a pinch of salt," said he. "My goodness, it's been salted already," she objected. The old man scowled at her. "I don't mean table-salt or cow-salt; you know what kind of salt I mean." The lady did, but pretended ignorance, until finally the old fellow decided he was being trifled with. "Salt-*PETER*, dang it!" he shouted, and stalked away in disgust. Another hillman, discussing the home manufacture of gunpowder, was always careful to say *potash* instead of saltpeter, if any womenfolk were within hearing.

When a man has some astonishing experience or sees something novel and extraordinary, he says, "Well, that's a new ring on my horn!" Sometimes it is "a new wrinkle on my horn." But since the word horn often means penis, in the presence of ladies a gentlemanly hillman is content to say, "Well, that's a new one on me!"

There's something a little off-color about the noun rhubarb. In some particularly strait-laced settlements the best people don't use the word at all; they say *pie-plant* instead. Emerson Higgins, Sulphur Springs, Arkansas, pointed out a reference to this meaning in a ribald folksong:

> *The cat couldn't kitten an' the slut couldn't pup,*
> *An' the old man couldn't git his* rhubarb *up.*

B. A. Botkin found a related stanza in an Oklahoma version of "Turkey in the Straw":

> *Cat had a kitten, the kitten had a pup,*
> *Say, old lady, is your rhubarb up?*
> *There's a plenty of rhubarb all round the farm,*
> *And another little drink won't do us any harm.*[27]

Okra is another vegetable which often carries a sexual significance. A man in Carroll County, Arkansas, was swaggering around with some young girls. "Look at old Sam, *a-struttin' his okra* for them town gals," a country woman said scornfully.

[27] *American Play-Party Song,* 335.

Taboos and Euphemisms

Many mountain women never use the word stone; the commoner term is rock, anyhow. Schele De Vere observed the same reluctance in other parts of the South, and refers to "a young lady who was so refined that she avoided saying *stone*."[28] The use of stone to mean testicle is found in the King James Version of the Bible,[29] a work with which the mountain people are more or less familiar.

The noun ball is acceptable everywhere, but the plural must be used cautiously. Asked to identify some small wild-fowl on the river near Cotter, Arkansas, a guide said, "Them's butter-ducks, ma'am." Those ducks (*Glaucionetta albeola*) are called *butterballs* from Maine to Florida, but the Ozarker thought this name should not be mentioned when there were ladies in the boat. *Balled-up,* according to Mencken, was once improper but is now making steady progress toward polite acceptance;[30] this is doubtless true in the more sophisticated sections of the country, but balled-up is still bad taste in the Ozarks.

Knocker is sometimes used to mean testicle. Pigs' testicles are sold as *mountain oysters, pigs' knockers,* or *lamb fries.* An old gentleman drinking great quantities of water at Hot Springs, Arkansas, remarked, "It's good for your *knockers,*" meaning that the water is aphrodisiac. A well-behaved Ozark boy would hesitate to mention knocker in a respectable conversation.

Jingle-berry is another backwoods word for testicle; there is an old song about a boy and girl who "set right down to *jingle-berry* tea."[31] The man who sang this song for me remarked: "You better write down sassafras tea, because it's ag'in the law to print words like *jingle-berry* in a book."

Even the common word nuts is in doubtful taste because it is sometimes used to mean testicles. I have often observed that in talking about machinery, when ladies are present, a hillman says bolts an' *taps* rather than bolts an' nuts.

Cod still means scrotum or testicles in the Ozarks, and children giggle over such words as codfish and cod-liver oil. I have seen little girls blush when called upon to point out Cape Cod on a schoolroom map. A young man in Springfield, Missouri, described a certain sorority dance as "a regular cod-buster," and another chap remarked that Bear Creek, after a shower, was "just about *cod deep.*" Country boys sometimes speak of

28 *Americanisms,* 554.
29 Deut. 23:1.
30 *American Language,* 2nd ed., p. 176.
31 Cf. my *Ozark Folksongs,* III, 154.

having the *clabber-cod,* some condition of the testicles associated with venereal disease. A druggist in Joplin, Missouri, told me that his rural customers often ask for a *cod-holder* when they mean a suspensory. It is not the thing to refer to an elderly hillman as an old *codger* anywhere in the Ozark country.

A paper bag is always called a *sack*[32] or a *poke,* since bag means scrotum in the hill country and is too vulgar for refined ears. It is said that bag has the same indecent connotation in certain parts of Kansas.[33] The male organs are frequently known as the *prides,* and the word pride has thus acquired a certain obscene significance. The term privates means genitals; I have seen a mature woman, mother of a large family, burst out laughing when a former soldier spoke casually of *buck privates.* The word parts, too, is so often used to mean genitals that it is no longer a "nice" word in mixed company.

I know certain old folk in southwest Missouri who use the word craw to mean scrotum, or perhaps it means the scrotum and testes together; there is an ancient tale of a pioneer who sat naked on a log "with his old craw a-hangin' down."

Some people flinch at the word original, which means a horse with defective sex organs, and is sometimes applied to a man in a similar case. The term also refers to a male animal which has been *cut proud,*[34] incompletely or unsuccessfully castrated. The innocent verb alter is not used in the presence of strange women, because alter in the Ozarks means to castrate, and is rarely used in any other sense.[35] In mixed company the hillman often says de-horn when he means castrate; I have heard men threaten to *de-horn* a sex-mad evangelist who had been annoying their womenfolk. And yet the noun horn means penis, not testicles. The verb means to cuckold, as in the sentence, "Poor Henry was *horned* afore the weddin' was two months old." Unsatisfied sexual desire in the male is called either *stone-ache* or *horn colic.*

Many of the old-timers use the term *red onion* to mean the female genitals. "Jim's out a-playin' the red onion" means that he's running after disreputable women. There is a Red Onion Cave near Flat River, Missouri, and Red Onion used to be a common name for a dance hall or honkytonk in the Missouri and Oklahoma mining camps.

[32] *Dialect Notes,* Vol. II (1904), 420.
[33] Mencken, *American Language,* 2nd ed., p. 152.
[34] Cf. *Dialect Notes,* Vol. V (1923), 217.
[35] *Dialect Notes,* Vol. VI (1928), 60.

Taboos and Euphemisms

The word satchel is best avoided because it means the pudendum, also known as the pussy, twat, snatch, monkey, moosey, or twitchet. Weldon Stone, in an Ozark novel, refers to a woman who is invited to come near the fire and "warm her *twitchet*," to which she replies that it's warm enough already.[36] A man who is interested in nothing but woman-chasing may be described as *satchel-crazy*, *twitchet-struck*, or *pussy-simple*. The verb monkey around seems innocent enough, but some very careful people object to it as rather "brash" for use in mixed company. Since the noun monkey refers to the female genitals, *monkeyin' around* suggests some kind of sexual approach or even a direct contact with the vulva.

When a woman's husband has been absent for a long time, she may be suffering from *back trouble,* but this would never be mentioned in general conversation. Backache is harmless enough, but *back trouble* is something else again.

Many women avoid the word pain, apparently feeling that this word refers chiefly to the pains of childbirth. One of our neighbors often spoke of a *hurtin'* under her ribs or a *misery* in her side. But she didn't have pains, being a respectable widow and beyond the age of childbearing anyhow.

The preterite hung must be used with caution in elegant backwoods talk, because it has a sexual meaning in many wisecracks and anecdotes. I once heard a tie-hacker say of a bedraggled little puppy: "No wonder he looks so miserable; he just passed the *place where his pappy was hung.*" The common expression "till the last dog is hung" means only a long time in many parts of the United States, comparable to "till Hell freezes over." But in the Ozarks it is a filthy utterance, unfit for refined feminine ears.

When the word ill is applied to a woman, it usually means that she's in a bad temper, but sometimes it refers to menstruation, and unwell is always used in this latter sense. A man or boy could never be unwell in the Ozarks.[37] I met a woman near Fayetteville, Arkansas, a university graduate, liberal and tolerant of most Yankee vulgarisms. But she was horrified to hear the word unwell in a general conversation, and refused to believe that even a Northerner or an Englishman could use it to mean anything other than menstruation.

Courses means menses, too, and must be avoided in polite talk. I once knew a preacher who denounced "The Little Mohee" as a "dirty" song because of the lines:

[36] *Devil Take a Whittler,* 167.
[37] *Dialect Notes,* Vol. VI (1928), 60.

I'll turn back my courses
Far o'er the blue sea.

Flowers is also used with reference to catamenia. Dr. Morris Fishbein noted this, and regards it as a modern slang term.[38] It is found in Webster, however, and in the King James Bible.[39] The *Oxford Dictionary* quotes from a work of about 1400: "A woman schal in the harme blede for stoppyng of her *flowrys.*" The wife of a state official once appeared in Searcy County, Arkansas, with a large stain on her gown. "Law sakes," whispered an old woman in the audience, "the pore gal has done *flowered* her dress!" A physician in Pineville, Missouri, asked a woman when she had last menstruated. "I ain't seen no *flowers* in four months," she told him.

A young girl in Shannon County, Missouri, remarked at breakfast, "Well, *old grandpaw come last night.*" Everybody looked shocked, one of the children giggled, and the poor girl flushed scarlet. Her remark was perfectly innocent, meaning only that there had been a heavy frost. But the expression reminded people of *old grandmaw's* coming, which refers to menstruation.

The Ozarker seldom uses the words virgin or maiden, since these terms bear a too direct reference to sex. A teacher of botany in Jasper County, Missouri, says that he is afraid to mention the *maidenhair* fern in his high school classes. "I can still use the word *orchid*," he added smiling, "because neither the students nor the members of the school board have any idea of its original meaning."

Harmless is sometimes used as a synonym for virtuous; to call a young girl "a harmless little thing" means that she is a virgin.

Decent is supposed to describe women who have no sexual experience outside of lawful wedlock, but the term is not used in polite conversation between the sexes. "Fifty years ago," writes H. L. Mencken, "the word *decent* was indecent in the South; no respectable woman was supposed to have any notion of the difference between decent and indecent."[40] Decent is still a bit on the indecent side in the Ozarks.

The adjective *feisty,* used in some parts of the South to mean saucy or truculent, is generally applied to females in the Ozarks and means flirtatious or provocative. At Fayetteville, Arkansas, Joseph W. Carr found that

---

[38] *American Speech*, Vol. I (1925), 24.
[39] Lev. 15:24 and 33.
[40] *American Language*, 2nd ed., p. 152.

a *feisty* girl is "tomboyish, fast."[41] A lady in Galena, Missouri, tells me that "a *feisty* woman may not be *fast*, but she's a little too frisky to be nice." In Green County, Missouri, "*feisty* is used to describe a vivacious girl whose morals the neighborhood is beginning to question."[42] In McDonald County, Missouri, *feisty* means "irritably facetious or snippy," according to Jay L. B. Taylor, who thinks it derives from *fice*.[43] Marge Lyon says that a girl who attracts attention by "dancing too briskly or acting in an indecorous manner" is likely to be called *feisty* and suffer a loss of reputation.[44] Perhaps the meaning varies in different localities, but *feisty* is a word that must be used with considerable caution.

Similar to feisty is the noun *split-tail*, a disrespectful name for an active young woman. A split-tail is not necessarily a woman of bad morals, but rather one who is too lively, perhaps inclined to some sort of indiscretion.[45]

Cagey, pruney, rollicky, and *horny* are the conventional words for sensual, and are not used in polite conversation. Jay L. B. Taylor reports that horny means "carnal minded" in McDonald County, Missouri,[46] but I have heard it used only with reference to sexual desire. Although the noun horn means penis, the adjective horny is applied to either sex. The Devil is often called Old Horny, but not in polite conversation between men and women.

The word fleshy does not mean fat or corpulent, but only concupiscent in the hill country. I know a woman at Forsyth, Missouri, who was mortally offended when some tourists described her husband as "a rather *fleshy* man."

Rim, according to Taylor's word list from McDonald County, Missouri,[47] means "desirous of sexual intercourse, wanting to be bred," and applies particularly to sows. I have heard *rim* and *rimmin'* and *over-rim* used with reference to many females, including young girls. I am not sure just what these words mean, but they are not regarded with favor by respectable country women.

---

[41] *Dialect Notes,* Vol. III (1906), 136.

[42] Wilma Wade, *Publication of the American Dialect Society,* No. 2 (1944), 55–56.

[43] *Dialect Notes,* Vol. V (1923), 206.

[44] *Fresh from the Hills,* 136.

[45] Cf. Waldo Lee McAtee, *Rural Dialect of Grant County, Indiana: Supplement* (Washington, 1942), 9.

[46] *Dialect Notes,* Vol. V (1923), 211.

[47] *Dialect Notes,* Vol. V (1923), 219.

When a mountain man says of a woman that "her *comb sure is red,*" he means that she's in a state of sexual excitement.[48] No well-bred hillman would use this expression in polite society. Joseph W. Carr heard *red in the comb* at Fayetteville, Arkansas, where he says it means "anxious to marry."[49] It is a phrase from the barnyard; a fowl with a bright red comb is thought to be healthy and sexually active, while one with a pale comb is in poor condition.

The term peach orchard carries some obscure reference to sexual excess. General Daniel E. Sickles, of Civil War fame, used to be described as "the hero of the Peach Orchard," a phrase which sent any Ozark audience into gales of laughter. Clara B. Eno says that Howard County, Arkansas, "contains the largest Peach Orchard in the United States,"[50] but this passage in Miss Eno's book seems very funny to Ozark children, who cannot refrain from giggling over it. A very passionate, licentious woman is said to be "peach orchard crazy."

A candidate for Congress once said that his opponent, a handsome fellow and popular with the ladies, was "wild as a boar in a peach orchard." Perhaps he meant *borer* instead of boar. The phrase "peach orchard boars" is applied to men who appear sexually passionate and unrestrained. I have seen an old letter from Phelps County, Missouri, in which some visitors from St. Louis are said to be "wilder than Petrosse's boars," but have heard no explanation of this expression. It may be that there's some connection between *Petrosse* and *Peach Orchard*. However, the significance of these expressions is so widely understood in some sections of Missouri and Arkansas that it is a serious breach of the proprieties to say peach orchard in polite conversation with respectable women.

Some obscene significance attaches to the word tomcat. It is quite correct to remark that a young man is *talkin'* or *settin' up* or *sparkin'* or *courtin'*, since all these terms may imply an intention to marry. But to say that a boy is *tomcattin' around* means that he is seeking illicit romance,[51] and such activities must not be mentioned in genteel conversation.

The brothels in the mining camps are called *cat-houses,* and the vans used by traveling prostitutes are known as *cat-wagons.* An old freighter told me that Joplin, Missouri, was called *Chippy's Delight* in the early days, because the whole town was full of *ram-cat alleys.* Carr reports that *blister*

[48] *American Speech,* Vol. V (1929), 19.
[49] *Dialect Notes,* Vol. III (1906), 153.
[50] *Historic Places in Arkansas* (Van Buren, Ark., 1940), 41.
[51] *Dialect Notes,* Vol. V (1927), 478.

is "not uncommon" in Washington County, Arkansas, as a term for an "immoral woman," and that a brothel is called a *franzy-house.*[52] I have heard these terms, but believe that they are rare nowadays.

White-livered does not mean cowardly, as in some other sections of the country, but lascivious; a woman who has lost several husbands by death, while remaining youthful and vigorous herself, is called a *white-livered widder.*[53] This superstition is found in some other parts of the United States and in England. Although the *Oxford Dictionary* does not give the definition above, the *English Dialect Dictionary* does: "A white-livered woman is popularly supposed to be almost as dangerous as was the poison-natured Indian beauty sent as a present to Alexander the Great. How the whiteness of the liver is to be detected is not clear. . . . At any rate, if you discover that a young woman is white-livered do not on any account marry her, because the whiteness of her liver is of a poisonous nature, and you assuredly will not live long with a white-livered young woman as your wife. If she does not die, you will!"

To describe a girl as *fork-ed* is to call her bold, brazen, "crazy about men." Shakespeare speaks of the *forked plague,* meaning cuckoldry: "This forked plague is fated to us all, when we do quicken."[54] I have seen young girls leave a dance because the fiddler began to play "Fork-ed Deer." When Buster Fellowes played this tune on a radio program, Bill Ring announced it as "Frisky Deer."[55] Even such a phrase as "the *forks* of the creek" suggests the pudenda. Asked to plow the Widder Spelvin's garden-patch, my neighbor was reluctant to leave his own farm work. "If she'd let me plow *at the forks of the creek,* it would be different," he said with a leer.

Many of the old fiddle-tunes are fitted with suggestive lines. A dancer who has once heard these obscene old verses comes to associate them with the music, and seems to hear them again whenever the tune is played. A man at Cyclone, Missouri, once told me that "old folks mostly think the witches have something to do with it," and I have heard other hillfolk offer similar explanations. "Them fellers can make a fiddle talk, all right," said an old gentleman, "but it sure talks dirty!" A village preacher told me that certain dance tunes would "make an old man's *hair* stand on end," and any young woman who listened would be "a-squirmin' round like a mink" in no time at all. Many backwoods Christians, even today, regard

[52] *Dialect Notes,* Vol. III (1905), 70; *ibid.,* Vol. III (1906), 136.
[53] Cf. my *Ozark Superstitions,* (New York, 1947), 172.
[54] *Othello,* Act III, scene 3, line 276.
[55] KWTO, Springfield, Mo., May 3, 1947.

the fiddle as the Devil's own instrument. Mary Elizabeth Mahnkey, Kirby-ville, Missouri, says of "The Irish Washerwoman" that "it had innocent words, but the vulgar parody was so widely known that decent girls would leave a dance if a single bar of that tune was played." The same is true of several other old dance tunes.

Any direct reference to aphrodisiacs is in very bad taste. It seems odd that men who would never mention rabbit-fat, or ginseng, or snake-root tea[56] in mixed company feel that it's quite all right to talk about "medicine for my wife's kidneys." I have heard aged men, about to take a snort of whiskey, say, "Well, this is *for my wife's kidneys!*" C. C. Williford published a letter from an old fellow who recommended the *rabbit-ice* that appears on horsemint or dittany-weed. "It's something like swamproot," he wrote, "and I always take it in the spring *for my wife's kidneys.*"[57]

The hillman sometimes eats pigs' testicles, which he calls mountain oysters, but these are believed to contain a powerful aphrodisiac and must not be mentioned when ladies are present.[58] "In 1870," writes B. W. Rice, "very few young country women would eat oysters."[59] Even today I know Ozark girls who like oysters or lamb-fries at home, but would never order them in a public restaurant. Eggs are supposed to excite sexual desire also, and it is not quite proper for a modest mountain woman to admit that she is especially fond of them.

Many expressions and allusions link the noun gravel with sexual contact. Ask a hillman where he is going and he replies, "To git some *gravels* for my goose," meaning that he is in search of sexual satisfaction. When a widow remarries, the neighbors say, "Well, Florrie has throwed away her *gravel-medicine*,"[60] a play upon the notion that frequent sexual intercourse cures diseases of the female kidneys and bladder. To speak of a man's *turning over the gravels* means that he is in robust health, full of vigor; one who can urinate with such force that the stream of urine scatters pebbles on a gravel-bar is in pretty good condition. "Uncle Jim's been kind of puny all winter," I was told, "but he sure does *turn over the gravels* now!" Because of these and other set phrases and axioms, the word gravel must be used rather carefully in mixed crowds, and the well-intentioned "furriner" had best not use it at all when ladies are present.

The term shag, used as the name of a dance step, seems very shocking

[56] Cf. my *Ozark Superstitions*, 103, 112.
[57] *KWTO Dial*, Springfield, Mo., December, 1949, p. 13.
[58] *American Speech*, Vol. V (1929), 19.
[59] *Arcadian Life*, March, 1936, p. 3.
[60] Cf. my *Ozark Superstitions*, 103.

to the old-timers, who know the word only in its ancient sense of a sexual attack. Professor Ramsay points out that *shag* appears in Mark Twain's bawdy *1601,* and that it is still current in the Ozarks.[61] In Taney County, Missouri, I have heard a tourists' week-end party called a *shaggin'-match.* A man in southwest Missouri was nicknamed *Shag,* and an old-timer told me that "he come by his name honest," since he had fourteen children. A *shaggy dog* means either a bitch in heat or a male looking for female companionship. In Fayetteville, Arkansas, I once heard a man designate obscene tales as *shaggy-dog* stories.

The verb *bother* has the same significance as shag, but implies that the female is unwilling or at least reluctant. The wife of a Hot Springs, Arkansas, policeman testified demurely, "My man he *bothers* me every day, an' three times of a Sunday." A granny-woman at Pineville, Missouri, remarked of a certain bride, "She says she wasn't *bothered* till November, but I bet she comes fresh before All Fools' Day!"

Correspond is sometimes used to mean copulate and is therefore regarded as a doubtful word by very "nice-spoken" hillfolk. This must be an old British usage; the *Oxford English Dictionary* gives "sexual intercourse" as an obsolete meaning of correspondence.

When a hillman says that he got him a *piece,*[62] he means that he has had sexual intercourse, and thus the intrinsically harmless term piece is unfit for refined backwoods society. The verb *diddle,* which is commonly used to mean cheat or defraud in some parts of the United States, signifies copulate in the Ozarks and is not mentioned in the best family circles.

Even such an innocent verb as tread must be avoided, because it still means copulate. Combs noted this in the Appalachians also, where *"tread* is a dangerous word in highland speech, meaning to cohabit."[63] Major E. H. Criswell, Lexington, Missouri, has heard the term in his neighborhood, but thinks that it applies only to fowls. However, there are many elderly people in southern Missouri who regard it as a "dirty" word, and I once heard a politician publicly criticized for *"treadin'* half the schoolmarms in Dallas county."[64] I have seen mountain children in church giggling over a line in the hymn "Onward, Christian Soldiers," which reads "Brothers, we are *treading* where the saints have trod." The past tense trod, oddly enough, seems to have no indecent significance.

[61] *A Mark Twain Lexicon,* 202.

[62] Cf. *Dialect Notes,* Vol. V (1923), 217.

[63] *Publication of the Modern Language Association,* Vol. XLVI (1931), 1322.

[64] Cf. *American Speech,* Vol. V (1929), 20.

Some strait-laced Ozark folks wriggle a little at any reference to *the short rows*. This expression is often used in connection with copulation and means a brief interval just preceding the orgasm. "We was just *gittin' into the short rows*," said a backwoods philanderer, "when I heerd the front gate slam!" The phrase is perhaps derived from plowing in irregular clearings, where the last few rows to be plowed are the shortest.

The word roger, as used by many young people in the Ozarks, is a verb meaning to manage, to control. Taken for a ride in a new car, a lady asked the driver: "Do you think you can *roger* this thing all right?" But among the old-timers *roger* means copulate, particularly among sheep and goats. Compare *roger* in this latter sense in William Byrd,[65] also the references to *roger* as meaning sexual intercourse between human beings in *A Mark Twain Lexicon*.[66] There are many elderly people in the Ozarks today who regard *roger* as a "dirty" word, and are shocked to hear it used by respectable young men and women.

The verb wing means to court or woo: "They do say Job Henders is *a-wingin'* Polly Howard now." Some hillfolk avoid this as rather indelicate, "too much like a gobbler draggin' his wing at a hen-turkey."

Sprunch is another term for the sexual advance of a male, a much stronger term than *spark* or *wing*. Some hillfolk use *sprunchin'* to mean copulation, but I think it often refers to some preliminary sex activity rather than to coitus proper.

The old expression *ride and tie* originally referred to two men who had only one horse; one man rode for awhile, tied the horse and walked on; the other passed him on horseback, then after a proper interval *he* tied the horse and walked a spell. Crumb reported *ride and tie* from southeastern Missouri,[67] and I have heard it in many parts of the Ozark country. The saying is often used figuratively to describe a scandalous triangle involving two men and one woman, so that it is not quite the thing to mention in elegant backwoods conversation.

Rose O'Neill, Day, Missouri, told me that one of her neighbors always used *deceiver-woman* to mean an unfaithful wife, apparently regarding it as a very delicate and "refined" expression.

Such terms as passion and passionate are never used save with reference to sexual desire, and must be avoided in polite conversation. A lady in Springfield, Missouri, told me how shocked she was, as a girl, to hear a

[65] *Diary,* March 29, 1711; March 30, 1711; May 16, 1711.
[66] *University of Missouri Studies,* XIII (1938), 191.
[67] *Dialect Notes,* Vol. II (1903), 327.

"furrin" preacher speak of the *passion* of Christ. One horrified old woman in the congregation cried out, "Why, He didn't *have* no passion! He was without sin!"

Even the word love is considered more or less indecent, and the mountain people seldom use it in its ordinary sense, but nearly always with some degrading or jocular connotation. If a hillman does admit that he *loved* a woman, he means only that he caressed and embraced her.[68]

Ravish and ravage always mean rape among the old-timers, and such words are not used in decorous social gatherings.

Even bed is not a term to be used by "nice" girls before male strangers. Refined backwoods ladies never "go to bed"; they think it is more delicate to *retire* or even to *lay down!*[69] Crumb says that in southeast Missouri *"lie down* is considered more polite than *go to bed."*[70]

There are no crabs in the Ozarks, but the word is applied to *Pediculus pubis,* and since this parasite is most active in the areas about the sex organs, the name has acquired an indecent connotation. The tourist may talk of shrimps and prawns and lobsters without let or hindrance, but the first mention of *crabs* is greeted by an awkward silence, or by embarrassed efforts to change the subject.

School butter is a backwoods expression that must not be used in refined speech, but nobody seems to know just what it means. Ruffians who ride by a schoolhouse in the backwoods sometimes call out *"school butter!"* whereupon the big boys of the school rush to attack them. If the teacher is a man, he leads the pursuit, which always ends in a bloody fight if the miscreants are overtaken. Judge John Turner White, Jefferson City, Missouri, recalled that this sort of thing was common at rural schools near Springfield, Missouri, in the eighteen sixties and seventies. "I don't know what *school butter* means," said Judge White, "or how the expression originated, but it was a deadly insult."

An old man at Cyclone, Missouri, told me that *"school butter* is a fightin' word, like son-of-a-bitch, only nastier."

Wayman Hogue says that "the word *school butter* was an insult to the whole school," and quotes a little rhyme:

> *School butter, chicken flutter,*
> *Rotten aigs for the teacher's supper.*[71]

[68] Cf. *Dialect Notes,* Vol. V (1923), 214; *ibid.,* Vol. VI (1928), 62.

[69] *Dialect Notes,* Vol. III (1905), 92; *ibid.,* Vol. V (1923), 213; *ibid.,* Vol. VI (1928), 59.

[70] *Dialect Notes,* Vol. II (1903), 319.   [71] *Back Yonder,* 37–38.

Elbert Short, of Crane, Missouri, says that when he was a boy it was a "terrible slur" to shout *butter-cup* around a schoolhouse. I have talked with perhaps fifty men and women who have heard the cry *school butter* or *butter-cup*, and they all agree that it was a deadly insult, but I have never been able to get any satisfactory explanation of its meaning. Some people connect it vaguely with the common term *duck-butter*, which means semen or seminal fluid.[72]

Pregnancy is seldom mentioned when both men and women are present, even among fairly intimate friends. If no women are about, a hillman may remark to a comparative stranger that his wife is *ketched*, or *pizened*, or *springin'*, or *sprung*, or *too big for her clothes*, or *knocked up*, or *comin' fresh*, or *lookin' piggy*, or *otherwise*, or *teemin'*, or *with squirrel*, or *fallin' apart*, or *fallin' to pieces*, or *in a family way*, or *that she has swallered a watermelon seed*, but these phrases are not for polite conversation between the sexes. At Granby, Missouri, when a man's wife was about to be delivered of a child, a friend said to the husband, "Well, Tom, it looks like *your bees are a-swarmin'*." To say that a woman is *about to find pups* means that she is going to have a baby, but a man would not use this one with reference to his own wife. A pregnant woman is supposed to stay at home and keep out of sight, never intimating to any man except her husband that she has the least inkling of her own condition. When an unmarried woman becomes pregnant, her friends say "she stumped her toe," meaning that the whole thing was somehow accidental.

Up-an'-comin' is a common term for pregnant, and sometimes one hears a superlative. A man near Eureka Springs, Arkansas, remarked that his wife was the *up-an'-comin'est* woman in Carroll County. "She gits knocked up," said he, "every time I hang my pants on the foot of the bed."

When a girl in our town quarreled with her lover, a local gagman remarked that "Lizzie has missed the bus." *Buss* means to kiss in the Ozarks, and Lizzie's boy-friend was a *bus* driver for the new consolidated school district. Also the phrase *missed the bus* meant that Lizzie was pregnant. This Shakespearian triple play on words amused the villagers no end, although the average tourist probably wouldn't see anything funny about it.

In some parts of the Ozark region *straw* means childbirth. A woman who is *called to straw* is about to have a baby.[73] I first assumed that it re-

[72] *American Speech*, Vol. VIII (1933), 48.
[73] *American Speech*, Vol. VIII (1933), 48.
[74] *American Speech*, Vol. XI (1936), 317.

ferred to a straw mattress, just as "hit the hay" signifies "go to bed." But many natives, including physicians and midwives, at widely separated points in Missouri and Arkansas, assure me that *straw* means the act of parturition or the muscular movements involved in the expulsion of the foetus.[74] It is sometimes used as a verb, as in the sentence, "Mable's a-strawin' right now, an' the granny-woman ain't here yet!" The *Oxford Dictionary* gives the phrase *in the straw*, in childbed; and *out of the straw*, recovered after childbearing.

A midwife is usually called a *granny-woman*, and *granny* is often used as a verb, referring to the actual delivery of the child. "I got a *granny-case* for ye, Doc," cried a young husband, rushing into a physician's office. The word is sometimes used with reference to the lower animals, and I have heard a hillman speak of *grannyin'* a cow. A "furriner" came to Christian County, Missouri, and was very successful in raising poultry for the Springfield market. "Shucks," said one of his envious neighbors, "chickens is a woman's work. That feller ain't nothin' but a *chicken-granny*." These *granny* words, particularly the verb combinations, are seldom used in general conversation between the sexes.

Slink is not a good word for genteel talk, because to the Ozarker it means to abort or produce a miscarriage.[75]

The adjective illiterate is best avoided by amicable strangers, because many hillmen confuse it with *illegitimate*. Many old-timers speak of illiterate babies, when they mean children born out of wedlock. A boy at Reeds Springs Junction, Missouri, made no secret of the fact that he couldn't read or write. But in 1942, when the local draft board rejected him because he was *illiterate*, this chap flew into a rage, cursed everybody in sight, and offered to fight the sheriff! He thought the officials were publicly branding him as a bastard. Sometimes illiterate seems to mean illegal or illicit; abortions are often referred to as illiterate or illiteral operations.

The word bastard must not be used in ordinary talk, but *woodscolt*, which means the same thing, is not prohibited. If one says of a child that it was got *on the wrong side of the blanket*, the meaning is that it was born out of wedlock or that its father was not the husband of its mother. The idea is that such a child was begotten casually or hasty-like on top of a bed, rather than between the blankets by decent married folk.

The noun man, used with a feminine possessive, is always taken to mean husband. An Ozark woman's legal mate is invariably known as *her man*. I shall never forget a sprightly widow from "up North some-

[75] Cf. my *The Ozarks*, 83.

wheres" who shocked her Arkansas neighbors by referring to a hired farmhand as *my man John.*[76]

A woman who asked for *acker fortis* in the drugstore at Pineville, Missouri, was much embarrassed; not because aqua fortis is used in the treatment of itch, but because *fortis* sounds like fart! The latter is a very objectionable word, of course. The refined hillman would say *break wind* or *poot* instead.[77] L. J. Hedgecock remembers that near Oronogo, Missouri, about the turn of the century, a boy "accidentally let a little *capoot,* as we used to say."[78] Ethel Reed Strainchamps, referring to her childhood in Polk and McDonald counties, Missouri, reports: "We used the words *poop* and *poot* with their onomatopoeic significance in regard to bodily discharges, and we were as horrified and amused to come across the word *poop deck* in our grade school textbooks as we were by the words *ass* and *hockey.*"[79]

The noun *jill-flirt,* according to Webster, means "a light, wanton woman," but in the Ozarks it means merely one who *poots* noisily and frequently. This is caused by a cut or wound connecting the vagina and the rectum, usually a tear suffered in childbirth. As James R. Masterson puts it, "A gilflirt is a female in which the perineal orifices are exceptionally close together."[80] W. O. Rice defines *jill-flirted* as "having the vulva lacerated in delivery."[81] A female in this condition has little control over the expulsion of gas from the lower bowel.

In Scott County, Arkansas, an elderly preacher left a social gathering rather suddenly. "I had to make a branch," he said in a loud whisper on his return, meaning that he went outside to urinate. Many Ozarkers "go out *to see how high the moon is,*" and one occasionally finds such euphemisms in print.[82]

Modest Ozark women do not say urine, but use the old word *chamberlye,*[83] even when talking to a physician. Shakespeare made one of his characters say "your chamber-lye breeds fleas."[84] Sometimes the hillfolk use

[76] *American Speech,* Vol. VIII (1933), 51.
[77] *Dialect Notes,* Vol. V (1926), 402.
[78] *Gone Are the Days* (Girard, Kan., 1949), 18.
[79] *American Speech,* Vol. XXIII (1948), 264.
[80] *Tall Tales of Arkansaw,* 324.
[81] *Dialect Notes,* Vol. II (1902), 237.
[82] Cf. Walter F. Lackey, *History of Newton County, Arkansas* (Independence, Mo., 1950), 289. The same expression is reported from Greene County, Mo., in *Western Folklore,* Vol. X (1951), 6
[83] *American Speech,* Vol. V (1929), 17.
[84] *1 King Henry IV,* Act I, scene 1, line 23.

chamber-lye to mean a mixture of urine and sweet oil, administered to infants as a remedy for colic.[85]

When a caller asked for the daughter of the house, an old granny said, "Just set down, young man. She's out *a-teasin' the cat.*" Granny meant that the girl had gone to an outdoor privy and would be back shortly. This remark was regarded as a dreadful breach of the proprieties and scandalized the whole family. They explained that the old lady was in her dotage and didn't realize what she was saying. "Lena just went out to *make water,*" said the girl's mother.

Near Oronogo, Missouri, in the early nineteen hundreds, modest young people hesitated over the pronunciation of piano. "I usually said pie-anna," writes L. J. Hedgecock, "because when I said *pee-anna* it embarassed me, as if I were telling Anna to do something that wasn't any of my business."[86]

The principal of a high school in McDonald County, Missouri, was astounded and shocked to find the verb *piss* in the school copy of *Webster's Dictionary,* and refused to believe my statement that the word is used eight times in the Authorized Version of the Bible.

When two persons are very intimate and have no secrets from each other, the hillman says that they *piss through the same quill.* This is an old proverbial expression. Roger North wrote: "So strangely did Papist and Fanatic, or the Anticourt Party, p——s in a Quill; agreeing in all Things that tended to create Troubles and Disturbances."[87] The word *piss* is never used in polite conversation, but the most respectable Ozark woman may say that Mr. and Mrs. Jones have *split the quill,* meaning that they have separated. Sometimes one hears *split the quilt,* and Crumb found *split the blanket* used with the same significance in southeastern Missouri.[88]

A variety of elm tree which carries a large amount of sap is known as the *piss-ellum,*[89] but this name is not mentioned in parlor conversation. *Piss-ant* is a common Ozark verb, since the backwoods lumberman often piss-ants his logs down to the river; that is, he pulls and pushes and prizes them down without the use of wheels. As a noun, piss-ant is sometimes pronounced *peezent,* and the term *step-ant* is used by some squeamish persons. Otto Ernest Rayburn told me of a gentleman at Lonsdale, Arkansas, who mentioned *step-ants,* and an impudent little boy asked what the

[85] *American Speech,* Vol. VIII (1933), 48.
[86] *Gone Are the Days,* 59.
[87] *Examen,* 1734, I, ii, sec. 78. Cf. *Oxford English Dictionary.*
[88] *Dialect Notes,* Vol. II (1903), 331.
[89] *Dialect Notes,* Vol. V (1923), 206.

name meant. "They bite," the man answered, "they make you *step* when-ever they get on your legs." McAtee discusses this matter of *step-ants* at some length.[90]

Ozark women and children often say *number one* when they mean urinate, and *number two* when they mean defecate. This is derived from a custom in the rural schools, when a child signals the teacher by holding up one finger or two in asking permission to "go out." It seems very odd that the teacher should need to know which of these functions the child expects to exercise. But I have seen these finger signals myself, and am told that they were formerly common in country schools all over the Ozark region.

The noun pot is seldom used alone, because that might remind people of a urinal or chamber-pot. In combinations like flower-pot, pot-metal, melting-pot, and so on the word is quite respectable. The ordinary iron vessel which hangs in the fireplace is called a *dinner-pot.*

Of a man engaged in some energetic but futile enterprise a newspaper columnist wrote, "He was just wishing in one hand and spitting in the other, to see which one would get full first."[91] This is a transparent euphem-ism, since *wishing* and *spitting* refer to micturition and defecation; the ex-pression in its original form is so well known that everybody understood the newspaper reference.

A casual mention of hockey will paralyze any Ozark audience, for the word hockey means nothing but dung in the hill country. "There is a game that they play on the ice in the North, which we who were brought up in the South almost instinctively blush at the mention of," writes Bur-ton Rascoe.[92] Mr. Rascoe used to live in Seminole County, Oklahoma. But it seems that this odd use of *hockey* is known in many Southern states.

When a well-bred country boy is walking with his girl, and sees that she is about to step into some cow dung, he says, "Don't cut your foot!" This euphemism is known to everybody in the backwoods and is some-times used figuratively even in the pulpit. But if a man says, "I *cut my foot,*" he generally means, "I have stepped into something filthy." If the nice boy mentioned above were forced to speak of cow dung specifically, in the presence of ladies, he would call it *cow-chips, cow-clods,* or perhaps *a cow-pile.* I have heard educated people in the Ozark towns say *rich dirt* when they meant rotted cow dung to be used as fertilizer.

[90] *Nomina Abitera* ([Chicago], 1945), 19.
[91] Spider Rowland, *Arkansas Gazette,* Little Rock, Ark., June 3, 1948.
[92] New York *Sun,* October 30, 1931.

Taboos and Euphemisms

Any mention of laxative drugs is considered in very bad taste, and I shall never forget a country druggist who was horrified when I called loudly for Pluto Water while he was selling candy to some young girls.[93] I remember also a grown-up mountain woman, the mother of several children, who blushed scarlet when she heard *physics* mentioned as a part of the high school curriculum.[94] Women of the same type see no harm in a public mention of the *back-door trots*, which means diarrhea. The expression *he had to go out* means that he had to defecate, and is seldom used with any other meaning. E. R. Strainchamps, who was brought up in McDonald County, Missouri, says that *"go out* really referred to the act of elimination, and we were likely to say 'He *went out* in his britches.' "[95]

The noun ass must be avoided because it sounds exactly like the Southern pronunciation of *arse*,[96] and even such words as aster and acid are sometimes considered suggestive. A girl in Stone County, Missouri, once told me that she was a photographer's *assistant*, but she made the initial vowel very long, and placed a great stress on the first syllable. There is a widely circulated tale about the woman who asked a druggist for *rumpsafetida;* it was asafetida that she wanted, but she thought *rump* was more refined than the *ass* sound in asafetida. The plant that the dictionaries list as *arse-smart* or *ass-smart* (*Persicarier hydropiper*) is regularly called *smart-weed* in the Ozarks.[97]

Distant relatives, those beyond fourth cousins, are often called *ass-hole kinfolks.* I heard a politician say that "them folks up Thompson Holler are all *butt-hole* cousins to Uncle Billy Jeffers," but this was regarded as pretty coarse language. One may use *button-hole cousins*, or *button-hole kinfolks*, without offense. When a hillman speaks of his *feudin' kinfolks*,[98] he means people who are not blood relatives at all, but who are allied with him in some economic or political activity.

The best people in the backwoods never use *bum* as a noun meaning hobo, or as an adjective meaning inferior. The word bum means buttocks to the old-timers in the Ozarks, and is to be avoided in polite conversation.[99]

The noun tail is frowned upon, too; Carr reports that "shirt-tail

[93] *Dialect Notes*, Vol. VI (1928), 63.
[94] Cf. my *The Ozarks*, 85.
[95] *American Speech*, Vol. XXIII (1948), 264.
[96] R. M. Bach, *Vulgarisms and Other Errors in Speech* (Philadelphia, 1869), 34.
[97] Cf. McAtee, *Nomina Abitera*, 11–12.
[98] Cf. *Arkansas Gazette*, Little Rock, Ark., May 3, 1942.
[99] *American Speech*, Vol. XI (1936), 314.

parade" is regarded as indelicate even at the University of Arkansas, "night-shirt parade" being considered much more refined.[100] Near the mouth of the Arkansas River was a settlement called Shirt-Tail Bend,[101] a hangout for whores and gamblers who preyed on the rivermen. A Little Rock newspaper refers to "that notable locality politely known as *Shirtle Bend*."[102]

Some hillfolk still shy at the word leg and usually make it limb if the speaker is a woman or the member under discussion is feminine. Professor Carr observes that leg "is commonly regarded as indelicate" at the University of Arkansas.[103] Farmer discusses the matter at some length,[104] but the general idea is that since women's legs are concealed by their garments they should not be exposed in speech. The younger women do not conceal their legs nowadays, but something of the old taboo still lingers in the common dialect; legs are to be seen perhaps, but should not be talked about. Too much chatter about stockings is considered rather indelicate, but a Missouri schoolteacher tells me that hose is even worse, since it somehow suggests the male genitals.

Very old-fashioned people don't like to use the word breast, so that bosom, which is not common in ordinary American conversation, is still the proper term in the Ozarks. The real old-time term for the female breasts is not bosom but *dinners;* young smart-alecs say *bubbies,* but elderly folk regard this as vulgar. A schoolmarm in southwest Missouri has truly enormous breasts, and is known as "Big Dinners" by almost everybody in town.

An educator in Joplin, Missouri, noticed that children from the backwoods districts always giggled at the words *titmouse* and *tomtit,* evidently because of some fancied relation to teat, which is always pronounced *tit.* Some people named Titsworth, who came from Iowa, were astounded to learn that their family name was considered rather indelicate by the neighbors.

The amusing thing about all this is that a woman who regards the word bull as an insult will use such inelegant verbs as spit, belch, and puke right out "before God an' all His boarders." I have heard the wife of a prominent attorney tell her daughter to "git a rag an' *snot* that young-un,"

[100] *Dialect Notes,* Vol. III (1905), 94.

[101] Cf. Thomas Bangs Thorpe, "The Big Bear of Arkansas," *Spirit of the Times,* March 27, 1841, p. 43.

[102] *Arkansas Gazette,* Little Rock, Ark., February 18, 1949.

[103] *Dialect Notes,* Vol. III (1905), 87.

[104] *Americanisms Old and New,* 346.

meaning to wipe the child's nose. On another occasion she remarked to a total stranger that her husband had "done got drunk an' *benastied his britches.*"

So much for prudery in the Ozark dialect. Perhaps a century or so of isolation is responsible for an abnormal development of this sort of thing. Or it may be that the mountain folk simply retained a pecksniffian attitude once common to the whole country.

In any case, it is obvious now that the influence of tourists and "furriners" is killing the old folk-speech. The newcomers are laughing the ancient taboos and euphemisms out of existence. A few more years, and the Ozark hillfolk will be talking just as "brash an' nasty-like" as the rest of us.

6　The Dialect in Fiction

THE OZARK DIALECT as used by novelists, dramatists, magazine writers, and newspapermen varies widely, of course. Some of those who write about the Ozarks know nothing of the dialect, and several of the most popular of them have never even heard it spoken. A few writers are natives of the Ozark region and revert to the authentic folk-speech without much difficulty. Others have made a careful study of backwoods talk and have done tolerably well with it.[1] This chapter gives illustrative quotations from most authors who have used the Ozark speech and attempts some appraisal of many such writers.

When Albert Pike came to Van Buren, Arkansas, in 1833, he asked a backwoodsman about the opportunities for a schoolmaster in that region.

> "Why," said the man, "if you would set in, right straight, I reckon thar might be a right smart chance of scholars got, as we have had no teacher here for the best end of two years. Thar's about fifteen families on the creek, and the whole tote of 'em well fixed for children. . . . You must make out your proposals to take up school; tell them how much you ask a month, and what you can teach; and write it out as fine as you can (I reckon you're a pretty good scribe) and in the morning there's to be a shooting match here for beef; nearly all the settle-*ment* [laying the accent on the last syllable] will be here, and you'll get signers enough."[2]

Pike followed this fellow's advice, obtained subscriptions for twenty "scholars," and actually taught the Van Buren school for at least one term.

[1] For a discussion of the linguistic value of literary dialect, see Summer Ives, *Tulane Studies in English*, Vol. II (1950), 181–82.

[2] "Letters from Arkansas," *American Monthly Magazine*, Vol. I (January, 1836).

The Dialect in Fiction

One of the first popular dialect writers was Thomas Bangs Thorpe, author of "The Big Bear of Arkansas," the most celebrated anecdote ever published about this region. Follows a sample of the Ozark speech of the eighteen thirties, according to Thorpe:

> The season for b'ar hunting is generally all the year round, and the hunts take place about as regular. I read in history that varmints have their fat season and their lean season. That is not the case in Arkansas. Feeding as they do upon the *spontenacious* productions of the sile, they have one continued fat season the year round; though in winter things in this way is rather more greasy than in summer, I must admit. For that reason, b'ar with us run in warm weather, but in winter they only waddle. Run a b'ar in this fat condition, and the way it improves the critter for eatins is amazing. It sort of mixes up the ile with the meat until you can't tell t'other from which.[3]

Another pioneer humorist lived at Gainesville, Arkansas, as early as 1858 and wrote for the Little Rock *True Democrat* under the pseudonym "Snooks."

> Thar is a new fashion lately interduced inter our sexion which I do not believe the likes of war never seen afore. Jiminie, criminie! I wish ye cud of seen our gals dressed in there whoops, jist ter see how darned foolish they looks. They stands out like a yung baloon ... In the fust place, they are invented so as to facilitate a free passage of air and tharby impart comfort to the ladies in the heat of summer; also a woman need not war so many clothin' to keep from exposin' her good or ill shape, as the case mout be.[4]

The Ozark hillbilly of the stage first appeared in the *Arkansas Traveler* dialogue ascribed to Sandford C. Faulkner; this was printed between 1858 and 1860,[5] but the earliest text now available was published in 1876. The Squatter is explaining to the Traveler how come the whiskey's all gone:

> "Stranger, I bought a bar'l more'n a week ago. You see, me and Sal went shars. After we got it here, we only had a bit betweenst us, and Sal she didn't want to use hern fust, nor me mine. You see I had a spiggin

---

[3] *Spirit of the Times,* Vol. XI (March 27, 1841), 43–44.
[4] Quoted by Masterson, *Tall Tales of Arkansaw,* 110–11.
[5] Masterson, *Tall Tales of Arkansaw,* 186, 358.

in one eend, and she in tother. So she takes a drink out'n my eend, and pays me the bit for it; then I'd take one out'n hern, and give her the bit. Well, we's getting along fust-rate till Dick, durned skulking skunk, he born a hole on the bottom to suck at, and the next time I went to buy a drink, they want none thar."[6]

Perhaps the best of the early Ozark novels was written in 1884 by the Reverend John Monteith, but his attempt to record the dialect was not particularly successful.

"I'm agin skewls an' edication. Afo' the waw, we had peace an' plenty, an' a thousand cattle on a hill. We worked a leetle, an' some had niggahs tew work fur 'em. Hit was a beyewtifil pictur'. But hits done spild now. . . . An' whut fur does a man work? Hits to make a crap, haint it? Then the cawn an' the side meat, an' the shoulders you don't want fur yoreselves tew eat, yo' sells tew them that has money tew buy an' maouths tew feed. Hits maouths tew chaw thet we want. Now, sah, skewls is again maouths. The chillern get new ideas in the skewls, an' they don't want no more cawn or bacon. They wants geyew-gaws, gintlemen, geyewgaws, an' thems not raised in the field; they come from the city, an' I reckon the divil makes 'em."[7]

The Ozark natives that I know do not pronounce *afore* and *nigger* in the Monteith fashion. The hillman does not say *sah*, but sir. I have never heard a real Ozarker say *waw* when he meant war. Words like school are pronounced correctly, and the diphthong in mouth and house is not much modified. Monteith's omission of the *e* in picture is meaningless; most Ozarkers pronounce it *pitcher*, anyhow.

Alice French, better known as Octave Thanet, writes chiefly of the canebrake country of Arkansas but sometimes brings a hillman into her stories. Miss French's dialect is much better than the Reverend Monteith's.

"He hed one er his spells, an' he run out en the woods an' got soppin' wet an' cotched cole an' 'pears like hit gits a leetle mucher all the w'ile. Abe Davis, he war with me, but he went on the high road, an' I come down yer fer a shoot, so I'd hev some squirrels to tote home. We heerd the shoot, but folks is allus shootin' in the bottom."[8]

[6] *The Arkansas Traveler, Arranged and Corrected by Colonel S. C. Faulkner,* (Little Rock, 1876).

[7] *Parson Brooks, a Plumb Powerful Hard-Shell* (St. Louis, 1884), 39.

[8] "Whitsun Harp, Regulator," *Century Magazine*, May, 1887, p. 124.

The verb *tote* is used more or less all over the South, but most Ozarkers say *pack* instead. *Fer a shoot* is not heard in the sections of Arkansas with which I am familiar; the man would probably say, "I come down in hyar a-huntin'." Elsewhere in her story Miss French uses *knaw* as the preterite of know, where most hillfolk say *knowed*. I have not heard house pronounced *heouse*. There may be some advantage in spelling can't *caynt* instead of the usual *cain't*, but it is certainly a mistake to make the hillman say *waynt* when he means *want*.

Opie Read spent the best years of his life in Arkansas and wrote at least one good hillbilly novel.[9] The dialect isn't bad, although he uses a good deal of eye-dialect such as *uv* for of, *wuz* for was, and so forth. Read's spelling varies sometimes, as when he puts *wa'nut* and *wannuts* in the same line. He uses too many *r* sounds, I think: *er* for *a*; *yer* for you, *ther* for the; *merself* for myself; *ernuff* for enough; *erway* for away; and *inferdel* for infidel. He sometimes writes *viddults* or *vidults* when he means victuals. The verb *funter*, evidently meaning to putter or work ineffectually, is new to me. I don't understand why Read uses *col'n* for colonel; the Ozarker pronounces it *kernel*, just as most Midwesterners do.

Here's a sample from another of Opie Read's works:

A traveler in Missouri, noticing a large number of people following a wagon, rode up to an old fellow who sat on a fence and asked the cause of such a large procession.

"W'y, they air takin' Sam Bates out ter the graveyard."

"He must have been a very popular man."

"Wall, I should reckon he was."

"Held a high position, I suppose."

"Stood at the top."

"What was his business?"

"Chopped co'd wood fur a livin', I b'lieve."

"What, do people in this country pay so much attention to woodchoppers?"

"Look yare, my friend, Sam was the handiest man with a fiddle thar was in this neighborhood. He could jest natchully make a fiddle cluck like a hen. I don't know how it is whar you come from, but in this here community we don't pay no attention ter whut er man does fur er livin'. We measure him fur whut he is wuth ter society."[10]

9 *Len Gansett* (Chicago, 1888), 15, 29, 41, 95, 116, 358, 370, 383.

10 *Opie Read in the Ozarks, Including Many of the Rich, Rare, Quaint, Eccentric, Ignorant and Superstitious Sayings of the Natives of Missouri and Arkansaw* (Chicago, 1905), 50–51.

Twenty-five years later, Opie Read was still writing dialect. Here's a paragraph from his autobiography:

"I 'lowed I'd killed you tuther night, but it was only a wolf that was a tryin' to git inter my smokehouse. But the Lawd willin', I mout meet you some time when nobody ain't lookin'."[11]

J. N. Baskett tells a story of central and southern Missouri, but his notion of dialect goes no further than the misspelling of a few simple words. Nor is he consistent even in his errors:

"I've thought of this uh lot. . . . Wonderful stretchy thing's er fish-worm. Yer think yuh get a whopper here, but out on the creek yer find him nothin' but er string uh skin 'bout a foot long."[12]

It is difficult to see why the article *a*, unchanged before whopper and foot, becomes *uh* before lot and *er* before fish-worm and string. *Uh* seems to mean *of*, as well as *a*, and *yer* and *yuh* are both substituted for you. There may be people in Missouri who talk such a jargon as this, but I have not met them. Baskett wrote another Ozark book later on, but the dialect is no better than that in the first one.[13]

J. Gabriel Woerner records the Ozark idiom in this fashion:

"Both on 'em insulted me . . . that d——d Hessian, an' ek'ly that slick-tongued Kurnel. . . . Let's show 'im up fur the white-livered abolitioner 'at 'e is, protectin' that 'ar d——d Dutch upstart, an' sid'n with niggers agin' white folks."[14]

Woerner manages the dialect very well, considering that he was born in Germany. But I see no reason for misspelling colonel. The omission of *th* in *that*, and *h* in *he*, is not common among the hillfolk of my acquaintance.

Rose Emmet Young tells a story of the country near Joplin, Missouri, centering about a mythical village called "Poetical." The dialect is very poor. When the usual "city feller" asks about the distance to the village, a mountaineer answers:

[11] *I Remember*, 186.
[12] *At You-All's House* (New York, 1899), 90.
[13] *Sweetbriar and Thistledown* (Boston, 1902), 340.
[14] *The Rebel's Daughter* (Boston, 1899), 143.

"Yass, I cand tell you. It's six sights and a right smart chanst f'm here to Poetical, stranger."

Naturally the gentleman from New York wants further light, and this is what he gets:

"W'y, it's this-a-way—you'll git sight of Poetical f'm six hills, an' whend you git to the bottom of the sixt' they's a right smart chanst you won't be to Poetical evum yit awhile. You cand see far in this air. It's some mild f'm here to Poetical, an' sharp ridin' at that."[15]

There may be men in the Ozarks who say *yass* when they mean yes, but I have yet to hear a hillman say *evum* for even. They do say *mild* sometimes instead of miles, but most Ozarkers use *mile* for both singular and plural. The *cand,* which the author seems to use for both can and can't, is not heard in the Ozarks. Miss Young also puts a final *d* on other words which properly end with *n,* so that we have *whend* for when, *begand* for began, and *writtend* for written. It is no wonder that the poor Yankee didn't understand what the people were talking about. I shouldn't have understood it either, and I lived in the Joplin district for many years.

One of Harold Bell Wright's novels deals with Stone and Taney counties, Missouri, where some of the characters were still living in the nineteen twenties, and were known to me personally. The following extract is typical of Wright's dialect:

"Ain't nothin' to a flat country nohow. A man jest naturally wears hisself out a walkin' on a level 'thout ary hill t' spell him. An' then look how much more there is of hit! Take forty acres o' flat now an' hit's jest a forty, but you take forty acres o' this here Ozark country an' God 'lmighty only knows how much 'twould be if hit war rolled out flat. 'Taint no wonder 't all, God rested when he made these here hills; he jest naturally had t' quit, for he'd done his beatenest an' war plumb gin out."[16]

Wright falls into the common error of supposing that *it* is nearly always turned into *hit.* But his dialect is superior to that of most Ozark novelists.

[15] *Sally of Missouri* (New York, 1903), 292. Cf. *American Speech,* Vol. II (1927), 284–85.
[16] *The Shepherd of the Hills* (Chicago, 1907), 16.

Grover Clay gives us a story of the hill country south of Springfield, Missouri, but the dialect is not as good as Wright's:

> "The grey cow broke the fence agin, and wuz a eatin' the corn. Hester fixed hit, but she says hit wuz rotten, and there wuz no new rails to fix hit. She says, she d'n know what to do 'bout hit. . . . Hev hit for dinner. . . . Hit must be 'bout 'leven o'clock, haint hit?"[17]

The real Ozarker uses *hit* only at the beginning of a clause, or where some particular emphasis is required. Such alliterative forms as *hev hit* and *haint hit* do not fit the hillman's notions of euphony and are not heard in the Ozarks. Another of Clay's singular mistakes is the use of has in the first person singular, as "I's been a workin'." I have never heard a mountain man use this form. There may be people in the Ozarks who say *purdy* for pretty, and *wid* for with, but I have never met up with 'em.

Clyde Edwin Tuck's novel is supposed to be set in Taney County, Missouri. I lived in Taney County for several years, but never heard any such talk as this:

> "I'd bin dyin' ter see yer fer long spell."
> "What did yer want to see me fer?"
> "Ist cause."
> "Ist cause why?"
> "Wall, 'ter ax yer of they's any reason why we couldn't git splict."
> "Whut'd ma say?"
> "She need'nt ter know tel we done been splict."
> "Then I'd git a whoopin'."[18]

When one turns been into *bin,* he is simply changing the appearance of the printed word, not altering the sound of it. Tuck's work is full of this meaningless eye-dialect; he writes *uv* for of, *cum* for come, *frum* for from, and *tarnashun* for tarnation. The use of *splict* instead of spliced is a more serious error, because it suggests a short *i* and a *kt* sound which are altogether out of place here.

John Homer Case was engaged in running a tomato cannery at Lebanon, Missouri, but found time to write a novel on the side. As one of his

---

[17] *Hester of the Hills: A Romance of the Ozark Mountains* (Boston, 1907), 410. Cf. *American Speech,* Vol. II (1927), 286.
[18] *The Bald Knobbers, a Novel of the Ozarks* (Indianapolis, 1910), 206.

contemporaries observed, he might have done well to stick to the cannery. The following paragraph illustrates his method of handling the dialect:

> "I don't suppose there's any varmints that would hurt you 'thout it was two-legged ones, for the wolves are too cowardly and the panters are gettin' scarce. And, from the way they said you held them timbers at the razin', it looks like you might pull a panter clean in two, anyway."[19]

The hillman does pronounce panther with a *t* sound rather than a *th,* but the *a* is usually long, so most writers spell the word *painter.* It's hard to see much merit in *razin'* for raising, which sounds exactly like *raisin* to me.

Byron A. Dunn tells a story of guerrilla warfare in Missouri, but there is nothing noteworthy in his dialect:

> "Who be yo'un? . . . Don't be alarmed, pard. I reckon yo'un and I air in the same class. Yo'un knows we'uns air to make it hot for the Yanks in Palmyra. . . . I kalkerlate to have a hand in that little job at Palmyra myself. Have three or four debts to pay, one agin old Allsman. He'll never peach agin if I lay hands on him."[20]

You-uns is a common plural in the Ozarks, but I never heard the singular form *yo'un.* Alarmed is unusual, as most natives would say *skeerd* or *scairt.* I never heard *pard* except in a few old songs and dance calls. The Ozarker doesn't use *knows* in the second person singular, and he is much more likely to reckon than to "kalkerlate."

John Breckenridge Ellis makes his Arkansas hillmen say *yap* when they mean yes, and *nuck* when they mean no. Nobody familiar with the dialect will see much merit in such passages as the following:

> "Yap. Now you be there, both gents, for neither of you has had any fun, since to the Ozarks here you came. And they's going to be such doings at this lark as scarcely ever was saw in the neighborhood. A medicine-man has got a date to reach Ozarka the day previous, and people will come in droves to buy of his liniments, he being a knowed character and his liniments inspiring, whether applied to hoss or man, and so far as that goes, to woman either."[21]

---

[19] *Jean Carroll: a Tale of the Ozark Hills* (New York, 1911), 83.

[20] *The Courier of the Ozarks* (Chicago, 1912), 183.

[21] *The Little Fiddler of the Ozarks* (Chicago, 1913), 308. Cf. *American Speech* Vol. II (1927), 287–88.

I have yet to hear mountain men calling each other *gents,* except in the set phrases of old dance calls and the like. Neither have I heard any such sentences as "since to the Ozarks here you came." The word lark, in the sense of a social gathering, is strange too; the real hillman would probably say *doin's* or *frolic.*

Happy Hollow Farm, by William R. Lighton, is a fine back-to-the-land story about an urban couple who bought a farm near Fayetteville, Arkansas, in 1908. Full of factual material about crops and livestock, with penetrating comments on the Ozark way of life, there is not much dialect, but it is interesting as far as it goes. The author remarks that some natives passed "with a drawled *Ha-owd'y!* The inflection can't be set upon paper." Here is a sample of Lighton's dialect writing:

> "Ha-owd'y! You-uns all up?" Which was a kindly inquiry as to the state of our health. "Ha-owd'y, Jake! Yes, we-uns are all up." . . . "I reckon I better be cuttin' you-all a little jag o' wood this mawnin'. We-all is needin' coffee."[22]

I have heard *howdy* pronounced in three syllables, right enough, but why the apostrophe after *d?* Lighton is certainly correct when he says that "the inflection can't be set upon paper." Note his use of *you-uns, we-uns, you-all,* and *we-all.* The hillfolk that I know rarely say *we-uns,* but there's no denying that it is heard occasionally around Fayetteville, even today.

A backwoods Missouri girl in one of W. A. Kennedy's novels is made to converse in this fashion:

> "Next to nuthin' . . . Mam and Pap, they'ns went over to the mill to tote corn, and I come mighty nigh hevin' a fit les' they'ns 'd git home late. . . . Nope. We'uns don't hev much fun, but yer bet whin somethin' does come 'long. . . . Now don't that knock yer persimmon? 'Course, I'd rather chin with a boy. Them'se my sentiments, long as you've put it straight. Don't you like the gals?"[23]

You-uns is common, *we-uns* and even *us-uns* are sometimes heard, but I think the pronoun *they'ns* is rare in the Ozark country. The verb tote is used occasionally, but most Missourians *pack* their corn. I can see no reason for the final *e* in *them'se,* which evidently means *them is.*

Alice Curtice Moyer-Wing, who used to ride through the Ozarks on

[22] New York, 1915, pp. 35, 128–29, 318.

horseback, lecturing in favor of woman suffrage and prohibition, wrote an article for a St. Louis newspaper in which some Ozark dialect appeared:

> I remarked that I shore was tickled over this nice weather and that I dreaded to see it turn cold, when Bill he up and says: "Shore, granma, old people always dreads winter." Then I fixed up my own snack that I bought an' paid fer, because Mandy Shoemaker don't do things to suit me, and she says: "Old people is shore plumb childish," she says, "and old maids is petickler." Now they jist ain't nothin' that makes me tarder than talk like that. Why, as fur back as I can remember, I han't been crazy about winter. But I reckon I ort to keep still about it now fer fear somebody'll lay it to gittin' old. And I still like to have the stuff that I eat handled kinder clean, but I reckon now that it's a sign of childishness er of bein' a old maid. It's plumb sickenin'.[24]

Augustin W. Breedon, who spent his youth in Stone County, Missouri, represents the Ozark dialect as follows:

> "Hit's jest a lot of onery, lazy folks, mostly moonshiners an' hoss-traders, a-livin' up yere on this hawg-back whar the land is so pore an' rocky that the river bottom farmers don't want hit even fer pasture. ... The furdest house is where Zack Kady lives. He's got three growed-up daughters an' one that's married to Fil Siler, an' Fil's got two purty goodsize girls, an' that makes five, an' they have a daince up thar might nigh ever' Saturday night."[25]

The dialect writing of A. M. Haswell is very good indeed, when we remember that he was born in Burma and never saw the Ozarks until he was twenty-one years old. One of the characters in his first novel is represented as saying:

> "I was jest on the way to preach a sarmint at Red Bird big meetin' and were singin' a bit to keep the old mare and myself awake. Never 'lowed to pick up no jiners out hyar in the woods. So you wants to jine, does ye? ... Yes sir, ye are about two mile furder from Turtle

23 *The Master of Bonne Terre* (New York, 1917), 205–206.
24 Sunday Magazine, St. Louis *Post-Dispatch*, December 20, 1918, p. 13.
25 "Tom Allison's Hard Lesson," *Comfort Magazine*, January, 1924, p. 16.

Creek than ye were when ye left Chadwick. Say, stranger, what mout your name be?"[26]

I think Haswell's excessive use of the old pronoun *ye* is a mistake; certainly such a phrase as *does ye* is out of place here. *The old mare and myself* is a bit odd, too; a real Ozarker would probably say *me an' the old mare*.

Mark S. Gross makes one of his Ozark hillmen say:

> "Oh, waal, I reckon they's differ'nt names in differ'nt places. . . . Yep, this here's the trail shore 'nough. See that big bluff through the trees? When we git to the top o' that you kin see Ha'nted Holler cl'ar as a pitcher."[27]

Gross writes much better dialect than some of his more widely advertised colleagues, but it seems to me that the two *a*'s in *waal* are unnecessary; *wal*, with the *a* almost as as in hat, is better. Note that he uses *pitcher,* rather than the *pictur'* of Monteith and others.

Charles J. Finger lived near Fayetteville, Arkansas, for some years, but very little Ozark dialect appears in his writings. The following extract is from a story called "Eric,"[28] of which Finger wrote me: "In this tale I try as best I can to reproduce the original Ozarkian in his speech, his prejudices, his beliefs, his hates."

> "I aint had no book learnin', an' look at me . . . I'm just plum crazy to tell about the things what I see . . . Even the kids don't never play . . . Paw's chock full of pizen hate . . . Well, the women folk they take a dip down at the creek, for there aint no bath tubs hereabouts."

The real Arkansawyer says *chuck* full, not chock full. I have never heard a hillman say *folk,* or use *dip* to mean bath with reference to human beings. Finger was an Englishman who had lived in many countries and spoke many languages; but the details of local American dialects escaped him.

Rose Wilder Lane's first novel of the Missouri Ozarks is, from a literary point of view, much superior to any of the others I have mentioned thus far. In the matter of dialect, however, it is not much better than the works of Harold Bell Wright.

[26] *A Daughter of the Ozarks* (Boston, 1920), 25, 259.
[27] *Haunted Hollow* (St. Louis, 1924), 18.
[28] *In Lawless Lands* (New York, 1924), 178–85.

"I aim to have money in bank, an' good house built, an' prospect of thrivin' future. . . . Shorely it does require brave heart to farm in these yere hills. I oncet knowed intrepid farmer of Douglas county, that nary danger daunted. Yet end of that pore man was, he fell off edge of his cornfield an' broke his neck. . . . It was not true. Them words you spoke to me when last we spoke together, they were not true."[29]

The outstanding defect of Miss Lane's dialect writing is the omission of such words as *a*, *an*, and *the*; the real mountain man doesn't omit the articles. "It was not true" does not sound just right; most hillmen would say *hit warn't so*. The dialect in Miss Lane's later novel, *Cindy*, seems rather better than that of *Hill-Billy*, but she still slights both definite and indefinite articles in a fashion unknown to the hillfolk of my acquaintance.[30]

Herbert N. Roe and William E. Landers tell a story of the country near Jane, Missouri, in the early days. Landers lived in this neighborhood as a boy, but the book is concerned with girls and gunplay, rather than the mountain dialect. A young farmer speaks as follows:

"Don't reckon nobody wants nuthin' fer the cabin. It belongs to Preacher Thomas, an' he has gone fer a long spell. He took to moonshinin' an' the folks wouldn't stand fer it an' made him git. Stills an' preachin' jest don't go together, I reckon. . . . I wanted to tell you that the river yonder is way up an' ye'd best not try ter cross if yer goin' that away. By day atter tomorrer it'll be down. Ye'd best stay where ye are."[31]

Landers wrote another novel in which the dialect seems a bit broader, but it is still recognizable Ozark speech. He uses *ter* for to, *jes'* for just, *ez* for as, *er* for or, *'en* for then, *hollar* for hollow, *co't* for court, *hoss* for horse, *anybuddy* for anybody. *We-all* and *you-all* are common, the latter apparently referring sometimes to the second person singular. *Youns* appears also, as a plural only. Many dialect writers use *air* for there, but Landers makes it mean *here*, as in "these air times" and "this air kentry."[32]

[29] *Hill-Billy* (New York, 1925), 93, 278, 286.

[30] *Cindy, a Romance of the Ozarks*, 6, 41, 121.

[31] *Ginger* (Kansas City, Mo., 1927), 77, 334.

[32] *Whiterock, a Story of the Ozarks* (Kansas City, Mo., 1932), 49, 100, 101, 102, 133, 134, 152, 203, 274.

Rose L. Hamilton's novel shifts from the zinc-mining district about Joplin to the wilds of Stone County, Missouri, in the early eighteen nineties. Beyond such expressions as "I-golly" and a few references to *pokes* and *frog-stickers* there is no attempt to reproduce the Ozark speech, and the book holds little interest for students of dialect.[33]

The same is true of *Marise*,[34] a juvenile story by Louise Platt Haucke. But the dialect in Mrs. Hauck's novel, *Wild Grape,* is considerably better, particularly in the handling of *it* and *hit.* She says "hit *air* a nice night," where most hillfolk would say "*hit's* a nice night" or "hit *is* a nice night," and her use of *whobody,* apparently meaning whom, is not Ozarkian. The occasional omission of the articles, as "he'll be here with sheriff afore hunger nips us," is reminiscent of Rose Wilder Lane.[35]

Acres of Sky, by Charles Morrow Wilson, is a novel about the War Eagle country near Hog Eye, Arkansas. Wilson is a native Ozarker and a very good writer; he knows the dialect better than most of the regional novelists. It seems to me that he uses *it* and *hit* in a rather haphazard fashion. It may be that the hillfolk on War Eagle do make the pronoun *you-uns* apply to one person sometimes, although I don't think I ever heard it so employed. But these are small matters. On the whole, Wilson's dialect is very good indeed.[36]

Fenetta Sargent Haskell tells a sentimental tale of the Ozark foothills, somewhere southwest of St. Louis. Like Monteith, Clay, Wright and others, Mrs. Haskell assumes that the word *it* is nearly always pronounced *hit.* She avoids many of the dialectal pitfalls into which her literary betters have fallen, but she uses *ter* for to and *er* for or throughout and makes *yer* serve as both *you* and *your.* The repeated use of *it does so, you have so, there is so, I do so,* and *they do so* is unusual, to say the least. The same is true of *tooken,* when an auctioneer says that "no article is ter be tooken from the premises"; surely a real hillman would say *taken* or *tuck.* Mrs. Haskell makes a hillman use *you-all* in addressing one person; this agrees with my own findings, although many eminent writers contend that you-all is never used for the singular.[37]

In a magazine story entitled "Drought," Eleanor Risley gives a sample of an Arkansas backwoodsman's talk:

[33] *Fickle Fortune, a Romance of Life Among the Ozarks* (New York, 1928), 89, 183.

[34] Indianapolis, 1929, pp. 185, 298.

[35] Philadelphia, 1931, pp. 91, 93, 123, 153, 232.

[36] See pp. 116–17, 118, 340.

[37] *In a Cup of the Hills* (Boston, 1930), 10, 31, 37, 41, 62, 64, 137, 139, 167, 198.

"I thought I'd jist break hit ter you kinder, before you git ter town. The bank, hit failed yesterday. The one where yore money is. . . . I caint leave out ther snuff. Hit's ter pleasure my womern. She's purty puny this winter. . . . Course I kinder expect tracks, fur the fellers that is cotched fur makin' liquor go past my place ter get ter ther reservation an' hide erwhile. But effen thar's iny thar they'll hev ter kim down. Thar haint nothin' like thar commonly is ter eat this y'ar in ther mountings. . . . Afore ye leave we wants ye ter know that we haint ben treated right. We haint goin' ter make no trouble, because we caint. But we wanted ye ter know hit."[38]

Charles Hillman Brough, sometime governor of Arkansas, published the following as part of an interview with Uncle Lum Gibson, who lived near Fayetteville. Lum Gibson is remembered by many old settlers to this day, and there is an oil painting of him in the Quapaw Club at Little Rock.

"Them damn fool Perfessers at that University of yours 'ar squanderin' th' taxpayers' money by teachin' th' boys an' girls thet th' earth goes round. Thet's sheer nonsense, Vol, fer you 'member thet you an' me used t' ride on th' flyin' jenny when we was boys. When we rid close up t' th' pole, it didn't shake us up much, but ef we got on th' hobby horse on th' rim o' th' jenny, it shuk us up like th' devil. Now, Vol, some says thet th' earth is five hundred miles acrost. Some says it's a thousand miles fr'm here t' China. You an' me in this Prairie Grove Valley 're right in th' center of th 'earth, an' ef what them Perfessers re sayin' is true, it wouldn't whirl us around much. But ef th' earth is round instead o' flat, an' goes 'round th' sun, those pore devils thet live on th' rim o' China would hev their eyeballs shuk out."[39]

J. W. Vincent's *Tales of the Ozarks*[40] is a book of seven short stories based upon pioneer reminiscences. The following is an extract from the second tale, "What Jack Carrender Found:"

"Now don't you be skeered, Miss Sally, you not knowin' me's easy mended," said big Jack, and he told her his name. "As to the good

[38] *Atlantic Monthly*, May, 1931, pp. 627–36.
[39] Quoted by Allsopp, *Folklore of Romantic Arkansas*, II, pp. 354–55.
[40] Linn Creek, Mo., 1931, pages not numbered.

lookin' part, I haint never seen a posy that was a patchin' to you, even if you air a little flustered. But that haint the p'int. Ef you was old, an' humly, an' as cross as a crippled cat, I'd help you ef I knowed how. I've heerd of Murray's mill, but I thought hit was over on Gasconade. I live in Webster county, an' I don't know these settlements frum Chiney."

Elsewhere in the book Vincent uses *yere* for here, *mought* for might, *maby* for maybe, *desarve* for deserve, *hev* for have, *hosses* for horses, *thankee* for thank you, and *kaint* for *can't*.

My old friend Charles A. Cummins, veteran Ozark newspaperman, had his own strange ideas about writing dialect:

"Uz I rickillict, hit wahr 'way back yander—the day attar thar election—when James Buchanan wahr elected president. Thar had been one uv them onseasonable spells like this hyar October when ducks an' geese wuz flyin' 'bout tryin' tar find thar way southward, when people wuz goin' in thar shirt sleeves, talkin' who would be elected. Well, dirickly the polls opened—they wuz votin' in a log shack on what air now McDaniel avenue—hit begun tarnin' cold an' spittin' snow. By mornin' the snow wuz a foot deep on a level; that night it wuz two feet deep an' by mornin' thar thermometer wuz forty degrees below zero an' ice in Jordan crick 18 inches thick."[41]

Back Yonder, an Ozark Chronicle, by Wayman Hogue, is probably the finest nonfiction book ever written about the Ozarks. Hogue was raised in the wilds of Van Buren County, Arkansas, and his speech is that of the eighteen eighties. "In writing the dialect," says he, "I have quoted each word exactly as I have heard it spoken." A backwoods preacher holds forth as follows:

"Bretherin an' sisterin, I feel that this is goin' to be the greatest meetin' that this holler has ever had. I feel that before this meetin' closes that ever' sinner is goin' to come an' jine the church, an' that we air goin' to run the devil clean outen this whole settlement. Ricko- leck though, my good frien's, the devil is not idle. He knows what's goin' on an' you can see his works ever'whar. When I went to mill yistidy, I seed two young men a-settin' under a tree a-playin' kyards.

[41] Springfield, Mo., *Press*, November 2, 1932.

I heard two ole man a-talkin', an' they cussed about ever' other word. I seed a young womurn an' ever'thang about her wuz pride. Pride in her walk, pride in her talk, an' pride in her looks. Yes, my frien's, the devil has got this world by the tail with a downhill pull. He's here, he's thar, an' he's ever'whar."[42]

Personally, I see no good reason to write *wuz* for was, because everybody in the Middle West and most of the South pronounces this word just as the Ozarker does. But anybody who has heard the old-timers talk will recognize Mr. Hogue's transcription as the real thing. He learned the dialect as a child and spoke it himself for many years. Compare this with the writing of Rose Emmett Young, John Breckenridge Ellis, and L. S. Davidson, or the gibberish of Guy Howard in *Give Me Thy Vineyard,* and you'll see what I mean.

Charlie May Simon, author of many fine juvenile books, lived in the Ozark backwoods for some time and is familiar with the mountain speech. Here is a sample of her dialect writing:

"I jist wanted to say ... that when I hearn youens war a livin' here, I 'lowed there war a goin' to be trouble. But I see youens know how to mind yore business, an' I wan ter shake hands with you an' say I'm yore friend. .... Youens hadn't ort to plant yore beans on flowerpot day ... caze they'll all turn to blossom an' won't make beans.... Pappy caint buy me shoes to wear to school, an' I want to larn books. .... I give her some pole cat grease fer her cold, an' she perked right up.... She's a gittin' better. I know she's a goin' to git well."[43]

An Ozark book, entitled *Straw in the Sun,* is Charlie May Simon's best work; it is full of valuable information about the hillfolk, but there's very little dialect in it.[44]

Some Ozark newspapers try to use the dialect in their news stories. Orville L. Young, a farmer of Webster County, Missouri, was charged with the murder of Wayman Clark on September 13, 1933. In the course of the trial, the prosecuting attorney asked Young what he had eaten on the day of the killing. This is the way Young's testimony was recorded by the local press:

[42] See pp. vii, 130–31.
[43] "Retreat to the Land," *Scribner's Magazine,* May, 1933, pp. 309–512.
[44] See p. 218.

"Wal, if you've got t' know, hit was some dried beans and a lot of other grub. . . . They had some fried taters an' some biskits—that's all I et—they mighta had some other stuff, but I didn't run acrost hit. Oh yeah, an' they had some sop, too. I poured hit over my biskits."[45]

Here's a specimen of the dialect in the backwoods counties of Missouri, as set down by Edith Roles Jacobs:

"Hit was that purty little man come down from Springfield to keep the school. . . . Well, the four of us finally got Gum off him, an' breshed off the school teacher, an' wiped some o' the blood off him, an' got some water from the spring an' throwed on him. . . . Gum come to hisself, partly. An' he took a look at that pore little no-account book-learner that he knew Hildy wouldn't a-thunk of twice."[46]

Thames Williamson's *The Woods Colt* is unusual in that the entire book—not merely the quoted matter—is written in dialect.[47] Since I read this novel in manuscript, and most of my suggestions about the dialect were accepted by the author, there is no point in my criticizing it here. The difficulties and complexities of the Ozark speech so impressed Williamson that he wrote an article, "The Novelist's Use of Dialect," in which he discusses the whole subject at some length.[48]

Here is a bit of Ozark dialect according to Allen Oliver, who worked on a Springfield, Missouri, newspaper in the nineteen thirties. Oliver's real name was Dickson Terry, and he was born and raised in Bentonville, Arkansas.

"Thar wuz lots of excitement down tew the railroad depot Sunday afternoon. . . . Hit seems thet when the train pulled in fum St. Looey, thar was a gent aboard who had been a-takin' on a leetle mite too much moonshine likker. . . . He stud right thar in the coach and made hit knowed to all who was present that he had to hev two quarts uv whiskey immediately on account of he had a friend in the lower berth who was a-dyin'. . . . All the folks down tew the depot jest laughed at the dern fool."[49]

[45] Springfield, Mo., *News & Leader,* September 17, 1933.
[46] Kansas City, Mo., *Star,* October 22, 1933.
[47] New York, 1933, p. 288.
[48] *The Writer,* Boston, January, 1935, pp. 3–5, 28, 40.
[49] Springfield, Mo., *Leader & Press,* March 27, 1934.

William Boks Riggs makes his pioneer Missourians use a lot of pretty fair dialect.[50] They generally say *acks* for ask, and *acksed* for asked; this past tense form is not too common nowadays, but I have heard it many times. *Brersh* for brush, meaning undergrowth, is still used occasionally in southwest Missouri, although the intrusive *r* is not so common as formerly, if we are to believe the old chroniclers. But Riggs has an Indian fighter say *nunc* when he means no, and one of his backwoods girls uses *unc-un*, which also seems to be a negative. I have never heard *nunc* or *unc-un*, in the Ozark country or anywhere else.

The Voice of Bugle Ann,[51] by MacKinlay Kantor, is a fine fox-huntin' story, "a fictionized version of a feud reported in the Springfield, Mo., papers," according to a dispatch from St. Louis.[52] There is little dialect in Kantor's story, but that little is authentic. Note the careful distinction between *dog* and *hound*, also the fox-hunter's avoidance of the word bitch.

Emily Newell Blair was born in Carthage, Missouri, and spent most of her early life in the Ozarks. In her writings she makes sparing but very effective use of the dialect. Avoiding the most striking and outlandish expressions, which she knows as well as anybody, Mrs. Blair is content to say *caint* for can't, *Miz* for Mrs., *sot* for set, *yander* for yonder, and the like.[53] There are no conspicuous errors in her dialect, as in the writings of others who have dealt less cautiously with the Ozark speech.

Here is the Ozark dialect as set down by Robert L. Morris, professor of English at the University of Arkansas; it is from a play entitled *Readin', a Scene in the Arkansas Ozarks.*

> "I'm hyar, an' thanks fur bein' in frum that bilin' sun I'd say. If I'd had any sense I'd sent you, but you're the gal would linger on the way, spring time bein whut hit is now. . . . I'd sent your paw fur that music machine, but knowing the spunk he is agin bright-music, he'd say he plum' forgot hit, ur hit was broke down ur Minnie Wiles wanted to play on hit, ur somethin' else whut happened to come to his head. . . . Shore, he's too much a scripture man to do a thing like that. . . . I'm awful glad you snuk off an' got it nohow, cause he cain't say much, now hits hyar."[54]

[50] *Missouri in the Making* (Kansas City, Mo., 1934), 49, 170.
[51] New York, 1935, pp. 79, 128.
[52] St. Louis *Post-Dispatch*, February 9, 1936.
[53] "The Mob," *Liberty*, September 14, 1935; reprinted in my *Ozark Anthology*, 147–73.
[54] *University Review* (Kansas City, Mo.), Winter, 1936, p. 126.

Morris has a sharp ear for substandard English, and he certainly heard plenty of dialect at Fayetteville. But I think he uses *hit* in some cases where most backwoodsmen would say *it*. And why should a writer spell from, *frum,* when country people all over the Middle West pronounce the word pretty much as the Ozarkers do?

Girl Scouts in the Ozarks, by Nancy Clemens, is a juvenile story of Stone and Taney counties, Missouri.[55] The following passage in her book records the speech of a native guide in Marvel Cave:

> "I used t' fool round thar when I was jest a boy," Leather said. "I got lost in th' dang thing once myself. Busted my light an' had t' foller th' taller out."
>
> "Follow the tallow!" echoed Sally Lou, puzzled. "What do you mean?"
>
> "Th' taller th' tourists drops off o' their candles," Leather explained. "I jest kinder crawled along, a-feelin' round on th' rocks ahead o' me. I follered th' taller trail till my knees was wore plumb down t' th' bone, an' I shore was glad t' git back t' whar I could see daylight ag'in."

As in the case of Thames Williamson's *Woods Colt,* I read this story before it was printed, and made a number of suggestions about the dialect.

Here is a sample of the Ozark speech recorded by Pearl Spurlock, of Taney County, Missouri.

> So one time there was a big, fine carload of New Yorkers who came to the Ozarks. They saw a barefoot hillbilly woman out in the yard washing her clothes. They stopped the car. The young man went in and asked, "Lady, what was this little village we just came through?" She says, "I–dun–know. I haint never been thur." "Well, you knew about George Washington." "No, I never did know him." "Well, undoubtedly you knew about Abraham Lincoln?" "No, I never heard tell of him nuther." "Well, lady, you know that there is a God and that he died for you, don't you?" "Well, if his last name is Damn, I've heard my ole man speak of him a heap of times, but I didn't even know he wuz sick."[56]

Isabel France does a newspaper column called "The Hills of Home" for several Arkansas papers. Here is a specimen of her dialect writing:

[55] New York, 1936, pp. 156, 233.
[56] *Over the Old Ozark Trails* (Branson, Mo., 1936), 36.

Now whenever you are a-sparkin' an' mention somethin' about th' stars, hits a shore sign yore a-wantin' to be kist effen yore th' gal. An' effen yore th' boy hits a shore sign yore a-aimin' to try to kiss her.

Th' ole horse got half-way crost th' creek-ford an' stopped to git hisself a drink. Th' young folks didn't hear th' gal's brother, th' masterest person to tease, come a-ridin' his horse right up a-hind 'em, but he did hear his sister up an' say "Oh, aren't the stars numerous tonight?"

Th' mountain boy, too green to make shuckin's fur roastin' ears, instead uv kissin' her, looked up at the stars an' sez "Gee yeah, an' aint thur lots uv 'em!"[57]

Mrs. France insists upon using too much eye-dialect. But she is thoroughly familiar with the Ozark idiom, and knows more about these matters than most of the people who write scholarly papers on the subject.

Mae Traller, of Everton, Missouri, handles the Ozark speech expertly in her newspaper stories:

"Yisterday I got me a new pair o' britches over to Lem Tucker's store, and as Mary allus has to cut 'em off in the laigs, she cut one laig and fixed it at the same time she was watchin' the cookin' of her grub. And be-dog my cats! Hyah, hyah, hyah! when she come back from cookin' to fix the rest of my britches, she got all flabbergasted, and instead o' cuttin' off tuther laig, she cut off the same one, leavin' tuther long enough to drag my tracks out and flung 'em over to me. She never noticed till I had 'em on ready to come over here—hyah, hyah, hyah! And so I dug this green shirt that she'd colored fer cyarpet rags, outen the smokehouse and come in style, be-dog my cats!"[58]

Thomas Hart Benton is a native Ozarker, familiar from childhood with the mountain speech. He reports the statement of "an old Ozark Missourian" who was not impressed with the good qualities of the Arkansas hillfolk:

"These here Arkansawyers are a mean lot. I've heerd tell that a long time ago, Memphis, over thar in Tennessee, got all full of whores and whoredogs and the good people not bein' able to sleep or do business

[57] *Southwest Times-Record*, Fort Smith, Ark., November 15, 1936.
[58] Kansas City, Mo., *Star*, August 30, 1937.

fer their racket gits up one night and wint an' rounded 'em all up on a raft and towed the raft over the river to Arkansas and told them whores and whoredogs that wuz the place they'd have to live in, and if they come back to Memphis they'd git shot. Them people, they say, wuz the ancestors of Arkansas."[59]

Ward Allison Dorrance was a professor at the University of Missouri, and his book *Three Ozark Streams* is a story of vacation float trips on Missouri rivers. Here is a sample of his dialect:

"Now thar's ole Doc Wilson up the middle prong. Reckon you'uns wouldn't know him? Married a Johnson, cousin o' m' wife's? He mought hev a boat. Kind o' disremember, but danged if I don't think he *has* got one! Sort of an ole scow it is, just the kind of a boat you fellers needs. . . . Willie Craidie, he furnished Doc lumber fer thet boat, but Doc he hain't never used hit none. Doc's got a nephew up in Sin Louie. . . . Reckon you-uns wouldn't know him? Little feller, right fat. . . . I've ben up to Sin Louie m'sef. Shucks, yes. Scofts o' times. Don't nobuddy talk t'ye on the street. I wuz right glad t' git back. Wal, now, thishyur nephew, he comes down hyar a-week-ends, fishing . . ."[60]

Fred Starr's *From an Ozark Hillside* is a book of brief essays and sketches, reprinted from Starr's column in a Fayetteville, Arkansas, newspaper. Starr's remarks about the backwoods dialect are good on the whole, but he says that "the word *fit* is often used for fight" and illustrates this in the sentence, "he'll fit ye at the drap of a hat."[61] I have never heard a native Ozarker so express himself. *Fit* is the preterite or past participle, not the present or future. The hillman that I know might say, "I *fit* last night," or, "I *have fit* lots of times," but he wouldn't say "I will *fit*."

This is the way Lucille Morris reports the dialect as spoken in Taney County, Missouri:

"Grandpap had warned me not ter come through this country, for thar was lots of trouble, and strangers allus war gittin' inter it. But I paid him no mind. I rid right inter Forsyth. Hit shore warn't much of a town in them days. Two stores. I stopped at one of them, and the first

[59] *An Artist in America* (New York, 1937), 84–85.
[60] Richmond, Mo., 1937, pp. 1–2.
[61] Siloam Springs, Ark., 1938, pp. 35, 38.

thing I knew a man spoke ter me and used a string of cuss words. I whaled loose and hit him with two knucks. Tore his neck open and knocked him down so hard it busted the board he fell on. I 'lowed he was dead, and so did everybody else. The sheriff come and took me ter a little shop and sot me down on a workbench. Then he went ter look 'bout the dead man. I figgered I'd better take out. So I got my horse and rid five miles to my grandpap's. The man didn't die, and nobody ever bothered me 'bout it."[62]

In a magazine yarn entitled "One Man in His Time," Edward Parrish Ware deals with the hillfolk of northwest Arkansas. The tale shows considerable knowledge of the Ozark country, and the dialogue is very good indeed. Ware uses *sut* for soot, speaks of a *gaum* of spiderwebs, and refers to Epsom salts as *them* in true backwoods fashion. The mountain dialect is played down a bit for the slick-paper readers, but there are no serious errors in it.[63]

South of Joplin, by L. S. Davidson, is a story of the mining district near the Missouri–Oklahoma border.[64] The dialect seems strange to me, although I lived in that vicinity for many years. Miss Davidson uses *cain* for can throughout; I have heard *kin* for can, and *cain't* for can't, but *cain* is new to me. *Fer* is regularly used to mean for, and sometimes it is substituted for *far.* *Air* means *are* on one page but serves as *or* on another. There is no consistent distinction between *it* and *hit;* such sentences as, "I know *hit,"* are common all through the book. The term *chili-whelp,* which the author says means the child of a prostitute, is unknown to my acquaintances in the region. Miss Davidson's use of *sot*—"you cain *sot* in the kitchen" and "if we stay *a-sottin'* "—is unlike anything I have heard in the Joplin district. Never have I heard a Missourian say *thot* when he means *that,* although Miss Davidson's characters use this pronunciation constantly.

The careful dialect writing in Otto Ernest Rayburn's work is a welcome contrast. Rayburn has spent all his time since 1920 in the Ozarks, and he has an attentive ear for the quirks of backwoods speech:

"I don't begredge a feller a little hawg meat once in awhile but I like t' see him git it honest-like. If'n a man's up agin it, I'll go right into my smokehouse an' share what I got with him. But this here stealin's gittin'

[62] *Bald Knobbers,* 16–18.
[63] *Esquire,* September, 1939, pp. 54–55, 169.
[64] New York, 1939, pp. 71, 168, 290.

fur too common in th' county. Th' jedge thought so, too, an' he wus aimin' on puttin' a stop t' hit. We'uns knowed he had his back up right frum th' time he rapped fur order in the court house. . . . Both of 'em got on the stand an' swore they had seen Luke in th' Bull Crick settlement that very day."[65]

It seems to me that there is no merit in writing *wus* for was, nor *frum* for from. And I never heard an old-time Ozarker say *crick* when he meant creek. But Rayburn's use of the dialect is fundamentally sound. His characters always talk like hillmen, not like the synthetic "hillbillies" of fiction.

There is a lot of good dialect writing in *Yesterday Today, Life in the Ozarks,* by Catherine S. Barker.[66] She lived at Batesville, Arkansas, in the nineteen thirties and circulated among the hillfolk as a case worker for the Federal Emergency Relief Administration. Mrs. Barker knows the Ozarker, and she tells the truth about him without any sentimentality. The book is heavily loaded with dialect, and almost every line of it rings true.

Wilderfess,[67] by Pascal R. Guntharp, is a first novel, "written by a man who was born and raised in the Ozarks," according to the blurb on the jacket. The mountain speech is authentic in the main. It seems odd that Guntharp's hillfolk say *retolect* instead of recollect. He uses *ont* to mean both *won't* and *want. Orger* for auger is a bit strange, and so is *ustful* for useful. But I know what Guntharp has in mind when he turns where into *hwhar,* and tomorrow into *to-mar.* Some of Guntharp's best dialect is not in quotes, and it seems to me that much of it may be unintentional.

Marguerite Lyon came down to the Ozarks from Chicago, but she handles the dialect very well indeed:

> "A widder with two young 'uns has a hard time gittin' along any-wheres," said Pinky. "And hyer in the hills, it's twicet as hard. A widder has a tough row to hoe. Folks is allus gossipin' about her. Talkin' about her. She aint got no friends. Wimmin is agin her. Menfolks don't dast speak out, 'r their wimminfolks 'd kick up a fuss. . . . We-uns hain't a-goin' to pick no berries. The guv'ment gives us all we-uns need. . . . We brang you-ens some wild grapes. . . . Well, a feller there, he wuz a-runnin' f'r somethin', 'n he told me how to mark that big sheet with all them names on it. So I jis' tuk m' baby 'n went, an' they never ast me no questions."[68]

[65] *Ozark Country,* 10–11, 12, 352.
[66] Caldwell, Idaho, 1941, 263.
[67] Kansas City, Mo., 1941, pp. 84, 175, 243, 249, 364.

In a later book Mrs. Lyon devotes an entire chapter to the Ozark speech, and her comments are interesting and amusing.[69]

May Kennedy McCord, a native Ozarker who has heard rich dialect all her life, reports the speech of a backwoods woman demanding a divorce:

"Tightwad Souders ain't nothin' but a red-headed hedgehog no-how. For one thing, he's ornery. Downright ornery. . . . An' more'n that, he's always a cucklin me. If he hain't a primpin' up to go to the picnics an' dances an' all the gatherin's he can hear of, or a goin' over to that old strollop's place on Razor Ridge a swappin' calves, then he's tryin' to set up to Beaver's hired girl right under my nose! I've never seen a man with sich a hankerin' for the wimmin. He's got some sort of a flibberty-gibberty petticoat with seven ruffles on it in his mind ever' wakin' minnit. An' if he ain't awake, he snores so loud a body can't bed with him."[70]

Mrs. McCord writes a bit hastily sometimes, but she knows her stuff. She never falls into any ridiculous dialectal errors, as so many of the "furrin" novelists do.

Lennis L. Broadfoot, a native of Shannon County, Missouri, sets down a bit of old-time conversation:

"We purtnye have to be able to do a little of this, an' a little of that, an' so an' so, to be able to muster up a livin' in these ol' stony hills. I know I have done a lot of different things, an' I'll bet you a coonskin that I've got a record that thair hain't many other fellers got. I have been a preacher, a photographer, I've been married six times, an' killed three hawks at one shot. I first started out to preach for a livin', but gee whiz, I soon see'd that warn't goin' to git me nowhere, 'cause all I ever got out of it wuz maybe a night's lodgin' with some ol' brother who fed me on corn bread an' gravy. I hardly ever even see'd a chicken leg."[71]

Guy Howard, a Campbellite minister from Iowa, came to the Ozarks and preached in many backwoods settlements in southern Missouri. He

---

[68] *Take to the Hills*, 103, 250, 252, 278.
[69] *Fresh from the Hills*, 131–37.
[70] *American Mercury*, April, 1942, pp. 467–68.
[71] *Pioneers of the Ozarks*, 158.

set down his experiences in a book which contains a good deal of dialect.[72] Howard's use of *hit* for *it* is a bit strange, as in the sentence "Hain't nothin' wonderful 'bout *hit* if *hit's* a wood's colt." A girl in childbirth screams "Oh, oh, *hit* hurts! *Hit* hurts!" And a native uses *snuck* when he means steal: "If ye kin *snuck* hit, ye kin have hit. . . . I'm agoin' to ask Gran'paw to *snuck* you a pair of slippers when he goes to town." The hillfolk that I know sometimes use *snuck* as the preterite and past participle of sneak, but I've never heard it used in the Howard fashion. Except for a few slips like those noted above, it seems to me that the dialect in this book is better than that of many more pretentious works.

Later Howard came forward as the author of *Give Me Thy Vineyard*, subtitled *A Novel of the Ozarks*.[73] In this book the hillfolk are made to say, *"I'se* worried" and *"I'se* tired" and *"I'se* afeard." One character asks, "What do he think we-uns is?" *You'ns* and *you'all* are used indiscriminately, in both singular and plural. We find *yo'*, *you'ns*, and *you'all* applied to one man. The pronoun *hit* is misused throughout the book. There are ridiculous errors on almost every page. The dialect in *Give Me Thy Vineyard* is the worst I have ever seen in print. It is difficult to understand how Mr. Howard, who wrote some fair-to-middling Ozark dialect in his *Walkin' Preacher* of 1944, could turn out such nigger-minstrel drivel in 1949.

William Martin Camp's novel deals with country folk near Berryville, Arkansas. The dialect is authentic in the main, but one gets the impression that it is somehow secondhand, adapted from earlier Ozark books rather than acquired through actual contact with the hillfolk. There are a few odd pronunciations—*raffle* for rifle, *ho'dy* for howdy, *study* for steady, *lea'n* for leave. No real Ozarker would speak of "that clump of brushes," as Camp's heroine does. Most hillmen would say "take keer o' yourself" instead of "*keep* keer o' yourself." Camp makes the same errors in the use of *hit* and *it* that have been pointed out earlier.[74]

Amos R. Harlin comes from a pioneer Ozark family and spent his youth in Howell County, Missouri. A relative of the Harlins is quoted as saying that Amos put the backwoods dialect into his book only because the publishers insisted, that he would have preferred to use "straight English" throughout. However this may be, Harlin is certainly familiar with the Ozark speech, and has made a great effort to record it accurately. His use of *yhar* for year and *yhere* for here seems a bit fantastic to outsiders,

---

[72] *Walkin' Preacher of the Ozarks* (New York, 1944), 251, 256, 273.
[73] Grand Rapids, 1949, pp. 12, 17, 29, 41–42, 52, 101, 131, 141, 210, 223, 246, 287.
[74] *Skip to My Lou* (Garden City, N. Y., 1945), 5, 84, 190, 250, 401.

but anybody who has lived in Howell County knows the sound he is trying to set down on paper. Harlin uses *ere* to mean are, though most dialect writers spell it *air*. But he also uses *ere* for or, which seems rather odd. It also seems to me that Harlin makes too much use of the verb *be*. He says *I be* for I am, *ye be* for you are, *he be* for he is, *they be* for they are, *thar be* for there is, *this be* for this is, and *be that all?* instead of is that all? I have heard very little of this *be* business in the Ozarks. Rufe Scott, who has lived in Stone County, Missouri, for seventy years, says that it was formerly more common than at present. It is easy to pick a few flaws in dialect writing. But Harlin's book is honestly written by a sensible man thoroughly familiar with the country and the people. Every student who is interested in the Ozark dialect and folklore should read it.[75]

Weldon Stone's *Devil Take a Whittler* is a fanciful tale about a whittler in the Arkansas backwoods who has some dealings with the Devil. The author is a Texan who has spent eleven summers in the Ozarks. The dialect writing is good throughout, and not overdone. Even Old Nick speaks like a real Ozark hillman. This writer makes none of the usual errors. There are a few strained spellings, as when a character speaks of making something out of "an old sow's *yeer*." Stone says *bow-and-spike* as the real Ozark boy does, instead of bow-and-arrow. He knows such words as *ying-yang* and *twitchet*, and is not afraid to use them. There are some good backwoods comparisons, perhaps a bit bowdlerized, such as "clean as a coon's pretty thing."[76] The story is not really Ozarkian in spirit, but the dialect is authentic and well written.

Backwoods Teacher, by Joseph Nelson, is the chronicle of a native Arkansawyer who taught a country school near the Missouri–Arkansas line. There is a great deal of dialect in this book, and it is extremely well done, with some illuminating discussion of *you'ns, you-all, your'n's's*, and so on. Such terms as *dulge* for dig and *progue* for probe are new to me, and it may be that these are neighborhood words, current in a comparatively restricted area. Joseph Nelson is one of the best writers of dialect who ever worked in this region. *Backwoods Teacher* is required reading for all serious students of the Ozark speech.[77]

Constance Wagner's *Sycamore*[78] is set in a small resort town in north-

[75] *For Here Is My Fortune,* (New York, 1946), pp. 8, 19, 27, 28, 46, 49, 50, 52, 54, 56–57, 64, 97, 122, 136, 138, 140, 175, 182, 226, 244, 251, 266, 270, 290.

[76] See pp. 9, 40, 167, 252.

[77] Philadelphia, 1949, pp. 32, 60–63, 64, 81, 84, 105, 106, 109, 116, 124, 129, 132–33, 134, 137, 140, 162, 185, 193, 242, 284, 288.

[78] New York, 1950, pp. 53–60, 137–39, 158, 160–61, 192–93, 250.

west Arkansas. The author has lived in Eureka Springs for about ten years. This is the finest novel, in my opinion, that has ever been published about the Ozark country. But it deals largely with townspeople rather than country folk; the backwoods idiom is deftly but sparingly used. The dialect that appears is authentic and effective, but there isn't much of it.

I do not presume to discuss the literary merits of these stories, being concerned only with the dialect. But my bookish friends say that most of the Ozark novels are badly written, and the few which are not badly written contain little dialect. It has been suggested that there is a definite negative correlation between the ability to make use of dialectal peculiarities and the power to write good fiction. Well, I wouldn't know about that. I record the theory here, for what it may be worth.

It seems to me that some stage and screen comedians have been more successful with the mountain speech than the people who write books and magazine stories. Bob Burns of Van Buren, Arkansas, the Weaver brothers, who grew up in Christian County, Missouri, and Margaret Lillie, from the hills of eastern Oklahoma, all speak authentic Ozark dialect when they choose. The radio comics known as "Lum and Abner," of Polk County, Arkansas, do pretty well with it. In the lower reaches of the profession are scores of fellows who mutilate folk songs on the air and plug regrettable compositions of their own for the jukebox trade. But even in this wretched caterwauling one hears an occasional echo of the real thing. The worst of the radio hillbillies are better than the characters in many Ozark novels.

7 Unusual Words and Meanings

Backwoodsmen in the Ozarks frequently bring out good English words of a type seldom used by illiterates in other parts of the country.[1] As Allen Walker Read says: "It appears that many words which elsewhere are book-words or 'high-brow' words are used in the Ozarks in ordinary popular speech."[2]

Where else, for example, would you hear an unlettered woodcutter use the verb *cavil?* Not in New England certainly, nor in the Middle West, nor anywhere in America except the isolated hill regions of the Ozarks and the southern Appalachians. Our hired man, who couldn't read and didn't know enough to pour cider out of a boot, remarked that "them fool women is always *a-cavillin'* about somethin'." The principal of a small-town high school, a graduate of the University of Missouri, told me that "*cavil* is hillbilly slang, not good English at all."[3]

A friend of mine in the backwoods of McDonald County, Missouri, had gotten into trouble with the law. For several months he kept out of sight, and his wife told everybody that he had gone to Oklahoma. I rode up to the cabin one day and asked if she'd had any news, but the woman shook her head. "Tom's kind of *dilatory* 'bout writin' letters," she murmured. Our eyes met, and suddenly we burst out laughing. I knew that Tom was only a few hundred feet away, probably watching us at that very moment. The talk of letters was nonsense, because both Tom and his wife were completely illiterate. The woman's use of *dilatory* was a fine touch, and how she came by such a word is something to think about. In the same neighborhood I have heard it as a verb: "Amos he just kind of *dilatoried* around, an' never did git his corn planted."

---

[1] Cf. Charles Morrow Wilson, *Backwoods America,* 64.
[2] *Missouri Historical Review,* Vol. XXIX (1935), 265.
[3] *American Speech,* Vol. IV (1928), 56.

The verb partake, with *partuck* as the preterite and past participle, is commonly used in the most isolated communities. I recall one man who said: "I don't never *partake* of no whiskey, except if I'm a-ailin'." This same fellow told me that he had never seen a locomotive, but he had seen plenty of airplanes—a strange situation, when one stops to think of it. It was this man's son who described his wife as a docile critter, pronouncing *docile* with both vowels long and no noticeable accent on either syllable.

One often hears bemean, as in the sentence, "I hate a feller what's always *a-bemeanin'* of his kinfolks." The word forsake, too, is in common use among the hillfolk, who speak of a girl as *forsaken* or *forsook*, meaning that she has no suitors.

Another of my old neighbors near Pineville, Missouri, was very fond of the word proffer. "Judge Lampson's wife *proffered* to git me a bait of victuals," he said, "but I told her I better be a-comin' on home."

The noun caucus is rarely heard in the hill country, but the verb forms are common, meaning to chatter unintelligibly or to talk earnestly about matters of no importance. A barber in northwest Arkansas told me that "them fellers set on a rock an' *caucussed* pretty near all day." He was speaking of two Indians who conversed in a language he couldn't understand.

An onset means a contest or a struggle, and one may speak of a *master onset* between two dogs in the street. The good English word fray, meaning a fight with deadly weapons, is still common in the Ozark country.[4] Slay is often heard, too, and generally means to slaughter in large numbers. An expert gigger certainly can *slay* fish when the water's right, and a hot day in August is the best time to *slay* weeds. I have never heard slew or slain in the Ozarks; the preterite of slay is *slayed*, but sometimes it is pronounced to rhyme with crowd.

One of my wife's relatives at Pineville, Missouri, was known far and wide as "a plumb *contentious* woman." This was said quite without heat, merely as a mention of the lady's most outstanding characteristic.

A sudden breeze stirred the tops of the big cedars along Bear Creek, near Day, Missouri. An old man looked up. "That there wind *denotes* rain," said he. I nodded in agreement, and ventured the opinion that a little rain wouldn't do us any harm. "Maybe not, but I hope it *ceases* afore mornin'," he answered. "Me an' Lizzie are a-figgerin' on goin' to town."

Once in Lanagan, Missouri, I heard an illiterate old woman say, "Hit's a plumb *tragedy* for me to eat sparrowgrass,"[5] meaning that asparagus

[4] Cf. *Missouri Magazine*, February, 1938, p. 10.
[5] *American Speech*, Vol. IV (1928), 57.

produced a diarrhea. The hillfolk often use *tragic* and *tragical* in similar sentences.

At Keener, Arkansas, an illiterate farmer said to a storekeeper that he'd like to have all his small purchases put together "in one big poke, if it won't *discomfit* ye too much." He laid a heavy stress on the final syllable.[6]

Years ago I met a boy limping along the road between Big Flat and Fifty-Six, Arkansas. "I don't mind walkin','," he said, "but these new shoes is *destroyin'* me." I have often heard destroy used in this meaning since then, by Missourians and Oklahomans as well as Arkansawyers.

In refusing some proffered food at table, a well-bred hillman says, "I wouldn't *choose* any." Mary Elizabeth Mahnkey, of Kirbyville, Missouri, used to make it: "No thanky, I don't *choose* any." As far as I can recall, I have heard this only with reference to food and drink.

The verb *quote,* in the Ozarks, is just a rather formal term for say, tell, or speak; it does not mean repeating the words of another. A man testifying in court at Galena, Missouri, said of another witness: "That feller *quoted* a mistruth!" This meant simply and plainly, "That fellow lied," and every man in the courtroom so understood it. The witness did not mean that the fellow merely repeated a lie that someone else was responsible for.

A neighbor told me of a young matron who was having difficulty in making her little boy behave himself: "Maisie *affirms* she's a-goin' to whup the baby, but he never moves till he sees the limb!" One of this woman's relatives remarked: "We just drink branch-water till it gits *fouled* 'long about April, an' after that we pack water from the spring."

Dilapidate is common in such sentences as: "Bruce has just let his house *dilapidate* till it ain't fitten to live in." It was a wooden house, too, with no stonework except the fireplace. Once I heard a farmer bragging about his dog: "You just orter see old Bulger *dilapidate* a groundhog!"

"I just stopped to *squander a opinion* with them fellers" means to talk or argue idly, without any real interest. *Spend a opinion* is also heard and apparently carries the same meaning.[7]

A shell-digger on White River, near Cotter, Arkansas, was telling me that irregularly shaped pearls, which he called slugs, sell for $7 per ounce. "But it sure does *require a abundance* of them things to *comprise* a ounce," he said soberly.

In Taney County, Missouri, I heard a man say, "Them folks down to

[6] Cf. Wentworth, *American Dialect Dictionary*, 165.
[7] Cf. Charles Morrow Wilson, *Backwoods America*, 65.

Protem took up *vilifyin'* each other, an' then they got to fightin', an' killed one feller right in the church-house." *Vilify* and *vilified* are common all through the Ozark country.

The hillman regularly speaks of a *deserted* house, where most Americans would say an *empty* house or a *vacant* house.

The verb *creen* signifies to lean or twist sidewise, and is evidently an abbreviated form of careen, a word seldom used by farmers or woodsmen in other parts of America. A man told me that his father drank too much applejack, and "went *a-creenin'* round all evenin', till finally he fell right spang in a hog-waller."[8] A boot or shoe which is badly worn on one side and does not stand upright is said to be *creened*.

Beguile is another common verb. A little boy observed that "old man Landers he don't play at no dances nowadays; jest fiddles round home to *beguile* the time."

The word acclimated is common and properly used, though it is generally pronounced *climated*.

One often hears the verb tarry in the sense of wait, loiter, or remain. Speaking of an early snowfall, a man at Eureka Springs, Arkansas, said: "Yeah, we got a little skift yesterday. But it didn't *tarry* long." He meant that the snow melted immediately.

It always amused me, somehow, to hear *costive* used to mean either constipating or expensive.[9] An attorney in McDonald County, Missouri, complained bitterly that the local moonshine was "too *costive*," because it retailed at four dollars a gallon. In the midst of an argument in court, this same lawyer shouted to the jury, "You reckon I cain't *discern* right from wrong?"

An illiterate farmer in Kansas or Illinois would not be likely to say *megrim* when he meant headache, but this word is quite common in the Ozarks.[10] I've heard it all the way from Mena, Arkansas, to Poplar Bluff, Missouri.

All the women in a certain community were reputed to have syphilis. Doubtless this was an exaggeration, but one village boy said to another, "You better *shun* them Pokeroot Holler gals, on account they ain't healthy."

The expression *I dare say* seems odd in the mouth of an illiterate woodchopper, but we often hear it. One of my friends got very drunk at a dance, and I intimated that he would do well to go home and sober up. "*I dare say*

[8] *Dialect Notes*, Vol. V (1927), 473.
[9] *American Speech*, Vol. VIII (1933), 48.
[10] *American Speech*, Vol. VIII (1933), 51.

I can dance as good as anybody in Barry County, an' maybe better," he answered with dignity.

Mary Elizabeth Mahnkey reported *methinks* used by her neighbors near Kirbyville, Missouri.[11] I have heard it myself, in both Missouri and Arkansas, but not often.

Constance Wagner told me that she knew a boy in Eureka Springs, Arkansas, who used the word *perchance* and used it correctly. This is not uncommon, in some of the most backward and isolated settlements. If I should go about saying *methinks* or *I dare say* or *perchance,* it would seem ridiculous and affected. But these country boys use such terms quite naturally, and they get away with it. The expressions *I assure you* and *I warrant you* are also common in the backwoods of Missouri and Arkansas and are used by men who can neither read nor write.

The verb *wrest* is unusual in the ordinary American illiterate's vocabulary, but in the Ozarks one often hears such sentences as, "I was that weak, Doc, I couldn't *wrest* a 'tater off'n a baby!"

The Ozarker seldom *thinks* about any serious subject but prefers to *reckon* or *study* or even to *ponder.*[12]

Our Baptist preacher, a poor fellow who can hardly write his own name, is known as one who *comprehends* book learning and is able to *clarify* the most difficult and ambiguous passages in the Bible. When a flashily dressed photographer came to the village, this preacher warned him publicly not to *delude* any of the local virgins.

An old woman once told me of a little rhyme or *posey* her son had copied into a friendship book: "Jim he wrote it off for me, an' the schoolmarm she *rectified* it," meaning that the teacher corrected errors in spelling and punctuation. This boy, by the way, was described as "a apt scholar." The word *scholar* means pupil in the Ozarks, and is often applied to children in the lower grades who have not yet learned to read.

The adverbs *candidly* and *actually* are often heard in the ordinary conversation of very ignorant people. *Wearisome,* with the first two syllables pronounced *wary* or *worry,* is not at all uncommon.

One of my neighbors, convalescing from a serious illness, was said to *meander* around, a reference to his wavering, uncertain gait.

The word oracle is common in the backwoods. I knew a man whose wife ran a boardinghouse, and one day he announced to the guests, "My old woman is the *oracle* around here, an' don't you never forget it!"[13]

[11] Springfield, Mo., *News,* December 2, 1938.
[12] Cf. Thames Williamson, *The Writer,* January, 1935, p. 28.
[13] *American Speech,* Vol. IV (1928), 57.

Sometimes oracle is used as a sort of title and means boss or dictator as well as fount of wisdom.

The verb *pen*, meaning to write, is often heard among the older people, and I have heard *penned* used as an adjective. "It wasn't no printed dodger," a man said of a communication from a high official, "it was a regular *penned* letter in his own handwrite."

A lady in Galena, Missouri, was *noticeable vexed* because her canned peaches turned bitter. Her husband was an irritable, dyspeptic fellow; he was described as a man who *took umbrage*. Crumb reports the verb *peruse* from southeastern Missouri, where he says it is "a favorite word among the very ignorant."[14]

I have noted many other "book-words" which impressed me in the speech of the ignorant, illiterate hillman, such as *aver*,[15] *loiter, withstand, genteel, betide, agile, honorable, reconcile, exhort, dote, devote, intoxicate, diligent, diligence*, and *generate*.[16]

Almost as striking as the Ozarker's liking for "literary" words which are not common in the speech of illiterates elsewhere is the way he uses familiar words with some fantastic connotations, very different from their ordinary meanings in other sections of the country. This is one reason why the hillman's speech so often baffles visitors from the North and East. They may be acquainted with every word he says and still not get his meaning at all.

Invite a backwoodsman to have a drink from your flask, and he answers promptly, "I *don't care* to." It sounds like a definite refusal, but that isn't his meaning at all. He means, "Thank you, I'll be delighted to have a drink." When a man says, "I don't *care* to chop wood," the meaning is, "I don't *mind* chopping wood." A young man in Forsyth, Missouri, said to his sweetheart: "I don't care to see you dancin' with thet feller from Kansas City," meaning that he did not *object* to her dancing with the city feller in question. Looking at a fine new car, an Arkansas hillman remarked, "I wouldn't care to have one of them myself," meaning that he would very much like to have one.

When I first came to the Ozarks, I was astounded to hear the word *whore* applied to women who were obviously nothing of the sort. The hillman speaks of any woman who has sexual relationships outside of marriage as a whore.[17] Webster indicates that this usage was at one time com-

---

[14] *Dialect Notes*, Vol. II (1903), 324.
[15] Charles Morrow Wilson, St. Louis *Post-Dispatch*, June 9, 1930.
[16] Cf. *Missouri Magazine*, February, 1938, p. 9.

mon elsewhere; after the usual definition of *whore* as a prostitute, he adds, "formerly, any unchaste woman." The old word *whore-master,* in some sections of the United States, means a pimp, but the Ozarker uses it for any man who habitually associates with loose women.

When a man is said to sing or talk *coarse,* it means that he has a bass voice; if he can sing *fine,* he's a tenor. The stranger is puzzled at hearing of a fellow who "sings mighty fine, but can't carry a tune." It seems odd to hear a nice young girl say publicly, "I like a man that talks *coarse.*" A woman who sings *shallow* has a high, shrill voice, treble or soprano. May Kennedy McCord, of Springfield, Missouri, told me of a backwoods preacher who shouted during a song service: "Pitch it shaller, Sister Henderson! The Lord loves *shaller* music!"

Glib, in the Ozarks, does not refer particularly to speech. It means active, brisk of movement. Rose O'Neill, of Day, Missouri, heard a neighbor say: "Granny's eighty-seven year old, but she's still *glib as a quail.*"

When applied to a human being, the adjective *low* means short of stature: "The new preacher is a *low,* fat man."[18] One often hears a man described as *low an' little with it,* meaning that he is not only short but slender. A schoolmarm at Hollister, Missouri, was a "heavy-set woman, kind of *low an' wide out.*" The compound *low-down* is another thing, and means contemptible. A hillman might describe his best friend as *low,* but he would never say *low-down.*

Common is synonymous with unpretentious, unassuming, democratic. The hillman is always expecting people with money or education to "put on airs." The highest compliment that can be paid a rich man, a professional man, or a man in high political office is to say that he is *common,* or perhaps *common as an old shoe.*

To say that a woman is *neat* means that she is discreet, careful about the conventions. A young widow with two children lived near us, and she was always at great pains to get home before dark. It wasn't that she was afraid to be out at night, but for the sake of her reputation in the community. "Folks talk about a widder-woman if she ain't *neat* about things like that" was her way of putting it.

Much is a transitive verb meaning to praise, to flatter. One of our neighbors said to her husband: "Don't keep *a-muchin'* that young-un all the time, you'll spoil him." The man was playing with his three-year-old son.[19] *Make over* is often heard, with the same meaning.

[17] Cf. my *The Ozarks,* 55–56.
[18] Cf. Wentworth, *American Dialect Dictionary,* 370.
[19] *American Speech,* Vol. V (1929), 19.

Bereft is often used in the sense of insane, mentally unbalanced. To say that a man is bereft means that he has lost his mind. An acquaintance of ours had several times been confined in the asylum at Nevada, Missouri. When he came home for a visit, one of his neighbors remarked: "The folks claim Jim's all right now, but he looks plumb *bereft* to me. Why, he runs through the woods every night, a-howlin' like a wolf!"

Ill does not mean in poor health, but vicious or bad-tempered. "My woman," said a man at Walnut Shade, Missouri, "gits *iller* every day she lives!" Another fellow observed that "them Tompkins boys is the *illest* critters on the creek."

Wicked refers to speech only, and it means profane or blasphemous. One of the mildest, kindliest, most charitable men I ever knew, with no bad habits save cursing, was generally recognized as the *wickedest* man in our village. And there were plenty of murderers and law violators in the place, including one convicted rapist and two bank robbers.

The word *big*, applied to a man, means fat—what an Easterner would call stout. *Stout*, in the Ozarks, means strong, not corpulent or obese. A very small man, even a dwarf, might be both *big* and *stout* as these words are used in the hill country. One of the *stoutest* men in our neighborhood was "a little skinny wiry feller."[20] *Portly,* to the hillman means handsome and dignified; a very thin man may be quite portly.

Brown means brunet, having dark eyes and hair; it is applied chiefly to women and children. A young man at Forsyth, Missouri, said: "I always liked *brown* gals better'n these here blond-headed ones." I replied with a wisecrack about the multiple advantages of Negro girls, but he didn't understand me. There are many adults in the Ozark backwoods who have never even seen a Negro.

When a hillman is *bored*, he is not wearied or afflicted with ennui, but chagrinned or humiliated.[21] A boy said, "I sure was *bored* when I found out that Paw had been in the pen for stealin' hogs." Another young man in our village didn't like to go into the barbershop, because the loafers there "was always *a-borin'* him about his gal."

Hack and *wad* are transitive verbs which mean pretty much the same as *bore*. One of our friends was terribly hacked when some tourists laughed at his new Sunday-go-to-meetin' suit.[22] And a girl said in my hearing: "That there joke sure *wadded* Maw."[23]

[20] Cf. *Dialect Notes*, Vol. V (1926), 404.
[21] Cf. *Dialect Notes*, Vol. V (1923), 202.
[22] *Dialect Notes*, Vol. III (1905), 82.

Unusual Words and Meanings

Tree is a verb in the Ozarks, as when the dogs force some animal to take refuge in a tree. The term is quite correct even when no tree is involved, and one often hears of coons or wildcats *treed* in dens under the limestone cliffs. Panthers, in the early days, were generally treed in caverns. As I write these lines, I hear my own pot-hounds barking; they have probably *treed* a rabbit in the brush pile behind the garage. A woman in Crane, Missouri, told me that her terrier would "*tree* moles, then dig 'em out an' kill 'em right in the front yard."

A *bait* is usually a meal,[24] sometimes merely a light lunch or a snack. One of my neighbors was asked to ride into town and fetch the doctor. He consented amiably enough, but said, "Afore I start, I better git me a little *bait o'* victuals."[25] A *bait-can* is a dinner bucket. In Camden County, Missouri, *bait* is reported as "a large amount; usually refers to food."[26] A *dog's bait* generally means a big dinner, but sometimes the term is applied to an excessive amount of anything.[27] A hillman had a long argument with his wife, and ended the whole affair by saying, "I've stood for a lot of this here foolishment, but enough is enough, an' too much is a *dog's bait!*" An old man came past our cabin one day, scratching with both hands. "I sure did git a *dog's bait of chiggers* in that old orchard," he said by way of explanation.

The Ozarker uses *grandmaw* as a verb, and it means to steal timber. In Howell County, Missouri, they say a young fellow accused of cutting ties on some rich man's property denied everything at first, but finally admitted that "*grandmaw* might have cut a few sticks over thar." Another explanation is that, asked where his firewood came from, a hillman answered "off'n grandmaw's place," meaning land belonging to some non-resident capitalist. Nancy Clemens[28] identifies this with the common expression "grannying timber."[29] In the *Missouri Conservationist*[30] is an article entitled "Grandmawing Doesn't Pay," with the explanation that "here in the hills the act of cutting timber that doesn't belong to you is known as *grandmawing,* and the people who do such things are called *grandmawers.*"

23 *Dialect Notes,* Vol. V (1926), 404.
24 *Dialect Notes,* Vol. III (1905), 69.
25 *Dialect Notes,* Vol. V (1926), 398.
26 *Publication of the American Dialect Society,* No. 2 (1944), 53.
27 *American Speech,* Vol. VIII (1933), 48.
28 Kansas City, Mo., *Star,* August 21, 1938.
29 *American Speech,* Vol. XI (1936), 315.
30 Jefferson City, Mo., July, 1948, p. 6.

The word *music* doesn't mean music at all, but rather a musical instrument. An old lady said to a man carrying a guitar, "Fetch your *music* into the house, the dew might warp it."[31] A brass band, or even an orchestra, is still known as a *band o' music.*

A *target* is not a mark to shoot at, but a rifle of small caliber, such as that used in target shooting.[32] "Fetch me the *target* out of the wagon," a man shouted to his wife, "there's a squirrel in this here tree." It appears that target rifle has been reduced to *target,* just as chamber pot has become *chamber.*

Several means not two or three or half-a-dozen, but a much larger number. When a hillman says that he trapped *several* possums last winter, he may mean thirty or forty. The country newspapers often say "several from here attended the show," when they mean a sizable crowd of fifty or a hundred persons. The phrase *a good few* is often used in a similar meaning, and a woman testified in court at Springfield, Missouri, that she was acquainted with *a great few* of the people who live in a place called Elsey.[33]

My neighbor who *"carried* his whole family plumb to Bentonville" did not actually pack or tote his wife and children; he merely led or accompanied them.[34] At Camp Pike, Arkansas, an Ozark lieutenant hailed a sergeant from Massachusetts. "Take these thirty-eight men," said he, "an' carry 'em over to headquarters." The building we called headquarters was several hundred yards distant, and I shall never forget the look on that poor Yankee's face. This meaning of carry was common long ago in England. Pepys writes: "My landlord carried us through a very old hospital."[35]

The term foreign or *furrin* is applied to anything or anybody outside the Ozark region. A man from Illinois, Iowa, or Indiana is just as surely a *furriner* as if he came from Germany or Switzerland.[36] Country bankers often speak of "*furrin* checks," meaning those drawn on banks in Chicago or Indianapolis. Rose O'Neill, of Day, Missouri, told me of a neighbor who said, "A furriner is a feller that comes from *fur off* somewheres."

One often hears the word *spouse* in the backwoods, but never with the meaning of a husband or wife. It is always applied to a small child.[37]

---

[31] *American Speech*, Vol. V (1929), 19.
[32] *Dialect Notes*, Vol. V (1923), 223.
[33] Springfield, Mo., *Leader & Press*, June 25, 1940.
[34] Cf. Fred Starr, *From an Ozark Hillside*, 36.
[35] *Diary*, February 27, 1659.
[36] Cf. my *The Ozarks*, 5; also Starr, *From an Ozark Hillside*, 35.
[37] *American Speech*, Vol. V (1929), 20.

One of our neighbors was trying to make his eight-year-old son pull weeds out of the corn, but the boy didn't want to do it. "Oh, let Freddie alone," said the boy's grandmother. "He's just a little *spouse,* an' ain't big enough to do no hard work yet."

The best man at a wedding, the fellow who stands up with the bridegroom, is called a *waiter.* The old-timers say that bridesmaids used to be called *waiters* too,[38] but I have not heard this myself. A physician *waits on* a patient—attends him, that is. When an honored guest or a visiting preacher is invited to *wait on the table,* it means to ask a blessing on the food, to say a prayer before eating.[39]

The mountaineer shows his inherent contempt for the law by using *judge* to mean clown or fool.[40] Occasionally one hears such a remark as: "Them city gals sure did make a *judge* out of old man Peters." Sometimes the judicial title is turned into an adjective: "Zeke's least boy is the *judgiest* chap I ever seen." *Chap,* by the way, means a small child, and is never used in the ordinary English sense.

A *taw* is not a marble, as it is to children in the North, but rather a girl, a man's partner at a dance or play-party. Mary Elizabeth Mahnkey, of Mincy, Missouri, quotes an old-time dance call:

> *Swing Sally Goodin, swing grandmaw,*
> *An' don't forget to swing your* taw.

Botkin heard the term *taw* at dances in Oklahoma and thinks it must be "from marble usage."[41] When C. R. Black of Springfield, Missouri, published a book on square dancing, the cover carried a picture of Black and his pretty wife with the caption, "Me and my Taw."[42]

The word *hickory* means a whip, a switch, and has no specific botanical significance. A school teacher at Pineville, Missouri, told me that "sassafras makes the best hickory, if ye kin git it."[43] I have heard a graduate of Washington University speak of punishing a child with "a little peach hickory." Joseph W. Carr found both *apple hickory* and *peach hickory* common in northwest Arkansas.[44] A man who taught school near Jane,

[38] Cf. Wentworth, *American Dialect Dictionary,* 687.
[39] *American Speech,* Vol. XI (1936), 318.
[40] *Dialect Notes,* Vol. V (1923), 212.
[41] *American Play-Party Song,* 114.
[42] *Square Dancing Ozark Style* (Springfield, Mo., 1949), 38.
[43] *American Speech,* Vol. V (1929), 18; XI (1936), 315.
[44] *Dialect Notes,* Vol. III (1906), 124, 150.

Missouri, used a thin switch in ordinary discipline, but he kept a heavy *leather hickory* for the big boys.

According to Webster, *skewbald* is an adjective meaning piebald or spotted, but in the Ozarks it's a noun. It means an animal, usually a horse, which has one light eye and one dark eye. The noun *rogue* and the adjective *roguish* are not often applied to human beings; they refer to cattle and other animals that break through fences. The adjective *breachy* carries the same meaning.

The word *natural* is a noun, and usually designates a congenital idiot or imbecile. "Maggie's baby looks like a *natural* to me, but she says it ain't." This must be an old usage; Shakespeare makes Trinculo apply the name to Caliban: "That a monster should be such a *natural!*"[45]

A *professor* is not a teacher, but a person who has "got religion," one who stands up in church to testify or profess. A neighbor once told me that he and his wife had been *professors* for seven years, though neither of them could read or write. The *Oxford Dictionary* gives this meaning, with quotations dating back to 1597.

The hillfolk seldom *address* a letter, they *back* it,[46] doubtless a heritage from the days when there were no envelopes and the address was written on the back of the sheet, the corners being fastened together with wax. Professor H. M. Belden, of the University of Missouri, is probably the greatest ballad scholar in America, but when he found "*bake* it and stamp it" used with reference to a letter in an old ballad manuscript, he surmised that *bake* probably meant date![47]

The word *clever* has nothing to do with intelligence, but means friendly, accommodating, or generous. Of a pretty girl in our neighborhood it was said, "Milly don't know enough to come in out of the rain, but she sure is *clever*."[48] One of the *cleverest* men who ever lived in Pineville, Missouri, is definitely feeble-minded. A similar usage is reported from northern Missouri.[49] The word is sometimes applied to inanimate objects; a song once popular at backwoods singing schools contains a reference to "a *clever* old barn."

A narrow-minded man is one who has a single purpose, a one-track mind, an obsession. "Tom says he's a-goin' to kill me," a hillman told our sheriff, "an he's just *narry-minded* enough to do it!" Catherine S. Barker

[45] *The Tempest,* Act III, scene 2, line 37.
[46] *Dialect Notes,* Vol. V (1926), 398; *American Speech,* Vol. XVI (1941), 21.
[47] *Ballads and Songs* (Columbia, Mo., 1940), 488.
[48] Cf. *Dialect Notes,* Vol. V (1926), 398.
[49] *American Speech,* Vol. X (1935), 291.

of Batesville, Arkansas, says that "a *narrow minded* person is one who is not very bright,"[50] but I don't think I ever heard the word used in that fashion.

Proud often means no more than pleased. When a hillman says, "I'm mighty *proud* to meet you," he doesn't mean that you are better than he is or that he considers it an honor to make your acquaintance. He uses the expression when he is introduced, just as a lowlander would say, "How do you do?" The word proud is frequently used where country folk from other parts of the United States would say glad, as "I'm sure *proud* it didn't rain on us today." I use the word in this sense myself sometimes, without thinking of it as dialectal. *Glad* seems rather feeble and childish, after you've heard *proud* for two or three decades.

Rose O'Neill, of Taney County, Missouri, tells me that some old-timers use proud to mean neatly or carefully dressed. The word proudful is sometimes used in this sense. "I seen them folks was a little more *proudful* than common" means only that they were wearing better clothes than usual.

The adjective *prideful* means vain or conceited, and *prides* is used to designate the genitals, particularly in the male. I don't think the average hillman ever connects the word *proud* with *pride* or *prideful* at all.

The hillman who speaks of a child or a young girl as *ashamed* does not use the word in the ordinary sense, with an implication of embarrassment or even guilt. The word means modest, unassuming, sometimes timid or bashful.[51]

In the Middle West people generally use *wonderful* and *marvellous* to describe something pleasant or at least harmless. But it is not the case in the Ozarks. Of a woman who died in childbirth it was said that "she suffered somethin' *wonderful*." A hillman may speak of a *wonderful* big storm that destroyed his property. Nancy Clemens, Springfield, Missouri, quoted a farmer who had been hurt in a motor accident: "No bones broke," said he, "but I sure was scratched up *marvellous*."

The term *pig trough* carries some obscure reference to foster-brothers and foster-sisters and is sometimes used in a slighting way to insinuate that the eldest child in a large family is illegitimate. Dr. W. O. Cralle, of Springfield, Missouri, tells me that an unmarried girl whose younger sisters have caught husbands is said to be "dancing in a pig trough."[52] On

---

[50] *Yesterday Today*, 130.
[51] *American Speech*, Vol. VIII (1933), 47. Cf. Starr, *From an Ozark Hillside*, 36.
[52] *American Speech*, Vol. XI (1936), 316.

election day in Syllamore, Arkansas, I heard a man say: "If you vote for my boy, I'll dance in a pig trough at your wedding." None of these *pig trough* references is clear to me, but I set them down here for the record.

When the hillman says *poverty,* he means the actual lack of food. "Bob says that there dog had the distemper, but I reckon it was just *poverty* what killed him." The above sentence is just a polite way of saying that the dog starved to death. I have several times heard of hogs and cattle that were isolated by high water and died of *poverty.* Meriwether Lewis uses *poverty* to mean leanness or feebleness,[53] the effect rather than the cause.

The old folks believe that *yarn* designates woolen cloth or any sort of woolen garment. An old fellow said: "Next week I aim to put on my *yarn,*" meaning his heavy winter underwear. When a woman "leaves off her *yarn*" in the spring, it means that she discards a warm petticoat, woolen drawers, or perhaps even a knitted undervest or jacket.

Most of the old-timers use sorrow where ordinary Americans would say sorry, as in the sentence: "I'm right *sorrow* I cain't go fishin' with you-uns today." Taylor thinks that *sorrow* is only "the written form of sorry" in McDonald County, Missouri,[54] but I have not found it so. A man who came to play my phonograph at Pineville, Missouri, always referred to an ancient fox trot as "Who's *Sorrow* Now?" although he was quite able to read the *s-o-r-r-y* in large print on the label. Many mountain people use *sorry* as an adjective meaning inferior. I don't think I ever heard *sorrow* used substantively by any of the old-timers in the Ozarks.[55]

A stopper is not a cork for a bottle, but a drink of liquor. "Just a little *stopper* now an' ag'in won't hurt nobody," a gentleman assured me.[56] Stew is not a dish of meat and vegetables, but a toddy of whiskey, ginger, and hot water. The old-timers made a ceremony of drinking *stew* on Christmas and New Years mornings.[57] The noun wash means a swallow of water taken after a drink of whiskey; it used to be called a *chaser* in the North. I have heard *rinse* or *rench* used in the same meaning, as when a man asked the bartender for "a double bourbon, with a beer *rench.*"

Yankees use jag as synonymous with spree or binge, but in the Ozarks a jag has nothing to do with intoxication.[58] It means a light load, a com-

[53] E. H. Criswell, *Lewis and Clark, Linguistic Pioneers* (Columbia, Mo., 1940), 67.
[54] *Dialect Notes,* Vol. V (1923), 221.
[55] *Dialect Notes,* Vol. V (1926), 403.
[56] *Dialect Notes,* Vol. V (1927), 478.
[57] Cf. my *The Ozarks,* 66.
[58] Cf. *Dialect Notes,* Vol. V (1923), 211.

paratively small quantity: "Tell Jim to fetch me up a little *jag* of cook-wood." I think *jag* is more often used with reference to hay and firewood than anything else. But William R. Lighton, who used to live near Fayette-ville, Arkansas, spoke of "a little *jag* of potatoes,"[59] and a man in Carroll County, Arkansas, told me that his wife wanted "a *jag* of rich dirt" to put in a flower bed.

The noun gum means a hollow receptacle, such as a beehive[60] or a rabbit trap made of a hollow log. Sometimes it means the wooden curbing of a well or spring. Joseph W. Carr mentions somebody who said, "You ought to have a *brick gum* around that spring."[61] The old folks say that black gum trees were generally used in pioneer days, hence the name. A *gourd gum* is a large gourd used as a container for meal, salt, soap, or some other household substance.[62] When the hillman wants chewing gum he doesn't use the word gum at all, but calls for *wax*.[63]

When a hillman says *house,* he doesn't necessarily mean the entire building, but rather the main room. "Come into the house" is an invitation to enter the living room, which contains the fireplace, and the invitation may be addressed to a guest who is already in the kitchen or the lean-to bedroom. In a double log cabin, where two similar *pens* are connected by a breezeway or dog-run, the word house may apply to either room. A man sitting in one may remark that "the old woman's in the other *house*."[64]

The old-timer seldom uses the term fireplace, but prefers to say chim-ney. "Put some wood in the *chimney*" means to replenish the fire. "A *chimney* beats a stove all to hell, when it comes to cookin' 'taters," said one of my neighbors. Mantelpieces are always *fireboards* in the Ozarks.[65] The glass in a window is a *light* instead of a pane. An opaque curtain is a *blind,* not a shade. A porch or veranda is usually called a *gallery*.

Surround means to go around, to detour.[66] It is quite possible for one man to *surround* a building or even a large tract of land; he just walks around it. Motorists often find it necessary to *surround* a big rock which has fallen on to the road; this means that they turn to one side in order to miss the obstruction.

---

[59] *Happy Hollow Farm,* 62.

[60] *Publication of the American Dialect Society,* No. 2 (1944), 53.

[61] *Dialect Notes,* Vol. III (1906), 128.

[62] *Dialect Notes,* Vol. III (1906), 138.

[63] *Dialect Notes,* Vol. III (1906), 163; V (1923), 224; also Fred Starr, *From an Ozark Hillside,* 36.

[64] *American Speech,* Vol. V (1929), 18.

[65] *American Speech,* Vol. XI (1936), 315.

[66] *Dialect Notes,* Vol. V (1926), 404.

The noun ramp doesn't mean an inclined plane or passageway, as it does to most city dwellers. In the Ozarks a *ramp* is a wild onion or garlic (*Allium tricoccum*), doubtless derived from the English ramson, or perhaps from rampion which Webster defines as "a plant of the bellwort family cultivated in Europe, its succulent root eaten as a salad."[67] The word is known in many parts of the South. A high school near Beckley, West Virginia, was almost disrupted because the children persisted in "munching ramps en route to classes." The school principal said that "the ramp odor could be likened to that of a polecat," and he punished the "ramp-eaters" severely.[68] There is an adjective, *rampy,* which the Ozark folk apply to milk or butter that tastes of garlic or wild onions.

Diddling means cheating or outwitting, according to Webster. But in the Ozarks it refers to sexual intercourse, and nothing else.[69]

"Mary's *a-workin' the piller-pokes*" serves as an announcement that the girl is engaged to be married. Literally, it means "embroidering the pillow-slips." To say that "Mary is *a-piecin' quilts*" may mean that she is contemplating marriage; it does not necessarily imply, as the *piller-poke* figure does, that the date of the wedding is all set.

The verb enjoy is used in the sense of entertain, and one of my neighbors remarked just after a number of guests had left his cabin, "We done our best to *enjoy* 'em, but they was the sorriest company I ever seen."[70] *Sorriest* means poorest, most inferior. On another occasion the same man complained, "We been a-havin' too damn' much company here lately; the old woman's just *hosted* plumb to death!"[71]

Mistook or *mistuck* is the hillman's word for mistaken. But when he says "I was *mistook*" or "I was *mistuck*," the Ozarker doesn't mean that he made a mistake, but that he was mistaken for somebody else. A man came to a physician to have some bird shot picked out of his back. "I was *mistook,* Doc," he explained. "The feller that shot me figgered I was one of them Ashcraft boys." It wasn't the shooter who was mistaken, but the man who was shot. I once consulted an educated fellow about this, a backwoods boy who had become a college professor. "Yes, *mistook* is often so used," he said. "There's a kind of logic to it, at that," he added thoughtfully.

When the hillman speaks of tutoring a child, he doesn't refer to book

[67] *American Speech,* Vol. VIII (1933), 51.
[68] *United Press* dispatch, May 22, 1948.
[69] Cf. Wentworth, *American Dialect Dictionary,* 161.
[70] *Dialect Notes,* Vol. V (1926), 399.
[71] *Dialect Notes,* Vol. V (1926), 400.

learning. Tutor, in the hill country, means to indulge, to pamper, to spoil.[72] Of a worthless boy in our neighborhood, an old man said: "It's his maw's fault. She just *tutored* that young-un since he was knee-high to a duck, an' now he ain't worth killin'." One definition of tutor in the *English Dialect Dictionary* is "to humor, to coax."

The Ozarker often uses the word *reverend* to mean full strength, undiluted. A village druggist, selling a dose of castor oil, asked: "Do you want it *reverend,* or shall I put some sody-pop in it?" The phrase *reverend so* is also common, as in the sentence: "Jim always drinked his whiskey *reverend so,* an' he taken his quinine the same way."[73] Some people write *or ever an' so,*[74] but it sounds like *reverend so* to me. Occasionally one hears it shortened to *so.* Invited to have a cocktail, a man at Galena, Missouri, said, "I'd ruther have whiskey *so,* with plain water for a wash."[75]

Reverence is a verb, with the meaning of *tolerate.*[76] The proprietor of a general store in Benton County, Arkansas, was denouncing a ruffian who had been annoying local merchants. "If a feller done *me* thataway," said the storekeeper, "I wouldn't *reverence* him for a minute! I'd split his head with a hatchet, an' kick the corpse right out in the road!"

Some old-timers use a noun that sounds like *knowance* and means knowledge. Told that his nearest neighbors were notorious criminals, sought by the federal authorities, an elderly farmer said, "Well, maybe so, but I sure ain't got no knowance of it."[77] Charley Cummins, veteran Ozark newspaperman, sometimes used this word in his copy, but he usually spelled it *knowins.*[78]

It is quite all right to describe a baby or a small child as cute. But to say that a grown-up girl is cute means that there's something funny about her legs.[79] Joseph W. Carr says that *cute* is a euphemism for bowlegged, since "the latter adjective is regarded as indelicate" at the University of Arkansas.[80] Sometimes, among very prudish folk, *cute* is regarded as an oblique reference to the lady's morals. Visiting Yankees will do well to avoid the word altogether.

[72] *Dialect Notes,* Vol. V (1927), 478.
[73] *American Speech,* Vol. V (1929), 19–20.
[74] Cf. Wentworth, *American Dialect Dictionary,* 508.
[75] Cf. D. S. Crumb, *Dialect Notes,* Vol. II (1903), 330.
[76] *Dialect Notes,* Vol. V (1927), 476.
[77] *Dialect Notes,* Vol. V (1927), 475.
[78] Springfield, Mo., *Leader & Press,* September 19, 1936.
[79] Cf. Berrey and Van den Bark, *American Thesaurus of Slang* (New York, 1942); also Wentworth, *American Dialect Dictionary,* 152.
[80] *Dialect Notes,* Vol. III (1905), 76.

As a verb, cute means to flatter, to praise excessively. O. O. McIntyre told of an Arkansawyer who said that his daughter had been *"cuted* too much" by her admirers. He also mentioned a girl who peeked around the corner of an Ozark cabin at Riley Cooper. "She's tryin' to *cute* you," an old man explained to the visitor.[81] Sometimes one hears the verb *cuter,* which means to discuss or debate fruitlessly. A man in Pineville, Missouri, said to me: "Well, if we're goin' a-fishin', let's go. It aint no use to stand here *a-cuterin'* 'bout it."[82]

I have never heard an old-timer use the verb *snub* in the ordinary transitive sense. Snub means to weep, to sob, to snivel: "Them kids been *a-snubbin'* round all day, because somebody went an' run over the pup."[83] Judge Tom Moore, of Christian County, Missouri, reports that "the defendant *snubbed* some,"[84] as a description of a backwoods culprit's behavior.

The word *about* is used in certain combinations which seem strange to visitors from the North and East. A man in Forsyth, Missouri, said: "Maw used to call me an' Fred up *a morning about* to make the fire." That is, she called the two boys on alternate mornings, so that the task was evenly divided. Which reminds me of the two men in Christian County, Missouri, who were enraged because their old car wouldn't start. "By God, I'll chop the damn' thing to pieces!" one yelled. "Good idea, Tom," cried the other. "Fetch the ax, an' we'll *take a lick about!"* He meant that they would take turns a-chopping.

The Ozarker who falls off his horse or out of his hayloft is always said to *catch a fall.* I met a man at Fayetteville, Arkansas, who told me he had broken his leg "whilst we was puttin' the roof on our new church-house" in a near-by village. "The boys told me I was apt to *ketch a fall,"* he said, "but I didn't pay 'em no mind."

A. M. Haswell, of Joplin, Missouri, recalls the alphabet rhymes in the old Blueback Speller. The final stanza was: "Z is for Zaccheus, he clomb up a tree, his Lord for to see." At the bottom of the page, says Haswell, some youngster had written, "The tree was tall, he *caught a fall,* and didn't see his Lord at all."[85]

One version of the "Old Dan Tucker" dance song includes the line: "The limb it broke and he *caught a fall."* The phrase *caught a fall* occurs

---

[81] Syndicated column, June 16, 1930; September 23, 1935.

[82] *American Speech,* Vol. XI (1936), 314.

[83] Cf. *Dialect Notes,* Vol. II (1903), 330.

[84] *Mysterious Tales and Legends of the Ozarks* (Philadelphia, 1938), 97.

[85] Springfield, Mo., *News & Leader,* April 16, 1933.

also in a "Frog's Courtship" song from Washington County, Arkansas.[86]

The words gracious and precious are sometimes used in an odd fashion. In a bar near Joplin, Missouri, a man said, "I've heerd a *gracious plenty* of that kind of talk," meaning that a previous speaker had better shut up or change the subject. And a lady in Springfield, Missouri, referring to some political appointment, said to the Governor of Missouri: "I don't want that job! Wouldn't have it as a *precious gift!*"

Salivate has nothing to do with saliva; it means to mangle, to shatter, to ruin. "Bugler sure did *salivate* that there groundhog," said a man whose dog had just killed a woodchuck.[87] An Arkansas boy who was wounded in World War II explained the circumstances of his injury: "I was comin' round the corner of a stone house, with a jug in each hand, when a Goddamn' Dutchman *salivated* me with one of them burp-guns."

The word master, in the backwoods, is nearly always an adjective, meaning biggest, most impressive.[88] One of my old friends "ketched the *master* possum ever saw in these parts." A woman in Pineville, Missouri, said: "If Jake keeps on aggervatin' my boy, he'll git the *master* whuppin' a feller ever packed!"

The verb shout is used chiefly with reference to religious meetings and is not synonymous with call, yell, or holler. When backwoods Christians get to shoutin', they dance or jump or roll in a religious frenzy. Usually this is accompanied by loud yells, but it is quite possible for a worshipper to *shout* without opening his mouth, or making any sound at all.[89] Sometimes hillfolk *shout* at funerals, too. Mary Elizabeth Mahnkey tells of a little boy going with his elders to a buryin' ground. "Granny'll shout," he said. "Granny's nigh ninety, but she'll shout."[90] And *shout* she did.

The Ozarker is rather fond of talking about skeletons, but the word means only skull in his dialect. On digging into some old Indian graves, a Missouri farmer said, "There was leg-bones and rib-bones and backbones all over the place, but nary sign of a *skeleton.*"[91] When I lived in Stone County, Missouri, I kept a Bluff-Dweller skull on my desk. The people who came to see me often made some remark about this, and more than half of them called it a *skeleton*. They were not ignorant or illiterate folk, either; many of them were school teachers and the like.

[86] Cf. my *Ozark Folksongs,* I, p. 409.

[87] Cf. *American Speech,* Vol. XI (1936), 317.

[88] Cf. *Dialect Notes,* Vol. II (1903), 320; II (1904), 419; V (1923), 214.

[89] Cf. H. R. Sass, *Saturday Evening Post,* October 3, 1942, pp. 17, 69. He explains that *"shout* isn't a sound made with the mouth, but a kind of ecstatic sacred dance."

[90] Springfield, Mo., *News,* May 18, 1940.

[91] *American Speech,* Vol. XI (1936), 317.

The noun scenery means a picture, usually a photograph, not necessarily a landscape. Rose Wilder Lane, of Mansfield, Missouri, told me that she heard a hillman say of a family group portrait: "That sure is a purty *scenery* of them children."[92] Sometimes the word means a sight or a spectacle. A man near Galena, Missouri, was showing his sawmill to some tourists; the visitors did not seem much impressed, and the owner was a little irritated. "It's a heap bigger *scenery* when it's a-runnin'," he said.

A grocery is not a place where one buys groceries, but a saloon, a grogshop. In pioneer days when a man had whiskey to sell, he just painted the word GROCERY on a board and nailed it to the front of his cabin. A newspaper story deals at length with a *grocery* that flourished at Buffalo, Missouri, in 1858.[93] The term was heard in northwest Arkansas as recently as 1941.

When a backwoods woman says "factory," she usually means cloth, generally unbleached muslin. A little girl told my wife: "Maw made me a *factory* dress, an' dyed it yaller with hickory bark." Carr found the word domestic used to mean cloth in northwest Arkansas, and adds, "it is also called *factory*."[94] Some hillfolk use *factory* to mean cannery, a place where tomatoes are put into tin cans. One often hears *cannin'-factory* and even *tomater-factory*.

The noun ballet is pronounced pretty much like ballot; it doesn't mean ballad, but only the written words of a song. "My least boy he wrote out the *ballet* of that song, but he couldn't git it versed off right." The combination *song-ballet* or *song-ballad* is also common.[95] A Little Rock newspaper prints a list of old-time Arkansas words, alleging that *ballad* or *ballard* means recipe,[96] but I have not heard this meaning in the Ozarks.

Careless sometimes means careful, as when a mother warns her child: "Be *keerless* now, that gun's terrible easy on the trigger!" This sort of thing shows up in a few other words. "My old man is so *forgetless* nowadays," a woman told me, "that I cain't trust him to do our tradin' at the store."

The word happen is used rather oddly sometimes. Instead of saying that "Joe *had* a bad accident" or "*suffered* a bad accident" or "*met with* a bad accident," the Ozarker says, "Joe *happened to* a bad accident t'other night." D. S. Crumb long ago reported this usage from southeastern Mis-

---

[92] *American Speech*, Vol. VIII (1933), 51.
[93] Springfield, Mo., *News*, May 7, 1934.
[94] *Dialect Notes*, Vol. III (1907), 230.
[95] Cf. H. M. Belden, *Song-Ballads and Other Popular Poetry Known in Missouri* (Columbia, Mo., 1907), 1.
[96] *Arkansas Gazette*, May 10, 1942.

souri.[97] When the hillman asks, "How in the world happen that?" he means "How in the world did that happen?"

A woman at Anderson, Missouri, was shocked by the news of an atrocious murder. "Jesus Christ!" she cried out. "That feller took a ax an' cut the baby's head off! Why, it's plumb *ridick'lus!*" One often hears ridiculous, as an adjective or an adverb, used to mean shocking or outrageous rather than worthy of ridicule. Carr and Taylor say that in Washington County, Arkansas, ridiculous means "outrageous, indecent."[98]

Some jokers told a foolish boy in our neighborhood that the sheriff had a warrant for his arrest, and just then the officer happened to come along. The boy fled wildly into the woods. "Pore Andy sure did *top the brush* gettin' away from there," said one of the bystanders, who laughed till the tears rolled down his face. To *top the brush* is to leap or run through undergrowth, as a deer does sometimes. The expression *ride the brush* is something else again; it refers to the activities of men engaged in illicit love affairs.[99] The idea is that men on such errands ride through the woods, keeping away from the roads to avoid being seen.

A scorpion, in the Ozarks, is a little blue-tailed lizard (*Eumeces quinquelineatus*), quite harmless.[100] The real scorpion (*Centuroides vittatus*) is called a *stingin'-lizard.*[101]

In some settlements the word democrat has nothing to do with politics, but means an ox yoke or a yoke-like device to prevent a breachy or roguish animal from getting through a fence. I have seen cattle, pigs, and even geese with triangular wooden *democrats* fastened around their necks.

Neck is often used to mean throat. My wife and I entertained some neighbors at a fish fry on a gravel bar, but the evening was spoiled when one of our guests "got a big bone stuck in his *neck.*" In Forsyth, Missouri, a girl told me, "Doc he just put some cotton on a stick, an' swabbed out my *neck.*"

In Taney County, Missouri, the word qualified means aristocratic, belonging to the *quality folks.* In many parts of the Ozark country, *fine-haired* carries the same significance.

Ooze is a noun, which usually means some kind of medicine made by concentrating herb teas or decoctions. *Slippery-ellum ooze,* for example,

---

[97] *Dialect Notes,* Vol. II (1903), 315.
[98] *Dialect Notes,* Vol. III (1907), 235.
[99] Cf. Constance Wagner's novel, *Sycamore,* 139.
[100] *Dialect Notes,* Vol. II (1903), 328.
[101] *Dialect Notes,* Vol. V (1923), 222; *American Speech,* Vol. XI (1936), 317.

is made by macerating the inner bark of the elm in water and then boiling it down to a thick paste.[102] *May-apple ooze,* a violent purgative, is similarly derived from mandrake roots.

The phrase *in a manner* generally means to a certain extent or degree, as when a countryman admits, "Maybe I was *in a manner* drunk."[103] Sometimes it seems to mean nearly, virtually, or almost. "Them biscuit is *in a manner* done," a housewife said, "an' we'll have 'em on the table in a minute."

The Ozark people do not use the word token in its modern sense. In the back hills, a token is an omen or portent of something supernatural, a sign of some impending calamity. When an albino deer was seen near Forsyth, Missouri, in 1939, many of the old folks "figgered it must be a *token.*" Webster gives this meaning as archaic or dialectal.

The noun hazard generally means an animal that breaks through fences, as a breachy cow. Sometimes it is applied to human beings of a wild or unkempt appearance. A woman in Barry County, Missouri, once told me, "Aunt Sula has run through the hills till she looks like an old *hazard.*" Sula earned her living by gathering medicinal herbs and roots and was always pretty dirty.

Most tourists think that pone is cornbread, but to the old-time Ozarker it is often a lump of flesh, a swelling.[104] A woman said of her burned wrist, "I busted the blister, an' next mornin' it turned red, an' now there's a big *pone* round it." Sometimes the word means only a roll of fat: "Paw eats too damn' much. Just look at them *pones* round his middle!" In some cases *pone* refers to muscle as well as fat; I have heard a hillman speak of the big pones on a professional boxer's arms and shoulders.[105] The verb *pone* is less common, but it seems to mean pelt. I once heard a boy say: "I wish we had some good rocks, to *pone* them town fellers with!"

One of the most popular men in a certain settlement was the superintendant of schools, a "furriner" from a northern state. This man's wife was behaving very foolishly, quite without her husband's knowledge. Our town marshal, who belonged to the same lodge, tried to give the schoolman a hint that the wool had been pulled over his eyes. "I told Bob he was *about ready for shearin',*" the officer said, "but it seems like he didn't ketch my meanin'. Ain't it funny how them high-educated fellers cain't understand

[102] Cf. my *Ozark Superstitions,* 92.
[103] *American Speech,* Vol. V (1929), 18.
[104] *Dialect Notes,* Vol. V (1923), 217.
[105] *American Speech,* Vol. XI (1936), 316.

plain English?" Well, I don't know whether it's funny or not, but it certainly is true.

Some of the high-flown "book-words" in the Ozark dialect are archaisms, and many of the unusual meanings attached to ordinary words are very old, too. The reader who is interested in such matters will find related items elsewhere in this book, particularly in Chapter IV and Chapter IX.

8 Sayings and Wisecracks

AMONG THE MOST striking features of the hillman's speech is his habitual use of picturesque comparisons, outlandish metaphors and similes, old sayings and proverbs, cryptic allusions to esoteric mountain lore, and bucolic wisecracks generally. Some of these expressions are very old, used in their old form. Others are changed to fit the current situation, while many are brand new spontaneous creations. Some specimens of this figurative speech may be found in the works of novelists who have written about the Ozarks, such as Rose Wilder Lane, Thames Williamson, and Charles Morrow Wilson. But they have received little attention from serious students of the dialect.

The Ozarker is not content to observe that any object is cold; he likes to say that it's *cold as a witch's tit*, or *a well-digger's ass*, or *a banker's heart*. A dead man, or even one who is merely unconscious, is said to be *cold as a wagon-tire*, or *cold as a pump-handle*, or *cold as a hammer*. One of my neighbors found a sick man in the road near Pineville, Missouri, and in telling of it later he said, "That feller was just a-layin' thar, *cold as a frog*." A friend of mine in Joplin, Missouri, was "knocked *cold as a turnip*" by a policeman with whom he had an altercation. *Cold as a snake* is common everywhere.[1] Served some very poor coffee at a village restaurant, a hillman spat it out upon the floor: "That stuff's *weak as well-water*," he said, "an' *colder'n kraut* besides!"

One often hears such comparisons as *hot as a 'tater, hot as a fire-cracker, hot as a parsnip*, or even *hot as fire in a pepper-mill*. Sometimes these expressions are meant literally, but often they refer to temper or temperament, rather than actual physical temperature. A gambler who says, "I'm *hotter'n a pistol*," means only that he is having a run of luck; to describe a young woman as *hotter'n a pistol* is to say that she is sexually excited,

---

[1] Joseph W. Carr, *Dialect Notes*, Vol. III (1906), 131.

while the same expression applied to an elderly man may mean that he's in a towering rage. A fellow in Stone County, Missouri, said that he was *hot as a run-down goat;* this is a euphemism, I think, and "run-down" isn't really the word. A lady in Galena, Missouri, often used the phrase *hot as a red hen;* I leave it to the reader to guess what she meant by that figure. *Hot as a hen layin' a goose-egg* is another common expression. A lusty young country girl, talking with a boy, seemed a bit amorous; "Lucy's *hot as a red beet* an' pantin' like a lizard," said a disapproving old woman.

In Taney County, Missouri, an aged woodsman was examining a new axehandle; running his fingers along the polished surface, he looked up with a smile and said dreamily, "*Smooth as a schoolmarm's leg!*" Spider Rowland testified that the whiskey made near Fouke, Arkansas, is *smoother than a baby's cheek.*[2] Such expressions as *slick as a lizard, slick as a greased pig,* and *slick as a peeled onion* make sense. But what about *slick as a hound's bottom?*

The Ozarker who wants to describe very rapid movement often says *quick as greased lightnin',* or *quicker'n chain lightnin'.* Several times I have heard *quick as double-geared lightnin',* and once a man told me that something happened *quick as a double streak of greased lightnin'.* When Tom Jeffers' shanty caught fire in the night, a neighbor said, "Tom busted out of that house *quicker'n two gods could skin a minner!*"[3] Another common expression is *quick as a minner could swim a gourd.* Spider Rowland used a variant, *quicker than a minner can swim a dipper.*[4] Near Hot Springs, Arkansas, when a lizard crawled up his pants-leg, an old gentleman "shucked out of them britches *quicker'n a snake goin' through a holler log.*" In the same locality a woman boasted that she could bake a pie "*quicker than you can say God with your mouth open!*"

A farmer in Garland County, Arkansas, once said that a wiry little gambler was *nimble as a weasel;* this figure can only be appreciated by one who has seen weasels in action.

Any creature or process that moves slowly is *slow as an old cow, slow as smoke off'n a manure pile,* or *slower than sorghum at Christmas.*[5] The noun *slow-run* is an old name for molasses,[6] and molasses doesn't flow readily in cold weather. I once heard a politician say, in a public address, that "the Arkansas legislature is *slower than pond-water.*"

[2] *Arkansas Gazette,* Little Rock, September 11, 1948.
[3] Cf. Carr, *Dialect Notes,* Vol. III (1905), 69.
[4] *Arkansas Gazette,* Little Rock, January 26, 1949.
[5] *Arkansas Gazette,* Little Rock, May 3, 1942.
[6] Amos Harlin, *For Here Is My Fortune,* 96–97, 173.

The expression *big as a skinned horse* is common, and it's true that a skinned horse looks pretty big, especially in the moonlight. A man with new false teeth told me, "A raspberry seed under my plate feels *big as a cucklebur.*"

When a man says "this country was *rough as a cow's tongue* in the early days," he means that there was a lot of fighting and hell-raising in the vicinity. Some young men at Protem, Missouri, were said to be *rougher than corncobs.* The expression *tough as a boot* is well known; *tougher than a wood-hauler's boot* is common too, although wood-haulers are shod just like the rest of us. An elderly man in Pineville, Missouri, complained that his beefsteak was *tougher than the law.* A friend tells me that he probably meant "tougher than the law *allows,*" but I'm not sure about this; the old gentleman had "run with the wild bunch" in the Territory when he was young. Maybe he remembered the hard-riding deputy marshals who worked out of Fort Smith under Isaac C. Parker, the "hangin' judge" from Missouri.

A schoolmarm from Blue Eye, Missouri, told me that her pupils were all *meaner than snakes,* and I believe they were, at that. When a man says that something or somebody is *meaner than dockroot,* he refers to the fact that dockroot is tough and difficult to get rid of. *Mean as gar-broth* is common, but here the word signifies no more than poor or inferior, since the hillman feels that gars are unfit for human food.[7] Worn-out land is often said to be *as mean as gar-broth* or *as thin as gar-broth.*[8]

Referring to his own sons, who were always going into Joplin and fighting with the police, a man declared, "Them boys is *mean as their hide will hold!*" This is a pretty strong saying. He meant that it was physically impossible for them to be any more vicious; given size and strength, they would lay waste whole continents. A woman at Picher, Oklahoma, had the same idea of physical limitation in mind when she said, "If Joe ever gets to be a *bigger* liar, he'll have to *put on weight!*"

It is easy to see what is meant by *busy as ants at a picnic* or *busy as a stump-tailed cow in fly-time.* Very common are such comparisons as *busy as a hen with one chicken* and *busy as a goose with nine rectums.* One often hears *busy as a fiddler's elbow,* but it isn't really his elbow that is meant. The greatest newspaper in Arkansas[9] assures us that *busy as a buzz saw in a pine knot* means "really occupied." Many Ozarkers serve as guides

---

[7] *Missouri Conservationist,* September, 1949, p. 6.

[8] *American Speech,* Vol. V (1929), 18.

[9] *Arkansas Gazette,* Little Rock, May 3, 1942.

for city fishermen, and *busy as a guide on a riffle* recalls a johnboat in fast water, with the boatman paddling frantically to keep from crashing on the rocks.

Lively as a tick in a tar-pot and *active as a spider on a hot stove* need no detailed explanation. A farmer fighting bumblebees was said to be *brisk as a chinch on a griddle; chinch* is the old-timer's word for bedbug. *Restless as the tip of a cat's tail* is a common expression meaning nervous or distraught. A man told me that his wife, who had lived through the great tornado at Green Forest, Arkansas, was *jumpy as a pregnant fox in a forest fire* every time she heard the wind whistle at night.

Useless as a one-horned cow seems a rather odd figure, but the hillfolk say that a cow which has only one horn is a nuisance to the cattleman, because it can never mingle with a normal herd. *Useless as brains in a preacher's head* reflects the deplorable skepticism of modern youth. *Useless as tits on a boar hog* is another common expression of futility.

Asked if he thought it was likely to rain, an old man squinted doubtfully at the "clabbered" sky. "This weather is *uncertain as a baby's butt,*" he answered. "You cain't tell *what's* a-comin'."

Ugly as a mud fence is common, though there are very few mud fences in the Ozarks. Joseph W. Carr reported *ugly as a mud fence stuck with tadpoles* from Fayetteville, Arkansas.[10] Mary Elizabeth Mahnkey, of Mincy, Missouri, once mentioned an Indian woman who was *ugly as a rail fence, stake-an'-ridered with tadpoles.* There is a sort of pun in this, since the *riders* on such fences are really *poles.*

"Every one of them Simpson gals is *ugly as a gouge,*" said a lady in Galena, Missouri. The word gouge means a kind of crooked chisel, also a swindler, and I'm not sure just what the lady meant. But I've seen the Simpson girls, and they certainly won't win any beauty contests.

Sharp as a razor and *keen as a briar* are common everywhere, but in the Ozarks one often hears *dull as a frow,* a reference to the tool used in riving out shingles and clapboards. *Duller than a widder-woman's ax* is common also, and needs no explanation. An unsatisfactory knife is *so dull you could ride to mill on it.*[11]

A man who is very much inebriated is said to be *drunker than a fiddler's bitch, drunker than a boiled owl, full as a fall corncrib,* or *drunker than two judges.* In Washington County, Arkansas, people used to say *drunker than Cooter Brown,* but nobody seems to know who Cooter Brown was.

[10] *Dialect Notes,* Vol. III (1905), 99.
[11] *Arkansas Historical Quarterly,* Vol. VI (1947), 124.

Full as a tick[12] and *full as a bullbat in fly-time* are common expressions, but usually mean full of food rather than liquor.

Tighter than Dick's hatband does not refer to drunkenness, but is said of a door or window that is difficult to open, or of anything else that fits very tightly; some hillfolk regard this expression as vulgar, and won't let their children use it. A man in Forsyth, Missouri, told me that "on Sunday everything in this town is shut up *tighter'n a jug*." A stingy man is often said to be *tight as a new boot* or *tight as beeswax*. But when a village woman remarked that her husband was *tighter than two drumheads,* she meant only that he had refused to donate seventy-five cents to the support of a Holy Roller preacher.

If any particular items are very abundant, the hillman says they're *thick as peckerwoods in a deadening;* a deadening is a place where the trees have been killed by girdling but not felled. Peckerwood means woodpecker, but it also means the sort of farmer who "collars" trees in the backwoods, instead of clearing land for his cornpatch. *Thick as crows at a hogkillin'* is pretty common, also *thick as worms in a bait-gourd, thick as whores at a buryin', thick as fleas on a pot-licker,* and *thick as warts on a pickle.* One often hears *thicker than fiddlers in hell,* and sometimes *thicker than Hammons in hell,* though I could never find out who the Hammons were. It has been suggested that Hammon may be a variant pronunciation of Haman,[13] but I'm not satisfied with this explanation.

A very large number or quantity is implied in *more than Carter had oats,* as when a neighbor cried out, "We've got more trouble than Carter had oats!" The back-country newspapers spell Carter with a capital, as if it were a family name.[14] But the Kansas City, Missouri, *Independent* observed that some local nabob "has more money than the most affluent carter ever had oats."[15] In northwest Arkansas one hears *more than Thomas had corn,* and this expression is sometimes seen in the newspapers.[16]

If melons or pumpkins are much more numerous than usual, the hillman says, "We got 'em under the bed," or "there's two for every fence-corner."[17]

---

[12] Cf. *Dialect Notes,* Vol. V (1923), 207.

[13] Cf. Esther 7:10.

[14] *Dialect Notes,* Vol. V (1926), 401.

[15] July 6, 1940, p. 3.

[16] *Arkansas Gazette,* Little Rock, May 3, 1942.

[17] *Missouri Historical Review,* April, 1950, p. 229.

Sayings and Wisecracks

A guest in a backwoods cabin noticed that the table was piled high with fried chicken, vegetables, jellies, and so on, but there was only a very small pat of butter in sight. "Go heavy on the butter, stranger," said the hostess, "we got plenty more down cellar, *in a tea-cup.*"

When a villager remarked that "honest carpenters are *scarce as preachers in paradise,*" the carpenters and even the preachers knew what he meant. Carr heard *scarce as snake's feathers* in Washington County, Arkansas, where he says it means "extremely rare."[18] The hillman who answered a demand for money with the question, "Won't hen's teeth do?" meant that cash was nonexistent at his house. Clink O'Neill, of Day, Missouri, used to quote one of the Bear Creek philosophers: "As long as you got money, it's a plenty; but when it's all gone, it *gits awful scarce.*"

When phrases like *green as grass, green as a gourd,* and *green as goose-dung* are applied to a human being, they mean nothing more than rustic or countrified. At Pineville, Missouri, I heard a member of the Missouri Legislature say that his brother "was *so green you could scrape it off'n him with a cob.*" The phrase *sap-green* means only young and inexperienced; a lady in Springfield, Missouri, remarked: "I was just a *sap-green gal* in them days."[19] Looking at some potted cacti, a woman said to me, "Them things ain't dead, they're *green as pizen!*" The indecorous expression *blue as a possum's cod* is known to almost everybody in the hill country, and a possum's scrotum *is* blue, believe it or not.

Pink as a spanked baby's ass is common, also *red as a gobbler's snout in spring.* Any black object may be described as *black as a kettle in hell* or *black as Coaley's butt.* Coaley is an old-time name for the Devil. In Yell County, Arkansas, children say *black as Coaley's tail,* and a boy from that neighborhood told me that black dogs are usually named Coaley.

A boy in Forsyth, Missouri, was describing a pretty girl from the Bear Creek neighborhood. "Why," he said wonderingly, "her skin's *as white as the inside of a toadstool!*" A young woman at Hollister, Missouri, was said to be *pretty as a new-laid egg.* There is a kind of clean, satisfying symmetry about an egg, and this girl certainly had it. It is not unusual to hear an attractive young girl described as *pretty as a speckled pup* or *pretty as a bug's ear.* These backwoods beauties are often vain, and I remember one who was said to be *proud as a peafowl with two tails.*

A woman once remarked to me that her daughter's boy-friend was *strong as acker fortis;* I learned that *aqua fortis* is an old name for nitric

18 *Dialect Notes,* Vol. III (1905), 93.
19 *American Speech,* Vol. XI (1936), 317.

acid, which the hillfolk mix with grease and quicksilver to cure the itch, but I'm not sure just what sort of a fellow the lady was describing. The phrase *strong as a new rope* may be applied to anything from home-cured tobacco to a belief in the second coming of Christ.

The hillman is not satisfied to say that a woman is elderly, or even old; he generally says that she's *older'n a tree* or even *older than God.* To hear a timid little woman described as *mute as a mouse* seems reasonable enough. *Soft as silk* and *sweet as honeysuckle* are complimentary expressions. But to say that a lady is *sweet as a moss rose* means that she has halitosis or offensive body odors and *stinks worse'n a buzzard roost.*

An expression like *happy as a heifer in the corncrib* seems plain enough, but what about the rural preacher who was said to be *happy as a dead pig in the sunshine?* In the same vein perhaps are these expressions: *safe as a possum in a pie, pleased as a skunk in a churn,* and *calm as a hog on ice.*

When a man is peevish or irritated, but powerless to do anything about it, he is said to be *mad as a coon in a poke.* A vivid picture is presented in the phrase *miserable as a toad under a harrow.* A woman once told me that her husband was *tickled as if he'd found a hair in the butter,* meaning that he was pretty damn' mad about something.

Jack Short, of Galena, Missouri, was talking about a long-haired, bearded fellow who lived near the mouth of Mill Creek. "He's *hairy as a summer groundhog,*" said Uncle Jack, "an' kind of *favors a badger,* too."

One often hears *lazy as a shingle-maker,* though the shingle-makers I have known worked about as hard as the rest of us. *Tedious as fishin' for sun-perch* is full of meaning to a man who has tried this kind of fishing.

A motorist ran over a hound on the highway, and Mary Scott Hair, of Hurley, Missouri, remarked that the dog was *as dead as Pompey.* "And that's pretty dead," she added.

A man in Washington County, Arkansas, was injured by a locomotive, which cut off his leg *clean as a whistle.* Such comparisons as *clean as a June rabbit* and *clean as a hound-dog's tooth* are heard all over the Ozark country. Near Berryville, Arkansas, I heard the expression *clean as Penny's nose,* and it really means clean. A boy washed himself several times before he could pass his mother's inspection, then she said, "Yes, you're *clean as Penny's nose now,* even behind the ears!"

Loose as a goose refers to diarrhea. *Bare as a bird's butt* is understandable, but *naked as a jaybird* is not, since the jay is well feathered. But there are hillfolk who seldom use the word naked without mentioning jaybirds. I heard a man in Joplin, Missouri, describe some city girls in evening

178

dresses, saying: "They're all *naked as jaybirds!*" Guy Kilpatrick makes a British sailor use the expression *naked as a jailbird,*[20] which may or may not have some connection with our Ozark expression. *Naked as a plucked goose* is sometimes heard. *Ragged as a buzzard's ass* does not seem to be grounded in anatomical fact, but it is common all through the Ozark country.

Years ago, in company with a native deer hunter, I came upon a ramshackle frame house, deep in the Arkansas wilderness. It was obvious that nobody had lived there for a long time, but my friend imagined that he saw a wisp of smoke come out of the chimney. Because of this, he insisted upon searching the place while I sat under a tree in the yard. In a few minutes he came out. "Did you find anything?" I asked. "Not a damn' thing," he answered. "It's *empty as a dead man's eyes.*"

Inviting a neighbor to visit her, a woman in Stone County, Missouri, shouted, "Come on over, Lulie, an' stay all night. You're just *as welcome as water.*" Has the reader ever been really thirsty?

Of a lively young woman in Farmington, Arkansas, it was said, "That gal's goin' to hell, *straight as a martin to his gourd.*" One must see the swinging martin houses made of gourds and watch the birds enter them, in order fully to appreciate this comparison.

Near Southwest City, Missouri, a boy was telling me of a trick some village loafers had played on him. "Them fellers put a cucklebur under my saddle," said he, "an' I was *throwed higher'n a kite.*"

An old woodsman, reminiscing vaguely about some great adventure of his youth, remarked by way of introduction, "The snow was *deeper than the world* that winter."

Many lengthy items are compared to well ropes. I have heard automobiles, sermons, police records, lizards' tails, and even the beard of a wild turkey gobbler characterized as *long as a well rope.* This is understandable in a village where nearly every house has a "dug well" near the door, and the water must be pulled up by main strength. One has no idea how long a well rope can be until he draws a few buckets of water.

Such figures are extraordinarily numerous in ordinary backwoods conversation. During a two-day float trip near Noel, Missouri, in the early nineteen thirties, I heard the following: *calm as a cucumber, cool as a cucumber, freckled as a turkey egg, sour as owl droppin's, crooked as a dog's hind leg, crooked as a barrel of snakes, easy as shootin' fish in a rain barrel, fine as frog hair, healthy as a alligator, poor as buzzard dung,* and *dry as a*

[20] *Saturday Evening Post,* March 10, 1945, p. 64.

fish-hawk's nest, also twelve other similes which cannot be printed in this book.

Many an Ozarker fortifies a wild statement with one of these phrases: *sure as I'm a-standin' here, sure as I live an' breathe, sure as you're born, sure as God made little apples, sure as a goose goes barefooted, sure as a dead man stinks, sure as snakes crawl, sure as a gun's iron,* or *sure as a wagon-wheel's round.* Such expressions serve as mild oaths. "The Goddamn' Republicans is a-goin' to grab everything," said a man in Hot Springs, Arkansas, "just *as sure as meat'll fry!*"

An extraordinary woman in southwest Missouri had just died, and I was talking with an old-timer who had known her well. "When I heerd Lucy was dead, I felt plumb turrible," he said slowly. "It was just *like stoppin' runnin' water.*"

A big overgrown boy upset something every time he came into the house and invariably left the door open behind him, no matter what sort of weather we were having. "Tommy acts *like he was raised in a sawmill,*" his mother said. One often hears *raised in a barn* or *raised in a hog-lot* used with the same meaning.

A fat little man with a square head and no neck worth mentioning was under discussion. "He looks *like a young jug with a cork in it,*" said a sharp-tongued old woman.

When the biggest barn in our village seemed to be endangered by a grass fire, an old-timer cried out, "Folks, if that barn ketches, it'll *make hell look like a lightnin'-bug!*"

Of a cowed, ragged little man one of my neighbors said, "He looks *like the dogs had him under the house.*" A poor fellow appeared with his clothes torn and his face all bloody and was greeted with: "Howdy, Walt. You look *like you been a-sortin' wildcats.*" Asked how he felt the day after a big celebration, a bedraggled farmer in Eureka Springs, Arkansas, answered: "I feel *like a bobcat that's been drug tail-first through a briar-patch.*" Another very untidy chap was said to "look *like he'd been chawin' terbacker, an' spittin' ag'in the wind.*" A man who looks *like he'd been chawed up an' spit out* is disheveled, to put it mildly.

A farmer in Washington County, Arkansas, was describing his hired man: "Pete always walks *like he was belly-deep in cold water,*" a crack which described the man's gait perfectly. A woman in Springfield, Missouri, was said to "strut *like she had a corncob between her legs.*" A Little Rock newspaper describes a citizen of Miller County, Arkansas, as "a big

[21] *Arkansas Gazette,* Little Rock, September 11, 1948.

double-jointed guy, who walked *like he had a pumpkin* under each arm."[21] One also hears "he walks *like he was comin' through brush*" and "he was steppin' out *like a chicken in high oats.*" A man at Old Linn Creek, Missouri, was said to "dodder along *like a hen with a busted lay-bag.*" To indicate greater speed one says "he was runnin' *like a striped-assed ape,*" or "he passed us *like a bat out of hell,*" or "he come through town *like a canebrake afire.*"

Once a crowd of young horsemen galloped past our house on Christmas Eve, yelling and firing their pistols in the air. "They was runnin' *like the mill-tails of hell,*" said a man who sat beside me on our little porch. I don't know just what this means, but it struck me as a very effective figure at the time.[22]

A lanky farmer blundered into a yellow jackets' nest, and got several stings. His wife saw him "cavortin' around" down by the gate, but couldn't make out what was wrong. "He was actin' *like a windmill gone to the bad,*" she said later.

Judge Tom Moore, of Christian County, Missouri, refers to someone "staggering around *like a buckeyed calf,*" meaning an animal which has been poisoned by eating buckeyes.[23]

When a big truck plunged off the highway near our cabin, an eyewitness testified that "it busted through that five-rail fence *like a bull through a cobweb.*"

Sleeping in a tumble-down shanty, we found our blankets covered with snow one morning. "Jesus Christ!" a lady exclaimed, "the wind blows through this house *like a Goddamn' corncrib!*"

At Noel, Missouri, an armed man believed to be Matt Kimes, the Oklahoma desperado, frightened some tourists at a dance hall. "Them city folks was a-millin' round *like bees fixin' to swarm,*" a local peace officer told me next morning.

A backwoods dandy in Benton County, Arkansas, a handsome young fellow whose mustache was "curled to a barber's fancy," said complacently, "Them Bear Holler gals is a-chasin' me *like pigs after a punkin!*" Speaking of a popular young widow who frequented the taverns along the highway, an old woman said, "The boys follers that gal *like buzzards after a gut-wagon.*" Of another young widow who seemed anxious to marry our hired man, it was said that she "jumped on pore Tommy *like a duck on a June bug.*"

[22] Cf. *Dialect Notes*, Vol. V (1923), 214.
[23] *Mysterious Tales and Legends of the Ozarks*, 71.

A farmer near Pineville was bragging about "the best damn' tree-dog that ever sung on a trail." Some of the villagers seemed a bit skeptical, and the dog's owner looked around indignantly. "Why," he cried, "everybody knows old Bugler can smell out possums *like a horse-jockey can smell women!*"

In Boone County, Arkansas, a barefoot, bewhiskered young farmer said to his sweetheart, "The days when I don't git to see you are plumb squandered away an' lost, *like beads off'n a string.*"

Another young man in our town was complaining about his unrequited love. "I've *sot up till chicken-crow* with that gal," he said, "but it was just *time throwed away.*"

When a country boy wanted to marry the banker's daughter, he encountered considerable opposition. "By God, I'll *wade knee-deep in blood,* an' nobody cain't stop me!" he shouted. "I'll git that gal if I have to *tear the stars out of heaven!*"

Of a gabbling old woman in Poplar Bluff, Missouri, it was said that "her tongue is always a-waggin' *like the south end of a goose.*" A fragile little man with a deep voice was nicknamed Bumbler, and a neighbor explained that "whenever he talks, it sounds *like a bumblebee in a dry gourd.*" A farmer once told me that his wife "was a-singin' *like a hen fixin' to lay,*" a reference to the smugness and complacency that sometimes goes with pregnancy. May Kennedy McCord, of Springfield, Missouri, once remarked that a certain woman "looked *like she was fixin' to eat mush out of a churn,*" but I'm not sure just what Mrs. McCord meant.

To say that a woman "has got *a head like Collins' ram*" is an intimation that she's pretty stubborn. But who Collins was, or how his ram differed from other rams, I have been unable to find out.

Such a sentence as "Paw was a-yowlin' *like a painter with a sore foot*" is clear enough, if you remember that *painter* is the old-time pronunciation of panther. A farmer, returning home after a prolonged drunk in Joplin, was greeted with: "My God, you look *like a sick dog with a thorn in his foot!*" I knew a shabby little man in Rogers, Arkansas, who always looked *like the hindquarters of bad luck.* Paul G. Brewster found the same expression in Columbia, Missouri, applied to "a seedy or slovenly dressed person."[24]

Of a restless, amorous young hillman it was said, "Tom he just goes a-roamin' round *like a bug on a hot night.*"

A farmer in southwest Missouri was captured by the notorious Bar-

[24] *American Speech*, Vol. XVI (1941), 23.

row brothers and forced at pistol's point to act as a guide in helping the outlaws elude the state troopers. Later on, when the officers asked for a description of Clyde Barrow, the man answered earnestly, "He looked *like the Devil, redhot from home!*" A little boy who stumbled upon a bobcat snarling in a steel trap used a similar expression, saying that the varmint looked *like the Devil afore day!*

A man near Little Rock had a very large front yard. It was quite a task to keep the grass properly trimmed, even with a gasoline-powered mower. He was thinking of buying a few sheep, and letting them take over the lawn. "Sheep is a lot of trouble," an old farmer advised him. "They got to be took care of *like a preacher in pore health.*"

When a man said that a certain woman had *legs like a churn dasher,* I think he meant that the ankles were too thick and the calves not properly tapered. I saw the legs in question, and they looked like twin stovepipes.

A fat woman from Neosho, Missouri, is said to be *pooched out like a cat full of kittens,* although she's far too old for pregnancy. Of this same woman I heard people say, "she's got a gut on her *like a rain barrel,*" and, "her belly sticks out *like a fifer's eye.*" It is true that she "loomed up *like a backhouse in a fog.*" The old girl appeared in the village one day dressed up *like a sore thumb,* with a conspicuous, wide metal-colored belt round her middle. "Gertrude would *favor a barrel,*" said one of the town loafers, "if we could git a few more hoops onto her." All these cracks refer to a fat, clumsy figure, but to say that a woman "swelled up *like a pizened pup*" means only that she showed signs of anger.

The phrase *out like Lottie's eye* seems to mean defeat or extinction. If you knock a man senseless, he is said to be *out like Lottie's eye,* but the expression may also be applied to a flashlight which does not function. And once, after an election in Benton County, Arkansas, I heard a man announce happily that the Republican Party was *out like Lottie's eye.*

I have heard *wrinkled like Nellie's apron* used to describe a warped roof. There is a riffle on White River that is known as *Nellie's Apron;* an old story relates that a girl named Nellie was drowned and her apron was found in an eddy, but I am not sure that this explains the saying.[25] "Riffles are rapids, and eddies (whatever lexicographers may have to say) are the quiet stretches in between," explains W. A. Dorrance.[26]

After a tornado struck his cottage at Green Forest, Arkansas, a man said grimly, "What's left of my house looks *like the runnin'-gears of a*

[25] *Dialect Notes,* Vol. III (1909), 402.
[26] *Three Ozark Streams,* 13–14.

hawk's nest." When an airplane crashed and burned, my neighbor viewed the wreckage. "It looks *like the runnin'-gears of a grasshopper,*" said he.[27] This reminds me of a woman at Neosho, Missouri, who remarked that her small son had devoured a whole pie, "all except the *runnin'-gears.*" She meant that he had eaten everything but the bottom crust.

A young girl idly drew her fingernails along the bark of a sapling, as she chatted with her lover at the gate. "Nancy's a-sharpenin' her claws, *like a cat a-courtin',*" cried an old woman who was watching from inside the cabin.

A country boy, fuddled by too much applejack, burst into a neighbor's cabin by mistake; an old woman described the incident by saying that "Tom Hopper *blowed in like a storm,* an' them fool gals all hollered *like whores at a camp meetin'.*" Another witness pointed out, in Tom's defense, that he was "lit up *like a church-house,* so drunk he didn't know which from t'other."

A horse-trader of my acquaintance generally wore high-heeled boots, but had put on shoes with his Sunday suit to attend a funeral. "These here little shoes is a-killin' me," he whispered, "an' they *squeak like a new saddle* besides."

One of our friends was a rather quiet man, and his wife criticized him for "settin' there *like a bump on a log.*" A nervous chap "bats his eyes *like a frog eatin' fire*" or "blinks *like a toad in a hail-storm.*" An aged Indian has strangely brilliant eyes, which were described as "snappin' *like a terrapin's in a high wind.*"

The chief witness in a murder trial seemed very nervous, and the sheriff remarked: "Nellie is a-squirmin' round *like a worm in hot ashes.*" A man in similar case might be "sweatin' *like a bound boy at a corn-shuckin'*" or "*shakin' like a heifer with her first calf.*" I once saw a country boy so frightened that "his teeth was a-rattlin' *like a hog eatin' charcoal.*" I am told that swine really do eat charcoal on occasion, or even bituminous coal.

A lively young woman at Harrison, Arkansas, was described as "bouncin' round *like she had a briar in her tail.*" Of a man who sat dozing in a barber's chair until a pistol was discharged behind him, it was said that "Charley come out of that chair *like he had springs on his butt.*"

Once I was talking with a man in Boone County, Arkansas, and was called away suddenly in the midst of an earnest discussion of something-or-other. "I didn't know you was goin' to be snatched away *like the handle off'n a jug,*" he said peevishly.

[27] Cf. Paul G. Brewster, *American Speech,* Vol. XVI (1941), 24.

Workin' like a nigger means working very hard, and it seems odd that *workin' like a tow-head* carries exactly the same meaning. My landlady in Hot Springs, Arkansas, always cleans house *like she was a-fightin' fire,* which means fast and furiously; "she don't stop for wood, water, or coal," a neighbor said admiringly, using a figure doubtless borrowed from the railroaders. "Tom shucks corn *like he was a-killin' snakes*" has the same significance as the fire-fightin' simile.

Discussing a backwoods ruffian who used to break up religious meetings, I was told that "he run right into the church-house, *a-yellin' like a Comanche* an' a-pootin' *like a stud-horse!*"

"Listen, Paw," cried a high school student in northwest Arkansas, "that schoolmarm hates me *like a hog hates cholery,* an' that's how-come I cain't git no good grades." Another schoolboy said "it was a-rainin' *like all hickory,*" as an excuse for his absence the previous day.

When a teacher told a hillman that his son was always fighting the other pupils, the man said, "Well, I don't aim to have Bill a-settin' round *like Polly in the Primer,*" meaning that he didn't want the boy to be a sissy.

The expression *Ned in the First Reader* apparently carries a slightly different meaning than *Polly in the Primer.* A back-country newspaper commented editorially that President Truman "displays an ineptness that makes him look *like Ned in the first reader.*"[28]

"Our jail won't hold them fellers," said a sheriff of two notorious criminals. "We throwed 'em in once, but they busted out *like the bold hives.*" The bold hives is a skin disease which appears suddenly and is said to be nearly always fatal. The doctors all agree that there is no such ailment, but you'll find elderly people in every backwoods village who believe in it.[29]

One of my neighbors tried to keep his grown son on the farm, but the young man spent most of his time in the bars and dance halls around Joplin. "My boy sticks to them honkytonks *like a lean tick to a fat kitten,*" said the father. A woman once told me, "Jeff he sets up to that gal *like a sick kitten to a jam rock,*" a jam rock being the upright stone at each side of a fireplace.[30]

A drill sergeant at Camp Pike, Arkansas, admitted his inability to teach a certain rookie the manual of arms. "That feller's got four thumbs

[28] *Stone County News-Oracle,* Galena, Mo., March 5, 1948.
[29] Cf. my *Ozark Superstitions,* 111–12.
[30] *Dialect Notes,* Vol. V (1927), 475.

an' two left feet," he cried; "it's just *like poundin' sand in a rat-hole* to learn the damn' fool anything."[31] The expression *"just like chasin' a chigger round a stump"* may be used with regard to any fruitless endeavor. "Lizzie just looked at me *like I was dirt on a stick,*" said a rejected suitor in Pineville, Missouri.

"Jim Tuttle sure is a smart feller," said one of my neighbors. "Smart!" cried another, "smart where the hair slipped!" When I remarked that Jane was "a sweet little girl," an old woman laughed derisively. "Sweet!" she cackled, "sweet *like skippers in the bacon!*" The same woman said of a squat, repulsive-looking stranger, "That feller looks *like he was marked for a hog,*" meaning that the man's mother must have been frightened by swine before he was born.

One of our young men grabbed a pretty schoolteacher and tried to "wrastle her down," but she kicked him in the stomach and knocked the wind plumb out of him. "That schoolmarm like to a ruined me," he complained to me later. "I just stood thar with my mouth open, *like a widder-woman's pig!*"

Tantalized by a provocative but recalcitrant young woman, a hillman suddenly burst out, "I cain't stand no more o' this! It's *like smellin' whiskey through a jail-house winder!*"

A woman addressed her big lubberly son, whose "heart was plumb broke" over a disastrous love affair. "What do you aim to do now, Delbert?" she asked. "Just go meanderin' round *like a lost goose?*" If you have ever listened to a wild goose, separated from the flock and calling forlornly in the night, you'll see the beauty of this figure.

After a terrific row with his wife, a hillman said: "Everything will be all right in the mornin'. Bessie sleeps *like a goose.*" He meant that she would forget the whole episode. There is a widespread notion that geese begin life anew at every sunrise, remembering nothing of other days.

Some of the most striking comparisons are not appreciated by outsiders. In the summer of 1939 a drunk tried to break out of the jail at Galena, Missouri. He got one foot caught in the bars at the top of a door and hung head downwards, yelling for help. The officer who released the man from his predicament told me about it. "That boy's free leg," he said, "was wavin' round in a circle, *like a coon's tail when its neck's broke.*" This figure is very vivid to a coon hunter, because a coon with a broken neck invariably swings its tail in circles.

Down around Fayetteville, Arkansas, one often hears that somebody

[31] Cf. *Dialect Notes,* Vol. V (1923), 219.

is "actin' *like a fool on the door rock.*" A door rock is the flat stone which serves as a doorstep. The significance of this expression was not clear to me. "Does it mean that he's making a fool of himself?" I asked an old friend. "No," was the answer, "it means that he's bein' a fool a-purpose. He's just a-prankin' around pretendin' to be a fool, but he knows better all the time." I thought about this for a moment. "But what's the *door-rock* got to do with it?" I asked. "Oh hell, I don't know," my friend replied. "It's just one of them old sayin's."

Discussing a difficult and hazardous enterprise, a man told me, "It's just as *easy as puttin' butter up a wildcat's ass with a hot awl!*" Another chap in a similar situation cried out, "I'd just as soon *shin up a thorn tree with a armload of eels!*" Referring to some ticklish political maneuver, a Missouri congressman said, "It's a good deal *like climbin' a greased pole with two baskets of eggs.*"

An aged man in our neighborhood was horrified when his daughter asked him to join the Methodists. "Baptize me in *that* church?" he cried. "Why, I'd sooner look for Christian love in a tannery!"

Another hillman, offered highly paid work in the zinc mines near Joplin, refused to consider it. "I don't want no such a job as that," said he. "I'd ruther be in hell with my back broke!"

A poor chap in Taney County, Missouri, was too proud to accept "charity" from the federal relief agency. "I'd sooner get me a tin bill," he declared, "an' pick manure with the chickens!" The fellow used a shorter word than *manure,* but that's what he meant.

When an old-timer says bread, he means fresh cornbread or hot biscuits. "I'd sooner eat a wasp-nest," growled an elderly woodsman, when he was offered some ordinary bread from a city bakery. "I'd just as soon let the moon shine in my mouth, as to eat light-bread," spoke up another hillman. After a long silence, an old man said thoughtfully: "Well, light-bread's better than nothin'. *I've tried both.*"

An Ozarker who doesn't like cornbread is said to have *gone back on his raisin',* which is almost as bad as denying one's kinfolks. An Arkansas governor, at a public dinner, was admonished, "Don't go back on your raisin', Governor!" Whereupon the Governor grinned, dropped the roll he had selected, and took a corn muffin instead.

A young bride, exasperated by some ineptness on her husband's part, suddenly cried out to the entire household, "Jake don't know no more about lovin' than a dead horse does about Sunday!" This happened many years ago, but it is still told with delight by members of the family, including the bride's children and grandchildren.

187

Related perhaps is the saying that "he ain't got no more use for a wife than a toad has for spit-curls," and "you don't need a car no more than a tomcat needs marriage-license." A man said to me, "We ain't got no more use for a stove than a hog has for a side-saddle, but my woman keeps a-hollerin' about it, so I reckon I'll have to buy one."

A country boy from Oklahoma appeared in Fort Smith, Arkansas, dressed in cowpuncher clothes and saying that he was a professional bronc rider. "That feller?" sneered a local horseman. "Why, he couldn't *carry a bridle down the street!*" Another man who claimed to be a champion rifle shot was greeted with: "Him? Why, he couldn't *hit a bull in the rump with a fiddle!*" In McDonald County, Missouri, there was a yokel who had inherited some tools and set up as an expert gunsmith. "Him a gunsmith!" laughed one of the old-timers. "Why, that feller wouldn't *make a scab on a gunsmith's ass!*" The same idea is expressed in "he couldn't even *hold a light for a gunsmith!*" Another example of this sort of thing was directed at a barber in Siloam Springs, Arkansas. "That feller a barber? Hell, he couldn't *roach a mule for me!*" Of an Indian athlete who wanted to run at the county fair it was said: "Win the race? That feller? Why, he'll *be lucky to come in last!*"

Referring to any noisy but unprofitable enterprise, a hillman may remark, "Seems like there's *more holler than wool,* as the feller said when he sheared the pig."

I once heard a young farmer answer some derisive criticism with: "Well, tell me where to go, as the bullet says to the trigger."

Another old sayin' is "A gun's dangerous without lock, stock nor barr'l, as the boy said when his Pappy give him a lickin' with the ramrod."

"My son-in-law is so lazy," grumbled a man at Reeds Spring, Missouri, "that he stops plowin' to poot!" Another loafer said, "My brother is so unlucky, it would be money in his pocket if he'd never been born!" W. A. Dorrance reports a swift change in the weather. "A week ago," said he, "it was so cold that the wolves were *eating sheep just for the wool.*"[32] Enraged by some fancied slight, a young farmer in Stone County, Missouri, cried out: "Why, I'll kick that feller so high that the bluebirds'll nest in him!" I think this last crack has been bowdlerized a little.

A fellow in Baxter County, Arkansas, professed an enormous dislike for the Robinson family. "Hell is so full of Robinsons," said he, "that you can *see their feet stickin' out the winders.*"

"That man is so contrary," a woman told me, "that if you throwed

[32] *We're From Missouri,* 44.

him in the river he'd float upstream!" I have heard of a Missouri house-wife who was "so ugly that she had to *blindfold the baby before it would suck.*"

Speaking of some wartime beef, a hillman said, "It was so tough you *couldn't stick a fork in the gravy.*"[33] Related to this perhaps is the tale of a toddy *so strong that it couldn't be sweetened;* when a man tried to stir in some sugar, he bent the spoon double an' busted the cup!

A White River guide near Cotter, Arkansas, said he was so poor he couldn't buy worms for a sick hen, or hay for a nightmare. A gardener told me that "the soil down here is so triflin', you cain't hardly rust a nail in it." A man from Granby, Missouri, spoke of a farm *so infertile that two red-headed women couldn't raise a ruckus there.*[34]

A blacksmith in McDonald County, Missouri, got *so drunk that he couldn't find his own mouth without a leadin' string.* There are many of these fantastic descriptions of drunkenness. "I was so damn' dizzy," an-other poor inebriate told me, "that I had to hold on to the grass before I could lean ag'in the ground!"

A boy who offered to guide me through the White River bottoms near Calico Rock, Arkansas, suddenly realized that we were hopelessly lost. "These roads is so Goddamn' crooked," he said, "that a feller cain't tell if he's goin' somewheres or comin' back home."

E. E. Dale tells of a horse that was *"so pore you had to tie a knot in his tail to keep him from slippin' through the collar."*[35]

"The brush in that holler is so thick you cain't cock a pistol" is only a slight exaggeration. "Why, there ain't room enough to cuss a cat without gettin' ha'r in your mouth!"

In telling a long-winded ghost story an old woman said, "It was so still you could have heerd a cricket cl'ar his throat."

Just after a great electrical storm we found a drunk lying in the muddy road. "I don't know if I was lightnin'-struck or not," said he. "After the mare throwed me, I got so bumfuzzled I couldn't tell wet from windy."

Clink O'Neill, of Taney County, Missouri, quotes one of his neigh-bors who remarked, "There's so many chiggers here, that a *tick-bite* is kind of a enjoyment."

A little boy near Harrison, Arkansas, told me soberly that "the butter-milk got so sour it et a hole in the crock, an' all leaked out, an' that's how-come we ain't got no buttermilk."

[33] Cf. *Arkansas Historical Quarterly,* Vol. VI (1947), 123.
[34] Cf. my *We Always Lie to Strangers* (New York, 1951), 23–24.
[35] *Arkansas Historical Quarterly,* Vol. VI (1947), 125.

A dying woman in Crane, Missouri, smiled a little when some fool inquired about her health. "I'm so weak," she gasped, "I couldn't holler *sooey* if the hogs had me down."

In Barry County, Missouri, a horseman was complaining about a mudhole in the public road. "My mare got stuck," said he. "She sunk down so deep we couldn't git a jack under her."

Talking about a visitor from the North, a woman marveled at his capacity for victuals. "That feller eats so much," she said, "it keeps him skinny just a-carryin' the weight around." There was another fellow who had once been *so fat you couldn't see his eyes*, but was now *so skinny you could shade his butt with a match*. He attributed the change to his diet, since he lived almost exclusively on cornbread and hominy. "I've et so much corn," he told me, "that the tumblebugs have to shuck my dung!"

A certain kind of applejack made near Caverna, Missouri, was said to be *crystal clear, water white, simon pure, double run an' three times twisted.* The stuff was pretty strong. "That liquor is *so hot the sheriff himself cain't drink it,*" a bootlegger told me, and there was something like awe in his voice.

A man at Eureka Springs, Arkansas, was grumbling about the heavy rains, which had made a quagmire of the road in front of his house. "Even my lane," said he, "is so Goddamn' muddy it would bog down a snipe!" Anyone who has watched snipe negotiate mudholes can appreciate this expression. I have heard also of a field which got *so muddy it would bog a buzzard's shadow.*[36]

An angler from Kansas City asked if Greasy Creek was clear enough for fly-fishing. "Hell no," a farmer told him, "the water's so muddy you could track a coon right down the middle of the creek!"

Of a boy who had caught a skunk, it was said, "Lester smelled so bad that folks thought he was the cholery a-comin'."

A man in Seneca, Missouri, is said to be *so stingy he's afeared to set down.* He just stands on one foot and leans ag'in a post, to save the seat of his britches.

There are tales of a woman in Pineville, Missouri, who "walks so damn' slow that they have to set stakes to see if she's a-movin'."[37] One of the lady's neighbors said mildly, "Leony will never get the itch," meaning that she was too slow to catch anything, even an infectious disease.

"It's so dark in Wolf-Pen Holler," an old man assured me, "that the

[36] *Arkansas Historical Quarterly,* Vol. VI (1947), 124.
[37] Cf. *Dialect Notes,* Vol. V (1923), 220.

foxes ketch chickens at high noon, and the big owls hoot all day, and you can see lightnin'-bugs any time." I was told that on Roark Creek, in Taney County, Missouri, the country is *so wild they use wolves for watchdogs, an' the whoop-owls cross with the chickens.* A man near Hot Springs, Arkansas, said that "things is so disorderly out our way that we roof the cabins with bull-hides, an' use the tails for lightin'-rods."

A politician declared that "the boys down in my district are *so tough that the sheriff has to hire a bodyguard.*" I told this man I'd like to visit his county seat, but he said it was quite impossible. "The roads is so damn' steep," said he, "that you couldn't get over the mountain if you was ridin' a turpentined wildcat!"[38]

A fox-faced newspaperman in Springfield, Missouri, was described as *sharp enough to stick in the ground, an' green enough to grow.* One often hears that somebody is *mad enough to butt stumps* or *mean enough to bite himself.*

Of some adolescent boys it was said, "They're gittin' *big enough to kick up dust,* an' *drag one wing at a grass widder.*" One young fellow, it was said, "has took up *bellerin' an' pawin' dust* round the Widder Lee's place."

A man asked me how a certain young woman earned her living; I answered that I thought perhaps she was a waitress. "A waitress!" he cried. "Why, she ain't got manners enough to carry guts to a bear!" A boy in our neighborhood was rather stupid, and his own father said, "Allen is a good boy, but he don't know enough to drive pigeons to roost." There is an old saying about a fellow who *ain't got sense enough to poke acorns down a peckerwood hole.*[39] Of a certain prolific bachelor it was said, "Jim's daddied kids enough to start a school, an' he aint but twenty-two year old."[40]

In a little roadside café a truck driver complained loudly about the coffee. "Good God!" he shouted. "It's *too strong to tan bullhides!*" That was his way of saying the coffee was very weak. "Some folks don't realize," he said later, "that it don't take much water to make coffee."[41]

After an election in Benton County, Arkansas, a prominent citizen told his neighbors, "The Republican party is *too dead to skin.*"

Near Pineville, Missouri, there used to live a farmer almost seven

---

[38] Cf. my *We Always Lie to Strangers,* 21.
[39] Cf. *Dialect Notes,* Vol. V (1923), 219.
[40] Cf. Wentworth, *American Dialect Dictionary,* 153.
[41] Cf. *Arkansas Historical Quarterly,* Vol. VI (1947), 124.

feet tall. "Bob's kind of a awk'ard size," remarked a village loafer. "He's too big for a man, an' not big enough for a horse."

A man near Walnut Shade, Missouri, became violently insane, but because of some legal mix-up he was refused admittance to the state asylum. "Them doctors wouldn't let Floyd in," a neighbor said soberly, "on account he was *too crazy.*"

In Benton County, Arkansas, a farmer was denouncing the President of the United States. "As for that man Hoover," he shouted, "I think he's *the little end of nothin'.*" A lady in Blue Eye, Missouri, carried this figure even further when she spoke disparagingly of her estranged husband. "That there *thing,*" she said, "is smaller than the little end of nothin', *whittled down to a p'int!*"

"My man's always a-braggin' about his kinfolks," a woman told me, "but the truth is, they *don't amount to a poot in a whirlwind!*"[42] She meant that his was an insignificant, *one-gallus family,* described as *small 'taters an' few in a hill.*

A person, a garment, or even a house that looks worn and soiled is said to have *went through the soap kettle.* When my neighbor said "that Paisley gal *ain't fit for soap grease,*" he meant that she was altogether worthless; soft soap is made of waste fat which can't be used for anything else.

A gentleman in Washington County, Arkansas, was known for his invincible stupidity; it was said that "poor Charley was *behind the door when the brains was passed out.*" Of some children who had misbehaved, a woman remarked, "Them young-uns was *under the porch when they passed the manners.*" A preacher who couldn't sing explained, "I wasn't here the night they *passed the tune around.*" Speaking of a man who sang very badly, a woman said, "He orter have *a poke to carry the tune in.*" One sometimes hears, "He couldn't carry a tune in a basket with three handles!" I tried to sing a ballad one night at Farmington, Arkansas, and Lon Jordan said: "That tune sounds like you been *carryin' it on a shovel.*" Another bit of musical criticism is: "It sounds like the hogs must have got into that feller's tune-patch." Governor Jeff Davis of Arkansas once declared, "I cain't sing. I ruined my voice *a-hollerin' for gravy when I was a young-un.*"

There are numerous general statements, which I suppose might be called maxims or proverbs. One often hears hillfolk remark that *a short horse is soon curried.* My wife quoted this once as she cooked breakfast,

[42] *Dialect Notes,* Vol. V (1926), 402.

meaning that since we had little food, it wouldn't require much time to prepare it.

Of a disgraceful political incident in Joplin, a prominent citizen wrote: "We'd like to quit thinking about it for awhile, but we'll not forget it. *A dead skunk still stinks.*"

The significance of *no use cryin' after the jug's busted* and *old sins throw long shadows* does not require any explanation. *Little pitchers have big ears* is a warning not to talk of secret matters before children.

Such adages as *cat looks big till dog shows up* and *a squeakin' wheel gets the grease* are common everywhere. Congressman Dewey Short of Missouri stated his creed in a political speech: "I believe in putting the grease where the squeak's loudest." The Ozarker generally says *mouse in the meal* where an Easterner would use *fly in the ointment.* One often hears *there's two sides to every flapjack,* meaning that there are two ways of looking at any question. *There's another verse to that song* means "you haven't got all the facts; there's more to the story than you've been told." One of my old friends used to say *any pig will squeal when the Devil turns barber,* but the meaning of this is not clear to me.

A very unattractive girl in our village married a peddler. "There's never a goose so gray that she cain't find a gander," said one of the local granny-women. *Even a poor jug don't long lack a stopper* is another common saying, applied to aged or ugly women who succeed in getting husbands. An old settler named Rice quotes a variant: "No matter how battered a skillet is, *you can always find a lid to fit it.*"[43]

Advocating soft answers and inaction rather than violence, a woman said, "No use to fan fire."

When his friends congratulated him on a very successful business deal, a hillman answered modestly, "Even a blind hog will find an acorn once in a while."

Trying to seduce a married woman, one of our neighbors argued: "What's the difference? A slice off'n a cut loaf won't never be missed!"

A peddler of "herb remedies" used a different sales talk for newly married folk than for elderly people with large families. I asked him about this. "Well," he said, grinning, "you cain't run all the squirrels up the same tree."

It takes gizzard an' guts to get along in this world is a common saying. Another one is *still water runs deep, an' the Devil lays at the bottom.*

Several times I have heard *two wrongs never make a right, but maybe*

[43] *Arcadian Life,* Caddo Gap, Ark., March, 1936, p. 3.

three will. This crack has a strangely modern sound and may have been brought into the hill country in comparatively recent years.

It don't take no big bone to choke a cow means that small things can do a lot of damage.

There's a little rhyme that is often quoted as a kind of proverb:

> *A feller that's rich can ride a-straddle,*
> *But them that's pore must tote their saddle.*

The word *saddle* here means buttocks, just as the edible parts of bullfrogs are called "frog-saddles." The familiar welcome, "Light down an' *cool your saddle,*" is addressed to pedestrians and motorists as well as to *horse-backers.*

The old saying *there's a squirrel in the tree somewhere* means that something important is concealed; *look for a bug under a chip* has the same significance.

When an Ozarker says, "There must be somethin' dead up the branch," his meaning is roughly equivalent to "there's something rotten in Denmark."

Fred High, who lives near Berryville, Arkansas, used to quote an ancient saying: "This world is a goose, and *them that do not pick will get no feathers.*"[44]

A neighbor had a lot of trouble with his young son, who had several times been thrown into jail for some petty crime or other. When the boy announced that he wanted to leave home, an old friend of the family said, "They might as well turn Charley loose. *You cain't keep a squirrel on the ground.*"

The hillman who says, "I'll make a spoon or spoil a horn," means that he intends to take a long chance, to kill or cure, to put all his eggs in one basket.

The Methodists in our town staged a baby show to raise money for the church, offering a handsome prize for the prettiest baby. Meely Short's bald-headed infant lost to another child who had a lot of fine curly hair. *"Long hair, scrub stock,* is what my Pappy always said," sniffed Aunt Meely.

A woman in Pineville, Missouri, cried out in a moment of exasperation, "I sure *drove my ducks to a pore puddle!*" meaning that she had made a bad marriage, since her husband was a drunken idler who did not sup-

[44] *Forty-Three Years for Uncle Sam* (Berryville, Ark., 1949), 21.

port her. Of a similar case in Conway, Arkansas, I heard a man say: "Nancy sure *let her skimmer leak* when she married that feller from Little Rock."

A man named Price butchered an old boar, and the beast had a strong, rank odor. "You could smell the meat half-a-mile off," a young loafer said. "Yes," answered another, "an' *his two biggest gals got married that same week.*" Both men spoke in a sober, deadpan fashion, but everybody within hearing was delighted. This kind of insinuation gets a great laugh from any backwoods audience.

A girl in our neighborhood made a bad marriage, against her parents' advice. A few months later she wanted to call it quits and return to her old home. "No," said the girl's father, "you just go back to your man, an' *set on the blister.*" A local character got drunk at the county fair and traded his saddle mare for a decrepit mule and a pair of cowboy boots. His wife urged him to seek out the man who swindled him, and try to recover the mare. "No, I reckon not," said the poor fellow. "When a man gets his butt skinned, he's got to *set on the blister.*"

To say "that feller don't cull none of 'em" means that he isn't particular about women but just takes 'em as they come.

"My oldest boy *has done shod the horse all round,*" a country woman told me. I didn't know what she meant, but my old friend Gerald Pipes, who runs the dance hall at Reeds Spring, Missouri, explained it. "She just means that Jim's been married four times," he said.

A sprightly young widow lashed out at her kinfolk, who were braggin' up a wealthy suitor. "I wouldn't marry that feller," she said, *"if every hair on his head was gold!"* Another young woman said, "I wouldn't go to a dog-fight with Tommy, *if he had three silver legs!"* This last crack is probably a euphemism.

A young couple in McDonald County, Missouri, didn't get married until the girl was obviously pregnant. "They've done *made their crop,*" said an old woman, "an' now they're *a-buildin' a fence round it.*"

Discussing a scandalous triangle at Rockaway Beach, Missouri, a backwoods preacher said solemnly: "Hit was just *a case of a bull in the wrong pasture.*" Then the speaker gazed about him triumphantly, feeling that he had expressed it very subtly and delicately.

The old expression, "it's an odd mule in a strange stall," may be applied to almost any bizarre or incongruous situation.

In speaking of an acquaintance who was doing something both difficult and dangerous, a man said, "Jimmy better look out. He's *a-ridin' a mare an' leadin' a jackass.*"

"It's *pourin' short sweetenin' into long,* for Sally to use lipstick," a boy cried.[45] Taken literally, this would be to pour sugar into molasses, but the hillman uses it to mean gilding the rose or painting the lily. The speaker felt, with reason, that Sally's lips did not need any artificial color.

"That feller's a-tryin' to *cut a big hog with a little knife*" means that he is working under difficulties, with poor equipment.

To "talk turkey" is to speak frankly and sincerely. When one man says to another, "Let's *talk turkey,*" he means, "Let's put our cards on the table." The common expression, *"I'll talk turkey if you'll talk squirrel,"* is an offer to compromise, to split the difference; it does not mean "I'll talk turkey if you'll do the same."

In a dry season one is often reminded of the old saying, "You can haul corn as far as you can hear thunder." This means that a local drouth is not completely ruinous. If rain falls so near that you can hear the thunder, you can get food from somebody in the neighborhood, and your family won't starve.

After two disastrous crop failures, a hillman said, "It's just *scratchin' a pore man's ass,* tryin' to raise corn in this wolfish country!" Another farmer allowed that "a feller *can* make a crop here sometimes, but *it's a hard fight with a short stick.*"

To say that "Bill's *a-scratchin' where he don't itch*" may mean that Bill is under the influence of liquor. But sometimes it means that he's hysterical or disoriented, even to the point of insanity.

An official of a charitable organization delivered a rousing speech, all about the advantages of altruism and the like. An old woman sniffed. "Cain't fool me," she said, "that feller's just *a-tryin' to keep his own skillet greasy.*"

Speaking of a very old lady, a real pioneer mother who had weathered all sorts of hardships and was still in rugged health, a man remarked, "I knowed her sisters, an' the whole family. Them Bradley women is *hard to tear down.*"

Another old lady was recalling the hardships of her youth. "After my man died," she said, "old Smith foreclosed his mortgage. I moved out one day, an' he moved in the next. The last thing I done was to *kill the cat and throw it in the well.*" The woman did not intend this to be taken literally, but meant only that she wished no good fortune to the Smith family.

A nervous, high-strung hillman was *settin' up* to a girl near Kirby-ville, Missouri, but was annoyed by pigs that squealed so loud as to spoil

[45] Cf. Nancy Clemens, Kansas City *Star,* August 21, 1938.

his whispered *sweet talk*. Suddenly he sprang up in a rage. "I cain't do no sparkin'," he cried, "with them Goddamn' hogs a-fightin' under the house!" This happened years ago, but it is still remembered with laughter by the old-timers.

I knew a boy in Taney County, Missouri, who asked a girl to go for a walk down by the river. "I don't want to go way down there, Elmer," she answered, "it's *too far an' snakey.*" Never having heard this before, I thought it was the girl's creation. But E. E. Dale reports *too fur and snakey* as a familiar pioneer expression.[46]

One very hot day near Cassville, Missouri, I met an old woman almost at the point of collapse. "Ain't it awful?" she gasped, mopping her forehead with a red handkerchief. "I feel like *hell ain't a mile away, an' the fences all down!*" A related expression is: "That wind comes straight from Kansas, without a button-bush to stop it!"

A neighbor of ours, a pale, blue-eyed fellow, became an outlaw and got his picture in the city newspapers. The village patriarch looked at the headlines. "It don't seem possible Lon could be as bad as the papers make out," he said wonderingly. "Why, I knowed him when he was just a little *gander-eyed* boy!" Another man in the same town was very tall and thin, with a long neck and a conspicuously small head. More than once I heard him described as "one of them skinny, *gander-necked fellers.*"

To call a countryman a *possum-farmer* is to say that he lives on a farm, but devotes himself to hunting and trapping instead of agriculture.

"Them boys is *all vines an' no 'taters"* means that they look well and put up a good front, but are really worthless.

A man who "don't know beans when the poke's open" is an ignorant, stupid fellow. To say that a fellow "cain't see his hand before his face, with thick glasses on" does not mean that his vision is defective. When an old-timer remarks that a neighbor "couldn't find his butt with both hands, in broad daylight" he refers to an incurable clumsiness and ineptitude.

Our neighbor's son was a *thin an' ready feller,* about eighteen years old, of the type described as *fish-pole high an' gun-barrel straight.* A great favorite with the ladies, he was the best square dancer for miles around, and nobody ever heard him admit fatigue. "I've saw that boy plow from dawn till dark," a relative said admiringly, "then wash his feet an' dance till the roosters crowed for day!"

"My man he dances fit to bust a gizzard-string," a woman told me in her husband's presence. "Soon as my back's turned, he's out on the floor

[46] *Arkansas Historical Quarterly,* Vol. VI (1947), 127.

with them Horse Creek gals, just *a-makin' their dress-tails pop!*" She meant that he swung 'em with unnecessary enthusiasm. "You're a great one to talk," the husband retorted. "You've had them Pine Run fellers' *claws in your flanks* ever since you was big enough to caper!" This last was a reference to the waist-swing; a very strait-laced backwoods girl does not permit a partner to put his arm around her waist at all, but is swung by a handclasp only. The two methods of swinging are known as *biscuits* and *cornbread*, as in this old dance call:

> *Meet your pardner, pat her on the head,*
> *If she don't like biscuits, feed her cornbread,*

which means "if she doesn't wish to be swung by the waist, give her the old-fashioned hand-swing."

Pete Whetstone was telling somebody about the troubles of the Arkansas pioneers in the eighteen forties: "The way they have had hard times, is a *sin to Crockett.*"[47] This expression is still heard in the Ozarks, also *sin to the crickets, sin to Moses,* and *sin to the world.* These phrases mean something surprising rather than sinful. An old man gaping at a motor-driven saw cried out: "It's a *sin to the dogs* how that contraption cuts wood, ain't it?"[48]

A loafer near Fort Smith, Arkansas, remarked: "You orter seen old man Boggs a-tryin' to spark Sally Henderson. It was *a sight for the world!*" And Mrs. Olive Ellis, of Eureka Springs, Arkansas, told me that one of her neighbors described another's outlandish costume and hair-do as *"a sketch for the birds."*

Near Neosho, Missouri, I met an old man who had served under Sterling Price in the Confederate Army. "Pappy Price was the best general we had," said he, "an' us boys would have follered him to the *middle kits of hell.*" May Kennedy McCord thinks the word is *pits* instead of *kits.* She has a character say, "I hope I never see ye again, till I see ye a-burnin' in the *middle pits o' hell!*"[49]

Emmett Atkinson, of McNeill, Arkansas, refers to "the Irishman's fence that is *horse high, bull strong, pig tight and goose proof.*"[50] Doubtless this description did apply to a fence originally, but hillfolk nowadays use

[47] *Spirit of the Times,* January 19, 1850, p. 570. The phrase was used by George William Featherstonhaugh (*Excursion Through the Slave States* [London, 1844], 62).

[48] *American Speech,* Vol. V (1929), 20.

[49] Springfield, Mo., *News & Leader,* March 18, 1934.

[50] *Arkansas Gazette,* Little Rock, March 8, 1949.

it ironically with reference to a political scheme or a get-rich-quick proposal.

Enjoying a fine dinner at a camp on White River, I asked the hostess what kind of fish we were eating. She made no answer, but turned to her husband. "Them's what the boys call *jail-house fish,*" he said with a grin. He meant that they were channel catfish, caught out of season. The sale of game fish is illegal, so the hillman says that he caught 'em *with a silver hook.* Quail killed in violation of the law are called *mud-hens,* and contraband venison is always *goat mutton.*

"The trouble with that calf," said an amateur veterinarian from Carroll County, Arkansas, "is that it was *knocked in the head with the churn dasher.*"[51] This didn't make sense to me, at the time. But he meant that we had used too much of the cow's milk to make butter, and that the calf was undernourished.

I went to see a man in Little Rock who was recovering from a dangerous illness. "Oh, I just *et myself into the creek,*" he said. He had gorged himself with food and drink, and it nearly killed him. When cattle become foundered, farmers often drag them into a stream, believing that this relieves the condition. That's what the old gentleman meant by his reference to the creek.

"I remember you, all right," cried a hillman to an elderly lady whom he had not seen for fifty years. "Why, I'd *know your old hide in a tanyard!*" The poor woman looked horrified, and the rest of us whooped with helpless laughter. It isn't so funny, maybe, unless you could have seen the lady.

A dignified old woman from St. Louis became alarmed over the way our hack driver whirled along a narrow mountain trail and admonished him in no uncertain language. "All you got to do, lady," said he, "is to hold your head up an' *keep your tail over the dashboard.*" One often hears a hillman say "keep your tail in the water," which means no more than "be calm." When horses get sick or excited, the Ozarker leads them into a stream, and lets them stand in the water a while.

If a cow falls down, the farmer often pulls her tail until she gets up. A man who had become very drunk was found lying in the road one night. "If the boys hadn't come along an' *tailed me up,*" he said later, "I might have got run over, or somethin'."

A lady in Springfield, Missouri, was telling somebody about a horse. "He's black all over," she said, "except for a white spot *on the side next to*

[51] Cf. *Arkansas Historical Quarterly,* Vol. VI (1947), 129.

the fence." An inquisitive friend chose seven old-time horsemen at random, and asked them about this. Every one said that the right or *off* side of an animal is known as *the side next to the fence.*[52]

Many times I have heard farmer's say, "I believe in *whippin' my horse on the hairy side."* They tell me that this expression just points up the folly of punishing a stubborn beast by insufficient feeding.

Asking for a ride in an already crowded car, an old-timer said, "I'll just hang on *for a tar-bucket."* He meant that he would require very little space, and not cause any trouble. In pioneer days the wagons had wooden axles, and you could hear 'em squeaking for miles. A bucket of pine tar hung on the rear axle, to be used as a lubricant.

Uncle Jack Short, of Galena, Missouri, used to describe the Seventh Congressional District as a place "where the flitter-tree grows close beside the honey-pond." Mr. Short meant that the Seventh District is a fruitful region, where it is easy to make a living, a land of milk and honey. *Flitter* is a dialect word meaning pancake. "All is not gold that glitters," writes Fred High, "but lots of people come to Arkansas to eat the flitters."[53] The expression *flat as a flitter* is common throughout the Ozark country.

Dr. O. St. John, of Pineville, Missouri, once remarked that "Judge Sturges has heard it thunder a many a time," meaning that Sturges was pretty old. When a hillman tries to appear younger than he really is, the neighbors say "that feller's done *lost his measurin'-stick."* An elderly man in our village flew into a passion when somebody called him an "old gentleman." He drew a deep breath. *"Me old?"* he shouted, "Why, I'll eat the goose that fattens on your Goddamn' grave!"

A prominent citizen of our town had just died, and his widow said over and over to the neighbors: "Jeff was a man whut *never rolled up his sleeves!* He was a man whut *never took off his drawers!"* The first statement meant that he lived by mental effort and was not a mere laborer; the second that he was a decent, modest gentleman who respected his wife. This last crack seems to support certain odd findings in the famous Kinsey Report.[54]

Clink O'Neill, of Taney County, Missouri, told me of a day-dreaming hillman who murmured, "I wish I was *well fixed an' plumb genteel."* An Arkansawyer who suddenly came into possession of a considerable legacy

[52] Cf. *Dialect Notes,* Vol. V (1923), 216.
[53] *Forty-Three Years for Uncle Sam,* 33.
[54] Alfred C. Kinsey, *et al., Sexual Behavior in the Human Male* (Philadelphia, 1948), 366–67.
[55] *Arkansas Gazette,* Little Rock, January 8, 1950.

was asked if he was going to set up in some sort of business. "No, I ain't," he said positively. "I aim to live on Magazine Mountain the rest of my life, an' *roll down rocks on all mankind*."

When some prominent citizens of Springfield, Missouri, were abusing me in the newspapers, alleging that I had poked fun at the hillfolk and held the Ozark country up to ridicule, an old politician told me: "Them fellers is just *a-pourin' water on your wheel*." He meant that the newspaper publicity would help sell my books. This figure derives from the old-time gristmills, which were operated by a stream of water flowing over a big wooden wheel.

There is an old story about a farmer boasting of his splendid corn, declaring that he had produced this phenomenal crop by his own efforts, without any help from any source. "I reckon *the sun didn't hinder none*," said an old man dryly. There are many variants of this tale. Isabel France tells of a flour salesman, who was bragging about his own good qualities. "You'd *give the miller half the grist*, wouldn't you?" a hillman asked. "The folks laughed," writes Mrs. France, "until the salesman had to leave without his order."[55]

When a villager seems to be prospering, doing well in his business or profession, the hillman says, "That feller sure is *cuttin' the big jimson*." May Kennedy McCord says, "I think this means the jimson weed, which is very hard to cut, and requires smartness or skill or something of the sort."[56]

Urged to take some vitamin pills, an old friend in Galena, Missouri, said, "I believe I've got *all the vitamins I can chamber*," meaning all that he could use to advantage. Men used to speak of a shotgun that would *chamber five buckshot;* to put more than five into such a gun would not help, but even reduce its effectiveness.

"Tommy Burns started out for to spark the schoolmarm, but he *hit a knot* afore he got to goin' good." A vivid figure to anybody who has sawed wood. "Some say it was Frank Reeves that *throwed a sprag in his wheel*," my informant added. This last comes from the mines around Joplin, I think. Miners used to stop the little cars with a stick of wood thrust between the spokes, and the practice was known as *spraggin'*.

Asked if he would vote for Harry Truman in 1948, an Arkansas Democrat answered, "Yes, it looks like *duck or no dinner*," meaning that he didn't care particularly for Truman, but that the only alternative was certain defeat for the Democratic party.

[56] Springfield, Mo., *Leader & Press*, June 4, 1942.

A lady in Springfield, Missouri, expressed some doubt as to the results of the election. "Everybody says this is a Republican year," she said, "but you can't never tell. I'm goin' to wait *till the shoutin's over an' they gather up the singin'-books.*"

A more or less legendary Ozarker cried out, "The wolves killed my goats, hawks got the chickens, night-riders burned the barn, an' a preacher run off with my wife!" Also, he added, the dry weather ruined his crops, and the mowing machine was busted, anyhow. "By God!" said he, "I've got a mind to *quit farmin' and go to work!*" Another hillman, after a similar recital of mishap and catastrophe, ended with: "I'm goin' to get me a new jug, an' *drink till the world looks little!*"

"How does your tobacker taste today?" is a common greeting, which means "How are you feeling today?" Any man who chews the weed can understand this. It is not, as some tourists have imagined, an attempt to mooch tobacco.

A newcomer in Eureka Springs, Arkansas, met one of the villagers in the street, and said, "How are you today?" The hillman scowled. "I'm feelin' mighty mean," he answered, "an' *my stinger's about half out.*" In other words, he was half in the humor to fight anybody who crossed his path.

A boy from Pineville, Missouri, which has a population of 422, made a visit to Neosho, Missouri, a town of five or six thousand people. I expected him to be impressed by the size of the place, but he wasn't. "I hate *these little shike-poke towns,*" he said. The boy had never seen anything as big as Neosho. But he had heard of cities, and realized that Neosho is smaller than Chicago or New York.

The grown son of a farmer came home in a towering rage, reporting that some newcomers had insulted the whole family. "I ask 'em how was their sick cow," the boy told us, "an' one of them smart-alecs says, 'She's tolerable. How's all *your folks?*'"

Of a man who was always making passes at women, somebody said, "Bob acts like he had a *rough cob between the ears,*" meaning that the fellow had nothing but sexual adventure on his mind.

When a hillman says "you can *see the signs* on that feller," he is implying that the man is not long for this world. Often *the signs* augur a natural death from disease, but sometimes the phrase means that the man has dangerous enemies and may be murdered at any moment. In some localities, for one man to say that he *sees the signs* on another is regarded as a warning, perhaps even a threat.[57] I was personally acquainted with

202

three men who died by violence shortly after somebody had *seen the signs* on them.

Two villagers had hired a country boy to perjure himself, in order to give them an alibi in a murder trial. After their acquittal they didn't come across with the promised twenty-five dollars. "I got you-uns out of a bad mess, an' you better pay me," he said ominously. *"The creek might git up ag'in!"* The boy got his money at once.

Another country boy who believed himself defrauded by the "courthouse rats" at the county seat, said grimly, "If you fellers don't *tote right* with me, it'll be *too wet to plow!"* These sayings are not humorous, but are regarded as threats, and are taken quite seriously by those to whom they are addressed.

In southwest Missouri a man was arrested for stealing hogs. His lawyer assured the fellow that he couldn't possibly be convicted, since the prosecuting attorney had been "fixed" for fifty dollars. But the hog thief was still uneasy. "If I give you a hundred dollars more, do you reckon you could *plow a little deeper?"* he asked. "I'm not sure just what you mean," answered the lawyer. "I mean the circuit judge," said the defendant.

A reluctant witness in a murder trial told the sheriff that his life had been threatened by a brother of the accused. "Did he say he'd kill you?" asked the officer. "No, sir," answered the witness, "he didn't say nothing like that." The sheriff persisted. "Well, what *did* he say?" The witness looked around uneasily. "He said if I didn't keep my mouth shut, *there'd be a new face in hell tomorrow."*

A stalwart young woodcutter was having an affair with the daughter of our local rich man, despite the strenuous objections of the girl's parents. "Gifford's *a-huntin' trouble with a big gun,"* said a neighbor, "if he's a-foolin' with one of them Spelvin gals." I have heard *stirrin' up hell with a long spoon* used in the same meaning.

A friend of mine, engaged in an illegal and dangerous enterprise, said of an accomplice, "That damn' fool will *knock the shucks out of the bell,* if we don't watch him." He meant that the fellow might betray a secret, let the cat out of the bag. The hillfolk used to bell their horses before turning them out on the range. When a man wanted to ride for a short distance, without attracting attention, he silenced the bell by stuffing cornshucks into it.

"Wait till I see *which way the cat's goin' to jump"* probably derives

[57] Cf. May Kennedy McCord, Springfield, Mo., *Leader & Press,* November 27, 1934.

from the quilting party. When a quilt is finished, the women toss a cat in it; the girl toward whom the cat jumps will be the first to marry.[58] Nowadays the expression is used figuratively, with reference to almost any future event.

"If Baldy ever gets caught a-foolin' with the United States mail, it'll be *Katy bar the door!*" said a local character; he was speaking of a postmaster suspected of opening letters. He meant that Baldy would be in a tight spot, a serious predicament, a hell of a fix. In the course of an argument about religion, a man from Lincoln, Arkansas, said: "Well, if there ain't no Heaven, it'll be *Katy bar the door!*"

A city feller came into the drugstore and began to poke fun at the Ozark region in general and our settlement in particular. He said we were backward, ignorant, and quaint; all true enough perhaps, but not very tactful. "Stranger," said a tight-lipped villager, "you're *a-divin' in shaller water* when you talk that-a-way about my home town."

A backwoods fortuneteller in Wayne County, Missouri, once said to me, "You're forty year old, an' you've done *waded your deepest water*," meaning that the most difficult part of my life was past.

When a man says "I've been *through that weed-patch*," he means that he is familiar with that line of argument or that point of view.

A young farmer was accused of associating with a notoriously promiscuous woman, but he denied it indignantly. "I ain't no angel," said he, "but I *don't berry in no such a patch* as that!"

A lively young girl in McDonald County, Missouri, had no idea who her father was. "Mommy *run through a briar-patch*," she said humorously, "an' never did know *which thorn stuck the deepest*."

I remember a wealthy dowager from Kansas City who tried to *claim kin* with a snuff-chewing old woman at Pineville, Missouri. Both families had been reared near Pea Ridge, Arkansas, but the old woman was not impressed by fine clothes and big automobiles. "*Your gran'pap's dog might have run through my gran'pap's orchard*," she said sourly, "but that don't make *us* no kin."

A friend of ours was patient and persistent, but incredibly slow at everything. A neighbor said of him: "Charley ain't what you might call brisk, but he'll *lean ag'in the rack till the fodder falls*," a figure understandable to men who feed cattle.

Another local character announced, "I *don't chaw my terbacker but once*," meaning that he had made known his position, and did not intend to repeat the statement.

A crossroads mechanic had fixed my brakes, but they didn't function very well. "Tell him to *lick his calf over again,*" said an old woman. This means to repeat a performance not satisfactorily concluded.[58]

Mary Elizabeth Mahnkey, of Mincy, Missouri, once tried to buy some household relics from her neighbors. "They *had the big eye,*" she told me, meaning that they regarded the stuff as more important and valuable than it really was.[60]

When a woman runs out of flour before her dough is properly mixed, so that the *kneadin'* is too thin and there's no flour to thicken it, they say, "She has done *drownded the miller.*"[61] Elizabeth Edwards reports that in Caldwell County, Missouri, *to drown the miller* means only "to empty the flour bin."[62]

One often hears a man complain that "the *big gut is eatin' up the little-uns.*" It's just an inelegant way of saying, "I am extremely hungry."

A tight-fisted farmer had lost several hogs, and a chore-boy said, "He claims it was the cholery, but that cain't be, 'cause they lingered. Them hogs died of the *miss-meal colic,*" meaning that the owner did not feed them properly. I have heard *miss-meal cramps* used as a euphemism for hunger.

The average hillman likes pork better than any other meat. He will eat rabbits only when he can't get anything else. Speaking of the poverty which overtook him after a severe drouth, a farmer said, "My family et so many rabbits that winter, that the *twins was born harelipped!* The kids got so they'd *dive into a brush-pile every time they heerd a dog bark!* An' I done *more hoppin' than runnin',* myself!" But when a woman said, "That Johnson boy's got *rabbit in his feet,*" she meant only that he was restless, fond of leaving home and wandering about the country.[63]

The old-timers often speak extravagantly of the poverty and hardships of their youth. "We didn't have nothin' but *skim-milk an' wild onions* when I was young," said an old codger, without cracking a smile. "Us boys was *drinkin' branch-water an' eatin' sheep-sorrel* in them days," another told me solemnly. "My folks lived mostly on *pawpaws an' high wind,*" said an old granny, adding that "it was mighty hard sleddin' when the pawpaws didn't hit an' the wind died down."

[58] *Journal of American Folklore,* Vol. XLVI (1933), 6.

[59] Cf. Marguerite Lyon, *Fresh from the Hills,* 131.

[60] D. S. Crumb, *Dialect Notes,* Vol. II (1903), 306.

[61] This saying is found in the *English Dialect Dictionary,* with a similar meaning.

[62] *Publication of the American Dialect Society,* No. 2 (1944), 58.

[63] Cf. Fred Starr, *From an Ozark Hillside,* 37–38.

A well-to-do farmer told me seriously: "We're gettin' on pretty good here lately, but in the early days most of us *didn't have nothin' but feet on the ground*."

"We had a pretty hard time when Hoover was runnin' the country," said another man. "I recollect one winter when we just stood around lookin' at each other, *wonderin' which one to eat first*."

A man in Eureka Springs, Arkansas, declared, "The hardships us pioneers went through was plumb turrible. Why, some winters *we had to sleep with our own wives!*" This was a slighting reference to the sex habits of the tourists and newcomers who have invaded the Ozarks in recent years.

To say that "them fellers *belong to the Steele family*" means that they are dishonest. "They *come from Steele County*" carries the same meaning. There is a place called *Thief Holler* near Pineville, Missouri, but it was named long ago, and the people who live there "don't take it personal no more," as a prominent citizen assured me.

One of our fellow townsmen decided to run for Congress. "Well, I'm goin' to vote for Jim, an' I hope he wins," said a neighbor. "But it's *a long shot, with a limb in the way*." This figure is plain enough to a generation of riflemen and means that the candidate's chances of election are not too good.

Of a twelve-year-old boy who looted country stores and was sent to the reformatory, a man remarked, "Bobby kind of *soured on the cob*," meaning that the poor boy was *rotten before he was ripe,* or *spoiled before he was prime.*[64]

A farmer listened to a foul-mouthed Missouri politician for a while without any comment, then he said, "That feller *reminds me of the time the skunks littered under our barn*."

Aunt Sarah Wilson, who lived on Bear Creek, near Day, Missouri, and tended a little kitchen garden for more than fifty years, was getting pretty old. "Ain't you goin' to plant nothin' this spring?" some friends asked. "Naw, I ain't," she answered. "I've done *made peace with the ground*."

"It won't be long now," said an old gentleman at Tahlequah, Oklahoma, "till they'll be puttin' the green quilt over me." He meant that he didn't expect to live much longer.

Of a woman who ran a little store and made a lot of money, it was said, "That widder could *run hell for a camp-ground,* an' git rich at it!" One often hears "that feller would *tell the Devil how to run hell*" applied to some loud-mouthed know-it-all.

206

"To listen at Jim Henson talk," said a quiet little man, "you'd think he could *put out hell with one bucket of water.*"

In Pineville, Missouri, the boys were discussing an evangelist from Arkansas, noted for his fundamentalist sermons. "That feller talks so familiar about hell," said one wisecracker, "you'd think he was *borned an' raised thar.*"

A tourist came into our village pool hall, and instantly two local humorists began to talk of the hardships endured by city dwellers. "In them big towns," said the first loafer, "the people is forced to work all week for nothin'." The second villager shook his head. "Yes, an' that ain't the worst of it," he said. "The gamblers cheat 'em out of their pay every Saturday!"

"I don't like these here games where you got partners to fuss with," said a boy whose sweetheart wanted to teach him bridge. "I'd rather play *every dog for his dinner,*" every man for himself, that is.

A wealthy man in our community died and left most of his estate to a rattle-brained wife. "Shucks," growled a neighbor, "that money *won't last till it's gone,* if Lizzie ever gets her hands on it." A physician in Stone County, Missouri, asked the druggist to send for ten thousand pills, but the fellow only ordered five hundred. "Hell!" said the doctor. "Five hundred ain't enough! Why, they *won't last till they're gone!*" This expression always catches the ear of the tourist, and seems very funny to people who have never heard it before.

When my neighbor's wife kept pestering him with demands for an automobile, he cried out, "Car! Where in the hell would I get a car? You think I can *run it out of a hole with a ferret?*"

Another character, hearing some very poor singing in a roadside church, remarked, "Them damn' fools is a-draggin' it. They'll *never git butter that-a-way.*" I suppose this saying derives from the old-fashioned churn.

Boring with a big auger means doing things in a big way or on a large scale. An old fellow was telling me about a picnic he had attended in the eighteen nineties. "We had more'n two hundred people from all over the county," said he. "There was a fine dinner, an' horse-races, an' card-games, an' a wrasslin'-match besides. We was *borin' with a big auger* in them days."

High speed or celerity is indicated in the reference to a runner's garments sticking straight out behind. Our hired girl was warning me never

[64] Cf. Marguerite Lyon, *Fresh from the Hills,* 136.

to confide any secrets to a certain female. "Molly's *dress-tail won't never touch her bottom*," said the girl, "till she tells the neighbors everything she knows." And a man near Calico Rock, Arkansas, remarked: "That boy of mine *never let his shirt-tail fall* till he got one of them Perkins gals in bed with him."

Packin' the mail means doing anything in a rapid, vigorous fashion. Looking at a Carolina wren which was singing very loud, a boy said, "He sure is *a-packin' the mail*, ain't he?" Speaking of a dog running, a neighbor cried out: "Look at him pick 'em up an' set 'em down! That's what I call *packin' the mail!*"

There was a youngster in Benton County, Arkansas, who used to crawl about in the brush and catch rabbits with his hands. I asked the boy's father how the trick was done, and the old man answered that "Elmer just grabbed 'em *before they could git word to God!*"

A young ruffian near Marshall, Arkansas, attacked a federal officer in the street, but bystanders separated the two. "If the folks hadn't pulled me off," the boy said later, "I'd have whupped that feller *before Christ could have got the news!*"

Denouncing the owner of a flour mill, an old friend of mine said earnestly, "That corn-cracker of his'n *don't pass all it chaws*." He didn't intend this to be taken literally, though it is said that some early gristmills did contain a mechanical contraption to steal grain. He meant that the miller was tricky, unscrupulous, not to be trusted.

Near Galena, Missouri, I was sent to interview a woman whom I had never seen. "What does she look like?" I asked a villager. "Mabel's a low, yaller-headed woman," he answered. "She *cain't run fast, or she'd put her eyes out*." The idea was that Mabel had long, pendulous breasts, which would flop up and blind her!

To say "that feller's *got somethin' in his head beside nits*" means that he has considerable information, or some kind of technical knowledge. A man who's got *mountain sense* is reasonable, well balanced, sensible. *Mountain sense* and *rawhide wisdom* are sometimes used to draw a contrast with a fellow who has book learning but lacks these other qualities. "He *ain't no bug-eater*" is equivalent to "he's a level-headed chap, not a radical or extremist."

Referring to a lying, hypocritical, all-things-to-all-men sort of fellow, a woman told me: "Bobby's *got faces all round his head*."

Wishing to compliment the wife of a state senator, the villagers used to say, "She's *always the same every time you meet her*." This meant that she wasn't fickle or changeable; also that she didn't seem snobbish or inclined to put on airs.

A small-town idler told me that his wife was "a wild hog with a barb-wire tail." Asked what he meant by this, he said, "Well, she ain't *biddable,*" meaning that she wasn't docile, tractable, or perhaps obedient.

A fat woman who lived on Rumpus Ridge, in Stone County, Missouri, was said to be "four ax-handles across." Woodsmen measure timber by a mark on the handle of the ax. A log described as "four ax-handles across the butt" would be eight feet in diameter.

A country boy who had attained high military rank was little respected by the home folks, because of his arrogant, *stuck-up* manner. "Bert talks mighty big now, but he was *raised with a tick in his navel,*" said an old neighbor. He meant that Bert was brought up in the backwoods, like the rest of us.

Another local man who had *sand in his craw* and *grit in his gizzard* came back from the wars with many decorations. A silly woman asked if he had killed any Germans. The warrior scowled. "If I'd thought to save their ears," said he, "I'd *have a churnfull!* Do you think they give me these here ribbons for *pitchin' horse-shoes?*"

An old fellow who had a leg shot off in the Spanish-American War listened contemptuously to the boasting of younger veterans. Asked if he had ever been in battle, the old soldier made a wry face. "No," he answered scathingly, "I just *fell through the hay-hole at the livery-stable* in 1904."

Commenting on the demoralizing effect of alcohol, a farmer in Benton County, Arkansas, remarked: "Everybody's lappin' up this here moonshine nowadays. Some of these young gals from town get to drinkin' it, an' layin' out nights, an' the first thing you know *they're a-givin' milk!*"

When the wife of a young man had a premature baby, the husband stalked around, half-drunk, hinting darkly that he thought another fellow was probably the father. An old gentleman advised him to stop such foolish talk. "Look here, Henry," said the old man, "when you *ketch a varmint in your trap,* it's yourn!"

Any good-looking young country girl may be called a *fence-corner peach,* but the term often implies a low-class family background or questionable paternity. I asked an old friend about this, and he answered: "Well, the trees in the fence-corners was all *seedlin's,* you know. Just growed up accidental, not planted in no regular orchard. But they was the *best* peaches I ever tasted," and he grinned reminiscently.

An old gentleman, speaking of some village girls who used too much vivid lipstick, said that they reminded him of *jaybirds in pokeberry time.* A city man might think that it was the beaks of jaybirds which show crimson when the jays have been eating pokeberries. But it's the other end of the bird that's colored.

Near Pineville, Missouri, there lived a widow-woman who had an incredibly pretty daughter. Some of the young men paid the widow a great deal of attention. "Can't fool me," the old lady grinned, "they're just *a-baitin' the cow to ketch the calf.*" May Kennedy McCord prints a variant, *salting the cow to get the calf.*[65] Mrs. McCord quotes another old saying, addressed to someone who was bragging a little: "Oh, I've milked *many a heifer that was wilder than you,* in a gourd." A writer in *Life Magazine* says that *plowing with the heifers* is an Ozark expression for a preacher's attempt to reach the menfolk by getting their wives into church.[66]

A man in Eureka Springs, Arkansas, told about putting hobbles on an unbroken mare. "She could walk slow," he said, "but when it come to kickin', *there wasn't a pea on the vine,*" meaning that the animal couldn't kick at all. The expression *hobblin' a wild mare* is often used figuratively, sometimes with reference to human females.

Of a bibulous evangelist it was said, "He tried to mix preachin' an' whiskey-drinkin' an' *that dog won't hunt.*" Meaning that such a combination is not practicable.

A voter said of a local politician who sought support from both Democrats and Republicans, "Joe wants *anybody's* dog that'll hunt with him."[67]

If you ask a hillman about something that is none of your business, he often replies with a bit of traditional nonsense. To the question "What are you doing?" he may answer *fattenin' frogs for snakes,* or *makin' kitten-britches for tomcats,* or *punchin' peth out of elders.* Several times I have heard the expression *layin' rows for meddlers;* the *rows* are little fences used in snaring birds, and there is a kind of pun with *medlars,* which means meadowlarks. Joseph W. Carr found *layovers to catch meddlers, popovers to catch meddlers,* and *rearovers to catch meddlers* in Fayetteville, Arkansas.[68] Paul G. Brewster reports *layover to catch meddlers* from Columbia, Missouri, "said to inquisitive children who want to know what an object is."[69]

[65] *KWTO Dial,* Springfield, Mo., October, 1949, p. 8.
[66] December 25, 1944, p. 66.
[67] Cf. *Arkansas Historical Quarterly,* Vol. VI (1947), 127.
[68] *Dialect Notes,* Vol. III (1905), 86; III (1906), 151, 153. Cf. *American Speech,* Vol. X (1935), 282.

Sayings and Wisecracks

My friend Bob Wyrick, of Eureka Springs, Arkansas, was working in his garden when a loafer asked, "What you doin', Bob?" Wyrick looked up. "I'm *a-plantin' wheelbarrow seed,*" he answered shortly.

When a stranger persisted in asking about the man of the house, where he was and so on, the housewife did not want to answer; she thought the stranger might be a game warden or some other unfriendly character. After evading the question for some time, she said vaguely, "I reckon he must have *went down to the river a-huntin' crawpappies, an' cain't find his way back.*"

When a man goes out at night, without any explanation, it is said that "he's *a-hunting hoot-owls";* the hillman may use this expression himself, if anybody asks him where he has been.

In Springfield, Missouri, in the early days, when a citizen was asked, "Where are you going?" he was likely to reply, "I'm going to *see the willipus-wallipus.*"[70] Credulous strangers were told that the *willipus-wallipus* was an enormous obscene monster, kept in an iron cage behind the fire station; but it was really only a newfangled road-building machine, a sort of steam roller.[71]

The hillfolk study calendars and almanacs to see about the phases of the moon, the signs of the Zodiac, and the proper days for planting; but they pay little attention to the exact dates of past events. Ask a hillman just when something occurred, and he may answer, "Well, I reckon it was *when our least boy was about three-four months old.*" Ask the mother for the date of the child's birth, and she says, "Lem was borned *about cowcumber time,* the *year of the big freshet.*" Many mature, intelligent hillfolk don't know their exact birth dates, and neither do their parents. In the early days no records were kept, unless a religious family had them inscribed on the fly-leaf of the Bible. A lawyer in southwest Missouri needed the exact date of a woman's death, to enter in some legal papers. When he asked her surviving relatives, he was told, "Aunt Suly died *just past the peak of watermelon time.*" The dead woman's most intimate friend said, "She took sick *when we was just about knee-deep in August.*" Another neighbor thought that Aunt Suly had passed away right at *the start of kitchen-settin' weather,* which means the first chilly period of early fall, when people sit around the wood range in the kitchen.

[69] *American Speech,* Vol. XVI (1941), 21.

[70] Bill Arp (Charles Henry Smith) uses this term in *The Farm and the Fireside* (Atlanta, 1890), 325.

[71] Cf. my *We Always Lie to Strangers,* 48–49.

Even today, in the back hills, there are old-timers who pay no heed to dates, and some can't so much as tell you the current month. They are not particularly ignorant people, but they just don't give a damn'. Asked to name the months of the year, a woman in southwest Missouri answered, "Well, there's groundhog day, an' blow-month, an' Aprile, an' the time the meat give out." The early settlers thought of time in terms of weather, farm work, and the like: *sarvis bloom, buzzard comin', blackberry winter, frog squall, corn-plantin', court week, layin'-by time, camp-meetin' season, roastin'-ear time, fodder-pullin' days, hog-killin', first frost, 'lasses-makin' time,* and so forth. There is an old saying that the pioneer's indifference to time and dates was acquired from the Indians, but I don't know if there's any truth in it.

The words *daybreak, sunup, sundown,* and *mornin'* are used in the ordinary sense, except that *mornin'* is made to last until noon. The term *afternoon* is seldom heard, but the period just after the noon meal is sometimes called the *afterdinner.*[72] *Evenin'* in the Ozarks begins at noon and lasts until sunset.[73] A radio announcer at Springfield, Missouri, tells us that a certain market "is open every Sunday evening until six o'clock." Dusk is called *lamp-lighting time,* or *candle-light*—often divided into *early candle-light* and *late candle-light;* the expression *early candle-light* is still seen in the country newspapers, announcing church meetings and the like.[74] The word soon is regularly used as an adjective in the sense of early: "That feller is aimin' to git him a *soon start* in the mornin'."

Most hillfolk have clocks nowadays, but one may still find cabins with a notch cut in the floor, where the shadow of the door-jamb falls at high noon. The clock, if there is one, is often set according to the *noon-mark.*[75] Charles J. Finger, of Fayetteville, Arkansas, told me of a neighbor who answered a query about the time with: "It *wants three puncheons till noon.*" Finger explained that the man "was referring to the movement of a spot of sunlight through a chink across the puncheon floor." I have myself heard old-timers speak of "floor-boards" instead of hours, disdaining the figures on the clock dial.

"I ain't laid eyes on you *in a coon's age"* means "I haven't seen you for a long time." *A hound's dotage* and *a donkey's ears* are often used in the same sense. Jay L. B. Taylor reports that in McDonald County, Missouri,

[72] *American Speech,* Vol. VIII (1933), 48.
[73] *Dialect Notes,* Vol. V (1927), 472.
[74] Cf. *Dialect Notes,* Vol. II (1904), 418.
[75] *Dialect Notes,* Vol. V (1926), 401.

"since the hogs et up my brother" means "a very long time."[76] One often hears *since Heck was a pup,* and "I ain't been fishin' in *a month of Sundays."*

Speaking of a journey undertaken in his youth, an aged hillman said: "I don't know how many miles it was, and I disremember how long we was on the way. But we et three big deer, an' *greased the wagon four times.* That's how we measured distance in them days, by the *wagon-greasin's."* John Turner White, of Jefferson City, Missouri, told me of an old-timer who said, "If'n you don't take that there trip, it'll save *time an' axle-grease,* also wear an' tear on religion."

It was said of a certain family that "them folks *raise more corn than ever goes to mill,"* which means that they are making whiskey. "I hear Bob's *a-sellin' pumpkins"* is one way of saying that Bob is a bootlegger. During the Volstead era people did sell pumpkins, with bottles of whiskey inside, right in front of our courthouse.

Some hill farmers lack any sort of wagon roads, and tourists often ask how they get their crop out of the hills to market. "Stranger," one old man wisecracked, "we just turn our corn into whiskey, an' *fight* it out." The fact is that they use most of the corn right on the farm, to feed stock and make bread.

A local moonshiner jokingly called his corn-drippin's "Old Crow" after a well-known bonded whiskey, and it was known as *crow liquor* for miles around. When a newcomer complained of the bad roads and the difficulty of getting into the village, a crossroads humorist said, "It's too bad we ain't got no highway. But what's the difference? A feller can take a drink of that crow whiskey an' *fly* to town!"

A hillman took a drink out of a jug, and sighed happily. "That stuff is so good," said he, "a feller cain't hardly *bite it off."* Another expert agreed. "That's the *pure quill,"* he said, "you can *smell the feet of the boys that plowed the corn!"* But some squeamish folk don't like moonshine so well. "My God, do you call that whiskey?" cried an outraged customer from the city. "Well, it sure ain't gravy," answered the village bootlegger.

One of our neighbors always spoke of a special kind of moonshine as *Bottled in the Barn,* doubtless an imitation of Bottled in Bond. They tell me that a fellow near the Missouri-Arkansas line used regular printed labels bearing the words *Bottled in the Barn,* but I never saw one of these.

When Charles A. Fleming was running for the governorship of Arkansas in 1948, his opponents referred to him as a whiskey drinker. "I

[76] *Dialect Notes,* Vol. V (1923), 221.

like to take a little mountain dew, out on a fox hunt," said Mr. Fleming in a public address.[77] "I use it to rinse my mouth. Of course, I *don't spit it out.*"

"Pass me that there jug," said a fisherman on a James River gravel bar. "You mean the one *with the corncob in its mouth?*" asked the cook. "No," said the fisherman, "I'll take that little one *with the rope through its gill.*" This is a vivid figure to a riverman accustomed to stringing big catfish.

Some humorous phrases are found in the extravagant boasting that the hillman sometimes indulges in. I heard one of these fellows "declarin' himself" in a saloon at Joplin. "I'm a *curly-tailed wolf with a pink ass,* an' this is my night to howl," he yelled. "I was *borned, bred an' buttered* right here on Spring River! I ain't never been beat! I ain't never been tied! I ain't never been headed, even!" By *headed* he meant turned aside, diverted, as a driver heads cattle. I should have enjoyed hearing more of this, but the fellow began to fire his pistol into the ceiling, and the police took him away. He was no desperado, but an inoffensive young farmer who had a little too much whiskey under his belt.

One of my neighbors near Walnut Shade, Missouri, was said to have broken up a Holy Roller love-feast by shouting: "Whoo-pee! I'm the meanest man in Taney County! I'm the feller that *chaws 'em up an' spits 'em out!* I cut my teeth on a six-shooter, an' *killed three preachers before I was seven year old!*"

A magazine published at Jefferson City, Missouri, tells of an old-timer named Parmer, who was quite illiterate but who was elected to the Missouri Legislature, where he made his debut with the following speech: "I'm a *ring-tailed painter from Fishin' River,* wild an' wooly an' hard to curry. When I'm mad I fight, an' when I fight I whup! I raise my children to fight. I feed 'em on painters' hearts, fried in rattlesnake grease!"[78]

Wayman Hogue reports this "holler" from Van Buren County, Arkansas, about the turn of the century: "Hoo-ee! Drunk an' all dressed up, an' nowhar to go. I live on Round Mountain. I'm *all wool, warp an' fillin' a full yard wide,* an' I kin whup my weight in wild cats. Hoo-ee!"[79]

A character in Carroll County, Arkansas, used to get drunk at dances and boast: "I'm *all wool an' a yard wide!* Never rip nor ravel, run down at the heel, grow old, go out of fashion, or smell bad! Whoo-pee!"

---

[77] *Arkansas Gazette,* Little Rock, July 15, 1948.
[78] *Missouri Conservationist,* June, 1948, pp. 3–4.
[79] *Back Yonder,* 107.

Sayings and Wisecracks

Bob Wyrick tells me that a certain fellow at Green Forest, Arkansas, "declared himself" as follows: "Hi-yoop! I'm so tough I can scoot down a honey-locust back'ards, with two wildcats in each hand, an' never git a scratch! I got ears like a 'backer-leaf, sides like a wagon-bed, *iron ribs an' a steel backbone! I got a wire tail, an' it screwed on!* Hi-yoop!"

One seldom sees this sort of thing in the newspapers nowadays, but Mr. R. Cline, of Eureka Springs, Arkansas, published the following: "I'm *a ring tail tooter, iron backbone, steel ribs, suckled by a wolf with four rows of tits and holes punched for more!*"[80]

Just across the line in Missouri was a backwoods shouter who yelled: "Hi-yoop! I got *split hoofs,* an' *fourteen ribs to a side!* I'm rough on rats an' hard to handle!"

A waitress from Blue Eye, Missouri, said to an overattentive customer, "Let go my leg, or there'll be *a lump on your head that your hand won't cover!*"

A big yokel shook his fist under my nose, saying, "I'll put *a mark on you that won't rub off!*"

A girl warned me not to stop at a certain roadhouse, because some of the boys over there were *layin' for me.* I rather made light of this, and maybe bragged a little about my own abilities as a fighter, but she said seriously, "Them Bull Creek fellers don't fight, *they just kill an' drag out.*" Another character observed, "That gang will *cut your throat for two-bits, an' give fifteen cents of it back.*"

Another group of village ruffians had murdered a farm boy, and it was said, "They *bushwhacked* little Johnny Maxwell; didn't *give him a rabbit's chance.*"

Speaking scornfully of a troop of mountain boys who swaggered about with pistols and regarded themselves as desperate characters, a man in Taney County, Missouri, remarked: "Them fellers ain't bad, they just *smell* bad. I could take a right heavy feather pillow an' whup the whole bunch." He laid a faint stress on the word *heavy.*

A young man had a terrible fight with a stranger, and his friends brought him to the doctor's office; they feared that his *brains was a-leakin' out* and asked the physician to *cooper him up.* When the poor chap got to feeling better, somebody asked what started the fight. "I don't rightly know," said he. "I just met up with this feller in the road, an' we was a-fightin' *before the howdies was over!*"

Just as two gangs of young ruffians prepared to fight, the leader of

[80] Springfield, Mo., *News & Leader,* February 11, 1934.

one crowd shouted, *"Look to your primin',* boys! Here they come!" It was just a rough-and-tumble street fight, with no firearms involved. But the expression *look to your primin'* goes back to the days of the flintlock.

A prominent citizen of McDonald County, Missouri, was making wild threats against the sheriff, and when his friends tried to quiet him, he yelled, "I'll say my sayin', boys. An' that goes *on earth, in Heaven, an' else-where!"* The same man ended another tirade thus: "If he don't like it, he can lump it. An' if that don't suit, *let him put sugar on it!"* The noisy man's son was fearful that all this hollerin' would end in bloodshed. "The worst of it is," he said soberly, "that Paw'll do whatever he *says* he'll do, *come sweetenin' or come gunpowder!"*

"Why, I'll whup that bastard *till he runs rabbits!"* cried an infuriated hillman. "I'll make him *spit up somethin' he never swallered!"* Another man in a similar mood declared, "I can lick him with *fists, knives, guns, or giant powder! I'll fight him for *blood, money, marbles, or chalk!"*

Geraldine Parker, of California, Missouri, told me of an applicant for a country school who said, "I'm the best teacher on the creek! I can *read an' write, figger an' fight, fiddle, whup an' throw down!"* This is part of an old-time hollerin' boast, which somebody has cleaned up a little.

I once heard an Arkansas storekeeper roaring threats against a competitor. "Well, by God!" he yelled. *"There ain't no snakes* if I don't whup that feller! I'll *use his guts for galluses!* When I git through, *his hide won't hold shucks in a tan-yard!"* When the threatened man heard of this, he said calmly, "Let the pore old windbag holler. Why, he couldn't turn me over with a cant-hook, *if I was dead!"*

A little man near Walnut Shade, Missouri, had five daughters who married local desperadoes. The fellow swaggered about, secure in the knowledge that these five ruffians would back him up in any sort of trouble. One day he threatened an old bachelor named Ike Lowman. Finally Ike reached in his pocket and brought out a handful of .45-caliber cartridges. "Them's *my* son-in-laws," he said.

Referring to somebody who had wronged him and fled the country, a farmer cried: "I'll foller that son-of-a-bitch *to the high hills of Jubernaw!"* There are no hills of that name in Arkansas, Missouri, or Oklahoma; perhaps the expression is from the Bible, or some Masonic work, or an old story unknown to me. Or maybe it's just a malapropism, or a creation.

When a man is threatening or boasting about some big thing he is going to do, his fellows say derisively: "Yeah, you'll *raise hell an' put a chunk under it"* or "you'll *prize up creation an' put a chunk under it."* A chunk is a heavy block of wood, laid under the corner of a rail fence to serve as a foundation.[81]

A constable in a peaceful Missouri village suddenly encountered a group of wild-looking, armed strangers. "Where do you-uns live at?" he asked uneasily. "Mister, we come straight from Heaven," said one of the ruffians. "Just *greased our shirt-tail an' slid down a rainbow!*"

Some women were trying to dissuade an aged country sheriff from pursuing a gang of armed road agents; they spoke of the danger of his getting killed. "Well," said the old man, "I never did figger on dyin' in bed, *with a pink nightshirt round my neck.*"

Two of my friends had come into conflict with the law and were being chased by the state troopers and other officers. I expressed a hope that they might escape into the Cookson Hill country, just across the Oklahoma border. One of my wife's button-hole cousins observed that he thought this unlikely, because the fugitives could not travel fast enough. "Them boys ain't got a chance," said he, "unless they *make fewer tracks to the mile, an' more to the minute.*"

Of a man pursued by a swarm of hornets it was said: "Jack come a-tearin' down the road, *mentionin' hell-fire at every jump.*" Another story is that a half-blind old woman was puzzled by his antics, and shouted: "What's the matter?" The man yelled back, "Run, Aunt Sally! *Hell is out for noon!*" The victim admitted later that he was *in a burnt hurry,* an expression often applied to one in frenzied haste.

"*Was he runnin'?*" cried a spectator admiringly. "Boy if he'd just had *one feather in his hand, you could have called it flyin'.*" It was said that "Jack sure did *split the creek* a-gittin' home." This means merely that he moved very rapidly, not that there was a stream to be forded. "It's just *a manner of speakin',*" as an old friend told me later on.

In connection with this incident, we were discussing not only hornets, but other pests common in the Ozarks: ticks, chiggers, yellow jackets, centipedes, bedbugs, scorpions, and so on. "There's one good thing about hornets," a farmer said thoughtfully. The man who had been stung that afternoon replied profanely that he'd like to know what was good about 'em. "Well," said the hillman, "they *do* go to roost of a night."

Some hillfolk feel that a professional man should look the part. There was a time when doctors wore beards, preachers affected high hats, office-seekers could be recognized by their dress, and so forth. I remember a villager who was disappointed in the appearance of a famous politician

[81] Cf. Robert Steele Withers, *Missouri Historical Review,* Vol. XLIV (1950), 228.

who came to the Ozarks on a fishing trip. "If I'd been a-huntin' senators," he said disgustedly, "I *wouldn't have clicked my gun at that feller!*" A farmer near Galena, Missouri, said of a shabby little Campbellite evangelist, "If a man set out to shoot preachers, he *wouldn't bust a cap on nothin' like that!*"

A man in our settlement remarked, "Lucy's pappy is liable to get run over one of these days, *by somebody goin' for the doctor.*" This crack seemed very funny to us, because Lucy's father is the only qualified physician for miles around. But he doesn't *look* like a doctor!

A woodcutter came into the village restaurant, ordered a cup of coffee, and then produced a big sidemeat sandwich from his pocket. The outraged waitress stared at him. "Well," she said, "that's what I call *fetchin' a shingle off'n the house!*" I have heard the same expression applied to a man who drank from his own flask in a place where whiskey was being sold by the drink.

Commenting on the extravagant promises of a candidate for public office, an old man remarked, "Whenever you hear that *a chicken dips snuff, look under its wing.*" A Little Rock newspaperman, talking about the honesty and reliability of a certain editor, assured us, "If Tom says a rooster dips, you'll find *a snuffbox under its wing.*" In other words, whatever Tom says is true, even if it does sound a bit unlikely.

A rich man named Skaggs used to own a large game preserve in Taney County, Missouri. The neighbors say that he once caught a native who had just killed a deer, but the poacher pointed his rifle and made Mr. Skaggs return to the house. "That feller told old Skaggs *what God told John,*" a hillman said. I have heard this expressions many times, in Missouri and Arkansas. "It's out of the Book," a friend explained, "where God told John what to do, an' made him do it."

At Picher, Oklahoma, a traveling evangelist made a pass at a respectable widow who kept a boardinghouse. She ordered the scoundrel out at once and followed him into the street, shouting denunciations at the top of her voice. "She sure told that preacher *how the cow et the cabbage,*" said an admiring neighbor. This crack is sometimes strengthened by adding *stem an' all!* Near Carterville, Missouri, I heard a related saying about "how Peter et the turnips, *tops an' all.*"

C. R. McKennon, an aged Arkansas planter, was written up in the magazines because he sold a tremendous amount of cotton in one day, nearly a million dollars' worth.[82] It seems that McKennon, who never got

[82] *Time Magazine*, February 3, 1947, p. 88.

beyond the fourth grade in school, won a community spelling bee years ago at Dumas, Arkansas. He regarded this as a great triumph, and still boasts about it sometimes. "I sure showed 'em *where the bear set in the buckwheat,*" the old man said proudly to a reporter.

A witness in a hog-stealing case was unwilling to tell where he had obtained certain information. "I just *ketched it in the breeze,*" he said, meaning that his testimony was based on a rumor going around the neighborhood. Sometimes this expression refers to an unexplained pregnancy: "Lizzie's man has been dead for more'n a year, so she must have *ketched it in the breeze.*" I have heard also, in the same meaning, "she must have *got it in the water.*"

The hillfolk are not heavy eaters, and are often astonished at the amount of food the tourists consume. If a child eats too much, they say, "It looks like *that boy must be from Chicago!*"

Years ago I saw a young girl devour every morsel of food on her plate, and then polish the plate with a bit of bread. Her elders looked on in silent disapproval. After a long pause the father spoke: "Well, *it'll be a clear day* tomorrow." The girl flushed, and soon left the room. Since then I have heard this *clear-day-tomorrow* crack many times. It is always a criticism of greediness at table, and has nothing to do with weather prediction.

The old-timers are scornful of the villager's habit of lying in bed after sunrise. It was about eight o'clock when Porter Lucas, who runs a tomato cannery at Crane, Missouri, asked a farmer to have breakfast with him. "No, thank ye," said the man politely, "I done et, *in the fore part of the day.*"

Sometimes this habit of early rising is carried too far. A wealthy countryman retired and moved into town, intending to take things easy the rest of his days. But he persisted in getting up at five o'clock in the morning, just as he had always done on the farm. Finally his exasperated wife said, "Why don't you *sell the bed an' buy lanterns with the money?*"

Hollerin' down a barrel is somehow connected with paternity. When a young husband becomes a father, his friends make sly cracks about having heard him "hollerin' *Pappy* down the rain-barrel." References to childbirth, using the phrase *holler down a barrel,* often appear in the country newspapers. A local daily printed an item from Mountain Grove, Missouri, to the effect that "someone passed Arthur Akeman's place the other day and saw Arthur *with his head in a barrel* saying 'grandpa, grandpa.' "[83] A

[83] Springfield, Mo., *Leader & Press,* January 6, 1937.

woman who had never borne any children said of her husband: "Poor Jim's been *hollerin' down a rain-barrel* for a good many years now."

A story often credited to old Judge Green, in Howell County, Missouri, is about two men who had quarreled for years and engaged in a series of lawsuits. Finally one came at night and drove a stake in the other's lawn. Somehow this was mentioned in court, and the judge didn't know what was meant by "he driv a stake in my yard." Since the case depended largely upon this expression, court was adjourned while the judge investigated, presumably by consulting some of the old-timers. The final conclusion was that the act signified a defiant farewell; the stake-driver meant to say, "I'm leaving this vicinity for good, and to hell with you!" That's what the judge thought it meant, anyhow, according to the story.[84]

If a hillman is asked a question and doesn't know the answer, he often says, "Well, now, *that's a huckleberry over my persimmon*," meaning that the matter is just a trifle beyond his knowledge.[85] A lady at Elm Springs, Arkansas, tells me that her grandmother used to say: "It's just a huckleberry over your persimmon," which was equivalent to "you've bit off a *little* more'n you can chaw." Sometimes the expression is used ironically or sarcastically. I recall a poor fellow who couldn't read or write, or tell time by a clock, or figure out the dates on a calendar. But when some jokers asked him to solve a complex mathematical problem, he studied it carefully for a long time. "I reckon that's just a *huckleberry* over Ed's persimmon," said a bystander gravely.

An old man rode into town and told our sheriff, "The old woman's fixin' to *put a spider in my coffee*." He meant that his wife was preparing to poison him. I have heard *put a spider in his biscuit* and *put a spider in his dumplin'* used with the same meaning. The reference to a spider is not to be taken literally, but means any sort of poison. A wealthy farmer told me that he didn't believe in life insurance, because many people are murdered to collect the insurance money. "There's trouble enough in this world," he said, "without a man *buyin' spiders* for his family."

A young man in Stone County, Missouri, frequently failed to come home at night. He offered no explanation, and his people were a bit uneasy about him. "Oh, he's just *layin' out with the dry cattle*," a friend said reassuringly. When cows are dry, they don't come in at night to be milked; they just lie out in the woods wherever they happen to be. Some women, usually grass widows with no children or responsibilities, don't

[84] Cf. my *Ozark Superstitions*, 336–37.
[85] Cf. Horace Reynolds, *Saturday Review of Literature*, August 23, 1947, p. 27.

have to come home at night, either. So when a man is consorting with these foot-loose females he is said to be *layin' out with the dry cattle.*

In the early days many poor farmers had no feed, so they just plowed all day and turned the oxen out to graze at night. This was called *plowin' on the grass,* and the expression is still used with reference to one who works hard with insufficient capital or equipment. In 1944 a hillman said to me, "When them Japs try to fight the United States, they're just *a-plowin' on the grass.*"

A young waitress who lived near us in Hot Springs, Arkansas, had an opportunity to marry a wealthy widower, but refused. "If I *cain't be table-cloth, I sure don't aim to be dish-rag,*" she said scornfully.[86] I leave the reader to guess what she meant.

Many similar expressions are omitted from this chapter, because urban readers couldn't understand them.[87] Some of these esoteric items might be made acceptable by long-winded explanations, but others depend for their effect upon intimate experience, or fantastic local tradition, or a first-hand knowledge of backwoods life.

In Taney County, Missouri, a big hillman from Sowcoon Mountain came down to our community dance hall in search of feminine companionship. It happened that the place was full of high school girls, and rather scrawny, immature specimens at that. "Shucks," said the hillman disgustedly, *"the topwaters is a-shoalin', but there ain't a hoss in sight!"* The villagers roared with laughter, but a city feller who was present could make nothing of it. He asked me what all the people were laughing about.

But how could I tell him? It's no use to explain that a *topwater* is a small worthless minnow, and a *hoss* is a large highly prized fish, while *shoaling* is a frenzied sexual activity preliminary to spawning. These are the facts, but such facts are not funny.

Unless a man has actually seen topwaters and redhorse a-shoalin', he can never fully appreciate the Sowcoon Mountain wisecrack.

[86] Cf. Joseph W. Carr, *Dialect Notes,* Vol. III (1906), 160.
[87] Cf. *Ozark Guide,* Eureka Springs, Ark., Autumn, 1949, p. 47.

9 An Ozark Word List

THE WORDS AND PHRASES which follow are not rare or exceptional in the Ozarks. I have heard every one of them more than once, from several different persons, in widely separated places. To avoid needless repetition, I have omitted many items which are treated elsewhere in the book.

References to the writings of others often indicate that my findings differ from those of the author mentioned. In some cases, however, I have cited the work of other collectors, by way of re-enforcement, to show that I am not alone in reporting a certain term or expression as current in the Ozark region.

The titles of certain books and journals are abbreviated as follows: AS, *American Speech;* DN, *Dialect Notes;* EDD, *English Dialect Dictionary;* JAFL, *Journal of American Folklore;* OED, *Oxford English Dictionary;* PADS, *Publication of the American Dialect Society;* PMLA, *Publications of the Modern Language Association.*

The key to pronunciation and the respellings for pronunciation are based upon material in *Webster's New International Dictionary,* 2nd Edition (1934, 1939, 1945, 1950), by G. & C. Merriam Company, and are used by permission.

a: *v.t.* and *v.i.* Contraction of *have.* "I like to never *a* got here."

a: *prep.* and *prefix.* On, at. "We'll be here *a* Sunday," meaning next Sunday. "She lays *a*-flat of her back," meaning flat on her back.

acknowledge the corn: *phr.* To admit, to confess, to apologize. DN, V (1923), 199. See Bartlett, *Dictionary of Americanisms* (Boston, 1859), 3, for a fanciful explanation of this phrase. Cf. *own the corn.*

acorn calf: *n.* A runt, a poor specimen, a weakling. Applied to human beings as well as to cattle. AS, V (1929), 16.

aggerpervoke: *v.t.* To irritate, to provoke, to annoy. Perhaps a blend of *aggravate* and *provoke*. DN, V (1923), 200.

aggervex: *v.t.* Same as *aggerpervoke*. A blend of *aggravate* and *vex*. AS, VIII (1933), 47.

airish: *adj.* Cool, cold. "It's a-gittin' right *airish* here lately, on these high ridges." DN, V (1926), 397. Cf. *crimpy*.

alemand (ăl′ ĕ mănd) : *n.* A dance call. Botkin (*American Play-Party Song,* 203) thinks it is from the French *à la main*. C. R. Black (*Square Dancing Ozark Style,* 6) says that, at the call *alemand left,* "you take your corner, or left hand lady, by the left hand." A related call, which sounds like *alemandy goodelum,* is sometimes heard at the square dances. Cf. my *Ozark Mountain Folks* (New York, 1932), 80.

ambeer (ăm′ bĭr) : *n.* Tobacco spittle. "Old man Combs has always got *ambeer* on his chin." DN, V (1923), 200.

an: *conj.* If. "I wouldn't be surprised *an* he don't come down tomorrow." Also, "If it warn't for the *ifs* an' the *ans* I'd be a rich man today."

antick: *adj.* Playful, "fresh," sometimes wild or ungovernable. "Charley's gettin' too *antick* round them Burton gals" generally means only that he pinched the girls' legs, or something of the sort. AS, XI (1936), 314; PADS, No. 2 (1944), 17.

antick: *n.* Clown, buffoon. "That there young-un is a reg'lar *antick*." DN, V (1927), 472

anti-ganglin'. See *anti-gogglin'*.

anti-gogglin' (ăn tĭ găg′ lĭn) : *Adj.* and *adv.* Diagonal, diagonally, oblique, obliquely. "Bob walked *anti-gogglin'* across the square" means that his course was not directly across, but nearer the diagonal. Rural dressmakers use *anti-gogglin'* to mean "on the bias"—diagonal to the weave or pattern of the cloth. In some sections the word is pronounced *anti-goddlin'*. People in Greene County, Mo. (PADS, No. 2 [1944], 53) say that God created the earth with four corners and that a building not set "square with the world" is *anti-goddlin',* "against the wish or example of God." *Anti-ganglin', kitty-corner,* and *catty-corner* seem to be synonymous with anti-gogglin'. The adverb *catty-stranglin'* is a related form; May Kennedy McCord (Springfield, Mo., *News & Leader,* March 15, 1936) has seen an old deed in which a lot is described as *"catty-strangling* across" from another property. *Catty-wampus* and *cat-angular* are less common, but I think they mean cattystranglin'. A country sheriff told me that the body of a murdered woman "was a-layin' *catty-wampusly* in the kitchen." Taylor (DN, V

[1923], 205) says that *dianglin'* means diagonally in McDonald County, Mo. Cf. *sky-gogglin'*.

a-past: *prep.* and *adv.* Beyond. Often used figuratively. "Maybe Zeke didn't kill that feller, but I sure wouldn't put it *a-past* him." DN, V (1926), 398.

applicate: *v.t.* To pester one with requests. A girl said of an unwelcome suitor, "That feller just *applicated* me mornin', noon an' night, till Paw finally had to run him off'n the place." AS, V (1929), 16.

arbuckle: *n.* A sore, a boil. Perhaps a corruption of *carbuncle.* "This here *arbuckle* started from a chigger bite, Doc." DN, V (1927), 472.

Arkansas toothpick: *n.* A bowie knife, a large sheath knife, a dagger. AS, VIII (1933), 47. Allen Walker Read (*Missouri Historical Review,* XXIX [1935], 267) reports *Missouri toothpick* as meaning "a long knife," but I have not heard this.

arkansaw: *v.t.* To cheat, to take advantage of. When a hunter shoots a quail on the ground, the bird is said to be *arkansawed* (DN, V [1927], 472). My neighbor told me that a banker was trying to *arkansaw* him out of his farm. Cf. *ozark.* In some sections *arkansaw* means to sweep with a brush broom, or a bunch of green branches: "Just wait till I *arkansaw* the kitchen, afore ye set down" (As, XI [1936], 314). Sometimes it means wear out, or exhaust: "No wonder Billy looks young. He never done no hard work to *arkansaw* himself down." Postmaster McQuary, of Galena, Mo., ate lunch with me in a little restaurant, I reached for the check. "No," said he positively, "we'll go *arkansaw,*" meaning that each man pays for his own food.

Arkansawyer: *n.* A native of Arkansas. The newspapers often print *Arkansan,* but one never hears a hillman pronounce it to rhyme with Kansan (AS, VIII [1933], 47). Carr (DN, III [1906], 124–25) says "the adjective and the noun *Arkansan* are in disrepute because the word suggests *Kansan.* Kansas and the Kansans are very unpopular in Arkansas." He finds that "*Arkansawyer* is universal among the uneducated, and occurs even among the educated." He lists the pronunciation *Arkansawyan* as a compromise between *Arkansawyer* and *Arkansan,* but labels it "rare." On February 16, 1945, State Senator Julien James introduced a bill designating the people as *Ark-an-saw-yans,* but the Assembly would have none of it. John Gould Fletcher, a native of Little Rock and a distinguished literary figure, spells the name *Arkansawyer* (*Arkansas,* vii).

armstrong: *n.* A crude, primitive tool or implement. Taylor (DN, V [1923], 200) thinks it applies especially to the cradle used in cutting grain. Some old-timers call any outmoded tool an *armstrong*. I heard a barber in Crane, Mo., refer to his old-fashioned razor in this way: "Most men over fifty would rather shave with an *armstrong*, if they could keep it honed an' stropped."

auger-eyed: *adj.* Sharp-eyed, gimlet-eyed. DN, V (1927), 472.

baby-trough: *n.* A cradle, or a play-pen. At Zinc, Ark., the *baby-trough* was a sizable enclosure, in which women parked their babies while they worked in the tomato cannery.

back and forth: *phr.* To work in an aimless or futile manner. "Them boys just kept *a-backin' an' forthin'* all day long." AS, XI (1936), 314.

back-staff: *n.* A support. When a mountain man says that a certain tale "has got a *back-staff* behind it," he means that it is supported by substantial evidence. Cf. Tom Moore, *Mysterious Tales and Legends of the Ozarks,* 72.

back-stay: *n.* The background, history, or antecedents that explain an occurrence. A story or anecdote is much more interesting after some old-timer tells you the *back-stay*. Judge Tom Moore, of Christian County, Mo., says that the word was common at the turn of the century, but is seldom heard now.

bald face: *n.* Raw corn whiskey. Said to be a reference to *bald-face hornets;* they're hot, too. Tucker (*American English,* 233) found this word applied to whiskey as long ago as 1840.

barefoot bread: *n.* Hard cornbread, made without eggs or shortening. AS, VIII (1933), 47.

bare naked: *adj.* Naked, nude. "Them city gals was a-splashin' round plumb *bare naked!*" *Body naked, start naked,* and *mother naked* are also common. DN, V (1923), 201; V (1926), 398.

barrel into: *v. i.* To shoot into, to shoot at. "A big gobbler come runnin' out of the brush, an' Bob sure did *barr'l into* him." DN, V (1926), 472.

bastard oak: *n.* A variety of oak which some natives regard as a cross between the ordinary black oak (*Quercus velutina*) and the blackjack (*Quercus marilandica*). In some parts of Missouri, *bastard oak* means a variety of white oak (*Quercus alba*) used in making baskets. AS, VIII (1933), 47.

battlin' stick: *n.* A club with which pioneer women beat their clothes in washing them, since they had no washboards.

bawbee: *n.* A trifle, something of small value, like a cheap marble. Of a young ruffian it was said, "He'd kill you for a *bawbee,* an' eat you for two." Carr (DN, III [1906], 126) spells it *baubee.*

bawlin'-hound: *n.* A dog which bays when trailing coons, possums, foxes, and so on. "A genuine redbone *bawlin'-hound*" is highly prized by one of my neighbors. AS, V (1929), 16.

beat work: *phr.* To shirk, to avoid manual labor. A boy who wishes to learn a profession or engage in any white-collar enterprise is said to be "a-tryin' to *beat work.*" AS, VIII (1933), 47.

bedcord strong: *adj.* Very strong indeed. A reference to the stout cords which serve as slats and springs in the old-fashioned bedsteads. "Jim he's *bedcord strong* when it comes to book-learnin'." AS, VIII (1933), 47.

bed-post: *v.t.* To confine a small child by placing a bedpost on his dress or other garment. In Stone County, Mo., the county nurse and I entered a cabin where two children were sitting on the floor. They smiled but didn't get up. Their mother was out picking greens. "She's got us *bed-posted* down," said one, "so we cain't mess with the fire." Then I noticed that each child's shirt-tail was put under the bedpost, so that he couldn't move. Mirandy Bauersfeld (*Breezes from Persimmon Holler,* [Hollywood, 1943], 115) mentions this way of keeping children out of mischief. Mary Elizabeth Mahnkey, of Mincy, Mo., spoke of children's being "anchored with a bedpost on each child's dress-tail," and told me that this was a common practice in the backwoods.

beeler: *n.* A wooden maul used in splitting rails. The *beeler* is just a big mallet, distinguished from the *mankiller* maul which is made in one piece like a huge club.

begouge: *v.t.* To stab, to pierce. I heard of a woman who *"begouged* herself accidental"* with an ice pick.

benighted: *p.p.* of *benight.* To be overtaken by darkness. "We figured on gittin' to Joplin, but we was *benighted* just south of Tipton Ford."

bespoke: *adj.* Asked for, promised, engaged. When a girl is described as *bespoke,* it usually means that she's betrothed, but sometimes only that she is "dated up" for a particular dance or party. I once heard a countryman at Searcy, Ark., ask a lady on a bus: "Is this here seat *bespoke?*" AS, VIII (1933), 47.

betsey: *n.* This term is applied to various tools and utensils; but when a man calls for *old betsey* he generally wants either his rifle or the big maul used in driving fence posts. DN, V (1927), 472.

betsey bug: *n.* Any sort of large dark-colored beetle found in rotten wood. The blood of these insects is believed to be a cure for earache. AS, VIII (1933), 47.

betweenst: *prep.* Between. Still common in backwoods conversation. Used in the *Arkansas Traveler* dialogue, published at Little Rock, Ark., in 1876. Cf. Masterson (*Tall Tales of Arkansaw,* 188).

bingbuffer: *n.* A fabulous beast, said to kill other animals by throwing stones with its hinged tail. Cf. Jefferson City, Mo., *Daily Tribune,* July 23, 1891; *Missouri Historical Review,* XXXVIII (1944), 367.

bird-wire: *n.* A piece of thin wire, with a weight at one end. Cast into a covey of quails or other birds, this weapon is quite effective, and is widely used by boys in the Ozarks. DN, V (1927), 473.

bird-work: *v.i.* To leap forward, to progress by a series of stiff-legged jumps. "I seen Lem *a-bird-workin'* down the road; acted like the yaller-jackets was after him." AS, VIII (1933), 47.

biscuit weather: *n.* Snowy weather. A. B. Macdonald, of Kansas City, Mo., once explained this expression by remarking that "snow makes wheat, wheat makes flour, and flour makes biscuits."

blackberry squall. See *blackberry winter.*

blackberry winter: *n.* A late cold spell in May or early June, when the blackberries are blooming. AS, VIII (1933), 47. *Blackberry squall* is used in the same meaning. Cf. *Blackbird storm, buzzard storm, dogwood winter, frog storm, martin storm, oak winter, whippoorwill storm,* etc.

blackbird storm: *n.* A short cold spell in late spring, after the appearance of the blackbirds. Cf. *blackberry winter.*

blackguard: *v.t., v.i.,* and *adj.* To use vulgar or obscene language, or to tell smutty stories. "Them Tolliver gals just sets around an' *blackguards* all day long." DN, V (1927), 473. I have never heard *blackguard* as a noun in the Ozarks, but the adjective is common: "I'm ag'in this here *blackguard* talk right in the church-house!" One of my foul-mouthed visitors was described as "the *blackguardin'est* feller that ever set foot in this town."

blanny (blăn′ĭ): *n.* Cajolery. "Ab Lee's *blanny* sure did fool the schoolmarm." Perhaps from *blarney.* DN, V (1926), 398.

blink: *v.i.* To sour. "That milk'll *blink* sure if you leave it settin' out in the sun that-a-way." The adjective *blinky* is used to describe milk which is slightly sour.

block-and-fall: *n.* Block and tackle.

blowing horn: *n.* A scraped and polished cowhorn, which the fox hunter uses to call his hounds. AS, VIII (1933), 47.

blue darter: *n.* A small chicken hawk, usually the Cooper's (*Accipiter cooperi*) or sharpshin (*Accipiter striatus*).

bluegum moke: *n.* A Negro whose gums are bluish rather than red. It is said that the bite of a *blue-gum moke* means certain death. DN, V (1927), 473.

blue-john: *n.* Skim milk—milk from which the cream has been skimmed or separated. AS, V (1929), 16. When the stuff sours a bit, it is called *blinky blue-john*. A legendary giant who figures in numerous Ozark folk tales is known as *Blinky Bluejohn*. Cf. my *We Always Lie to Strangers*, 164–65.

board tree: *n.* A straight-grained oak, suitable for riving into clapboards or shingles. I once heard a moonshiner testify in court: "I was just out a-lookin' for *board trees* when the sheriff come a-runnin' up the holler an' 'rested me." Cf. DN, V (1923), 201.

bobble: *n.* An error, a mistake. The noun *misbobble*, oddly enough, means exactly the same thing. "A *misbobble* is what happens when you make a *mislick*," a woodcutter told me.

bodacious: *adj.* Outright, bold, brazen. "I never seen such *bodacious* dancin' in all my born days!" Fred Starr (*From an Ozark Hillside*, 36) says that *"bodaciously* means altogether, out and out, as: 'It ain't such a *bodaciously* good fence, but it's a heap better'n no fence at all.'"

bodark (bō' därk): *n.* The Osage orange (*Maclura pomifera*), also called hedge apple or bois d'arc, a common tree in some parts of the Ozark country. AS, VIII (1933), 48. John Gould Fletcher (*Arkansas*, 45) calls it *burdock*, but the real burdock is a biennial weed of the genus *Arctium*. Cf. PADS, No. 2 (1944), 54.

boggle: *v.t.* To bungle, to blunder. "Bill set up for a horse-doctor, but he *boggled* everything, an' killed more'n he cured."

boggy: *adj.* Confused or delirious, as under the influence of drugs.

bogue: *v.i.* To move slowly, to wander aimlessly about. "I cain't sleep. Reckon I'll just git up an' *bogue* around till sunup." AS, V (1929), 17; XI (1936), 314. There are many verbs to indicate purposeless, idle wandering. In the sentence, "I was just *a-santerin'* round," the verb may be replaced by *projectin', traffickin', boogerin', piddlin', shackin', asslin',* or *campaignin'* without any essential change in meaning. Cf. *cipher, cooter, sanko.*

bogue-sang: *n.* False ginseng. A two-year-old root of the pokeweed (*Phytolacca americana*), properly dried, looks very much like a genuine sang root. The root-diggers on Bear Creek, in Taney County, Mo.,

228

used to mix this *bogue-sang* with real ginseng, thus cheating the druggists who bought the stuff in quantity. Cf. my *Ozark Superstitions*, 113.

bolden: *v.i.* To swell. Cf. *boulden.*

bone idle: *adj.* Wilfully and incurably indolent. *Bone lazy* is also common, and I once heard a man described as a *pure bone loafer.* AS, VIII (1933), 48.

boo up (bōo): *v. t.* To praise. "Them fellers was *a-booin'* up the hotel down at Hollister, tryin' to tole folks away from my boardin'-house."

booger (bōog' ĕr): *n.* A louse, usually a head louse. But sometimes it means a ghost or some kind of supernatural monster. DN, V (1923), 201. Cf. PADS, No. 2 (1944), 28, 40; No. 13 (1950), 16.

bore for the simples: *phr.* A jocular expression referring to a stupid individual. "The old fool orter be *bored for the simples!*" One sometimes hears *tapped for the simples,* with the same meaning. The idea is that a hole in the skull might let some of the foolishness out. DN, V (1927), 473.

boulden (bōl' dĕn): *adj.* Swollen. Louise Platt Hauck, of St. Joseph, Mo., tells me that this is common along the Missouri-Arkansas border. I have heard it myself, but not often. Cf. *bolden.*

bounden: *adj.* Under legal or moral obligation. "It was my *bounden duty* to put that feller in jail," said a village constable who could neither read nor write.

bowel off: *v.i.* To have a diarrhea. "Tom he was a-pukin' an' *a-bowellin' off* somethin' turrible, so finally they sent after Doc Holton."

bowel-rack: *v.t.* To cut or wound so that the intestines are exposed. An acquaintance of mine was *bowel-racked* in a knife fight; I could see the contents of the intestines coming out between his fingers as he clutched his abdomen.

bowels: *n.* Feces, dung. "The baby's *bowels* looks mighty black an' dismal-like." AS, V (1929), 16.

box: *n.* Coffin. A washerwoman at Galena, Mo., disapproved of my white shirts. "I'd ruther see my *box* a-comin' as to iron these here shirts!"

box house: *n.* A house built of rough oak boards, as distinguished from a building of logs or matched lumber. AS, V (1929), 17.

brag dog: *n.* Favorite, pride, pet. "Jim had lots of hounds, but old Biggy was always his *brag dog.*" Used figuratively of children, pupils, and friends. I once heard a fox hunter in Joplin, Mo., refer to his mistress as "the *brag bitch*."

brake: *n.* A thicket, usually of cedar trees. The plural form is usually employed, as "in the Black River brakes" or "the brakes of Little Piney." AS, VIII (1933), 48.

branch-water: *adj.* Trifling, shiftless. *Branch-water folks* are people who camp anywhere and drink surface water; regularly settled hillfolk live near a well or spring.

bread: *n.* Corn, often used to designate the growing crop. "Bob got crippled up in the sawmill, so the neighbors just whirled in an' planted his *bread* for him." AS, VIII (1933), 48.

break: *v.t.* To loose hands. This term is used in many combinations by callers at the square dances. *"Break* an' trail," for example, means "loose hands and move in single file."

brickle: *adj.* Brittle, crisp. "If cowcumber pickles ain't *brickle,* they ain't fit to eat." Sometimes used as a verb, meaning to become brittle, to crack. "I sure don't want the icin' to *brickle* off'n that there cake."

brim (brĭm): *n.* Bream, a name applied to several fishes, usually the blue-gill (*Lepomis macrochirus*). Commonly used in the White River country of Arkansas. I have not heard it very often in Missouri. AS, V (1929), 17.

britches quilt: *n.* A quilt or comforter made of heavy woolen material. A lighter covering is known as a *shirt-tail quilt.* Cf. AS, VIII (1933), 33.

britchin's: *n.* Diapers, also known as *hippin's.* DN, V (1926), 398.

bronikal: *adj.* Bronchial.

broom me out! *interj.* An exclamation comparable to "Well, I'll be damned!" The expression *fry me brown*! is used in the same way.

brush-arbor whiskey: *n.* Cheap but potent moonshine, *popskull, foxhead.* Sold chiefly to the class of people who attend camp meetings and brush-arbor revivals. Cf. *farm liquor.*

brush drag: *n.* A crude seine made of willow boughs, tied together with bark. Meriwether Lewis (*Journal* III, 1, 14, 1805) tells of catching many fish in a *bush drag.* Sometimes *brush drag* is used to mean a primitive harrow, made of brush weighted with stones.

brush rack: *n.* A raft or platform of small sticks tied together. The term is sometimes applied to a rude brush shelter for chickens or swine.

buck-eye: *v.t.* To poison. The hillfolk use the roots of the buckeye tree

(*Aesculus glabra*) in poisoning fish. An animal which staggers or acts strangely is said to be *buck-eyed*.

budget: *n*. A parcel, a package. "The boss got too sassy, so I just picked up my *budget* an' walked out." AS, V (1929), 17.

buffalo: *v.t.* To beat with a firearm, to club with a revolver. Cf. *pistol-whip*.

buggy days: *n*. A term used by the old-timers, with reference to the period when there were no automobiles or good roads in the hill country.

build pigpens: *phr*. To deceive someone, to cheat a customer. Woodcutters pile firewood pigpen-fashion in their wagons, to make the load appear larger than it really is. I have heard a backwoods politician charge the President of the United States with *buildin' pigpens*. AS, XI (1936), 314.

build a smoke: *phr*. To fire a gun repeatedly. "Tom sure did *build a smoke* behind that feller, but he never did hit him."

bull goose: *n*. The leader, the boss, the head man. A native of Springfield, Mo., said to me: "Old Foster is the *bull goose* out at the Army Hospital," meaning that Colonel Foster was the commandant.

bump: *v.t.* To *jump* or *goose* bass, forcing them to leap into a boat. "This here *bumpin'* fish is ag'in the law nowadays." See *Esquire*, August, 1939, pp. 67, 149. Cf. my *We Always Lie to Strangers*, 220.

burn-out: *n*. A destructive conflagration. "They had a turrible *burn-out* in Reeds Spring. The lumberyard's plumb gone, an' two good houses."

bush colt: *n*. An illegitimate child, a bastard. Cf. *woodscolt*.

bush up: *v.i.* To hide. "Bill he went an' *bushed up* somewhere out back of the church-house." DN, V (1926), 398.

bussy: *n*. Sweetheart. This is heard occasionally, but I don't think it is common anywhere in the Ozarks now. DN, V (1926), 398.

busty: *adj*. Self-assertive, loud, boisterous. As, XI (1936), 314.

butternuts: *n*. Brown overalls or work clothes. Weeks (DN, I [1892], 325) reported *butternuts* from Jackson County, Mo. "To this day," he writes, "the natives in country neighborhoods so hate blue that they will not wear overalls of this color."

buttridge (bŭt' rĭj): *n*. A knife used by old-time blacksmiths in trimming horses' hooves; there was a long butt like a gunstock, which rested against the smith's shoulder and gave him more leverage. Evidently identical with *butteris* as given in Webster. Cf. Allen Oliver in the Springfield, Mo., *Leader*, July 23, 1936.

buzzard storm: *n.* A period of cold weather in spring, after the buzzards have returned from the South. Cf. *blackberry winter.*

by guess and by God: *phr.* More or less at random, without any accurate measurement. "We never did get this here town surveyed; just laid it off *by guess an' by God."* DN, V (1923), 203. AS, XVI (1941), 21.

by-word: *n.* One's favorite expression. A boy in our village shouted in the street that the schoolmaster was a son-of-a-bitch. Later the boy's mother explained that "Tommy didn't mean no harm. Son-of-a-bitch has been his *by-word,* ever since he was a baby." Cf. DN, V (1923), 203.

caddy: *n.* A box or trunk. In Taney County, Mo., I was told of a woman who "has got a whole *caddy* full of old books an' letters."

call: *v.t.* To recall, to remember. "I orter know that feller, but I cain't *call* his name." But if the hillman says "I dassn't *call* his name," the word means mention rather than recall. Sometimes it is used instead of pronounce, as when a man says, "I cain't rightly *call* that word," in reference to some strange term he has seen in print. DN, V (1926), 398.

candy-breakin': *n.* A social game where men and women are "paired off" by biting opposite ends of the same piece of candy. Cf. DN, V (1923), 203. JAFL, 49 (1936), 204–205.

candy snake: *n.* The so-called glass snake or joint snake (*Ophisarurus ventralis*), which is really a legless lizard.

canker: *v.i.* To become tainted, to decay. A fowl which has hung too long is said to be *high* or *cankered.*

caplock: *n.* A gun fired by means of a percussion cap, the form of muzzle-loader which followed the flintlock. AS, VIII (1933), 48.

captain: *n.* A strong-minded, domineering woman. "Jim sure did git him a purty woman, but she's too much of a *captain* to suit me." A lady in Stone County, Mo., was such a super-captain that people called her *general,* and this was regarded as very witty.

careless: *adj.* Reckless. A lawyer in Galena, Mo., said of some wild young men, "They're the *carelessest* bunch in this town."

careless weed: *n.* A certain tall, red-stemmed plant (*Amaranthus hybridus*), sometimes known as pigweed. It is said that the tiny seeds are deadly poison. I know a blind man who attributes his affliction to a single seed which blew into one of his eyes.

carry on: *v.i.* To behave in a noisy or boisterous manner. "I never seen folks *carry on* like them gals from Springfield." DN, V (1926), 398.

carry on a chip: *phr.* To humor, to pamper, to spoil. "They done *carried that boy on a chip* till he ain't no good for nothin'." AS, VIII (1933), 48.

catamount: *n.* The bobcat (*Lynx rufus*). In the West it appears that catamount means panther, but the word is not so used in the Ozarks.
Wayman Hogue (*Back Yonder*, 184) observes that "the wildcat, also
called the *catamount* and the bobcat, is about half the size of the painter." And S. E. Simonson (*Arkansas Historical Quarterly*, Winter,
1947, p. 419) says that in 1902 Mississippi County, Ark., "was full of
predatory animals, particularly bear, panthers, and almost innumer-
able bobcats or *catamounts.*"

cat-and-clay: *n.* A rude chimney made of sticks and mud. AS, XI (1936),
314.

cat-squirrel: *n.* The gray squirrel (*Sciurus carolinensis*), as distinguished
from the larger, reddish fox-squirrel. AS, VIII (1933), 48.

cave: *n.* A cellar. Many hillfolk store their food in natural caverns, but the
word *cave* is used to designate a "dug cellar." also.

cha-muck-a-muck (chá mŭk' á mŭk'): *n.* A relish of mixed pickles, highly
seasoned. May Kennedy McCord, of Springfield, Mo., says that it is
identical with what used to be called *chow-chow.* Some Indians at
Pack, Mo., told me that it is a Cherokee word.

chance: *n.* Accident. "Hit'll just be a *chance* if you-uns ever see that feller
again." Sometimes used to mean a considerable number. Boasting of
his exploits in the Civil War, a very old man said, "I killed a *chance*
of Yankees at Prairie Grove." DN, V (1927), 473.

chap: *n.* A child, usually a little boy. The plural is used for children of both
sexes. *Chap* never means an adult in the Ozarks. When I spoke of a
summer visitor as "a pleasant-spoken chap," one of my neighbors cried,
"*Chap,* hell! That feller's thirty year old, maybe forty!" DN, V (1926),
398.

charge: *v.t.* To command, to order. "Paw *charged* me to cut wood all day;
so that's what I done."

charge one's mind: *phr.* To burden one's mind with something. A hillman
was asked about the ages of his twelve children. "The woman'll know,"
said he. "I never *charge my mind* with such as that."

chaunk (chôngk): *v.t.* To crunch or crush between the teeth. "Don't spit
them grape-seeds out, just *chaunk* 'em." DN, III (1906), 130; III (1909),
393; V (1927), 473.

chawed rosum: *n.* Something conspicuously excellent. "This here gun,"
said a hunter brandishing a new rifle, "is the *chawed rosum* an' no mistake!" A backwoods matron stared at a pretty schoolteacher and

snarled: "That young hussy thinks she's the *chawed rosum,* but she don't look like much to me."

cheat: *v.i.* A term used in the square dance. *"Cheat* or swing" is a common call. When a male dancer *cheats,* he makes a feint, as if to swing a girl, and then leaves her untouched. Cf. my *Ozark Mountain Folks,* 74.

chimney sweep: *n.* A species of swift (*Chaetura pelagica*) which nests in chimneys. AS, VIII (1933), 48.

chinkapin: *n.* The dwarf chestnut (*Castanea pumila*). In some sections the term designates a variety of pin oak. Elsie Bates, of Hollister, Mo., told me that the children in her neighborhood called little black acorns *chinkapins* and ate them.

chips and grindstones: *phr.* Odds and ends, general merchandise. A workman who is paid in *chips and grindstones* gets no cash, but is forced to accept feed, groceries, dry goods, and the like. The phrase *whets and grindstones* is also used, with the same meaning.

chock: *v.t.* To put chunks or pieces of wood under something. Usually it is the wheels of a wagon. But I knew a man in Joplin, Mo., who *chocked* a trunk in his bedroom to make it "set level."

choke rag: *n.* An old-fashioned necktie.

chub: *n.* A sweetheart, a lover. Rose O'Neill, of Taney County, Mo., says that this was a common word along Bear Creek in the early nineteen hundreds and applied to either sex.

chucklehead: *n.* A blue catfish (*Ictalurus furcatus*), thinner and reputedly tougher than the ordinary channel cat.

chuffy: *adj.* Plump. "Lucy's man is a kinder low, *chuffy* feller."

chug: *n.* A slight depression in the road. "Hit rained just enough to fill all them little *chugs* full of water." DN, V (1927), 473.

chunk: *n.* A stick of wood, a short log. "Jeff he cain't shoot nohow, only if he rests his rifle-gun on a chunk." DN, V (1927), 473.

chunk: *v.t.* To waste, to discard. "Lon just kept *a-chunkin'* his money away, till purty soon he was pore just like the rest of us." DN, V (1927), 473.

churn: *v.t.* To beat, to drub, to paddle. "If that young-un don't behave, I'll *churn his behind* every step of the way home!"

cipher around: *v.i.* To loiter about, to get in people's way, to idle in public places. Major E. H. Criswell, of Lexington, Mo., says that a man who *ciphers around* "goes nosing into other people's business, trying to

234

detect something that will enable him to make trouble. He is a busy-body rather than an idler." Cf. AS, V (1929), 17.

citireen (sĭt ēr ēn'): *n.* An old resident, an old-timer, an old fogy of either sex. "You ask any of these old *citireens,* an' they'll tell you all 'bout it." AS, V (1929), 17.

citizen-rifle: *n.* The muzzle-loading Kentucky rifle. Probably so called to distinguish it from military weapons. DN, V (1926), 398.

civvy-cat: *n.* The civet or polecat (*Spilogale putorius*), or little spotted skunk, similar to the "phoby-cat" of the Southwest. DN, V (1927), 473.

clabber: *v.i.* and *adj.* Cloudy, as when the sky *clabbers* up before a storm. But sometimes it is used figuratively. Asked what he thought about the prospects of war, a backwoods congressman said, "It looks mighty *clabber* to me."

clean one's plow: *phr.* To handle very roughly, to thrash severely. "If that feller says one faultin' word to me, I'll *clean his plow!*" The Ozark farmer is accustomed to scour the rust from his plowshare by dragging it through a gravel bar. One who has witnessed the knock-down-and-drag-out fights of these backwoodsmen will appreciate the aptness of the figure. Cf. Marge Lyon, *Fresh from the Hills,* 136.

clearing: *n.* A social gathering, the real purpose of which is to clear land of timber and underbrush. Men bring axes and saws, and work hard all day. The host's part is to provide good food and perhaps some music and whiskey for a frolic in the evening. AS, V (1929), 17.

clew: *v.t.* To strike. "So then I just up an' *clewed* him side of the head!" DN, V (1927), 473.

clew-bird: *n.* A fabulous heron that sticks its bill in a gravel bar and whistles loudly through its rectum. The James River fishermen call it the *milermore* bird, because the noise it makes can be heard for a long distance. The variety known as the *noon-bird,* said to inhabit the Kiamichi Mountains of Oklahoma, whistles like a fire engine at high noon. Cf. my *We Always Lie to Strangers,* 68.

climate: *v.t.* To afford proper climatic conditions. "My folks they went to Nebrasky once, but 'peared like the North couldn't *climate* 'em." AS, V (1929), 17.

clout: *n.* Diaper. The combination *britch-clout* is heard occasionally. DN, V (1926), 398.

cobbing: *n.* A vigorous massage with a corncob soaked in grease or ointment. "A plumb good *cobbin'*" is indicated in certain skin diseases. AS, VIII (1933), 48.

collar: *v.t.* To girdle or deaden a tree by cutting off a strip of bark. "I don't aim to fell them trees. I'm just a-goin' to *collar* 'em."

come bad: *phr.* To acquire a venereal disease. "My boy's been a-runnin' with them Bull Creek gals, an' now he's done *come bad.*"

complected: *adj.* Having a delicate skin, easily burned by the sun. "Nancy she's *complected,* but the rest of them gals don't need no sunbonnets."

confidence: *v.t.* To trust, to place confidence in. "I don't reckon I could *confidence* any woman, since Ruby has done went back on me."

conjure: *n.* A supernatural spell. "Maw she thinks somebody has done laid a *conjure* on her."

conjure: *v.t.* To deal in magic or supernatural spells. The word also means to perform some ordinary task with unusual skill or celerity. Mabel Mueller, of Rolla, Mo., spoke of a neighbor "who can *conjure* a fine dress out of a gunnysack." A girl in Branson, Mo., showed me a large cake, which she said was *"conjured* an' baked" in her own kitchen.

conohany (kō nō hăn' ĭ): *n.* Hominy cooked with meat and nuts, seasoned with wild herbs. It is still favored by old-timers in the Cookson Hills of Oklahoma, where it is said to be a Cherokee dish.

cook-room: *n.* A kitchen. Since the kitchen is sometimes a separate building, even though built right up against the house, there is often no door between, and one must go outdoors to get into the *cook-room.*

coon: *v.t.* To crawl, to move on all fours. "The ford was washed out, so I just *cooned* a log that had fell acrost the creek." AS, VIII (1933), 48.

cooter: *n.* and *v.i.* A hard-shelled water turtle (*Emydidae*), but sometimes the word is applied to any sort of hard-shelled turtle or tortoise. I have never heard it used to designate the soft-shelled or the snapping turtle. As a verb, *cooter* means to move aimlessly about, as "I seen that Goddamn' preacher *a-cooterin'* round amongst the womenfolks." Cf. Mencken, *American Language: Supplement I,* 198; George P. Wilson, *Frank C. Brown Collection of North Carolina Folklore,* I, 529.

cord-wood: *n.* A sign of rustic or rural breeding. To say that a man has *"cord-wood* on his breath" means that he still bears marks of his backwoods origin. AS, V (1929), 17.

corn cracker: *n.* A primitive gristmill.

count: *v.t.* To consider, to regard. "Mary was always *counted* one of the fightin'est women in Polk County." DN, V (1926), 399.

coverlid: *n.* A counterpane, coverlet, bedspread. DN, III (1905), 75; V (1926), 399.

cow-itch: *n.* The trumpet vine (*Campsis radicans*), also known as *thimble blossom* and *bugle vine.*

crawdad: *v.i.* To crawl on one's belly, like a crawfish. "Me an' Ab had to *crawdad* purty near a mile to git a shot at them geese." AS, VIII (1933), 48.

crawdad bottom: *n.* Swampy land near seeps or springs, too wet for profitable cultivation. AS, XI (1936), 314.

cream-jug: *n.* A small pitcher used for cream. The Ozarker never calls a large pitcher a jug.

crib basket: *n.* A stout basket made of oak splints, used to carry corn. AS, VIII (1933), 48.

crimp up: *v.i.* To writhe in agony, to collapse from pain. "Tom sure did *crimp up* when that feller kicked him in the stummick." DN, V (1927), 473.

crimpy: *adj.* Cool, chilly. "It gits pretty *crimpy* on these high ridges of a mornin'." Cf. *airish.*

crowd the mourners: *phr.* To act prematurely, to show unseemly haste. Cf. DN, V (1923), 205; AS, XI (1936), 314.

cuckle: *v.t.* To cuckold. "Jim is a-fixin' to *cuckle* old man Blakemore." The injured husband is said to be *cuckled.* "They tell me that the old feller was *cuckled* afore he'd been married a week." AS, XI (1936), 314.

crud (krŭd): *n.* A disease usually marked by skin lesions and digestive upsets. According to *Time* (August 13, 1945, p. 76), "crud and creeping crud are U. S. servicemen's names for any and every kind of tropical skin disease." Here in the Ozarks some hillfolk say *crud* when they mean hives, others tell me it means diarrhea, or the *backdoor trots.* In Fayetteville, Ark., it is said that when a man has the *crud* "everything he eats turns to dung," and as a result he is undernourished. A man from Yell County, Ark., says that down his way *crud* means a respiratory disturbance, such as asthma or hay fever.

cull list: *n.* The unwanted or undesirable. When a mountain girl reaches the age of nineteen or twenty without finding a husband, she is said to be "on the *cull list.*" AS, VIII (1933), 48.

cush: *n.* A mixture of eggs, water, and leftover cornbread, fried in bacon grease.

cut a big gut: *phr.* To do something foolish, to make oneself ridiculous. AS, VIII (1933), 48.

cut a rusty: *phr.* To do something foolish or improper. "I sure did *cut a rusty* when I wrote that letter." DN, V (1927), 473. Lillian Short, of Galena, Mo., tells me that the phrase really means to *cut a fine figure,* but it is nearly always used sarcastically or ironically. There is a related expression in an old song, "The Cowboy's Dream:"

> *I'm scared that I'll be a stray yearling,*
> *A maverick unbranded on high,*
> *And get* cut in the bunch with the rusties
> *While the Boss of the Riders goes by.*

Margaret Larkin (*Singing Cowboy,* [New York, 1931], 181) says, "To be *cut in the bunch with the rusties* is to be herded with the poorest steers, the culls, the wild ones, the lean ones."

Clink O'Neill, of Day, Mo., thinks that the word is really *rustic,* but I have not heard it so pronounced.

cut a stick: *phr.* To run rapidly. Cf. *light a shuck.* AS, XI (1936), 314.

cut mud: *phr.* To make haste. One of our neighbors said to his small son, "You just *cut mud* for home, afore I take a hickory to you!" AS, XI (1936), 314.

cut your own weeds: *phr.* To mind one's own business. Cf. *kill your own snakes.*

cymlin: *n.* Any small gourd, also a kind of summer squash. Cf. Wentworth, *American Dialect Dictionary,* 559.

cymlin-head: *n.* A fool, a dunce, a gourd-head. DN, V (1926), 399.

dabblin' pan: *n.* A wash basin.

dance juber (jōōb′ ēr): *phr.* To leap wildly about. "The old man cut him a good hickory, an' he sure did make them boys *dance juber.*" AS, V (1929), 17.

dauncy (dôn′sĭ): *adj.* Lacking appetite, fastidious about food. Taylor (DN, V [1923], 205) defines it simply as "in poor health." Charles Morrow Wilson (St. Louis *Post-Dispatch,* June 9, 1930) says it means "unsteady about one's victuals." Olga Trail, of Farmington, Ark., thinks it means dizzy; a *dauncy spell* is a brief period of dizziness. Clarence Sharp, of Dutch Mills, Ark., tells me that in his neighborhood the word sometimes means stupid or confused. DN, V (1926), 399; PADS, No. 2 (1944), 55.

deadenin': *n.* An area in which the trees have been killed by girdling or collaring, but remain standing. When the trees are felled and cleared away, the *deadenin'* becomes a *clearin'*.

deem: *v.t.* To opine, to judge. DN, V (1926), 399.

derby: *n.* A young foxhound. A *derby dog* is a male under seventeen months, according to the Southwest Missouri Foxhunters Association; a *derby gyp* is a female of like age. AS, VIII (1933), 48.

devil's lane: *n.* When two farmers whose fields adjoin cannot agree to maintain a common fence, each man builds a fence on his own land. The space between the parallel fences, often only two or three feet, is called the *devil's lane*.

devil scratcher: *n.* Hellgrammite, larva of the dobson fly (*Corydalus cornutus*).

dido (dī' dō): *n.* A rowdy prank, a too exuberant caper. Cf. DN, V (1923), 205. When a country boy "goosed" the waitress in a roadside café, he was expelled at once, and the proprietor announced that "there'll be no such *didos* here." Marge Lyon (*Fresh from the Hills*, 135–36) mentions a girl who "danced too briskly" at a party, and was criticised for *"cuttin' a dido."*

dift: *v.t.* To strike, usually with the fist. "You orter seen me *dift* that feller! I knocked him plumb out of the wagon!" DN, V (1927), 474.

dinge (dǐnj): *v.i.* To become dingy or murky. "The river *dinged up* last night" means that the water is no longer clear.

dip: *n.* Sweetened cream, eaten with pie, apple dumpling, cobbler, and the like. Sometimes *dip* means a mixture of powdered tobacco and molasses; this stuff is taken on a chewed black-gum twig or *dip-stick*, like snuff. DN, V (1926), 399; V (1927), 474; PADS, No. 2 (1944), 42. Professor Carr, of the University of Arkansas (DN, III [1905], 101), lists dip in the meaning of syrup or sauce.

disencourage: *v.t.* To discourage.

disrecollect: *v.t.* To forget, to fail to remember.

disremember: *v.t.* To forget.

dobbin': *n.* The mud chinking between the logs of an old-time cabin. AS, XI (1936), 314.

doctor: *v.t.* This word is often used in a peculiar passive sense; it means to receive medical treatment, rather than to administer it. "I been *a-doctorin'* with old Doc Mollynix, but 'pears like he don't do me no good." AS, V (1929), 17.

doddly: *adj.* Nervous, shaky, unsteady. "I'm so *doddly* this mornin', I couldn't pour cider out of a boot."

dodge times: *n.* Odd moments, spare time. "I just work on these here baskets in *dodge times;* I ain't no regular basket-maker." The phrase *betwixt-an'-between times* is also common. AS, VIII (1933), 48. Cf. *odd-come-short.*

doggery: *n.* A saloon, a dramshop, a *grocery.* "That fool boy orter be a-workin' instead of hangin' around them *doggeries."*

dog fall: *n.* A tie, a draw. The term is commonly used with reference to fights or wrestling matches. AS, VIII (1933), 48.

dog-hair: *v.i.* To grow slender, by reason of too much crowding. A farmer said, "I'm afeared them oats is goin' to *dog-hair* on me. We done planted 'em too thick."

dog irons: *n.* Rude andirons, made by the country blacksmith. The term *fire-dogs* is also common.

dog-leg fence: *n.* A rail fence, with each panel of rails at an angle, giving a zigzag effect, "crooked as a dog's hind leg."

dog-run: *n.* The covered passage between the two parts of a double log cabin. The terms *dog-trot* and *turkey-trot* are heard occasionally. If the *dog-run* is open at both ends, it is sometimes called a *wind-sweep* or a *breeze-way.* AS, XI (1936), 314.

dogwood winter: *n.* A cold spell in spring while the dogwood is blooming. AS, XI (1936), 315. Cf. *blackberry winter.* Isabel France (*Arkansas Gazette,* April 11, 1948) says that *"dogwood winter* is a few hours flashback to winter while the mountain dogwood trees are in full blossom."

doless (dōo′lĕs): *adj.* Inactive, slothful, lazy. "Sally's beau ain't a *bad* feller, he's just kinder *doless."* AS, V (1929), 17.

donk (dôngk): *n.* Alcohol. "Them tourists puts *donk* into their sody-pop constant." AS, V (1929), 17.

donnick: *n.* A stone, usually one small enough to be thrown or used as a weapon.

doodle: *n.* A rounded heap or pile, sometimes a cone. A neighbor once told me that he "hid the jug under a *doodle* of fodder." One often hears a joke about *"doodles* of hay in a medder." Occasionally the term means a small knoll or hill. A boil or carbuncle is sometimes called a *doodle.*

door 'tater: *n.* The so-called Madeira vine (*Boussingaultia gracilis*), which has buds or fruit like tiny potatoes. This plant is grown in dooryards for shade and ornament, and is sometimes called *mignonette.*

dote: *v.i.* To anticipate with pleasure. "I sure don't aim to miss the circus next week; I just been *a-dotin'* on it all summer." DN, V (1927), 474.

doty: *adj.* Decayed, rotten. John Turner White, of Jefferson City, Mo., says that it is applied to posts or rails which "look sound on the outside but are rotten inside."

double cousins: *n.* When two brothers marry two sisters, the children are known as *double cousins.* Such relationships are very common in the Ozarks, and are considered somehow significant. In referring to each other these people seldom say simply, "He's my cousin," but rather, "We're *double cousins.*" The word cousin may indicate very distant relationship, but *own cousin* always means first cousin. The Eureka Springs, Ark., *Times-Echo* (January 27, 1949) prints a picture of a girl described as "a *double niece* of Rev. and Mrs. Herman Williams," but this usage is not common.

draggy: *adj.* Slow, tardy. "I like the job, but the pay's a little *draggy*" means that the worker is not getting his wages promptly. DN, V (1927), 474.

drammer: *n.* A moderate drinker. One who takes an occasional *dram,* but does not drink to excess. AS, XI (1936), 315.

draw a bite: *phr.* To prepare a meal. A woman calling at our house remarked: "Well, I must be goin'. Got to get home an' *draw a bite* for the old man." One of my friends was "mad 'cause he didn't git *a bite drawed on him,*" that is, nobody served his dinner. AS, XI (1936), 315.

draw an idea: *phr.* To perceive, to infer, perhaps sometimes to decide. "Soon as I laid eyes on that feller, I just *drawed a idy* he warn't up to no good." In an old song, "The State of Arkansas," are these lines:

> *He says you are a stranger,*
> *This* idea I do draw,
> *On yonder hill is my hotel,*
> *The best in Arkansas.*

drip-rock: *n.* Stone deposited by water, which forms stalactites and stalagmites in the Ozark caverns.

drop-in: *n.* A casual visitor, a transient. The keeper of a village hotel told me that he had four regular lodgers and averaged about three *drop-ins* a day.

drops: *n.* Liquid medicine, especially medicine to be largely diluted with water. Sometimes used to mean small pills or tablets. DN, V (1927), 474.

dry drizzle: *n.* A sprinkle of rain, a light shower. Cf. DN, V (1923), 206.

dry month: *n.* Four weeks of dry weather. A farm hand hired "by the *dry month*" gets his month's wages after he has worked twenty-four days; no pay for the days when it is too wet for work in the field.

dry wilts: *n.* A condition of extreme decrepitude or dessication. "That old feller's got the *dry wilts,* an' he looks plumb foolish a-runnin' after them gals." AS, V (1929), 17.

duckin's: *n.* Everyday clothes, usually overalls. AS, V (1929), 17.

dumb bull: *n.* A section of hollow log with rawhide stretched over one end, like a drum. This rawhide is pierced by a leather thong smeared with resin. When the thong is pulled, a deep roaring sound is produced. Popular at shivarees and similar parties.

dung out: *v.t.* To clean, to carry out rubbish. Refers primarily to barns or stables, where the matter removed really is dung. Often used humorously: "I told the old woman to *dung out* the shanty, afore company come." AS, V (1929), 17–18.

durgen (dûr' gĕn): *n.* An awkard, uncouth hillman, regarded as less polished and sophisticated than his neighbors. Webster gives *durgan* or *durgen* as Prov. Eng., a dwarf. And Merejkowski (*Romance of Leonardo da Vinci* [New York, 1902], 94) refers to "*durgans* and dryads, dwellers in trees." Some hillfolk say that the word derives from the old "Jack Durgan" plow, a primitive implement without any moldboard. Charles Morrow Wilson (St. Louis *Post-Dispatch,* June 9, 1930) says that near Fayetteville, Ark., *durgen* means "a clumsy fellow." In McDonald County, Mo., I often heard it as an adjective; the social activities of a certain family were said to be "just plumb durgen." DN, V (1926), 399; AS, XI (1936), 315. Cf. *uriah, jakey, soozy, koosy, pussy.*

dust: *v.i.* To move rapidly, a term much used at play-parties and square dances. Botkin (*American Play-Party Song,* 107) heard it in Oklahoma; he thinks it means "This way, come hither," and is derived from the Scotch *adist.*

duster: *n.* A vessel with small openings in the top, for salt or pepper. In many parts of the Middle West they are called *shakers,* but the Ozarker speaks of *salt-dusters* and *pepper-dusters.* There's a related verb, too. "The air's so damp here lately, that the salt don't *dust* very good."

edzact (ĕd zăkt'): *v.t.* To adjust precisely, sometimes to understand fully. One of my neighbors took a complicated machine apart, looked puzzled, and said, "I cain't *edzact* the damn' thing to suit me."

emmet: *n.* A big black ant. DN, V (1926), 399. Carr (DN, II [1904], 418) reports that the Ozarker uses *emmet* to mean an industrious person, but I have not heard it in this sense.

enduring: *adj., prep.,* and *adv.* Continuing, during. This is still common in Stone County, Mo. "We had a hell of a time *endurin'* of the war."

fair up: *v.i.* To become bright or clear, often used in speaking of the weather. "I reckon it'll *fair up,* come Sunday." AS, VIII (1933), 49. A man who had been quarreling with his wife said, "If she don't *fair up* in two more days, I'm goin' to leave the old heifer an' move down to the hotel!"

falling weather: *n.* Rainy or cloudy or unsettled weather. An old man in Joplin, Mo., assured me that this does not refer to the falling barometer; *fallin' weather* is when the smoke from the chimney *falls* right down to the ground, indicating rain or snow. DN, V (1927), 474.

farm liquor: *n.* Ordinary homespun whiskey, neither aged nor artificially colored. "Hit's just common *farm liquor,* boys, but it sure has got the power!" Cf. *field whiskey.*

favorance: *n.* Resemblance. "Soon as I seen the *favorance* betwixt them boys, I figgered they must be kin."

fawnch: *v.i.* To clamor, to raise a disturbance. A man in Stone County, Mo., was described as "poundin' on the table with his knife, just *a-fawnchin'* an' a-slaverin' for his victuals." From McDonald County, Mo., Taylor (DN, V [1923], 206) reports that *faunch* means "to rave, to make an outcry against." Marge Lyon (*Fresh from the Hills,* 135) says that if a hillman is *a-fawnchin',* he is "terribly disturbed about something."

feist (fist): *v.i.* To behave coquettishly or provocatively. "Them Lee gals don't do nothin' but *feist* all the way home from school."

fetchin': *adj.* In common use for emphasis, like *blinking, blooming,* etc. The following sentence is typical: "Four of them Tedlock boys jumped onto my Johnny, but he licked every *fetchin'* one of 'em!"

fiddler: *n.* A small mottled or spotted catfish, with a forked tail. Some rivermen believe that the *fiddler* is a young channel cat (*Ictalurus locustris*), which it actually is, but many regard it as a distinct species.

fiel'ark: *n.* The eastern meadow lark (*Sturnella magna*), called *medlar* in some parts of Arkansas. DN, V (1927), 474.

field whiskey: *n.* Common moonshine, not aged or colored. In Aurora, Mo., a woman told me: "Them boys was a-sellin' *field whiskey* right on Main Street, an' it a Sunday!" Cf. *farm liquor.*

finicky: *adj.* Over-nice, fastidious, sissy. Walter Williams (*Missouri Magazine,* December, 1928, p. 7) thinks that *"finicky* antedates sissy and mollycoddle" and says that Missouri girls do not care for *finicky* men.

fire-fishing: *n.* The practice of spearing or gigging fish at night, with burning pine knots for illumination. AS, XI (1936), 315.

fire of wood: *phr.* A small amount of firewood, just enough to cook one meal. "That boy has got to split three *fires o' wood* every mornin', before he goes to school." AS, XI (1936), 315.

fist: *v.t.* To beat with the fists. "The old woman she just *fisted* them kids somethin' turrible." DN, V (1927), 474.

Fist Holler: *n.* A mythical place where arguments are settled by fisticuffs. When two men are said to be "headin' for *Fist Holler,*" it means that they are about to fight. AS, XI (1936), 315.

fixy: *adj.* Well groomed, fastidious. A *fixy* girl is one who dresses with unusual care and "keeps her things nice."

flat 'backer: *n.* Plug tobacco. The term *sweet 'backer* is also common.

flatwoods: *n.* The comparatively level timbered plateaus between the high ridges. AS, XI (1936), 315.

flog: *v.t.* Used chiefly with reference to domestic fowl, it means to strike with the wings. Of a woman with a black eye it was said that "She went out to the chicken-pen, an' the old crower *flogged* her in the face." Some people dislike guineas because they *"flog* the chickens away from the feed."

flowzy (flou' zĭ): *adj.* Disarranged, untidy. "That Tandy gal's hair looks kind of *flowzy* tonight."

flying Dutchman: *n.* A primitive, homemade merry-go-round, also known as a *flyin' jenny.* A *circle-swing* is a bit more elaborate, with many seats. I saw a circle-swing, powered by a mule, in operation at Reeds Spring Junction, Mo., as recently as 1938.

flying-squirrel apron: *n.* A long apron, made like a dress but without sleeves. When it is untied in the back, the sides suggest the loose skin connecting the fore and hind legs of a flying squirrel. AS, XI (1936), 315.

flyin's: *n.* Short, coarse, hairlike wool, which flies or falls out of a carding mill. Frugal hillfolk used to knit socks out of *flyin's;* not so good as regular wool, but much cheaper.

fly-up-the-creek: *n.* The green heron (*Butorides virescens*), often called shikepoke or shitepoke. W. L. McAtee (*Nomina Abitera,* 25) lists thirty-four variants of the name *shitepoke.* AS, VIII (1933), 49.

folks: *n.* Blood relatives. "His paw an' maw was *folks;* first cousins, I think they was." AS, XI (1936), 315.

follow: *v.t.* Used with reference to one's trade, custom, or profession. "What do you *foller?*" means "What is your trade or occupation?" DN, V (1926), 400.

foot-washing: *n.* A religious ceremony. People take off their shoes and stockings, and wash each other's feet right in the church house. This is widely practiced by many of the Pentecostal sects, and by some backwoods Baptists. AS, VIII (1933), 49.

fore-parents: *n.* Ancestors, forebears. DN, V (1926), 400.

fore-stick: *n.* The log at the front of a fireplace. It is usually about half the size of the backlog. In building a fire, these two are put in position first, with smaller sticks between.

fossicate: *v.t.* To suffer from extreme heat, or lack of air, or both. A man from Yell County, Ark., said: "I like to *a fossicated* down in town yesterday." Perhaps it is somehow connected with suffocate.

fotch-on: *adj.* Imported, not produced in the neighborhood. "Them *fotch-on* beans ain't fit to eat!" DN, V (1926), 400.

fox-head: *n.* Moonshine whiskey. There is a variety of rye known as *fox-head,* and it may be that the name is derived from this. AS, VIII (1933), 49.

fractious: *adj.* Irritable, quarrelsome, contrary. "A feller that has fits is liable to be *fractious,* even when he ain't havin' 'em." DN, V (1927), 474.

fraid hole: *n.* A cave or excavation in which people take refuge from tornadoes. These places used to be called *cyclone cellars* in Kansas and Oklahoma. AS, VIII (1933), 49.

frazzle: *n.* A very small amount, most often used with reference to weight. "That there fish weighed sixteen pounds an 'a *frazzle*" means that it weighed a trifle more than sixteen pounds.

frazzle-headed: *adj.* A frazzle-headed person is one whose hair looks ragged at the edges, either uncombed or not properly cut.

fresh married: *adj.* Newly wed, recently married. A young matron was inclined to flirt with the tourists, and an older woman said, "That's a hell of a way for a *fresh-married* gal to be actin'!" AS, VIII (1933), 49.

fritter-minded: *adj.* Frivolous, erratic. "Them city folks is all kinder *fritter-minded,* I reckon." AS, V (1929), 18.

frog sticker: *n.* A pocketknife with a long, pointed blade.

frog storm: *n.* A period of bad weather in the spring, following several warm clear days. Cf. *blackberry winter.*

frolicate: *v.i.* To disport oneself at dances, which are called frolics. "I seen you *a-frolicatin'* up on Horse Creek 'tother night." AS, VIII (1933), 49.

from stem to gudgeon: *phr.* Completely, entirely. "Lizzie scrubbed that there shack *from stem to gudgeon.*"

from the knob: *phr.* Used for emphasis, as, "That feller is a sport *from the knob!*" Richard H. Thornton (*An American Glossary* [London, 1912], II, 969) found it in a Florida newspaper of 1840. DN, V (1926), 400.

fruit: *v.t.* and *v.i.* To result in, to produce an effect. "I told ye this God damn' hog-stealin' wasn't no good! Now it's *fruited,* an' here we are in the jailhouse!"

fuddle-britches: *n.* A wisecracker, a smart aleck. Cf. *Arkansas Gazette,* May 3, 1942. Perhaps sometimes it means a practical joker. Otto Ernest Rayburn (*Ozark Guide,* Eureka Springs, Ark., Autumn, 1950, p. 41) refers to "some clownish *fuddle-britches* who had humor bred in his bones." Cf. *jokey fellow.*

funeralize: *v.t.* To hold a funeral or memorial service; the *funeralizin'* is often postponed for months or even years after the actual buryin'. Cf. my *The Ozarks,* 64–65.

gaily: *adj.* In good spirits, or good health. "My chaps was sick this winter, but they're all right peert an' *gaily* now." DN, V (1926), 400. Cf. *gales, in the.*

gal: *v.i.* To seek feminine society. "Tom he always goes *a-gallin'* of a Sunday." *Gallin'* is more respectable than *tom-cattin',* but less so than *sparkin',* which latter term often implies serious matrimonial intentions. DN, V (1927), 474.

gales, in the: *phr.* Cheerful, in a good humor, even hilarious. "I knowed Paw was *in the gales;* he was laughin' so hard you could see his liver an' lights." AS, V (1929), 18. Cf. *gaily.*

gallynipper: *n.* The original gallynipper was a gigantic mosquito, according to the old-timers. The term is applied to other flying insects, particularly the crane flies (*Tipulidae*), which look like mosquitoes but are nearly two inches long. DN, III (1906), 147. Cf. *katynipper.*

gally-wampus: *n*. An amphibious monster, like a colossal mink, supposed to have inhabited central and southern Missouri in pioneer days. *Arkansas Historical Quarterly*, IX (1950), 70.

galoopus: *n*. A fabulous bird, like a great black eagle, said to lay square eggs. The old-timers tell tourists that the *galoopus* was once common in southwest Missouri. The astounding productivity of the soil in certain areas is attributed to the dung of the galoopus bird. Cf. my *We Always Lie to Strangers*, 66, 75–76.

gammon: *n*. Idle talk, untruths. Sometimes it means bacon, or salt sidemeat.

gammoner: *n*. A talkative, unreliable person.

gander berry: *n*. A variety of huckleberry, much larger than the ordinary kind. The names *buck berry, hog berry, whortleberry, goose berry*, and *he-huckleberry* are applied rather loosely to several species of *Vaccinium*. DN, V (1927), 474; AS, VIII (1933), 49.

gap: *n*. Used figuratively to mean opening, opportunity, encouragement. "Henry must have give them fellers some kind of a *gap,* or they wouldn't have said nothin' about makin' counterfeit money."

gathering: *n*. A boil or abcess. AS, V (1929), 18.

gaum (gôm): *n*. A mess, a muddle, a poor job. A jerry-built house or a garment badly tailored may be described as "just a plumb *gaum*." Starr (*From an Ozark Hillside*, 37) reports *gorm*, with the same meaning, to be common in Washington County, Ark.

gaum up: *v.t.* To soil, to smear. DN, V (1923), 208.

gee-whollicker: *n*. A wonder, a marvel, something amazingly large or fine, or otherwise surprising. Cf. *golly-whopper* and *sockdolager*.

giasticutus: *n*. A legendary bird of prey, with a wingspread of fifty feet and a habit of carrying off full-grown cattle. Cf. my *We Always Lie to Strangers*. 63–65.

git-flip: *n*. A humorous name for the guitar. AS, XI (1936), 315. Cf. *pick-fiddle*.

give-out: *n*. Announcement. "Did you-uns hear the *give-out* at the church-house last night?" DN, V (1926), 400.

glade-kid: *v.t.* To exaggerate. Near Pineville, Mo., there lived a fisherman named Glade Kidd, who told some pretty tall stories. Some joker doubtless coined this verb, which was used by hundreds of persons over a considerable territory. A girl at Neosho, Mo., answered some proposal of mine with the derisive, "You wouldn't *glade-kid* me, would you?" Cf. *jess-elliff*.

glob (glŏb): *n.* A rounded or semicircular piece. The Springfield, Mo., *Leader & Press* (March 19, 1936) tells of a barber who "amused himself by riding up and down on the hydraulic barber chair," the mechanism of which finally "pinched a *glob* out of his finger." AS, XI (1936), 315.

glut: *n.* The wooden wedge used in splitting logs. *Glut shoes* are homemade footwear, so called because they are made on a straight last which looks like a glut. A *glut shoe* fits either foot; there are no rights and lefts.

gnat-ball: *n.* A dense swarm of gnats or other small flying insects. A woman told me, "When that child was two year old, he stuck his head in a *gnat-ball,* an' he's been kind of sickly ever since."

go to the brush: *phr.* To defecate. This phrase is used by farmers who have outdoor privies, and even by people in modern houses. I have heard it spoken, more or less facetiously, by an Ozark politician in a New York hotel.

go-devil: *n.* The mole cricket (*Gryllotalpa borealis*). Cf. DN, V (1923), 208.

gollywhopper: *n.* A wonder, a marvel. "I fixed me up a *gollywhopper* of a speech, an' learnt the whole thing by heart." Cf. *gee-whollicker, sockdolager.*

gollywog: *n.* A mythical monster, like a giant salamander. Cf. my *We Always Lie to Strangers,* 48.

good heart, in: *phr.* Feeling well, in good spirits. "Paw was porely yesterday, but now it seems like he's *in good heart* ag'in."

goomer (goom' ēr): *v.t.* To bewitch.

goomer-doctor: *n.* A witch doctor, who professes to remove supernatural spells and curses. Cf. my *Ozark Superstitions,* 280.

goose: *v.t.* Same as *bump, q.v.*

goose-drownder: *n.* A cloudburst, a very heavy rain. AS, VIII (1933), 49. There is a tale of a mountain preacher who prayed: "Oh Lord, send us rain! We don't want no *drizzle-drozzle,* Lord. We don't want no *gully-washer,* nor no *fence-lifter.* What we need is a regular old *goose-drownder,* Lord!" C. C. Williford, weatherman at Springfield, Mo., tells of a farmer who used *toad-strangler* in the same meaning.

goozle: *n.* Throat. "She acts like she's got a fishbone stuck in her *goozle.*" DV, V (1927), 474.

gopher: *n.* A primitive plow.

248

gorge: *n.* A heavy meal, a large amount of food. "Jim sure et him a *gorge* of that there ham-meat." AS, V (1929), 18.

goslin's: *n.* The change of the masculine voice at puberty. A boy whose voice is changing is said to be "in the *goslin's.*" AS, VIII (1933), 49.

gourdy: *adj.* Green, green as a gourd. Cf. *Arkansas Gazette,* May 3, 1942. Sometimes used figuratively, to mean countrified or unsophisticated. "Betty's a nice girl, but don't you think she's a little too *gourdy* for our crowd?"

government socks: *n.* No socks at all. A farmer shows his bare foot and asks, "How do you like these here *government socks* we're all a-wearin' nowadays?" DN, V (1923), 209. Cf. PADS, No. 6 (1946), 16.

gowrow: *n.* A fabulous reptile, an enormous man-eating lizard, said to have terrorized rural Arkansas in the eighteen eighties. Cf. Otto Ernest Rayburn, *Arcadian Life,* June, 1935, pp. 18–19; *Arkansas Historical Quarterly,* IX (1950), 65–68.

grabble: *v.t.* To get potatoes out of a hill without uprooting the plant. People in the Ozarks do not *dig* their potatoes until late in the season, but they often *grabble* a few little ones in June. DN, V (1923), 209. Cf. PADS, No. 2 (1944), 9; No. 6 (1946), 15; No. 13 (1950), 17.

grand-rascal: *n.* A cheat, a grafter, a confidence man. The noun and adjective are pronounced as one word, with the accent on *grand.* AS, V 1929, 18.

granny cat: *n.* A small, square-nosed yellow catfish (*Pilodictis olivaris*). DN, V (1927), 474.

granny-woman: *n.* A midwife. Sometimes used contemptuously to mean an irritable, childish old man. DN, V (1926), 400.

grease light: *n.* A rude lamp made by placing a rag wick in a saucer or mussel shell filled with lard. Also called a *slut* or a *slut-lamp.* AS, VIII (1933), 49. Cf. *slut.*

green: *v.t.* To ridicule, to tease, to make the butt of a joke. "Them boys better quit *greenin'* Eddie, or he's liable to git mad an' hurt somebody." Cf. DN, V (1923), 209.

green fingers: *n.* The ability to grow vegetables and flowering plants. A woman whose garden always flourishes is said to have *green fingers* or *growin' fingers.*

greens: *n.* Something extra, without serious purpose or significance. "Them folks didn't have no money, but me an' Jim warn't doin' nothin' nohow, so we holp 'em out just for *greens*"—without any payment, that is.

grinnel: *n.* A long, slender fish taken in several Arkansas lakes. It is the dogfish or bowfin, also known as *grindle* (*Amia calva*).

grub hyson: *n.* Sassafras tea. Masterson (*Tall Tales of Arkansaw,* 188, 359) discusses this term as he found it in the old *Arkansas Traveler* dialogue. In Botkin's *Treasury of American Folklore,* 349, is reprinted the *Arkansas Traveler* as published in Little Rock, Ark., in 1876, with a footnote explaining that *grub hyson* means sassafras tea. Webster gives hyson as a Chinese word, meaning green tea, and adds that the early crop is called *young hyson.*

gull around: *v.i.* To court, to follow. "Tom he just kept *a-gullin' round* them Porter gals all summer." AS, V (1929), 18.

gum: *v.t.* To bite with toothless gums. "I ain't got no money to buy false teeth," an old woman told me, "so I just have to *gum* it." Sometimes pronounced *goom* (gōōm). AS, V (1929), 18.

gum crib: *n.* A cradle fashioned from a hollow log. An Arkansas politician, calling attention to his humble origin, told reporters, "Yes, gentlemen, I was borned in a log cabin, rocked in a *gum crib,* an' cut my teeth on a axe-handle!" AS, VIII (1933), 49.

hack: *v.t.* To achieve, to accomplish something. "I cain't quite *hack* it" is an admission that some specific task is beyond the speaker's ability. *Hack the jimson* carries the same meaning. Cf. *make the riffle.*

half-ham: *v.i.* To say that children go *half-hammin'* to school means that they use a kind of triple step, "a hop, skip, an' jump." Carl Withers found this in Wheatland, Mo., in 1940. May Kennedy McCord (Springfield, Mo., *Leader & Press,* June 9, 1942) got the following description from a man in her neighborhood: "You take a running start with both feet but land on the right one. Then cross the left foot behind the right ankle and jump again, landing on the left foot, with feet still crossed. Then make a third jump from the left foot and land on both. If you have made twenty feet in the three jumps, making them all as nearly as possible in one continuous movement, you are good. And this is what it meant to *half-hammon* down the street."

half-sole yourself: *phr.* To refill one's glass when it is only half empty. AS, VIII (1933), 49.

hang the moon: *phr.* To be very powerful or important. "Lucy thinks that fool boy of hern is God's own cousin! She thinks he *hung the moon!*"

happen-chance: *n.* An accident, a coincidence.

happen-so: *n.* An accident, a fluke.

happen-stance: *adj.* Haphazard, at random, perhaps even careless. Speaking of a patented chicken feed, a merchant said, "This here ain't no *happenstance* mixture; it's made scientific."

hate: *v.t.* This word often means only regret. A mountain man, on hearing of his mother's death, cried out, "Oh my God, I *hate* that!"

hazels: *n.* Hazelnuts. Taylor (DN, V [1923], 210) reports *haze-nut* from McDonald County, Mo., but I have not heard this. AS, XI (1936), 315.

hazel splitter: *n.* A wild, lean hog, a razorback. AS, V (1929), 18.

head: *n.* A copperhead snake (*Agkistrodon mokasen*). "Some feller up on Crane Creek stepped on a *head* this mornin'. They say his leg's swole up big as a stove-pipe."

head of the hall: *n.* The end of the room nearest the music, a term used in calling square dances.

head of the heap: *n.* The acknowledged leader. "Jim's always got to be *head of the heap,* or else he gits mad."

heading: *n.* A pillow. "Corncobs is all right in their place, but they sure make a sorry *headin'.*" DN, V (1927), 474.

heap: *n.* A large amount, sometimes a large number of persons or objects. Cf. *power, right smart, passel.*

hedge-bird: *n.* The loggerhead shrike or butcherbird (*Lanius ludovicianus*). DN, V (1926), 400.

heel it: *phr.* To walk rapidly. "You *heel it* over thar, an' tell 'em I cain't come." *Hoof it* is sometimes heard in the same meaning.

heir: *v.t.* To inherit. "Henry must have *heired* some money off'n his pappy's folks." DN, V (1923), 210.

hell's fuzzy: *interj.* An exclamation comparable to *hell's bells!* or *hell's delight!* both of which are common in the Ozarks.

hen-wood: *n.* The chittamwood (*Bumelia lanuginosa*), also called *yellow-wood* or *smoke tree.* Many old folks insist that Noah used this wood to build the Ark.

herby: *adj.* Having the flavor of herbs. In April the cows eat wild garlic and other weeds. A woman said to me, "The milk tastes kinder *herby,* don't it?"

hessian: *n.* A term of reproach, usually applied to a vicious or meddlesome old woman. DN, II (1906), 140; AS, XI (1936), 315. Cf. Mencken's *American Language: Supplement I,* 599–600. Also PADS, No. 2 (1944), 29, and AS, XVIII (1943), 72, 310.

hickory-limb oil: *n.* A whipping. Country schoolteachers speak casually of administering "a dose of *hickory-limb oil*" to an unruly pupil. The term *peach-tree tea* is used with the same meaning.

hide-out country: *n.* Any trackless, wooded wilderness. Such places were formerly inhabited by criminals *hidin' out* from the law. AS, VIII (1933), 49.

high-behind: *n.* A mythical lizard as big as a bull, a bloodthirsty enemy to all mankind. The names *nigh-behind* and *hide-behind* refer to the same legendary beast. *Arkansas Historical Quarterly*, IX (1950), 69. Cf. my *We Always Lie to Strangers*, 47.

high-headed: *adj.* Proud, arrogant, spirited. Usually refers to horses, occasionally to human beings.

hillbilly: *n.* A derisive name for the mountaineer, as contrasted with the valley-farmer and the city-dweller. Taylor (DN, V [1923], 210) reports it from McDonald County, Mo., as "expressive of contempt, or meaning ignorant." Rose O'Neill, of Taney County, Mo., told me that the term was not heard in her neighborhood until after 1900 and was not common until 1915. Carr (DN, II [1904], 418) found it in Fayetteville, Mo., in 1903. Tom Shiras, newspaperman of Mountain Home, Ark., says that he never heard *hillbilly* until 1906. Congressman Dewey Short, Galena, Mo., describes himself in public speeches as a *hillbilly*, but many hillfolk regard it as a fightin' word. John O'Neill shot and killed Elmo McCullars, of St. Louis, in 1934, because the latter called him a *hillbilly*. R. P. Weeks, who represented Douglas County in the Missouri Legislature, avoided the word hillbilly but admitted that he was a *flint-buster*. Others have referred to the hill people as *acorn-crackers, apple-knockers, briar-hoppers, bush-busters, brush-apes, elmers, ellum-peelers, fruitjar suckers, haw-eaters, hay-shakers, hog-rangers, puddle-jumpers, pumpkin-rollers, rabbit-twisters, ridge-runners, sorghum-lappers, sprout-straddlers, squirrel-turners, 'tater-grabblers,* and *weed-benders.* The terms *Arkies* and *Okies*, designating the "trashy" natives of Arkansas and Oklahoma, are much more recent, I think; I first heard of *Arkies* and *Okies* in Kansas City, Mo., in the nineteen thirties.

hind-sights: *n.* The Old Testament. May Kennedy McCord, of Springfield, Mo., recalls a backwoods preacher who announced, "I'll take my text from the *hind-sights* this mornin'."

hipped: *adj.* Disabled, crippled, seriously injured. The form *hip-shot* is also common, with the same meaning. DN, V (1926), 400.

hippin's: *n.* Diapers. May Kennedy McCord, of Springfield, Mo., tells me that it is used as a verb also, as in this sentence: "Somebody better go *hippin'* that there baby!" DN, V (1926), 400.

hip-swinney: *n.* A weakness of the back, similar to lumbago. Usually refers to horses, but I once heard a girl in Crane, Mo., remark that she couldn't dance, because she had the *hip-swinney*. At Hot Springs, Ark., a man told me that his wallet suffered from the *hip-swinney*, meaning that he had no money. Webster defines *sweeny* as "atrophy of the shoulder-muscles in horses." AS, XI (1936), 315.

hog-leg: *n.* A large pistol or revolver. "I'm ag'in this here packin' *hog-legs* to the dances, an' all such as that." DN, V (1927), 474. *Arkansas Historical Quarterly,* VI (1947), 121.

hog-killin': *n.* Any sort of hilarious celebration. "We had a regular *hog-killin'* at the dance t'other night."

hogmolly: *n.* A fish. A spotted sucker, the hog sucker (*Hypentelium nigricans*). The term is in common use among the Choctaws in Oklahoma, according to C. A. Cummins (*Outdoor Life,* September, 1928), and is heard all over the Ozark region. AS, VIII (1933), 49. Cf. *jess-ellif.*

hold your potato: *phr.* To be patient. "Just *hold your 'tater* now; I'm a-comin' quick as I can." *Hold your corn* is heard occasionally, with the same meaning. AS, XI (1936), 315.

holler: n. A hollow, a narrow valley, a cove. This word sometimes designates not only the hollow itself, but the stream which flows through the hollow. In some cases the stream has no other name; one does not fish in Mill Creek or Mill Branch, but in Mill Holler. Sometimes this condition is reversed, so that Horse Creek means not only the stream but the whole valley as well; the settlers do not live in Horse Creek Holler, but on Horse Creek. DN, V (1927), 475.

holler calf-rope: *phr.* To acknowledge defeat. When a boy is beaten in a fist fight or a wrestling match, he *hollers calf-rope* by crying, "Enough!" or, "I give up!" AS, VIII (1933), 49.

holler-horn: *n.* A disease of cattle, in which the horns or the bones of the tail are said to disintegrate. Cf. DN, V (1923), 210. Also my *Ozark Superstitions,* 50.

holly eve: *n.* Hallowe'en. AS, XI (1936), 315. Cf. Wentworth's *American Dialect Dictionary,* 299.

hone for: *v.t.* To desire, to crave. "I just been *a-honin'* for a good mess of fried catfish."

honor: *v.t.* To bow, a term used in calling square dances. *"Honor* your pardner" means "bow to your partner," and *"honor* to the left" means "bow to the left."

hoorah: *v.i.* To make haste, to hurry. *"Hoorah* now, an' git them dishes done." The accent is on the second syllable. There is a noun *hoorah,* with the accent on the first syllable, which means a loud noise, a great outcry. "Molly raised a turrible *hoorah* when she seen Joe in the jail-house." AS, V (1929), 18.

hoover pork: *n.* Rabbit meat. This is a reference to the lean years when Herbert Hoover was president, and many families could get no meat except rabbits.

hopper-tailed: *adj.* Having broad or prominent buttocks. Oddly enough, it generally refers to men, rather than women. "What does Bob look like? Well, he's a low, *hopper-tailed* feller." AS, VIII (1933), 49–50.

hoppinjohn: *n.* A dish of black-eyed peas cooked with hog jowl, a traditional New Year's dinner. The Ridgeway family, near West Plains, Mo., say that the name originated in Civil War days, when somebody named John was invited to *hop in* and help himself to the victuals! Cf. PADS, No. 2 (1944), 34. Also my *Ozark Superstitions,* 80.

horn: *n.* A measure of liquid. "I sure could use a *horn* of right good whiskey this mornin'." A lady in Galena, Mo., tells me that she has heard an ice-cream cone called "a *horn* o' puddin'."

hornswoggle: *v.t.* To cheat, to deceive. According to the *Stone County News-Oracle,* Galena, Mo. (May 31, 1939), it means to deceive without telling an out-and-out falsehood; the *News-Oracle* refers to a horse-trader "so artful that no man he had traded with could lay hold of anything the trader had said, and say with certainty that it was a lie." The term *hornscriggle* carries the same meaning. "Them town fellers has done *hornscriggled* old man Barton out of his farm." AS, VIII (1933), 50.

horny-head: *n.* A small chub-like fish (*Semotilus atromaculatus*). The male has short, horny protuberances on the scales about the head in the spring. AS, VIII (1933), 50.

horse: *v.t.* To lift, pull, push, move by force. An outboard motor *horses* a boat through the water; men with crowbars *horse* a big rock off the highway; a riverman *horses* a large fish into his boat. Sometimes the word seems to mean drive, as when a local ruffian stole four hogs, several miles from his farm, and *"horsed* 'em over home."

horse dose: *n.* A very large dose of medicine. "Old Doc Holton give me a *horse dose* of calomel, an' it damn' near killed me." A *horse quart* means a full quart, as distinguished from a *short quart* or "fifth." The phrase *horse measure* is sometimes heard in this connection.

horse-in: *n.* A marble game still popular in the Ozarks. Played in one big ring, it is similar to the game known as *Boston* in some sections of the Middle West.

house-plunder: *n.* Household furniture, carpets, bedding, kitchen utensils, and the like. "Git the *house-plunder* in the wagon, Lizzie. We're a-movin' to town." Henry Rowe Schoolcraft, who visited the Ozark country in 1818–19, remarked that *"plunder* is a common word here for baggage" (*Scenes and Adventures in the Ozark Mountains* (1853), 122).

hudder: *n.* The cap on a stack of wheat; it usually consists of two bundles put on crosswise.

hull: *n.* A shotgun shell, sometimes a rifle or pistol cartridge. Of a pump gun with a broken ejector, a hillman said, "This here weepon don't *shuck the hulls* no more." A *hull-sponger* is a hunter who mooches ammunition from his fellows. AS, XI (1936), 315.

hull-gull: *n.* A game played with pebbles, grains of corn, or other small objects, sometimes called *hully-gully.* Cf. JAFL, XLIX (1936), 199–200.

human-rifle: *n.* A muzzle-loading rifle of large caliber. DN, V (1926), 400. Probably so named because it was used to shoot human beings. Consider *hog-rifle, squirrel-rifle, goose-gun,* and so on. Cf. *Ozark Guide* (Eureka Springs, Ark.), Autumn, 1946, p. 33.

hunker down: *v.i.* To squat.

hush-puppy: *n.* A patty made of hash, with cornmeal in it. Emma Galbraith, of Springfield, Mo., tells me that the stuff was used "to hush the puppies that whined round the cabin door," hence the name. E. E. Dale (*Arkansas Historical Quarterly,* VI [1947], 122) says that "white sauce or cream gravy" was called *hush-puppy gravy* in pioneer days. The *Arkansas Gazette* (February 6, 1948) remarks editorially that to nominate a Southerner for vice-president "would be no more than throwing a *hushpuppy* to the South to keep it quiet."

idlesome: *adj.* Given over to idleness and sloth. "Tom sure is *idlesome* nowadays." Mary Elizabeth Mahnkey, of Mincy, Mo., says that *"idlesome* is an old word, and it means more than just *idle."*

Indian hen: *n.* The pileated woodpecker (*Dryocopus pileatus*), sometimes called the *Lord God woodpecker.* Cf. *woodcock, woodhen.* AS, VIII 1933), 50.

Indian pone: *n.* A cake made of flour or meal, like biscuit, except that it contains eggs. Cut into squares, it is served with a *dip* of milk and molasses. AS, V (1929), 19.

infare: *n.* A celebration on the day following a wedding, at the home of the groom's parents. The honeymoon, traditionally lasting two or three weeks, is called *infare days.* "It ain't right for a woman to grub sprouts durin' her *infare days.*" DN, V (1926), 400.

inkle: *n.* A hint, a tip, a bit of secret information. A woman once told me, "I got a *inkle* that gal of mine is fixin' to run off with Tommy Sturgis."

jacksalmon: *n.* The walleyed pike (*Stizostedion vitreum*), or the sauger (*Stizostedion canadense*). The latter name is used in some parts of Arkansas. Ozark Ripley (*Field and Stream,* October, 1928, 14) remarks that the name *California salmon* is occasionally used on White River, but I have never heard it. Corey Ford and Alastair MacBain (*Collier's,* April 6, 1940, p. 16) say that walleyed pike are called *jackfish* in this region, but I have not heard this name, either. AS, XI (1936), 315.

jakey: *adj.* Countrified, old-fashioned, uncouth. Cf. *durgen, soozy.*

jerp: *n.* A small quantity. Used especially with reference to sweets. "Aunt Sary always likes a little *jerp* of 'lasses on her bread." DN, V (1927), 475.

jess-ellif: *n.* The *hogmolly* (*q.v.*) or hog sucker (*Hypentelium nigricans*). It is said that the name was originally used in derision of a man named Jesse Ellif, supposed to have resembled this fish in habits or appearance. AS, V (1929), 19.

jibble: *v.t.* To cut into small pieces. Asked how to cook squash, a woman answered, "You just take an' *jibble 'em up,* an' then bile 'em." Another cook was talking about hash. "Sometimes I grind the meat, but mostly I just *jibble* it."

jillikens: *n.* Backwoods. "Them folks live away back in the *jillikens;* don't come to town but twice a year." This term used to be common in Ripley County, Mo.

jim: *v.t.* To damage, to mar, to deface. The Lamar, Mo., *Democrat* (September 5, 1939) describes a motor wreck on the highway: "Williams said it turned his Chevrolet over and sprang the frame, besides *jimming* it up."

jim-kay: *v.t.* To stuff with food. Somewhere near Joplin, Mo., a pioneer family had a pet pig, named James K. Polk, and the story goes that they fed the animal till it busted wide open. Since that time, if a guest is urged to eat more of this or that, he says, "Don't you *jim-kay* me, now!" Cf. *glade-kid, jess-ellif.*

jimplicute: *n.* A ghostly dragon or dinosaur, supposed to walk the roads at night. It is said that this creature was invented near Argenta, Ark., in the eighteen seventies, to frighten superstitious Negroes. *Arkansas Historical Quarterly,* IX (1950), 69.

joky fellow: *n.* A clown, a mental defective of a lively disposition. "Hank ain't no idiot; he's just a *joky feller."* Charles Morrow Wilson (St. Louis *Post-Dispatch,* June 9, 1930) says that "a *jokey* is a harmless imbecile." AS, IV (1928), 116.

jolt from Solomon's cradle: *phr.* This expression refers to wisdom or intelligence, and is generally used in the negative. To say that a man "never had no *jolts from Solomon's cradle"* means that he's rather stupid. *Never walked far with Solomon* has the same significance. AS, VIII (1933), 50.

joree-bird: *n.* The chewink, towhee, or ground robin (*Pipilo erythrophthalmus*). DN, V (1926), 400.

josie: *n.* A woman's garment, something like a long undershirt. The old-timers say it is derived from *joe-sack,* an old word for chemise or "shimmy." AS, VIII (1933), 50.

jower: *v.i.* and *n.* To argue, to quarrel, to wrangle. "Him an' her is always *a-jowerin'* about somethin'." The word is sometimes used as a noun: "They had a little *jower,* but everything's all right now." DN, V (1927), 475.

juckies, by: *interj.* A common exclamation of surprise or excitement.

judgematical: *adj.* A word akin to *quizzical.* Cf. *prezactly* and *edzact.*

juggles: *n.* Very large chips, seen about the camps of woodsmen who make railroad ties. To *box the juggles* is to cut these big chips loose from a tie that has been notched, after which it is smoothed up with the broadaxe.

juliper: *n.* The juice or gravy from a fowl or a roast of beef. "I mostly just baste the turkey, an' save the *juliper."* AS, XI (1936), 315.

jump the broomstick: *phr.* To marry. Sometimes perhaps it means to propose marriage. Cf. *Arkansas Historical Quarterly,* VI (1947), 127.

jump-up: *n.* and *adj.* A meeting at which extemporaneous speeches are delivered. I have heard the exercises on the "last day" of school called a *jump-up.* Certain wild chants popular in Holy Roller circles are known as *jump-up* songs.

june: *v.i.* To move briskly, to hurry. "A feller that works for old man Barnes has got to keep *a-junin'* from sunup till dark." Sometimes it seems to mean courting or sparking: "They tell me Jim Burke's *a-junin'* Sally Randall here lately." Cf. DN, V (1923), 212; AS, XXIII (1948), 305.

katynipper: *n.* Dragonfly, snake feeder. Any of the larger *Odonata*, particularly *Anax junius*. This term used to be common in Reynolds County, Mo. Cf. *gallynipper*.

keep close to the willows: *phr.* To be conventional, conservative, modest. Nude boys, swimming in the willow-bordered creeks, keep close to the trees to avoid being seen by passing tourists. "Jim's woman used to be kinder wild, but she *keeps close to the willers* now that the children's a-growin' up." Cf. Nancy Clemens, Kansas City *Star,* August 21, 1938.

keep your dobbers up: *phr.* To keep up one's courage. AS, XI (1936), 315.

keepin': *n.* Something reserved or saved. "This here jug is all the *keepin'* we got left from Christmas." DN, V (1926), 400.

ketchy: *adj.* Uncertain, unsettled. "The weather's kinder *ketchy*" means that it is unsettled, with some prospect of rain. A rural weather-prophet plays safe with the word *ketchy*. He means that it is more likely to rain than not, but he doesn't go so far as to say it *will* rain. AS, XI (1936), 315–16.

kill-devil: *n.* High-proof whiskey of poor quality. "*Kill-devil* don't do a feller's stummick no good, but it ain't so bad as this here limber-leg applejack." The term kill-devil is sometimes applied to very strong tobacco.

kill your own snakes: *phr.* To mind one's own business. Cf. my *Ozark Mountain Folks,* 95.

kingdoodle: *n.* An imaginary monster, similar to the "mountain boomer" or collared lizard (*Crotaphytus collaris*) except for its great size. Supposed to pull up saplings, tear down rail fences, and upset small buildings. *Arkansas Historical Quarterly.* IX (1950), 69.

kitchen-sweat: *n.* A country dance. "We was a-goin' to a kitchen-sweat over on Bear Creek."

kittle an' bilin': *phr.* The whole number, the entire group. "Them Tedlocks is no good, an' we're a-goin' to run the whole *kittle an' bilin'* out of the country." Sometimes it is shortened to *kit an' bilin'.* AS, V (1929), 19. May Kennedy McCord (Springfield, Mo., *News & Leader,* August 29, 1934) says "the whole *kit an' bile of us.*" I have heard *kit an' caboodle* in the same sense.

koosy (kōōs' ĭ): *adj.* Tacky, outmoded, in bad taste. Common in Stone County, Mo., where it is applied to women's clothing and household furnishings. Cf. *durgen, jakey, soozy.*

lally-gaggin': *n.* Love-making, coquettish or flirtatious behavior. AS, V (1929), 19.

lamentate: *v.t.* and *v.i.* To lament, to complain. "Jake was in here *a-lamen-tatin'* 'bout how his barn burnt up." AS, XI (1936), 316.

laplander: *n.* A person who lives on the Missouri-Arkansas border, "where Missouri *laps over* into Arkansas." DN, III (1906), 144; AS, V (1929), 19. The "boot-heel" country in southeast Missouri has long been known as Lapland and is the subject of many dull jokes. Cf. Mirandy Bauers-feld's *Breezes from Persimmon Holler*, 192, also *Missouri Conserva-tionist*, September, 1949, p. 6.

lard-stand: *n.* A large can or jar in which lard is packed. "A *stand of lard*," according to the Pineville, Mo., *Democrat* (May 29, 1931), was stolen from a house at Goodman, Mo. AS, V (1929), 19.

lashins and lavins: *phr.* A great quantity. "Them Hawkins boys has all got money, *lashins an' lavins* of it." DN, V (1927), 475.

last button on Gabe's coat: *phr.* The very last bit of anything; usually re-fers to meal, bacon, whiskey, sugar or some other household com-modity. If there is only one piece of meat left in the smokehouse, the hillman says: "Well, fetch out the *last button on Gabe's coat,* an' let's have at it." AS, XI (1936), 316. *Last shingle on the barn* is sometimes used with the same meaning.

lavish: *n.* A large quantity, a profusion. "If them fellers is a-lookin' for trouble, they'll sure git a *lavish* of it." DN, V (1926), 401.

lawrence: *n.* A lazy moocher, a loafer, a parasite. Of a man named Dixon McGee a woman said: "I reckon the old *lawrence* is hangin' round the pool-hall."

lay out: *v.t.* To plan, to purpose, to intend. "I *laid out* to go fishin' last week, but Paw made us cut sprouts every day." DN, V (1926), 401. *Lay out* also means to lie idle, or unused, as applied to cleared land not under cultivation. "I just had to let the east forty *lay out* this year."

layway: *v.t.* To waylay, to ambush. "I heerd them Pickett boys was aimin' to *layway* me on the road home." AS, XI (1936), 316.

lay whip: *phr.* To drive rapidly. I have heard it used seriously, in a moment of stress, in urging the driver of a motorcar to speed up. AS, XI (1936), 316.

lazy Suzan: *n.* An old-fashioned round dinner table, with the middle part made to revolve on a wooden pin. One serves himself by turning the platform upon which the victuals are placed. Such a table was used in a hotel at Gainesville, Mo., for many years. Cf. *Ozark Guide* (Eureka Springs, Ark.), May, 1944, p. 23.

lazy Tom: *n.* A rude water mill for grinding corn.

less and leaster: *phr.* Smaller and smaller. When anything is getting *less an' leaster,* it is dwindling away, like a lump of melting ice.

let fire: *v.i.* To discharge a firearm. "Willy hollered for 'em not to shoot, but Jim he *let fire* anyhow, an' killed him dead as a doornail."

let on: *v.t.* To pretend. "I just *let on* like I didn't care nothin' about it." Sometimes it means to show interest or knowledge. "I seen a gal settin' under a hawbush, but I never *let on,*" means that the speaker behaved as if he had not seen the girl. DN, V (1926), 401.

lick and a promise: *n. phr.* Temporary repairs, superficial treatment. To give anything *a lick an' a promise* is to fix it quickly for the time being, with the intention of completing the job later.

lickety-whoop: *adv.* At high speed. "Thar goes Elmer *lickety-whoop* down the road." One also hears *lickety-cut, lickety-split, lickety-scoot, lickety-brindle, lickety-whistle,* and *lickety-Christmas.* AS, XI (1936), 316.

lick-log: *n.* A fallen tree with big notches cut in the trunk to hold salt for the cattle. AS, VIII (1933), 50. Where a trough made of boards is used, I have heard it called a "built *lick-log.*"

lick your flint: *phr.* To prepare for a difficult task, to take precautions against disaster. "If you aim to play cards with them Turney boys, you sure better *lick your flint.*" It is said that in the days of the flintlock a rifleman moistened the flint with his tongue, to insure a good fat spark. AS, V (1929), 14.

lids: *n.* Covers or binding. "You cain't find it betwixt the *lids* of the Book!" The word book, in the Ozarks, generally means the King James Bible. DN, V (1927), 475.

lie a corpse: *phr.* To lie in state. "When anybody's a-dyin', or *a-layin' a corpse,* it seems like the roosters crows day an' night."

lie bill: *n.* A sworn statement, generally a written statement, which "gives the lie" to some previous testimony. These documents were not uncommon in pioneer days elsewhere. North Carolina (*Law Notes,* October, 1919, p. 138) has preserved the following: "In 1822 one William Jones had an entry made that *I do hereby acknowledge myself a Pub-*

lic Liar, and that I have told unnecessary lies on Jesse Worthington, and his family. A paper of this character is still in use in some rural communities in the South and is known as the *Lie Bill.*" Cf. DN, V (1923), 213. An old settler named Rice (*Arcadian Life* [Caddo Gap, Ark.], October, 1936, p. 11) was accused of stealing silver from a deacon; after a "church trial" resulted in acquittal, the deacon gave Rice "a *libel* written on paper cambric."

lie tale: *n.* A false and malicious story, as distinguished from a humorous *windy,* which is not intended to deceive anybody.

lift: *v.t.* To bring forward, especially to serve food and drink. I have heard a backwoods housewife say: "The dinner's all cooked, Paw. Are you-uns ready for me to *lift* it?"

light a shuck: *phr.* To depart in haste. "Soon as Zeke seen the sheriff a-comin', he *lit a shuck* for the big timber." AS, V (1929), 19. Cf. Marge Lyon, *Fresh from the Hills,* 133–35.

limb: *v.t.* To whip, to flog. "I'm a-goin' to *limb* hell out of that boy!"

limber sick: *adj.* Weak, unable to stand or walk because of illness. AS, V (1929), 19.

limby: *adj.* Having many limbs or branches. "Them is the *limbiest* cedars I ever seen."

lin: *n.* Linden tree, basswood (*Tilia americana*). AS, VIII (1933), 50.

line-side: *n.* Either the largemouth black bass (*Micropterus salmoides*), or more likely the spotted black bass (*Micropterus punctulatus*), which often has a black stripe along its side. Until recently this was the only common name, but now one hears *bass, green bass,* and *government fish,* since many streams have been stocked with fish from the state hatcheries. The small-mouth bass is still called a *trout* by the old-timers. DN, V (1927), 475. Cf. *trout.*

literary school: *n.* The ordinary public school, as distinguished from singin'-school, Sunday school, and so on. A veteran singin' teacher once told me: "Them schools I kept run all day long, just like a regular *literary school.*" AS, VIII (1933), 50.

liver-growed: *adj.* Subject to a mythical disease of the liver. I have seen sick children picked up by the heels and shaken vigorously, in the belief that the liver had grown fast to the body wall, and must be "shuck loose." AS, VIII (1933), 50. Cf. my *Ozark Superstitions,* 119.

live with the world: *phr.* To be concerned with worldly matters, material interests. Of a dreamy, impractical, absent-minded preacher it was said: "That feller don't *live with the world* no more. AS, XI (1936), 316.

load: *v.t.* To deceive with a *windy* or a tall tale. "The boys has been *a-loadin'* them pore tourists ag'in."

loafer: *v.i.* To loaf or idle about. "That boy just *loafers* around all day, an' comes home to sleep."

lolliper (lŏ′ lĭp ēr) : *n.* Something admirable or pleasing. "Look at that Paisely gal! Ain't she a *lolliper,* now?" DN, V (1927), 475. *Lollipaloozer* is sometimes used with the same meaning.

looby: *adj.* Clumsy, awkard, perhaps stupid. In Galena, Mo., I heard of a "great big fat *looby* boy that would step on himself an' fall down." Some hillmen put an *r* sound in this word, so that it sounds like *loobry*.

look: *n.* A view, usually from a slight eminence. Asked how far off a certain cabin is, the hillman may reply, "Three *looks* an' a couple of jumps." He means that the trail traverses three hills, and that the house in question is only a few yards beyond the crest of the third ridge.

loosenin' weed: *n.* A purgative or laxative herb.

Lord God: *n.* A name for the pileated woodpecker (*Dryocopus pileatus*). Both *Lord God* and *Good God* are on the label attached to a stuffed specimen at the University of Arkansas museum. See the discussion of this bird in W. L. McAtee's *Nomina Abitera,* 46–47. McAtee reports that it is called *wood God* in Arkansas. Cf. *Indian hen, wood-hen.*

love-apple: *n.* Tomato. This term is still heard occasionally, and the old-timers claim that it was in general use as recently as 1885. The first man to eat tomatoes at Green Forest, Ark., was regarded as something of a hero by his neighbors, who had always thought *love-apples* were poisonous. Cf. J. L. Russell's *Behind These Ozark Hills,* 26.

love-hole: *n.* A gully or ditch across the road. In the horse-and-buggy days, such a depression was supposed to throw lovers into each others' arms. DN, V (1926), 401. Cf. *chug.*

low-rate: *v.t.* To criticize adversely. "That feller better quit *low-ratin'* my kinfolks!"

lucky-bones: *n.* The two bony disks found in large crawfish. Many hillfolk carry these objects to bring good luck and ward off diseases. AS, VIII (1933), 50.

luggish: *adj.* Slow, heavy, sluggish. "Seems like the turkeys was kinder *luggish* that day, an' the boys killed seven of 'em right off." AS, VIII (1933), 50.

lumbrage (lŭm′ brĕj) : *n.* A loud rumbling or crashing noise. A woman told reporters: "I jumped out of bed when I heerd the *lumbrage,*" meaning the noise made by a drunken man as he fell down a flight of rickety stairs.

mad sow: *n*. A sow in heat. Butchered at this time, the meat has a strong odor. A man smelling some bacon in a store remarked, "It's either a old boar or a *mad sow*."

make: *n*. Figure. "Them thin dresses shows a gal's *make* too much." The past participle is also used in this connection; to say that a woman is "purty *made*" means that she has a good figure. AS, XI, (1936), 316.

make a fancy: *phr*. To make a good impression. "Jim's tryin' to *make a fancy* with them town gals tonight." AS, XI (1936), 316.

make ag'in: *v.t*. To injure, to damage. "I done quit chawin' tobacco; I seen it was *makin' ag'in* me." DN, V (1926), 401.

make bullet patches: *phr*. A man whose trousers fit very tightly over the seat is said to be *makin' bullet patches*. In loading an old-fashioned rifle, the hunter stretched his *patching* tightly across the muzzle before inserting the bullet, after which the surplus cloth was trimmed off with a knife. AS, VIII (1933), 50–51.

make out with: *phr*. Get along with, put up with, tolerate. Sometimes one hears *make-out* used as a noun, meaning makeshift. An old gentleman said of his new dentures, "I can *make out with* these here teeth, I reckon. But it's a damn' poor *make-out*."

make strange: *v.i*. To be amazed or astonished. Nancy Clemens, of Springfield, Mo., heard a farmer say, "I sure *made strange* when they showed me them bugs through the microscope." The sentence "she *made strange* of me" may mean "she didn't recognize me" or "she seemed surprised at my appearance."

make the riffle: *phr*. To accomplish a given task. The word *riffle* means rapids, fast water common in the Ozark streams, and these riffles are difficult to get through in a johnboat. The expression is generally used in the negative, as, "Bill tried for to be an auctioneer, but he couldn't *make the riffle*." Cf. *cut the mustard* (DN, V [1923], 205) and *hack it*.

mallyhack: *v.t*. To cut up, or to beat severely. "I'll *mallyhack* that feller within a inch of his life!" I have heard a man with many knife wounds and bruises described as *mallyhacked*. The word seems to be used only when the injuries are severe. Cf. *malahack*, Wentworth's *American Dialect Dictionary*, 376.

mammy: *v.t*. To transmit the mother's likeness to offspring. My neighbor, looking at a cat and kittens, said, "Well, she didn't *mammy* 'em," meaning that the kittens did not resemble the mother cat. The word *pappy* is used in the same way, meaning that the progeny *take after* the father rather than the mother.

mannerable: *adj.* Polite, having good manners. "He's a *mannerable* old feller, anyhow." *Mannersome* is sometimes used with the same meaning.

maple-head: *n.* Any man with a noticeably small head. This term is very common in Stone and Lawrence counties, Mo. The old-timers say that it began with a pioneer family named Maples. "The Maples boys all got funny little heads," said an old man at Hurley, Mo. "You can tell a Maples as far as you can see him."

martin storm: *n.* A late blizzard, at the time the martins return in the spring. Cf. *blackberry winter.*

mass dark: *adj.* Absolutely dark. "It's just plumb *mass dark* in that there cave." DN, V (1927), 475.

maw: *n.* Mother. *Mam, mammy,* and *mommy* are also common, the last used mostly by small children. Cf. *pappy.*

may-hop: *n.* The passionflower vine (*Passiflora incarnata*). The term *may-pop* is reserved for the edible fruit of this vine, which is also known as *wild apricot.* DN, V (1926), 401.

meat-house: *n.* Used figuratively to mean hopes or expectations. An old farmer, having agreed to finance his son's education at the village high school, issued this solemn warning: "But if you ever lie to me about them grades, down goes your *meat-house!*" Taylor (DN, V [1923], 206) found *cob-house* used with a similar connotation in McDonald County, Mo.

medlar: *n.* The eastern meadow lark (*Sturnella magna*). Cf. *fiel'ark.*

mellow: *v.t.* To beat, to pummel, to smash. "I'll just take a stick of wood an' *meller* that boy's head!"

mend: *v.i.* To gain weight. "That feller's *a-mendin'* mighty fast" does not mean that his health is improving, but merely that he's putting on weight.

mess-ahead: *adj.* Shiftless, improvident. "He's just one of them *mess-ahead* fellers" means that he is content to have only one mess of victuals in the house. AS, XI (1936), 316.

methiglum: *n.* Metheglin or mead, a fermented drink made from honey. Many Americans never even heard of metheglin, but the old folks in the Ozarks know all about it. Pepys (*Diary,* July 25, 1666) drank the stuff, as did Charles II, the same day.

middling: *adj.* Tolerable. "How's the old woman, Gabe?" asked a passing farmer. And my neighbor answered, "Oh, she's *middlin'*, just fair to *middlin'*." DN, V (1927), 475.

middlings: *n.* Pieces of side meat, salt pork. The term *middlin'-meat* is also common. AS, V (1929), 19.

milking stars: *n.* The constellation Orion. It is said that these stars are often conspicuous at milking time. AS, XI (1936), 316. Cf. *folding-star,* "a star rising at folding-time, an evening star." (OED).

ming-mang (mĭng′ măng): *n.* A mixture of butter and molasses, or sometimes butter and gravy. The old-timer likes to mix this on his plate, using a flexible steel knife for a spatula. Dorrance (*University of Missouri Studies,* X [1935], 86) found *mic-mac,* meaning a mixture, common among the Missouri Creoles. AS, XI (1936), 316.

misfool: *v.t.* To delude, to deceive. "Them folks didn't mean no harm; they was *misfooled* by listenin' at a crazy preacher."

misput: *v.t.* To mislay, to misplace, to lose. DN, V (1927), 475.

misremember: *v.t.* To forget. This is not common, but I have heard a few old-timers use it.

miss-woman: *n.* A refined, accomplished young woman, either married or single. "That feller can wash a shirt as good as any *miss-woman.*" Rose O'Neill tells me that she often heard this in Taney County, Mo., in the early nineteen hundreds.

mizzle: *n.* A very light shower, also called a *dry drizzle* or a *mizzlin'* rain. DN, V (1923), 215.

mollyjogger: *n.* A kind of minnow, probably the young of the *hogmolly* (*Hypentelium nigricans*). A group of men in Springfield, Mo., in the eighteen nineties, formed a fishing club known as the Mollyjoggers. J. F. Dunckel wrote a book entitled *The Mollyjoggers* (Springfield, Mo., n.d.) and explained (p. 83) that "there is a minnow inhabiting the James River, a horny-headed, spotted fellow, absolutely worthless, and this fish is called *mollyjogger* by the natives." It was the natives also who pointed out that the Springfield sportsmen behaved "just like a bunch of *mollyjoggers,*" and the name stuck.

mommix: *n.* A mess, a task badly done. "That there barber sure did make a *mommix* out of Pappy's whiskers." A verb form is heard occasionally: "Them fellers is *a-mommixin'* everything." Sometimes the noun seems to mean merely a state of excitement or confusion, as in the sentence, "No use to get yourself into a *mommix* about it." In Opie Read's novel *Lem Gansett* (p. 323) somebody told a Negro to put a new bottom in a chair, but the fellow *momoxed* the job. Read thought the word was introduced into the Ozarks by settlers from Tennessee.

morphodite (môrf' ŏ dīt): *n.* Hermaphrodite. Tucker (*American English,* 154) says this was used in eighteenth-century England. DN, V (1926), 401.

mountain boomer: *n.* A large collared lizard (*Crotaphytus collaris*), which the hillfolk believe to be venomous. DN, V (1927), 475.

mouse-bush: *n.* The pussy-willow (*Salix discolor*). The catkins do look rather like little gray mice.

mucher: *adv.* More, farther. In setting out a row of trees, a man said to his helper: "I reckon we better set that'n over just a *little mucher.*" The tree he indicated was a trifle out of line with the others.

muscle: *v.t.* To lift, to move. "You-uns can *muscle* that little rock easy." DN, V (1926), 401.

musicker: *n.* A musician, who plays a musical instrument or teaches music. *Musicianer* is also heard occasionally. DN, V (1927), 475.

mussel-head: *n.* One who is slow witted, not too intelligent.

name: *n.* Self-respect, character, reputation. A man on trial for murder was telling the court how the dead man had abused him. "He wallered me in the dirt, Judge, afore all them folks, an' I lost my *name* right thar!" DN, V (1926), 401.

nanny tea: *n.* A folk remedy, made by boiling sheep manure in water.

narrows: *n.* A pass or gap where the trail follows a narrow shelf, usually with a stream on one side and a high cliff on the other. Cf. DN, V (1923), 215.

near about: *adv.* Nearly, almost. "Jim was *near about* the best man in this country, when it come to makin' ties."

nigger runner: *n.* A fox chaser of a trashy, ignorant type; such a man knows nothing of the fine points of a foxhound, and real fox hunters don't like to associate with him.

nigh cut: *n.* A back road, more or less private, usually a narrow trail or bridle path. AS, VIII (1933), 51. Not always synonymous with *short cut.* A *nigh cut* between two cabins, both situated on the highway, may be longer than the main-traveled road.

nippety-nip: *adj.* and *adv.* Implies an equal sharing, a division comparable to half-and-half or horse-and-horse. "*Nippety-nip* in rural central Missouri," says the Kansas City *Star* (April 26, 1935), "seems to be a phrase corresponding to fifty-fifty, even-Stephen or something of the sort." After a motor wreck, one of those concerned was asked who was to blame. "Well," was the answer, "he was a-goin' too fast an' I didn't have no lights. I guess it was just a case of *nippety-nip*." One sometimes hears *nip-and-nip* and *nip-and-tuck* used to mean near equality in a contest, the equivalent of neck-and-neck.

nippy: *adj.* Stinging, sharp, or slightly bitter. Used of wine, cider, and other fermented drinks. AS, XI (1936), 316.

no-man's land: *n.* The earth and gravel washed from one farm to another by high water. The term was used in McDonald County, Mo., as long ago as 1882. Old-timers say that it originally designated a particular strip of bottom land in the Indian Territory.

nooby: *n.* A long knit scarf or muffler. Ruth Day, of Sparta, recalls that the pioneers used to wear "white *newbies* around their necks." Judge Ruppenthal (DN, IV [1914], 161) found *nubi* among the Russian-Germans in Kansas; he took it to be a Russian word, meaning "some article of wearing apparel, perhaps a fascinator." John H. Waterman (*General History of Seward County, Nebraska* [Beaver Crossing, Neb., 1916], 90) mentions pioneer women who "wore *nubias* in Winter." DN, V (1927), 476.

noodle: *v.t.* To catch fish with the hands, or with a short *noodlin'-hook* held in the hand. This is called *rock fishing,* since the fish are taken from holes under rocks. The Scotch highlanders *noodle* fish just as we do, but they call it *guddlin'.* Cf. *guddle,* EDD.

norate: *v.t.* To make public by word of mouth. Taylor (DN, V [1923], 215) thinks it usually means the spreading of "depreciatory rumors of a personal nature," but I have not found this meaning. The news of a sale or auction is often *norated around,* without any printed advertisement. Campbell (*Southern Highlander,* 145) says that in the Southern Appalachians "a man wishing to hold a public meeting has it *norated,* that is, the announcement of it spread by report." DN, V (1926), 401.

novel: *n.* Novelty, newness. "Lem never swaps nothin' till he gets the *novel* wore off'n it." DN, V (1927), 476.

oak winter: *n.* A late spring frost, after the oak leaves have appeared. AS, XI (1936), 316. Cf. *blackberry winter.*

odd-come-short: *n.* An indefinite time, an odd moment. "Thanks for the loan of the book; I'll fetch it back, one of these *odd-come-shorts.*" Cf. *dodge times.*

oddling: *n*. Something peculiar or abnormal in a harmless, inoffensive way. A pious eccentric is sometimes called "God's *oddlin'*." So is an agreeable, even-tempered half-wit.

oddments: *n*. Odds and ends. Mary Elizabeth Mahnkey (*White River Leader*, Branson, Mo., March 8, 1934) referred to "some *odds and endments* of handkerchief linen that she got out of her big old trunk."

off-bear: *n*. Progeny, offspring. "Doc Yokum has got *off-bears* on every creek in this county."

off-casts: *n*. Castoffs, something discarded. I have heard a woman, formerly a mistress of William Jones, described as "one of Bill Jones' off-casts."

olden: *adj*. Old, ancient. Used in several set phrases such as *olden times*, which means anything more than two or three generations back.

Old Master: *n*. God, or sometimes Jesus Christ, used without any intention of irreverence. The *Old Man*, or the *Good Man*, or the *Old Gentleman*—these names for God are used even by deeply religious hillfolk. Occasionally one hears the *Man Above*, or the *Old Man Higher Up*, or even the *Old Man Upstairs*. But the *Old Boy* means Satan. Other terms for the Devil are *Old Red*, *Old Rip*, *Old Sam*, *Old Coaley*, *Old Ned*, the *Other One*, the *Enemy*, the *Dark Stranger*, *Harry Scratch*, *Old Scratch*, *Old Horny*, *Old Blackie*, *Old Samson*, *Old Simpson*, and *Old Jimson*.

old none: *n*. Nothing, none. "That mare ain't much good, but she sure is better than *old none!*" AS, VIII (1933), 51.

once and occasionally: *phr*. Now and then. I asked a rabbit hunter if he ever killed 'em a-runnin'. "Yes, *once an' occasionally*," he answered, "but mostly I just arkansaws 'em." Cf. *arkansaw*.

one-gallus: *adj*. Poor, ignorant, of low origin and small attainments. Literally, of course, it means a single cord to hold up the trousers, instead of a belt or suspenders. "Them Tylers is a *one-gallus family*, an' always was."

one-poster: *n*. A bed built into the corner of a cabin, in such a way that only one post is necessary. An ordinary movable bed is called a *four-poster*. AS, XI (1936), 316.

on the floor: *phr*. Refers to the marriage ceremony. A couple actually being married are said to be *on the floor*. Or one may say: "Them two'll be *on the floor* before the pawpaws are ripe," meaning that they will be married shortly. *On the carpet* carries the same meaning. DN, III (1906), 149. Cf. Marge Lyon (*Fresh from the Hills*, 135).

on the lift: *phr.* Bedfast, unable to stand or walk without assistance. "Old man Byrd's *on the lift;* I reckon he'll make a die of it this time."

ontelling: *adj.* Erratic, unpredictable. "Sam is the *ontellin'est* feller I ever seen. Nobody knows what the damn' fool is goin' to do next." AS, XI (1936), 316.

oojit-nawsty (ōō′jĭt nôs-tĭ): *adj.* Good, pleasing, satisfying. Used in describing anything from hymn-singin' to corn juice. Common among the old-timers near Southwest City, Mo., who say it is derived from a Cherokee word. AS, V (1929), 19.

orance: *n.* A mysterious animal, which the villagers used to joke about in Greene County, Mo., back in the eighteen eighties. Some old settlers identify it with the *wampus,* a kind of legendary wildcat. Cf. my *We Always Lie to Strangers,* 52–53.

ornery, onery: *adj.* Inferior, mean, worthless. A stronger word than *sorry.* Applied to a human being, *ornery* generally means lazy and shiftless; sometimes it means ill-tempered.

out: *n.* Result, finish. "Jim he tried for to keep tavern, but he made a mighty pore *out* of it," which means that Jim was unsuccessful as a tavern-keeper. DN, V (1923), 216.

out: *v.t.* To cheat, to defraud. "He don't need no pension; he's just a-tryin' to *out* the government."

out-dugan: *v.t.* To outwit, to get the better of, to cheat. "Tom Fitzhugh will be *out-duganed* in no time, if he tries to trade with them Lassiter boys." Taylor (DN, V [1923], 216) says that in McDonald County, Mo., *out duganed* means "circumvented by questionable means."

out of heart: *phr.* Downcast, discouraged. AS, VIII (1933), 51.

overlay: *v.t.* To kill by crushing or suffocation, as when a sleeping mother rolls over on her babe. When a small man in our town married a very large woman, one of my neighbors said, "Don't you reckon that feller will get *overlaid?*"

own the corn: *phr.* To admit an error. AS, XI (1936), 316. Cf. *acknowledge the corn.*

ozark: *v.t.* To cheat, to defraud. A woman in Branson, Mo., said: "I've been *ozarked* out of my property," meaning that she was cheated by a realtor. Cf. *arkansaw.*

pair: *n.* A considerable number, a set of things. A necklace is "a *pair* of beads." A stairway is "a *pair* of steps." Five or six treble hooks, fastened together for use in snagging or grabbing fish, are called "a *pair* of grabs." A denture, whether in two plates or one, is often "a *pair* of teeth." At the Veterans Hospital in Fayetteville, Ark., I heard *"pair of cards"* instead of pack or deck. DN, V (1926), 402. AS, XI (1936), 316.

pappy: *n*. Father. *Pap, paw,* and *poppy* are also common. In some families the father is called *paw,* while *pappy* designates a grandfather or even a great-uncle.

parts: *n*. Region or locality. "My chaps ketched the biggest coon ever saw in these *parts.*" DN, V (1927), 476.

passel: *n*. A large number. "I seen a *passed* of furriners down to the depot." Not used to mean a large quantity or amount. DN, V (1923), 216. Cf. *right smart, power,* and *heap.*

paw-pawer: *n*. An outlaw, a fugitive. DN, V (1926), 401–402. C. L. Norton (*Political Americanisms* [New York and London, 1890], 86) says that "paw-pawers are equivalent to bushwhackers, current in Missouri. The paw-paw is a wild fruit of the genus *Asimina,* on which the bushwhackers are supposed to subsist." Dorrance (*Survival of French in the Old District Ste. Genevieve,* 55, 124) observes that the Missouri Creoles are called *paw-paws* or *paw-paw French* by their English-speaking neighbors, "a term intended to convey no flattery."

pea-rifle: *n*. A muzzle-loading rifle of small caliber, the bullet no larger than a pea. DN, V (1926), 402.

peckerwood: *n*. Woodpecker. In some parts of Arkansas it refers to rural whites of low origin, comparable to the *white trash* of the Deep South. DN, V (1927), 476.

peel: *v.t.* To slap or spank, as in punishing a child. "Quit that foolishness, Johnny, or I'll *peel* ye good!"

peewee: *n*. A wild turkey poult, still following the hen. In some parts of the Ozarks, *peewee* means the bank swallow (*Riparia riparia*) or the rough-winged swallow (*Stelgidopteryx ruficollis*), as well as the species of the flycatcher family, the eastern wood pewee (*Contopus virens*), to which the name properly belongs in the Middle West. AS, XI (1936), 316.

peezaltree (pē' z'l trē): *adj.* Inferior, uncultured, unsatisfactory. In McDonald County, Mo., one hears of *peezaltree* dances, *peezaltree* kinfolks, *peezaltree* clothing, and so forth. It is said to have started when a preacher in Pineville, Mo., mispronounced *psaltery,* and was henceforth known as the *"peezaltree preacher."* This mispronunciation is common in the South; Roark Bradford (*Collier's,* January 20, 1940) makes his characters say *p-saltree*. But I have never heard *peezaltree* used as an adjective except in southwest Missouri. Cf. *durgen, jakey*.

peg-rock: *v.i.* To tilt backward in a chair not provided with rockers. "Buck makes me sick with his everlastin' *peg-rockin'*; always looks like he's a-fixin' to fall over back'ards." AS, VIII (1933), 51.

personate: *v.t.* To call by name, to designate specifically. "That fool preacher done *personated* me right in meetin'! Said he was sorry I didn't come oftener!"

peter-bird: *n.* The tufted titmouse (*Parus bicolor*). Ralph Bates tells me this name is common near Kissee Mills, Mo., where the bird cries *peter-peter-peter* all morning.

pick-fiddle: *n.* A guitar. The terms *git-fiddle* and *git-flip* are also used, facetiously.

piedy: *adj.* Spotted. "The Indians'll pay good money for them *piedy* ponies." DN, III (1909), 401. Sometimes the combination *piedy-like* means in poor health, showing a spotty complexion. DN, V (1927), 476.

pilfer round: *v.t.* To examine or disturb property belonging to another; perhaps to look about with the intention of stealing something. Apparently it does not mean the act of theft. AS, XI (1936), 316.

pindling: *adj.* Weak, puny, slender. "Them Choctaw young-uns is all kinder *pindlin'*." DN, V (1926), 402.

pineries: *n.* Pine forests. The singular form is rarely heard. AS, VIII (1933), 51.

pine straw: *n.* Dead pine needles lying on the ground. AS, V (1929), 19.

pink-eye gravy: *n.* Gravy from ham or other pork, to which water or milk has been added. The name refers to the reddish globules of fat visible in the stuff. Known also as *red-eye gravy, black-eye gravy, white-an'-streaked gravy, piedy gravy, calico gravy, brindle gravy* (DN, III [1906], 128), *spotted gravy* and *grease gravy*. Some cooks pour a little coffee into the pan, which gives a richer color. Cf. *sop*.

pinnywinkle: *n.* A snail, a periwinkle. The term is often applied to a little dark snail (*Limnea stagnalis*) common in Ozark waters. DN, V (1927), 476. *Pinnywinkle fever* is a summer disease, also called *swimmer's itch*, said to be acquired by bathing in water which contains pinnywinkles. AS, XI (1936), 316.

pisoliver (pĭs äl' ĭv ēr): *n.* A revolving pistol, a revolver. Perhaps a jocular combination of pistol and revolver. The word *revolver* is seldom heard in the Ozarks; most hillmen say *gun* or *pistol*.

pistol-whip: *v.t.* To beat with a pistol. The Springfield, Mo., *News & Leader* (March 15, 1936) tells of one Harry Blee, who "allegedly *pistol-whipped* Walter Mease near Reeds Spring, Mo., May 2, 1935." The *Commoner Magazine,* Mena, Ark. (July, 1939), quotes a sheriff as saying that "he was going to *pistol-whip* Rosen to death." DN, V (1927), 476.

pitch gab: *phr.* To make flirtatious or suggestive remarks. "Molly sure is *a-pitchin' gab* at that city feller." Cf. Nancy Clemens in the Kansas City *Star,* August 21, 1938.

pitch it up: *phr.* To "put more pep in it" or "show more enthusiasm" or "be more energetic." Sometimes it refers to dancing.

playment: *n.* A toy, a plaything. The word *play-pretty* is also common.

play-party: *n.* A dance at which there is no instrumental music; the players sing game-songs or *swing-arounds* as they go through the complicated figures. JAFL, XLII (1929), 201.

play whaley: *v.i.* To blunder, to fail, to make a ludicrous error. "Tom sure *played whaley* when he tuck up with them card-players." It is said that this expression derives from "a bonehead family named Whaley," long famous in backwoods humor. Cf. DN, III (1906), 151; V (1923), 217; PADS, No. 2 (1944), 37.

plunder: *v.i.* To search, to ransack, sometimes merely to wander about. An old woman in Galena, Mo., returned from picking a mess of wild greens, and she was very tired. "It just kills me any more," she said, "to git out an' *plunder around* that-a-way."

pod: *n.* Belly, paunch. Of a very fat man in McDonald County, Mo., a neighbor remarked: "It looks like Lon's *pod* is about to bust on him."

poison fish: *n.* A little brown mottled sculpin or muddler (*Cottus carolinae*). Most hillmen know that these creatures are not poisonous, but they call 'em *p'izen fish* anyhow. AS, VIII (1933), 51.

pokeweed religion: *n.* The sort of religious excitement that springs up rapidly and seems impressive, but has no permanent value. The term *lightnin'-bug revivals* carries the same meaning. One hears also of *jimsonweed* Babtists, *cocklebur* saints, *toadstool* churches, and *buckbrush* parsons.

pole-buster: *n.* A very large fish, one that may break a fishing rod. "Swan Creek is full of regular old *pole-busters* this year."

polly-fox: *v.i.* To move quietly or stealthily, to pussyfoot. AS, XI (1936), 316. William Allen White (*Autobiography* [New York, 1946], 314, 516) mentions *polly-fox* and *polly-foxing* as occurring in Kansas.

poor-do: *n.* Grease, shortening. "Fetch me a sack of flour, an' some *poor-do* for to make gravy." This used to be very common in northwestern Arkansas.

poor-hog: *v.i.* To live in poverty. "We just been *pore-hoggin'* along, an' damn' near starved out last winter." AS, XI (1936), 316.

poot the rug: *phr.* To die. "Pappy's just about ready to *poot the rug;* says he don't figger on livin' till spring." AS, XI (1936), 316.

pop-call: *n.* A very short visit. "Yes, he come here to see Sally once, but it warn't no more'n a *pop-call.*"

pop-rind: *n.* A meat-rind baked crisp. When a large family is eating *pop-rinds,* the stuff cracks like a bunch of little firecrackers.

possum-grapes: *n.* A variety of small wild grapes (*Vitis cordifolia*). DN, V (1926), 402.

post-hold: *n.* A forked limb driven into the ground to hold fence posts while they are sharpened with the axe.

posy-pot: *n.* A flower-pot, often merely an old bucket or whiskey keg with holes punched in the bottom. AS, VIII (1933), 51.

potlicker: *n.* A dog of mixed breed, often a mongrel foxhound.

pour-down: *n.* A cloudburst.

pour-off: *n.* A waterfall.

poverty-poor: *adj.* Destitute, near starvation.

power: *n.* A very large amount. "There's a *power* of honey in that bee-gum." Cf. DN, V (1923), 217.

prank: *v.i.* To experiment, to manipulate. "That boy'll git hurt, *a-prankin'* with that there choppin'-axe." DN, V (1927), 476.

preacher's seat: *n.* A peculiar semirecumbent position. When boys in swimming "do the *preacher's seat,*" they leap into the water buttocks down, with the head and feet up.

prezactly: *adv.* Mary Elizabeth Mahnkey, Mincy, Mo., used to quote this word, always jokingly. I have heard it from other old-timers, too, but not often. Apparently it is a combination of *precisely* and *exactly.*

principally: *adv.* Chiefly, or mainly. "That boy ain't no kin, but we *principally* raised him" means that the boy lived longer at the speaker's home than with his parents. DN, V (1926), 402.

prize: *v.t.* and *v.i.* To pry, to snoop. *"Prizin'* round me" means "prying into my affairs," according to Clay Fulks of Mena, Ark. Some hillfolk use *prizin'* to mean objecting or complaining.

prong: *n.* One branch of a road or stream that has divided. "When you come to where the road forks, just foller the right hand *prong*." AS, VIII (1933), 51.

puke: *n.* A native of Missouri. Leopold Wagner (*More About Names* [1893], 28–29) says that "the natives of Missouri are universally styled *Pukes,* a corruption of the older name Pikes, which still obtains in California as the description of the migratory whites from the South owning to the idea that these originally came from Pike County, Missouri." May Stafford Hillburn, of Jefferson City, Mo., says that when the settlers first came to St. Louis, they gathered wild greens and suffered an epidemic of nausea; it was said that people moving into Missouri always got the *pukes,* hence the name for Missourians. According to the *Missouri Historical Review* (XXI [1927], 634–35), residents of St. Louis used to cross the river and gather Illinois *puke-root,* a remedy for fever and ague; the Illinois settlers called them *puke-hunters,* later shortened to *pukes.* May Kennedy McCord, Springfield, Mo., observes that when Missouri families move into any other state, they grow homesick and just go *a-pinin' an' a-pukin' round.* Therefore, says Mrs. McCord, people in other states call Missourians *pukes.* Ralph H. Pond (*Life,* November 23, 1942, p. 6) repeats "a straight story passed down from the early pioneers" to explain why Illinois people are called *suckers* and Missourians *pukes.* It seems that early settlers in Illinois learned to drink from scum-covered pools by sucking through a straw, leaving the surface undisturbed. Missourians just threw themselves down on their faces and drank the water scum and all; this made them sick and they vomited, hence the name *pukes.* A writer in *Fortune* (July, 1945, p. 118) has another explanation: "Apparently because many miners emigrated to Illinois lead mines in 1826, and as Missouri seemed to vomit them, it was called the *puke* state." Cf. Thomas Ford, *History of Illinois* (Chicago and New York, 1874), 68. Whatever the origin of the name, there are men in Arkansas and Oklahoma today who always refer to Missouri as the *Puke Territory* or the *Puke Nation.*

pulley bone: *n.* The wishbone of a fowl. AS, VIII (1933), 51.

pum-granny, plum-granny: *n.* A small, yellow-striped, fragrant, gourd-like fruit, used occasionally as food. I have seen them sliced and preserved in syrup or molasses. It is said that the name derives somehow from *pomegranate.* DN, V (1926), 402. Cf. Wentworth, *American Dialect Dictionary,* 466. Botanists in Missouri and Arkansas are unfamiliar with the vernacular name and are unable to identify the plant from my description. But any of my old neighbors on Bear Creek, in

Taney County, Mo., can tell 'em all about *pum-grannies.* Lola Byars Johnson, Benton, Ark., thinks it must be *Cucumis anguira,* called ornamental pomegranate, queen's pocket-melon, or vegetable peach.

pummies: *n.* Pomace, sugar cane stalks that have been pressed in a mill. "Cane *pomace* is now used as a mulch for strawberries in Barry County, Mo.," according to the *Country Gentleman* (December, 1939, p. 9). People who live in Barry County generally say, "Cane *pummies are* used," since they regard the word as a plural. Cf. DN, V (1923), 218.

pump-knot: *n.* A lump, a swelling. "Did you see that big *pump-knot* on Rafe's head? Looks like somebody hit him with a axe-handle." AS, VIII (1933), 51.

pure dee: *adj.* Genuine, indubitable. "No, them ain't no chigger-bites. That's the *pure dee* seven-year itch!"

pure quill: *n.* The genuine product, unadulterated, undiluted. A neighbor tasted my whiskey, and cried: "That's the *pure quill, an'* no Goddamn' water in it!" AS, XI (1936), 317.

push the collar: *phr.* To work very hard. Probably from the pushing of a horse's shoulders against the collar. "Joe's a good boy, but he don't *push the collar* like his pappy did."

pussy: *adj.* Countrified, awkward. "Aunt Bett is the *pussiest* old woman I ever seen." DN, V (1927), 476. Cf. *durgen, jakey, soozy.*

put the big pot in the little one: *phr.* To provide extraordinary hospitality, to feed a guest unusually well. "The preacher's a-comin', Maw! Kill the old rooster, an' *put the big pot in the little-un!*"

quern: *n.* A mortar, an Indian stone or metate used in grinding corn. Charles Morrow Wilson (St. Louis *Post-Dispatch,* June 9, 1930) says it means a hand mill.

quill: *v.t.* To blow. This is common usage in many parts of the South. Quentin Reynolds (*Reader's Digest,* December, 1939, p. 55) quotes a Southern engineer: "There never was a man who could *quill a whistle* like old Casey Jones." Dr. J. H. Young, of Galena, Mo., told me of a backwoods healer who *quills* a woman in labor by filling a turkey quill with snuff and blowing it in the patient's face; the theory is that the snuff makes the woman sneeze, and the babe will be born instanter! Farmers used to *quill* a sore on an animal by blowing some medicinal powder on it through a quill.

quill-wheel: *v.i.* To move about, to cover or patrol a large area. One of Rose O'Neill's neighbors in Taney County, Mo., said of a restless old woman: "She's always *quill-wheelin'* around." Miss O'Neill thinks the word may mean circling like a hawk.

rabbit 'backer: *n.* Dried rabbit dung, sometimes mixed with "long green" tobacco to make a milder smoke. AS, XI (1936), 317. The herb known as life everlasting or cudweed (*Gnaphalium obtusifolium*) is sometimes called *rabbit-tobacco.*

rabbit-ice: *n.* The flower-like ice formations sometimes seen on the stems of dittany weed; evidently a fine spray of liquid comes out of these stems near the ground and is frozen. Some Ozarkers believe that rabbit-ice has medicinal value. I have heard city folk call the stuff *frost flowers* and *ice orchids.* C. C. Williford (*KWTO Dial* [Springfield, Mo.], December, 1949, p. 13) says that "dittany is a small aromatic herb (*Cunila origanoides*) commonly called horsemint." But the weed generally known as horsemint in this region is a species of *Monarda.*

rabbit-twister: *n.* A rustic, a backwoodsman. The term refers to the practice of twisting rabbits out of hollow logs with a forked stick. AS, XI (1936), 317. Cf. *hillbilly.*

rack: *v.i.* To move rapidly, to make haste. "I seen Jimmy *a-rackin'* down the road like the Devil was after him."

rackensack: *n.* A derisive name for Arkansas. Cf. Carr, DN, III (1906), 152. Alsopp (*Rhymeries* [Little Rock, 1934], 99) says that the term "originated through a chance epithet disrespectfully applied by a Mississippian many years ago." Cf. Allsopp's *Folklore of Romantic Arkansas*, II, 87; also Masterson's *Tall Tales of Arkansaw*, 324, 352, 182, 195, 192, and 150. W. C. Holden (*Alkali Trails* [Dallas, 1930], 75) mentions the inscription on a mover's wagon:

> *Last fall come from* Rackin Sack
> *Got sorry and now go rackin back.*

rain crow: *n.* A bird whose cry is supposed to indicate rain. In most sections of the Ozarks, *rain crow* means the yellow-billed cuckoo (*Coccyzus americanus*). Cf. my *Ozark Superstitions* (1947), 248.

raise sand: *phr.* To create a scene or disturbance. "Paw sure will *raise sand* when he hears 'bout Lizzie a-sleepin' with the sheriff." The phrase *kick up sand* carries the same meaning.

ramack (răʹmăk): *v.t.* To search, to ransack. "I been *a-ramackin'* the whole country for sang-root, but I cain't find none nowheres."

rambunctious: *adj.* Impudent, loud-mouthed, objectionable. One of my neighbors said of a hired man: "Tom's a good worker, but he's gettin' so *rambunctious* here lately that I don't want him around my children."

ramp, rampse: *v.i.* To rush wildly about. The term is most often applied to bulls or other male animals, but sometimes to men. "A fresh-married feller ain't got no business *a-rampin'* round them tourist-camps."

rampooch: *v.i.* To engage in a kind of horseplay in which a boy is seized by his arms and legs, and his buttocks swung violently against a tree trunk. Cf. DN, V (1923), 218. *Rambutt, rambump, bump,* and *buck* DN, III [1909], 393) are used with the same meaning.

ramptious: *adj.* Wild, active, dangerous, like a mad bull. Cf. *ramp, rampse.*

ramrod: *n.* A leader, a boss, a person of great influence. "There's five fellers on the school board, but old man Burns is the *ramrod.* The rest of 'em does whatever he says."

raw: *adj.* Naked. "It got so hot the kids just sprinkled the bed, an' slept plumb *raw.*"

razorback, *n.* A half-wild hog. Most razorbacks are small and thin, with large heads and long legs. They rove the woods like range cattle, feeding largely upon *mast,* or acorns.

redding comb, reddening comb: *n.* An ordinary heavy comb, with which the mountain woman "reds out" snarls in her hair. AS, XI (1936), 317. A fine-toothed comb is called a *finin' comb* or a *booger comb.* Cf. *booger.*

red-eyed: *adj.* Obviously guilty, red handed. "The sheriff ketched Bill *red-eyed* this time, an' they got him in the jail-house right now."

red perch: *n.* One of the broad, varicolored sunfish (*Lepomis spp.*), also known as the pumpkinseed. AS, VIII (1933), 51.

red the guts: *phr.* To clean the intestines. At hog-killin' time the entrails are split open, cleaned, wound on sticks, and hung up to dry. They are used in making soap. AS, XI (1936), 317.

red up: *v.t.* To clean, to put in order. "I got to *red up* this here house if we're goin' to have company." Isabel Spradley, of Van Buren, Ark., thinks that the cabin should be *retted* up, but it sounds like a *d* rather than a *t,* to my ear.

regiment: *n.* A large number or quantity. "We didn't plant no garden this year, but we got a whole *regiment* of canned stuff in the cellar." The word *nation* is sometimes used with the same meaning.

ricebird: *n.* The goldfinch (*Spinus tristis*), often called the wild canary. The Ozarker does not use this word for the bobolink (*Dolichonix oryzivorus*), which is known as a ricebird in some parts of the South. AS, V (1933), 51.

rick: *n.* A pile of firewood eight feet long, four feet high, and as wide as the length of the sticks. A *cord* differs in that it must be four feet wide. The noun *rank* is sometimes used with reference to firewood and seems to mean either a rick or a cord, though James West (*Plainville, U.S.A.*, 33) says that a rank is "a half-cord" in Hickory County, Mo. *Rick* is also used as a verb, meaning to pile up. During World War II, I heard a wounded veteran say, "We killed so many Germans the boys just *ricked* 'em up like cookwood."

ride: *v.i.* To live as an outlaw, a fugitive from justice. "My pappy can remember when the James boys was *a-ridin'*, an' Jesse slept right here in our house a many a time." Perhaps it's a mispronunciation of raid. Emmett Dalton, the bank robber, published an autobiography in 1931, entitled *When the Daltons Rode*.

ride bug-hunting: *phr.* To ridicule, or to administer a sound thrashing. "The boys done *rid that old feller a-bug-huntin'*, an' he's goin' to get the sheriff after 'em." Cf. DN, V (1923), 202.

ridge-runner: *n.* A derisive term for the mountaineer, as contrasted with the valley-farmer. DN, V (1927), 476. Cf. *hillbilly*.

rifle-gun: *n.* A muzzle-loading rifle. In the larger bores these weapons are often called *human-rifles,* while those of smaller caliber are known as *turkey-rifles, hog-rifles, squirrel-rifles,* or *pea-rifles.* DN, V (1926), 402.

right smart: *n.* and *adj.* A considerable amount. "I raised a *power* of corn, sold a *heap,* an' had a *right smart* left." It is sometimes used with reference to distance. Ask a hillman how far off a certain village is, and he may answer, "Well, it's a *right smart* piece." As Taylor (DN, V [1923], 219) points out, *right smart* is not used to mean a large number of individual objects; the Ozarker does not say "a *right smart* of sheep, or horses, or cattle." Cf. *passel, power, heap*.

rim-reck: *v.t.* To destroy, to dismantle, to ruin. "If we let that feller into the Lodge, he'll *rim-reck* the whole business inside of a year."

ringer: *n.* At fairs and picnics boys on horseback carried wooden lances and rode full tilt at harness rings suspended by cords from a tree. When a rider succeeded in thrusting his lance through a ring, the performance was called a *ringer.* Cf. Mary Alicia Owen (*Missouri Historical Review,* XV [1921], 180). M. V. Lamberson, of Gentry, Ark., tells me that he saw one of these "tournaments" in connection with a Fourth of July celebration at Rocky Comfort, Mo., as late as 1907 or 1908.

risin': *n.* A boil, an abcess. "Maw had a turrible *risin'* on her neck." AS, V (1929, 20. Cf. *gathering.*

roasting ear, in: *phr.* Ripe, mature. Perhaps applied primarily to corn, but used with reference to other plants as well. Fully developed beans, for example, are said to be *in roastin' ear.* Isabel France (*Arkansas Gazette,* August 24, 1947) writes of "crowder peas canned *in the roasting ear.*" I have heard the phrase applied to water lilies, as "yonkapins *in roastin' ear,*" meaning that the pistils were fully matured.

rock-house: *n.* A shallow cave or shelter under an overhanging bluff. Hillmen often speak of storing their hay in a *rock-house,* or of using a *rock-house* as a stable. AS, VIII (1933), 51.

roguish: *adj.* Term applied to cattle that break through fences. Cf. *breachy.*

rollix: *v.i.* To frolic, to carouse, to philander. "Tub Rawlins has done left his woman, an' he's *a-rollixin'* round after them Horse Creek gals now." DN, V (1927), 476. There is an adjective, too, which sounds like *rollicky.*

rough: *n.* A grove, a thicket. Judge John Turner White, of Jefferson City, Mo., told me that two groves on the old White farm were known as the *Big Rough* and the *Little Rough.* "Where we got those names, I do not know," he added.

ruckus (rŭk' ŭs): *n.* A scuffle, a fight in which more than two persons are involved, a free-for-all. Sometimes one hears this pronounced *rookus,* but ordinarily the *u* is short. "Take care the jug don't get busted, fellers! Looks like there's goin' to be a little *ruckus* here."

ruddock: *n.* The redbird or cardinal (*Richmondena cardinalis*). Louise Platt Hauck, of St. Joseph, Mo., says this word was common at Blue Eye, near the Missouri-Arkansas line, in the early nineteen thirties.

rue back: *v.t.* and *v.i.* To trade back, to cancel a bargain. "We done swapped horses, fair an' square, an' now Ed he's a-tryin' to *rue back* on me!" DN, V (1927), 402.

rullion: *n.* A coarse, tough, unkempt person; I believe it is usually applied to unattractive women of low origin and loose morals. Pronounced to rhyme with *scullion.*

run: *n.* A small stream, a spring branch. Generally used with a specific name: *Puckett's Run, Rocky Run, Stillhouse Run,* and so forth. AS, VIII (1933), 51. The State Highway Department agents in Missouri do not understand this word, and their official designations are often tautological. A stream near Galena, Mo., has long been known as *Pine Run,* but a sign put up by the Highway Department makes it *Pine*

Run Creek! The term *branch* is another example of this; in Morgan County, Mo., there is a sign which reads *Clear Branch Creek*.

runnet: *n.* The stomach, or sometimes the gall bladder. Used in a jocular fashion. "Look out thar, Bill! You'll fall down an' bust your *runnet.*" AS, XI (1936), 317.

run the river: *phr.* To serve as a guide or boatman on the Ozark streams. "Lon he never does no work only *run the river,* an' maybe trap a little in the winter time."

sack: *v.t.* To refuse, to dismiss. When one of my neighbors announced "Lucy went an' *sacked* me," he meant that she had refused his proposal of marriage. Sometimes the preterite is pronounced *sackted*, in two syllables. Will Sharp (Springfield, Mo., *News*, May 31, 1941) says that girls used to knit a tiny *sack* and send it to a boy, as a sign that they wanted no more of his attentions. AS, V (1929), 20.

sandy: *n.* A trick, a bluff. "He run a *sandy* on me" means that he fooled me somehow or bluffed me into doing something against my inclination.

sang root: *n.* Ginseng, a plant which is still found in some parts of the Ozarks. DN, V (1927), 477.

sanko (săng′ kō): *v.i.* To walk silently, to pussyfoot around with no apparent purpose. Joe Beaver, of Eureka Springs, Ark., told me that he "used to *sanko* around in the woods" when he was a boy. Sometimes it means to assume a solemn manner, like that of a country preacher. "Deacon Jeems come *a-sankoin'* round, but I never paid no attention."

sarvis, sarvis-berry: *n.* The service berry or shad bush (*Amelanchier arborea*). Carr (DN, III [1905], 93; III [1906], 160) confuses *sarvis* with some kind of huckleberry, which is not the same thing at all.

sashay, sash-a-way, sashiate: *v.i.* To move briskly about. Used in calling the country dances, perhaps from the French *chasser.* Carr (DN, III [1906], 154) says that in northwest Arkansas *sashay around* means "to trifle, to cut up."

sassafrack: *n.* Sassafras. Used facetiously, or when talking with children. Cf. *Rackensack*.

saw off a whopper: *phr.* To tell a tall tale, to spin a *windy.* AS, XI (1936), 317. Cf. *whack*.

saying: *n.* A maxim, a proverb, a set speech. I have heard the Twenty-third Psalm described as "a mighty good sayin'." DN, V (1927), 477.

say on: *v.i.* A derisive or defiant expression, used in urging a speaker to continue. At political meetings and the like, men in the audience often shout, "Say on!" or "Tell on!" at an unpopular orator. AS, XI (1936), 318.

scadoodles: *n.* A very large number, or a very large amount. "I seen *scadoodles* of mussels in White River, just below Cotter." Perhaps a combination of *scads* and *oodles,* both of which are used in this region to mean large quantities.

scaley: *adj.* and *adv.* Inferior, low grade, contemptible. The prosecuting attorney in a Missouri village told me that the local rich man had "acted pretty *scaley*" toward his brother, who was a pauper.

scape-gallows: *v.i.* To idle about, to loaf. "Jim got let out of the army to work on his farm. But he don't do no work. He's out there now, just *scape-gallowsin'* around." Rufe Scott, of Galena, Mo., heard this term in his neighborhood, and says that it means "just keepin' ahead of the hangman." OED gives *scape-gallows* as a noun: one who has escaped the gallows though deserving it.

scarce-hipped: *adj.* Slender. "I seen that gal Jim's a-keepin' at the hotel; a *scarce-hipped* little bitch."

scatteration: *n.* A dispersal, a scattering. People in my neighborhood still talk of the *scatteration* which occurred when some boys threw a live hornets' nest into a Holy Roller meeting.

science: *adj.* Skillful, proficient, expert. "Bob sure is a plumb *science* fiddler." DN, V (1926), 403.

scoffle: *v.t.* and *v.i.* To ridicule, to scoff. "Maggie she kept *a-scofflin'* at me all evenin'." DN, V (1927), 477.

scoop-town: *adv.* An emphatic affirmative, comparable to "Sure!" or "You're damn' right!" Sometimes shortened to *scoop.* It is common near the Oklahoma border and is said to be of Cherokee origin. AS, V (1929), 20. Cf. *yooper.*

scope: *n.* A large area or extent. "They got a big *scope* of road to grade up this winter." AS, XI (1936), 317. Cf. Nancy Clemens, Kansas City *Star,* August 21, 1938.

scriber: *n.* A writer, a penman. "He's a right good *scriber*" means that his "handwrite" is easy to read. DN, V (1926), 403. In pioneer days, a *scriber* was an expert at notching logs for building cabins. Cf. my *The Ozarks,* 24.

scrooge (skrōōj): *v.t.* and *v.i.* To squeeze or crowd. "I'll just *scrooge* in here next to Miss Betsey." *Scrouch,* pronounced to rhyme with *crouch,* is also common. A woman who kept a boardinghouse in Stone County, Mo., often spoke of people being *scrouched* at her table; she meant that they were crowded, that their chairs were too close together. DN, V (1927), 477.

seep: *n.* A damp spot, produced by a stream which does not quite reach the surface of the ground. Some fine springs are developed by digging into these *seeps*. AS, VIII (1933), 52.

segashiate (sĕ găsh' ĭ āt): *v.i.* To move about, to progress. Usually jocular or facetious. Cf. *sashay, sashiate.*

set: *n.* Stand, growth. A man boasted that he had "a pretty good *set* of blue grass" in his front yard. A barber in Carroll County, Ark., remarked: "That feller has got a mighty coarse *set* of hair; it's just like wire."

set a spell: *phr.* To visit. "I don't relish them people much, but I *sot a spell* with 'em anyhow." DN, V (1927), 477. When a hillman invites you to "come over an' *set a bed-spell*" he means for you to stay until bedtime. AS, VIII (1933), 52.

set in: *v.i.* To begin. A farmer may *"set in* to pullin' weeds," and a man once told me that his wife had "done *set in* to raisin' hell." The sentence "it *set in* to rain" is very common. The term is often used with reference to the measurement of land: "My farm *sets in* right here, an' runs plumb to the creek." DN, V (1926), 403.

set one's budget down: *phr.* To come to a decision, to take a firm stand on any given question. "Hit ain't no use talkin' any more, Mister, 'cause I've done *set my budget down.*" AS, VIII (1933), 52.

set out: *v.i.* To seek a husband, to show a desire for matrimony. "Old Miz Thomas is *a-settin' out.*" I believe it refers chiefly to widows seeking to remarry.

set the fur: *phr.* To humiliate, to put a pretentious fellow in his place. "I sure did *set the fur* on Bill, tellin' 'bout the time he was throwed in jail."

set up to: *v.i.* To woo, to court. "Jake he's *a-settin' up to* a gal over on Gander Mountain."

set you acrost: *phr.* Help you across a stream. Used not only by the ferrymen, but by other Ozarkers. If the creek is too deep for easy wading, any passing teamster will offer to *set you acrost* in his wagon. AS, VIII (1933) 52.

shake-down: *n.* A makeshift bed, a pallet laid on the floor.

shaller: *v.i.* To become shallow. "The branch kinder *shallers off* just below the spring-house." Sometimes *shally* is used with the same meaning. AS, VIII (1933), 52.

282

shape notes: *n.* The peculiar notation which Ozark singin'-teachers still use, rather than the ordinary round or "sol" notes. The shape notes are sometimes called *buckwheat music.* Cf. my *Ozark Mountain Folks,* 248–49. AS, VIII (1933), 52.

sheep dumplings: *n.* Sheep manure. *Sheep dumplings* are used in the home treatment of measles and certain other ailments.

shell duck: *n.* The shoveller or spoonbill (*Spatula clypeata*). DN, V (1927), 477.

shell the brush: *phr.* Used in connection with political campaigns. "Bob's been *a-shellin' the brush* over in Barry county" means that he has done a lot of speech-making and hand-shaking over there. *Shellin' the woods* is often used with the same meaning.

shelly: *adj.* Inferior, of low grade, in poor condition. "An old *shelly* cow" is one that isn't worth much. I have heard it applied only to cattle, but believe that it sometimes refers to bony old horses as well. Mrs. Lillian Short, of Galena, Mo., tells me that some people say *hully* when they mean *shelly.*

shield: *n.* A sheath, a scabbard. "He was wearin' a cowhide *shield* with a big knife in it."

shiver: *v.t.* To propel, to throw, to fire. "They done *shivered* four bullets into Ab Yancey afore you could scat a cat!" DN, V (1927), 477.

shoal: *v.i.* To assemble for breeding or spawning, as suckers and other fish do in the Ozark streams. AS, VIII (1933), 52. Sometimes the word is applied to human beings. A village preacher once told me that serenades are sinful, "just an excuse for young folks to go *a-shoalin' round* of a night."

shoo-fly: *n.* and *adj.* The big bow of ribbon which some elderly women wear as a necktie. AS, VIII (1933), 52. Men and boys, in the early days, wore their hair "*shoo-fly* style," combed low on the forehead with the ends brushed back.

shoot: *n.* A person nearly mature. "Polly Brown's gettin' to be a *shoot* of a gal." DN, V (1926), 403.

shootin'-fixin's: *n.* Firearms and ammunition. Rarely heard now, but said to have been common in pioneer days. DN, V (1926), 403.

shuckle: *v.i.* To hurry, to bustle about. "I just let on like the house was afire, an' you orter seen them fellers *shuckle* out o' thar!" AS, VIII (1933), 52.

shut-in: *n.* The canyon formed by a stream with high banks on both sides. Perhaps the most conspicuous are the Black River *shut-ins* in Reynolds County, Mo., but there are many others in the Ozark country. AS, VIII (1933), 52.

side-hill hoofer: *n.* A mythical beast which runs around mountain tops, always in the same direction because the legs on one side of its body are longer than those on the other side. The *side-hill slicker* and the *side-hill walloper* are variants. These imaginary creatures play an important part in Ozark folklore. Cf. *Arkansas Historical Quarterly*, IX (1950), 71–72.

sidelin': *adj.* Leaning, inclined, not horizontal. A woman complained that her house, built on a steep hillside, was not level. "That shanty is so *sidelin',*" she said, "I cain't git a toe-hold nowheres."

side-line: *v.t.* To catch bass, usually bigmouth bass which are called linesides, by forcing them to leap into a boat. Same as *jumping, bumping,* and *goosing.* A man who makes a business of this kind of fishing is called a *side-liner.*

simmer down on: *phr.* To concentrate upon, to specialize in. A famous gigger once told me: "I aim to *simmer down on* redhorse from now on, an' let them damn' linesides go by." AS, VIII (1933), 52.

singin' convention: *n.* A competitive meeting of local groups of singers. Most of them sing only hymns. These gatherings were formerly called *singing matches,* but the term *convention* is regarded as more dignified. DN, V (1927), 477.

sink-taller whiskey: *n.* Liquor of a high alcoholic content. It is said that a piece of tallow floats in weak whiskey but sinks in high-proof spirits. AS, XI (1936), 317.

skift: *n.* The sled or sledge used in hauling stone, often called a *stone-boat.* Sometimes *skift* means a light fall of snow.

skillet-an'-lid: *n.* A Dutch oven, an iron dish with legs and a heavy cover grooved so that hot coals may be placed on top. The lid is usually pronounced *led.*

skin your eyes: *phr.* To be alert, to keep a sharp lookout. "You got to *keep your eyes skinned,* if you figure on gettin' a deer in this country." The phrase *peel your eyes* is also common.

sky-gogglin: *adj.* Crooked, irregular, lopsided, askew, aslant, awry. A *sky-gogglin* field is one with irregular borders, limited on one side by a meandering stream or by a road which winds around a bluff. Sometimes the word has particular reference to unusual or unexpected angles. Mrs. Bess Allman, of Galena, Mo., once told me that "the streets in Boston are all *sky-gogglin.*" I believe that *si-gogglin, skee-*

waddlin, sky-waddlin, and *sky-wampus* are very close to *sky-gogglin.* Charles Morrow Wilson (St. Louis *Post-Dispatch,* June 9, 1930) reports *hip-skeltered,* which apparently carries a similar meaning. Cf. *anti-gogglin.*

sky-ways: *adv.* This word must be somehow akin to *sky-gogglin.* I have not heard it often. But in a fist fight at Reeds Springs, Mo., it was said that somebody attacked the sheriff and "knocked him *sky-ways* an' crooked." Cf. *sky-windin'* in PADS, No. 2 (1944), 60.

slantendicular: *adj.* Not quite vertical, but nearly so. A *slantendicular* fence post is one that leans just a trifle.

slathers: *n.* A very large amount. "Them fellers has all got *slathers* of money." DN, V (1927), 477. Cf. *lashins and lavins.*

slattery: *adj.* Dirty, dilapidated, in poor repair. "Uncle Dick he lives in a old *slattery* house."

slaunchways: *adj.* and *adv.* Slanting, diagonally. DN, V (1926), 403. PADS, No. 2 (1944), 60–61. Cf. *anti-gogglin.*

slick: *n.* A certain kind of minnow (*Campostoma anomalum*). Boys around Protem, Mo., catch *slicks* in glass minnow traps, and sell them to city fishermen.

slicker: *v.t.* To beat or flog severely. "That boy's pappy just cut a switch an' *slickered* him good." A feud between the Hobbs and Turks families, in Hickory County, Mo., involved the horsewhipping of many persons. The "trouble" was known as the *Slicker War* and is so designated in several books of Missouri history. Cf. *Missouri Historical Review,* VII (1913), 138–45.

slump: *n.* A large, fleshy, untidy person. DN, V (1926), 403.

slut: *n.* A primitive lamp, made by attaching a rag wick to a pebble and setting it in a vessel of grease. The word in this sense has been traced back as far as 1609. An old man told me that such a lamp was properly called a *bitch,* but that folks nowadays thought *slut* was more refined! Cf. *grease light.*

smack out of: *phr.* Completely out of. A stranger asked for sugar to put in his coffee. "We're just *smack out* of sweetenin'," said his hostess.

smell the patching: *phr.* To be involved in a spirited conflict or struggle. In the old days when the patched bullet was forced into a rifle barrel, the shooter could often smell the burning cloth after a few shots were fired. Referring to a political meeting in 1940, a backwoods politician said, "I bet them fellers'll *smell the patchin'* at Springfield tonight!"

smidgin: *n.* A very small quantity. "That feller ain't got a *smidgin* of sense." DN, III (1905), 94; V (1926), 403.

snackin': *n.* A snack, a lunch, a small amount of food. "I ain't et nothin' all day, only a *snackin'* out of a poke." DN, V (1927), 477.

snap at: *v.t.* To extend credit, or lend money. "We got to pay cash for everything nowadays; the storekeeper ain't *a-snappin' at* us no more." AS, XI (1936), 317.

snawfus: *n.* A legendary creature, common in pioneer folk tales. Like an albino deer, with great white wings and flowering boughs for antlers. *Arkansas Historical Quarterly,* IX (1950), 70.

snibbling: *adj.* Dark, cloudy, rainy. "I cain't go nowheres on a bad, *snibblin'* day like this." DN, V (1927), 477.

snuff-mop: *n.* The chewed peach or black-gum twig used in dipping snuff. The term *snuff stick* is also heard occasionally. Cf. *tooth-brush.*

sobby: *adj.* Wet, soggy, mouldy. When stovewood is heavy or water-soaked, it is said to be *sobby.* The word applies also to dressed lumber that turns dark or mouldy.

sockdolager: *n.* Something surprising in size or quality. "Ain't he a *sock-dolager?*" cried a boy who had just caught a very large catfish. Cf. *gollywhopper, gee-whollicker.*

sog: *v.i.* If a stick of wood doesn't burn properly, but just turns black and smoulders, the hillman says, "That there ellum-wood ain't no good, it *sogs* too much." AS, VIII (1933), 52.

solid fellow: *n.* A suitor, a lover with serious matrimonial intentions. A girl who is "goin' with a *solid feller*" is said to be "keepin' *solid* company." AS, VIII (1933), 52.

something on a stick: *phr.* Something unusually fine or valuable. "Jim treats that old woman like she was *somethin' on a stick.*" Cf. Nancy Clemens, Kansas City *Star,* August 21, 1938.

soo: *n.* Suet, fat of beef or mutton. AS, VIII (1933), 52.

sooner: *n.* A child born less than nine months after its parents' wedding. Any native of Oklahoma may be called a *Sooner,* but this refers to the opening of the Cherokee Strip of 1893, and has no connection with birthdays.

soozy: *adj.* Countrified or uncouth, and at the same time ludicrously conceited. "We couldn't help laughin' at them *soozy* schoolmarms." DN, V (1926), 404; V (1927), 478; AS, IV (1928), 116. Charles Morrow Wilson (St. Louis *Post-Dispatch,* June 9, 1930) says that *suzy* means a bachelor, but I have not heard it in this meaning. Cf. *durgen, jakey.*

sop: *n.* Gravy, usually made from pork. The upper transparent grease is called *top-sop,* while the heavier opaque part is known as *bottom-sop.* DN, V (1927), 477. Cf. *pink-eye gravy.*

sot-work: *n.* Knitting, mending, needlework, and so on. One woman says to another, "Come over to our place. Bring your *sot-work* an' stay all day."

sour gnat: *n.* Any sort of small insect that gets into one's eye, causing severe pain. An ordinary gnat is bad enough, but a *sour gnat* or *p'izen gnat* is much more painful.

sowcoon: *n.* A jocular name for cyclone, like *bullgine* for engine. The word means female raccoon, too; there's a Sowcoon Mountain in Taney County, Mo.

spang: *n.* Gravy. Louise Platt Hauck, of St. Joseph, Mo., tells me that this word was in common use at Blue Eye, Mo., in the late nineteen twenties. I have heard *spang* used to mean a mixture of gravy and butter.

spew: *v.t.* To scatter or spread. "The wind blowed the line down, an' *spewed* Maw's washin' all over town." DN, V (1926), 403.

spike: *n.* An arrow. One hears little boys talking of "a bow an' *spike*" just as children elsewhere would say "a bow and arrow." The flint arrowheads found in the fields are known as "Injun *spikes*" and occasionally as "Injun darts."

split the quill: *phr.* To separate, to quarrel, to fall out. "Me an' Lizzie have *split the quill* for good this time, an' she says she's goin' to get her a divorce."

spunk: *n.* Dry, partially decayed wood. The pioneers used *spunk* to catch the sparks from the flint-and-steel gadgets which they carried in lieu of matches.

spunk-water: *n.* Rainwater which remains in cavities of trees or stumps, supposed to have some medicinal or cosmetic value. AS, VIII (1933), 52.

squander: *v.t.* and *v.i.* To scatter, to disperse. "That gun don't shoot true no more; the bullets just goes *a-squanderin'* round every which way."

squash: *v.t.* To crush. AS, XI (1936), 317.

squaw-wood: *n.* Small or badly cut firewood. Often used in a jocular fashion with a negative, as when a man selling stovewood says: "An' that ain't no *squaw-wood* neither."

squealer: *n.* A small catfish which produces a squeaking noise when taken from the water. Some say that the squealer is the so-called granny cat or yellow bullhead (*Ameiurus natilis*), but I am not satisfied with this identification. Perhaps other species of catfish squeal under certain conditions. Cf. my *We Always Lie to Strangers*, 229–30.

squee-jawed: *adj.* Distorted, misshapen, lopsided. DN, V (1927), 477. Cf. *sky-gogglin, whomper-jawed.*

squench: *v.t.* To extinguish, to obliterate, to subdue. Hal C. Norwood (*Just a Book* [Mena, Ark., 1938], 26) refers to a man who *"squenches* the thunder when he speaks!"

squinch owl: *n.* The screech owl (*Otus asio*).

squirmy: *n.* A lively young girl. "Them dance-halls is full of *squirmies* nowadays; growed-up women don't go there no more."

squirrel: *v.t.* To hoard, to conceal. "That old feller *squirrels* every nickle he gets his hands on."

squirrel-dumplin's: *n.* A facetious name for noodles. AS, V (1929), 20.

squirrel-hawk: *n.* Any large slow-flying hawk, usually the redtail (*Buteo jamaicensis*).

squirrel-turner: *n.* An expert with the small rifle used in squirrel shooting. DN, V (1926), 403.

stand: *v.t.* To contain or enclose in a standing position. Waldo Powell, of Reeds Spring, Mo., said of Fairy Cave: "Inside this majestic dome is a grotto large enough to *stand* a dozen people." The verbs *bed* and *sleep* are used in the same causative fashion.

starve out: *v.t.* and *v.i.* To die, to become extinct. *Starve* meant die in Queen Elizabeth's time, like the German *sterben.* The Ozarker still uses *starved out* in the old sense, without any direct reference to the food supply. "There used to be lots of rattlesnakes on that hill, but they all *starved out* years ago."

stash: *v.t.* To conceal, to cache. "Billy done *stashed* our jug in the brush, an' now the old fool cain't find it!" DN, V (1927), 477.

stay-bit: *n.* A snack, a bite of food between meals.

stay more: *v.i.* To remain longer. This is a polite expression, used when a guest is preparing to depart. "Don't be drug off, Jim. *Stay more!*" DN, V (1926), 404.

stewer: *n.* A stewpan, a metal vessel with a handle. Sometimes pronounced almost like *stir.*

stickery: *adj.* Prickly, covered with sharp points or *stickers.* "It's mighty *stickery* out back of the barn, with all them cuckleburs an' beggar-lice.

stid: *n.* A bedstead. May Kennedy McCord, of Springfield, Mo., quotes a young bride as saying: "Maw give me two *stids* an' the makin's for 'em"—the *makin's* being shuck mattresses, quilts, and coverlets. AS, XI (1936), 317.

stink bird: *n.* Any small bird which stays close to the ground. A man whose bird dog kept making false points, and finding no quail, told me, "It's them damn' *stink-birds* a-foolin' him."

stob: *n.* A sharp or jagged stump, an irregular piece of dead timber standing upright. A *stob-pole* is used in propelling a boat in shallow water; the boatman uses it to prevent collision with *stobs.*

stodge: *v.t.* To season, to spice, to flavor. A possum is not very palatable unless it is *stodged up* with red pepper, spicewood, and so on.

stone roller: *n.* A small sucker-like fish. Stone rollers are also called *rot-guts*, because it is said that their entrails turn black and decay within a few minutes after death. AS, VIII (1933), 52; XI (1936), 317. Some of the professors say that *stone rollers* are young hog suckers (*Hypentelium nigricans*), but the Ozark fishermen don't believe it, and neither do I.

stooped: *adj.* Leaning or inclined, often applied to trees on river banks. "Uncle Jack crope out on a *stooped* sycamore, an' gigged him a big redhorse." DN, V (1927), 477.

stradways: *adv.* Astride. Rose O'Neill, of Taney County, Mo., owned a fine saddle mare, and is remembered as the first woman who ever "rode *stradways*" in that vicinity.

strawberry friend: *n.* A moocher. Many city people visit their backwoods cousins only when strawberries are ripe, to get enough free berries for a year's supply of jam.

stretch the blanket: *phr.* To exaggerate, to tell a tall story. "Don't you reckon Ab was *stretchin' the blanket* a little?" said one of my neighbors, referring to a man who claimed he had killed a running deer with his derringer. Cf. *windy, whack.*

striffin: *n.* This name is applied to the membrane which lines an eggshell, also to the tough skin which protects the body of a mussel. "Pearls always lays at the end of the shell, just under the *striffin*," a shell-digger told me. Sometimes it means a membrane in the human body. A judge in Christian County, Mo., was asked the meaning of the word *epididymis.* "Oh, it's that *striffin* around the testicle," said he.

strollop: *n.* A rambling woman of doubtful morals. Perhaps a combination of trollop and strumpet. Sometimes one hears the verb: "Annie knows better than to *strollop* around with them town fellers." AS, XI (1936), 317.

strut: *v.i.* To swell. "Maw's foot is plumb *strutted* this mornin'." DN, V (1927), 478. There is a noun, too, as in this sentence: "Her foot is swole plumb to a *strut.*"

stud: *n.* A male fish, especially a game fish, such as bass or jacksalmon. Among coarse fish, suckers for example, the males are called *boars* and the females *sows.*

suck the hind tit: *phr.* To get the worst of anything, to occupy a disadvantageous position. I heard a politician say in a public speech: "You all know us Republicans has been *a-suckin' the hind tit* for fourteen year!" AS, XI (1936), 317.

sugar bread: *n.* Cake. Ralph Allen McCanse, a native Ozarker, used the term in this sense (*The Road to Hollister* [Boston, 1931], 40). May Kennedy McCord (Springfield, Mo., *News,* January 4, 1940) says that *sweet bread* is the old-time word for cake. AS, XI (1936), 317.

suggin (sŭg' ĭn): *n.* A hillman of inferior stock and low mentality. "Them Hornet Creek fellers is purty nigh all *suggins,* an' us folks don't neighbor with 'em." In English dialect one meaning of *suggan* is "a straw collar put around a dunce's neck." EDD.

sull: *v.i.* To sulk. Taylor (DN, V [1923], 222) reports the word from Mc-Donald County, Mo., with the meaning "to grow sullen, to refuse to talk. Also to balk, as a draft animal."

sulter: *v.i.* To smother, to suffocate. "I mighty nigh *sultered* down thar in the settlement." DN, V (1926), 404.

sun-ball: *n.* The sun. A man hiding from the law spent his days in a cave, never venturing out until after dark. "Jesus Christ!" he said to me one night, "I ain't seen the *sun-ball* in a month!" AS, VIII (1933), 52.

sun pain: *n.* A severe headache, which lasts all day but does not keep the patient awake at night. The natives attribute *sun pain* to malaria, but do not explain how it is relieved in the prone position. AS, VIII (1933), 52.

swag: *n.* A piece of low, swampy ground.

swage: *v.t.* To decrease in size, to reduce a swelling. When Marge Lyon (*Fresh from the Hills,* 135) sprained her ankle, an Arkansas school superintendent advised her to put the swollen foot in hot water "and get it *swaged* down." From *assuage,* according to Webster.

sweet-wood: *n.* Red cedar. "She keeps them fine clothes in a *sweet-wood* chest, so the moths won't bother 'em."

swiddle: *v.t.* To stir, to dip. Coral Almy Wilson, Zinc, Ark., tells of an old woman who *swiddled* some molasses off her finger into a guest's coffee. One of my neighbors often speaks of *"swiddlin'* out some clothes," meaning to rinse them. DN, V (1926), 404; AS, XI (1936), 317. Cf. *swoggle*.

swilge: *v.t.* To wash, to rinse, as a woman may *swilge* a churn. In some quarters, to *swilge out* means to take a vaginal douche.

swing-around: *n.* A game song, as sung by the dancers at a play-party. AS, VIII (1933), 52.

switch-cane: *n.* A kind of evergreen bamboo (*Arundinaria gigantea*). DN, V (1927), 478.

swoggle: *v.t.* To dip or stir. *"Swoggle* your dodger in them molasses, stranger!"* DN, V (1926), 404. Cf. *swiddle*.

take for the kitchen: *phr.* To withdraw from the conversation, to remain silent. A neighbor told me: "Them fellers got to talkin' purty deep, with big words an' all, so I just *tuck for the kitchen.*" He did not actually leave the room, but he declined to take any part in the discussion.

take rounders: *phr.* To walk around an obstacle, rather than scale it. Derived from an expression used by boys in playing marbles. Cf. *surround*.

take the mountain: *phr.* To start on a journey. Comparable to "hit the trail," as heard farther West. "Jim he *tuck the mountain* Sunday mornin', an' I ain't saw him since."

take the rag off the bush: *phr.* Sometimes this expression denotes only profound astonishment. One of our neighbors greeted his first airplane with: "Don't that *take the rag off'n the bush!*" Dean E. H. Criswell tells me that in Dade County, Mo., it means "to rant, rave or carry on in an exaggerated manner." When a farmer's daughter got into trouble with a drummer, her father "sure did *take the rag off'n the bush.*" AS, V (1929), 20.

take the studs: *phr.* To balk, to grow stubborn, to become immovable. "We was doin' all right till Deacon Jones got mad. But the old man has *tuck the studs* now, an' it ain't no use argyin' with him." AS, XI (1936), 318.

take with the leavings: *phr.* To withdraw hurriedly. "Things was gettin' too hot round home, so I just *tuck with the leavin's.*" AS, VIII (1933), 53.

talk to: *v.i.* To court, to woo. "The old fool was *talkin' to* Ellen Burke afore his wife was cold in her grave." DN, V (1927), 478.

talpa: *n.* The catalpa tree (*Catalpa speciosa*). There is a settlement called Talpa in Lawrence County, Mo., and R. L. Meyers (*Place-Names of Southwest Missouri,* 144) remarks that *"talpa* is a local, slangy form of catalpa."

tat: *v.t.* To gossip, to tattle. "You know I don't never *tat no tales,* Minnie, but I think you orter know how your man's been a-carryin' on whilst you was away."

tear off a strip: *phr.* To remonstrate noisily, to rave, to raise a disturbance. "If Nell's pappy knowed what she's a-doin', he'd *tear off a strip!*" Sometimes one hears *tear up jack,* with the same meaning. AS, V (1929), 20.

tear-out: *n.* A boisterous or hilarious meeting. "They had a regular *tear-out* down to the Possum Holler schoolhouse." AS, V (1929), 20.

tear the bone out: *phr.* To do anything thoroughly, to "go the whole hog." Often used in connection with house-cleaning and the like. Sometimes it means simply to throw a noisy party. "We sure did *tear the bone out* the night Judge Fuller got married."

teem: *v.t.* To pour, to drain. Mary Elizabeth Mahnkey, of Mincy, Mo., quotes one of her neighbors on the best method of pickling beans. "You do thus and so," she said, "an' then you *teem* the water off." Sometimes it is used to describe a heavy rain: "It sure was *a-teemin'* about four o'clock. I could hear the water a-pourin' off the roof."

tetchous: *adj.* Tender, sensitive, easily aroused. Usually refers to human beings or domestic animals, but it also means sensitive in a mechanical sense. A hair-trigger rifle is "so Goddamn' *tetchous* it ain't safe, unless you're used to it." DN, V (1927), 478.

thistle-bird: *n.* The goldfinch (*Spinus tristis*), a small bird which feeds upon the seeds of thistles and sunflowers. Sometimes called *wild canary* or *ricebird.* DN, V (1926), 404.

thousands: *adv.* Of large size or amount rather than of large number. "Them britches is *thousands* big, but they ain't noways long enough." DN, V (1926), 404.

thrifty: *adj.* Able to turn food into fat. This term is applied especially to swine which eat heartily and gain weight.

through: *n.* A series of doses of medicine. "I taken a *through* of calomel last week, an' now Doc's done fixed me up a turrible *through* of physic!" The words *course* and *round* are sometimes used in the same meaning.

throw an idea: *phr.* To make a suggestion, to offer advice. "I ain't tryin' to boss nobody. I just want to *throw a idy* an' see what you fellers think about it." Cf. *draw an idea.*

thumb-buster: *n.* A single-action revolver, the hammer of which must be drawn back with the thumb before each shot. AS, VIII (1933), 53.

tilting: *n.* A tournament, a contest between athletic teams or schools. *Tilting* was used by elderly folk at Doniphan, Mo., as recently as 1930.

timber doodle: *n.* The woodcock (*Philohela minor*). Also called the *night partridge.* AS, VIII (1933), 53. The Ozarker reserves the name *woodcock* for the pileated woodpecker.

time of books: *phr.* The study period in school. A teacher told me that she whipped a boy "for hollerin' in *time o' books.*" Once I went with a mountain man to interview the teacher of a country school. When we arrived at the building, he hesitated. "We better wait till recess, to see the schoolmarm," said he. "It won't do to go bustin' into the schoolhouse in *time o' books.*"

times, by: *phr.* Early, soon. "Jim riz up *by times* that mornin', 'cause we figured on goin' to town." Perhaps this is *betimes*; Pepys was always writing "Up *betimes,* and to the House of Lords."

tissick: *n.* A cold, an infection of the throat or lungs. Charles Cummins (Springfield, Mo., *Leader & Press,* September 18, 1933) always spelled it *tizzuk.* Perhaps a variant of *phthisic.*

toad-frog: *n.* A toad. The word frog is sometimes used with reference to both frogs and toads. DN, V (1927), 478.

toddick: *n.* This means either the portion of grain which the miller took as his fee for grinding it or the gourd which he used in dipping out his toll. Cf. Charles Morrow Wilson (St. Louis *Post-Dispatch,* June 9, 1930).

tomfuller: *n.* The old name for hominy, said to derive from an Indian word. Taylor Livers, a Cherokee who lives near Stilwell, Okla., tells me that *ta-fu-la* is Choctaw for "a kind of hominy, with pieces of meat mixed in."

tooth brush: *n.* A chewed twig used in dipping snuff. DN, V (1926), 404. Cf. *snuff-mop.*

tooth jumper: *n.* A mountain dentist of the old school, who extracts teeth by means of a mallet and a slender steel punch.

top-water: *n.* A little minnow (*Gambusia affinis*) which swims on the surface, eats mosquito larvae, and brings forth its young alive. The word is applied humorously to teen-age youngsters of either sex. Spider

Rowland (*Arkansas Gazette,* June 23, 1948) uses *top-waters* to mean small-timers, second-raters.

tote right: *phr.* To be fair, to conform to the local ethics. "I aim to *tote right* with everybody in this county, whether they voted for me or not," said a newly elected sheriff. The phrase *tote fair* carries the same meaning.

touch hands: *phr.* To unite, to co-operate, to stick together. This was a favorite expression of the late Jeff Davis, onetime governor of Arkansas.

tree-dog: *n.* A dog used in hunting coons, possums, and the like, as distinguished from a foxhound or a bird dog.

tree-top: *v.t.* To land a fish with unnecessary force, throwing it into the tree-tops. Figuratively, to attack any project with unusual vigor or enthusiasm. Of a girl who quite obviously "set her cap" for a village preacher it was said: "Minnie figures on *tree-toppin'* him!"

trigger up: *v.t.* and *v.i.* To primp, to dress up. "Molly's back in the shed-room, *a-triggerin' up* for that town feller." The adjective form is common: "Lucy's all *triggered up* tonight; I reckon Bob's goin' to take her to the dance."

trollop: *n.* A restless woman, a gadabout, perhaps inclined to be "fast." Sometimes used as a verb: "I sure wouldn't let no gal of mine go *a-trollopin'* round that-a-way." DN, V (1926), 404. Cf. *strollop.*

trotter: *n.* Foot, leg. Pickled pigs' feet are often called *pigs' trotters.* One of my neighbors struck a peddler in the face, and the blow "upped his *trotters,*" that is, knocked the man flat on his back.

trout: *n.* The smallmouth black bass (*Micropterus dolomieu*) also called *brownie, black bass, spotted bass,* and *swift-water bass.* There are no real trout in the Ozarks except rainbows, which have been introduced in recent years. AS, V (1929), 20. Cf. *lineside.*

truckle: *v.i.* To hurry, to move rapidly under orders, with some criticism of the mover implied. A woman said to her grown son, "You *truckle* outdoors, an' wash them feet." Common usage among the old-timers in Stone and Taney counties, Mo.

tuckin' comb: *n.* A comb that old women wear at the back of their heads. AS, V (1929), 20. In pioneer days, some long-haired men wore *tuckin' combs;* Major Elias Rector, of Fort Smith, Ark., was one of them. I saw an old man with a comb in his hair as recently as 1947, in Carroll County, Ark.

tudy-rose (tōō' dǐ): *n.* A design used in old-time quilts and fancy-work.

Someone has suggested that it is identical with the Rose of the Tudors. DN, V (1927), 478.

tumble-turd: *n.* A dung beetle (*Coprini*), a scarab, a tumblebug.

tunk: *v.t.* and *v.i.* To thump, to rap. "Them Kiowas is always *a-tunkin'* on drums," a farmer told me of his Indian neighbors. One *tunks* a watermelon to see if it is ripe. DN, V (1927), 478. The *English Dialect Dictionary* defines *tunk* "to strike, knock, rap."

turkey-pea: *n.* A little flowering plant, probably *Anemone caroliniana*. Children eat the tuberous roots, which taste rather like young peas.

turn: *n.* Disposition, temperament, type of mind. My neighbor said of a politician, a good mixer with a pleasing manner, "I sure do like that feller's *turn!*" A woman once remarked to me: "Sallie Porter's always a-raisin' hell 'bout somethin'. That's her *turn*, an' she cain't help it."

turnip kraut: *n.* Shredded, pickled turnips, as distinguished from ordinary sauerkraut, which is called *cabbage-kraut*. AS, V (1929), 20.

twigger: *n.* A man or woman who cuts twigs off cedars to sell for Christmas decorations. I never heard of *twiggers* until the middle nineteen thirties, when the word was common along the Missouri–Arkansas border.

unbeknownst: *adj.* and *adv.* "She done it *unbeknownst* to me" means "without my knowledge or consent." I have heard "unbeknownst behind my back" and even "unbeknownst *to* my back."

unbritch: *v.t.* To open a breech-loading firearm. "I *unbritched* the old shotgun, but both hulls had swole so bad I couldn't git 'em out."

under rail: *phr.* Fenced. The old-timers still speak of their land as so many acres *under rail*, though most of the fences are wire nowadays. AS, VIII (1933), 53.

up-and-gone: *adj.* Restless, prone to wander about, or to change employment. "Jim is one o' these *up-an'-gone* fellers, here today an' somewheres else tomorrow."

uriah: *n.* An ignorant, uncouth backwoodsman. I have seldom heard this myself, but Dean Virgil L. Jones, University of Arkansas, tells me that some of his students use it in the sense of *durgen, q. v.*

urr: *n.* A sudden impulse. One of my neighbors suddenly sprang out of bed and "chinned himself" on a rafter. His wife cried out, "What *is* the matter with you, Tom?" He crawled back into bed. "I just had a *urr* to do it," he answered sheepishly.

use: *v.t.* and *v.i.* To frequent, to loiter. "Them boys is always *a-usin'* round the barber-shop." DN, V (1926), 404.

vapors: *n.* An obscure disease which involves "nervous spells," fainting, and anemia. Many thin, delicate women "just pine away an' die of the *vapors.*" The *Oxford Dictionary* defines *vapor*: "depression of spirts, hypochondria, hysteria, or other nervous disorders," with a quotation dated 1662.

vault: *v.t.* To conceal in a safe place. Used chiefly with reference to money. One hears tales of gold coin being *vaulted* under a fence post, or beneath a hearth stone. AS, VIII (1933), 53.

vigrous (vĭ' grŭs): *adj.* Vicious, dangerous. Albert Price, of Pineville, Mo., says that the less common form, *survigrous*, is nearly always applied to "mean" dogs, stallions, or wild animals such as bears and panthers. AS, XI (1936), 318.

wade-and-butcher: *n.* A crude, heavy hunting knife, usually made by some country blacksmith. Perhaps this was originally a trade name. Several times I have heard it applied to a very large, heavy, thick-bladed straight razor.

wag: *v.t.* To carry with some difficulty. Theodore Garrison ("Forty-Five Folk Songs Collected from Searcy County," M.A. thesis, University of Arkansas, 1944, p. 14) says that "a small child in Searcy County is often compelled to *wag* her baby brother around with her."

wagon-bed: *n.* Charles Cummins (Springfield, Mo., *Leader & Press*, September 19, 1936) declares that you can always tell an Ozark freighter from a "furriner," because the native says *wagon-bed* where the outsider speaks of a *wagon-box.* I don't think I ever heard a real old-timer say *wagon-box.*

walk-way: *n.* A path, usually of gravel. Sometimes it means a wooden sidewalk.

wampus-cat: *n.* "A bloodthirsty animal of some kind, found only in the wildest sections of the Ozarks," according to G. H. Pipes' (*Strange Customs of the Ozark Hillbilly* [Reed Springs, Mo., 1947], 3–4). Cf. my *We Always Lie to Strangers*, 58.

warp: *v.t.* To bend, as in this sentence: "Get goin' now, afore I *warp* the poker over your head!" Sometimes this meaning is obscured: "Bob he up an' *warped* Henry in the mouth with his fist." Occasionally the verb reverts to its original Anglo-Saxon meaning, "to throw." A friend of mine hooked a big bass and *warped* it into the boat. A neighbor said, "Mary is just plumb *warped* on that feller," meaning that she was infatuated with him. As a noun, the word means a blow: "Wait till I give him a *warp* or two with this here hickory!"

wart taker: *n.* One who removes warts by charms or incantations. "I don't know if Gram French is a witch or not, but she's the best *wart taker* in this country." AS, VIII (1933), 53.

wash-off: *n.* A bath. When one remembers that the hillman has only a wash tub, in which he stands upright and rubs his body with a wet cloth, the term becomes singularly appropriate. The ordinary laving of the hands and face is known as *washing up.* DN, V (1926), 404.

wassy (wôs' sĭ): *n.* A wasp. The plural is *wassies,* and such compounds as *wassy-nestes* are not uncommon. The form *waspy* or *waspie* is heard occasionally. AS, V (1929), 20.

water boy: *n.* A winch with a long cable and bucket, used to draw water from a deep hollow.

waterloo bonney: *n.* A mythical fowl which the old-timers in Polk County, Ark., describe as a cross between domestic chickens and wild pigeons. The *bonneys* lived on Pigeon Roost Mountain, near Mena, and had one leg shorter than the other. The good looks and intelligence of the Polk County pioneers are attributed to the fact that they fed upon *waterloo bonneys* for several generations. Cf. E. W. Alley (*Arkansas Gazette,* October 5, 1947).

water turkey: *n.* The coot, or mud hen (*Fulica americana*). This term is common in southwest Missouri. The real water turkey or snakebird (*Anhinga anhinga*) seems to be unknown to the Missouri hillfolk, though not uncommon in central Arkansas.

wedge-floating: *adj.* Concentrated, strong. There is an old saying that camp cooks test coffee by dropping an iron wedge into the pot. If the wedge floats, the coffee is too strong. AS, VIII (1933), 53.

weep: *v.i.* To droop, to bend over. Usually refers to trees. An accumulation of ice and snow "makes the cedars *weep* a little." DN, V (1927), 478.

wet-weather horn: *n.* A horn which turns upward. "The old cow with the *wet-weather horn,* she went an' died."

whack: *v.t.* and *v.i.* To exaggerate, to tell a tall tale. May Kennedy McCord, of Springfield, Mo., was accused of *whackin'* when she spoke of a sow nursing sixteen pigs. Cf. DN, III (1906), 163. To *whack up* means to divide, as when my neighbor told his son to *"whack up* them goobers," so that each of the other children should have a share. The noun *whack* sometimes means a bargain, an agreement; "I offered to swap my knife for hisn, an' Joe he said it was a *whack.*" AS, V (1929), 21.

whet a banner: *phr.* To make a loud rattle with a whetstone, scraping it on a scythe or cradle. It is a sort of challenge to other reapers. The man who *whets a banner* is telling everybody within hearing: "I'm the best mower in the whole damn' country! I can cut more wheat than any other man in these parts!" The stone plays a lively tune, like a jig. AS, XI (1936), 318. Rayburn (*Ozark Country*, 147) mentions this; he spells the word *banter*, but it sounds like *banner* to me.

whey (hwā): *v.t.* To thrash, to beat severely. "If Sally was *my* daughter, I'd take a club an' *whey* her good!" AS, XI (1936), 318.

whickerbill: *n.* The prepuce, the fore-skin. Taylor (DN, V [1923], 224) says that *whicker bill* means mouth in McDonald County, Mo., but I have not heard it in this meaning.

whiffle-bird: *n.* A legendary fowl which always flies backward. Cf. May Kennedy McCord (KWTO *Dial*, Springfield, Mo., October, 1946, p. 3). Other birds of this type are the *ponjureen*, the *bogie-bird*, and the *fillyloo crane*, described in my *We Always Lie to Strangers*, 67–68.

whippoorwill peas: *n.* A variety of peas or beans, mottled exactly like the whippoorwill's eggs.

whippoorwill storm: *n.* A storm in late spring. "Whenever you hear a whippoorwill holler in April," the old folks say, "it's time to begin a-packin' in wood." In Oklahoma, says Floy Perkinson Gates (AS, VIII [1935], 80), "a *whippoorwill storm* is a cold rain attended by a driving wind and considerable bluster; it occurs in the spring after the season is well advanced." Cf. *blackberry winter.*

whip-stitch: *n.* A brief interval. "Bob's folks are a-sendin' him money every *whip-stitch*, but he won't even pay his store-bill."

whistler: *n.* A fabulous black panther, alleged to lure timber workers to their doom by whistling at them from cedar thickets. It is said that the Concatenated Order of Hoo-Hoo, a national fraternity of lumbermen organized at Gurdon, Ark., in 1892, derives its name from the beguiling cry of the whistler. *Arkansas Historical Quarterly*, IX (1950), 70–71.

whitefish: *n.* A mushroom. Many hillfolk won't eat any sort of mushroom, but those who do eat them usually prefer morels, which they roll in cornmeal and fry in deep grease. AS, VIII (1933), 53. The term *dryland fish* is sometimes applied to morels in northwest Arkansas.

whitening: *n.* Face powder. "Molly puts on too much *whitenin'*, an' it makes her look kind of puny." AS, V (1929), 21.

whitey-ganser: *n.* The hooded merganser (*Lophodytes cucullatus*), a species of fish duck. AS, VIII (1933), 53.

whittaker: *n.* A soft felt hat. Rarely heard now, but Marion Nelson Waldrip, a preacher who lived near Bentonville, Ark., in the eighteen eighties, told me the term was common. Just as, farther West, any good felt hat was called a Stetson.

whomper-jawed: *adj.* Distorted, misshapen. A deformed child is *whomper-jawed* even though its head is normal; I have heard a hunchback so described. The term is often applied to inanimate objects, such as crooked cabins, vehicles, and articles of household furniture. DN, V (1927), 478; PADS, No. 2 (1944), 62. Cf. *squee-jawed.*

whoop owl: *n.* Hoot owl, also called *whoopin' owl.* Any large owl that makes a lot of noise. Usually it is the great horned owl (*Bubo virginianus*), sometimes the barred owl (*Strix varia*) common along many of the Ozark streams.

widow-maker: *n.* The woodsman's name for a big dead limb that falls unexpectedly.

willipus-wallipus: *n.* A vague legendary monster, according to the old-timers. In the early days a road-building machine in Greene County, Mo., was known as the *willipus-wallipus* and was listed under that name in the official documents. *Arkansas Historical Quarterly*, IX (1950), 69–70. Cf. my *We Always Lie to Strangers*, 48–49.

winchester: *n.* Any repeating rifle of the lever action type. The maker's name doesn't matter; one hears of Marlin *winchesters*, Savage *winchesters*, Remington *winchesters*, and so on. The first repeater to become popular in the Ozarks was a .44 made by the Winchester Arms Company in 1873.

wind-jammer: *n.* A teller of tall tales, a windy-spinner, a blanket-stretcher.

windy: *n.* A tall tale. AS, VIII (1933), 53.

winter fever: *n.* Pneumonia. The *Arkansas Gazette* (February 23, 1949) mentions people's dying of this disease in the eighteen forties and explains: "*Winter fever* was pneumonia. The colloquial term was in general use. In that period it meant almost certain death." The term *winter fever* was still common in McDonald County, Mo., when I lived there in the nineteen twenties.

winter sucker: *n.* A full-bodied, dark-colored fish, the black redhorse (*Moxostoma duquesnii*), also known as the *oil sucker.* AS, VIII (1933), 53.

wish: *v.t.* A euphemism for bewitch. A girl tells me that an incurable disease has been *wished on her* by an old woman.

witch elm: *n.* The winged elm (*Ulmus alata*), which some hillfolk call *wahoo.* A. M. Haswell, of Joplin, Mo., says that a wahoo fork is used by water-witches, hence the name. Cf. my *Ozark Superstitions,* 85.

within: *prep.* and *adv.* In. Used where most Americans would say *in.* "It ain't no fun, a-settin' *within* this here jail-house all by myself."

woobles (wōōb' 'lz) : *n.* Feeble-mindedness, idiocy, foolishness. When a hill-man says that somebody should be *bored for the woobles,* he refers to an old notion that mental troubles might be relieved by boring a hole in the skull. AS, VIII (1933), 53. Cf. *bored for the simples.*

woodchuck: *n.* Woodpecker. The animal which is called a woodchuck elsewhere is always a groundhog in the Ozarks. DN, V (1927), 479.

woodcock: *n.* The pileated woodpecker (*Dryocopus pileatus*), still common in the backwoods. DN, V (1926), 405. The real woodcock is called a *timber-doodle* or *night partridge* in the Ozarks. Cf. *Indian hen, Lord God.*

woodscolt: *n.* A bastard. DN, V (1923), 224. Cf. *bush colt.*

wool: *v.t.* To tussle with, to worry as a dog worries a cat. "Them kids is always *a-woolin'* the baby around, pullin' its hair an' rollin' it in the dirt."

wope: *interj.* A mild exclamation indicating surprise. Perhaps it means *whoa!* or *stop!*

work-brickle: *adj.* Industrious, anxious to work. "Paw ain't so *work-brickle* as he used to be. I reckon he must be gettin' old." AS, IV (1929), 204.

wowzer: *n.* A legendary super-panther, said to kill cattle and horses by biting off their heads. Common in the tall tales told by the pioneers. Cf. my *We Always Lie to Strangers,* 57.

writing: *n.* A paper, a document. A village lawyer told one of our neighbors, "Don't never put your name to no *writin',* 'thout you show it to me first." Cf. DN, V (1923), 224.

yank: *n.* A little creeping bird called the nuthatch (*Sitta carolinensis*). Arkansawyers say that the name is a reference to its blue coat, but perhaps the bird's querulous chirp is responsible. DN, V (1926), 405.

yard grass: *n.* Bluegrass. AS, XI (1936), 318.

yarm: *v.t.* To thrust into, to insert. Sidney Johnson (*The Ozarkian,* Joplin,

Mo., July, 1926, 12) refers to a hillman who *yarmed* a load into his gun. DN, V (1926), 405.

yellow hammer: *n.* One of the names applied to the yellow-shafted flicker, or golden-winged woodpecker (*Colaptes auratus*). It also means, in some sections of the Ozarks, a scrub Jersey calf.

yes-sir-ee-bob: *interj.* A more emphatic affirmation than *yes-sir-ee.* The accent is on *ee* in both cases.

yonkapin (yŏng' kȧ pĭn): *n.* A yellow water lily (*Nelumbo lutea*). It is said that the Indians used to eat the seeds and that *yonkapin* is a Cherokee word. Vardis Fisher (*Children of God* [New York, 1939], 22, 24) has the early settlers in Pennsylvania call water lilies *water-chinquapins* or *wakapins.* DN, III (1906), 165; V (1926), 479.

yonker-pad: *n.* The round, flat leaf of the yonkapin. AS, XI (1936), 318.

yooper (yōōp' ẽr): *interj.* An emphatic affirmative, said to be of Cherokee origin. I have heard it many times near Southwest City, Mo., along the Oklahoma border. "Is that gal purty? *Yooper!*" AS, V (1929), 21. Cf. *scoop-town.*

zephyr: *n.* A woman's wrap or scarf. Usually a knitted or crocheted thing, worn over the head and shoulders. Similar to what used to be called a fascinator. DN, V (1927), 479.

Bibliography

Not many papers on the Ozark dialect have been published. The titles listed below make up the entire literature of the subject, so far as I know. Students who wish to go further will do well to read up on the related speech of the Appalachian highlands, in the writings of Josiah H. Combs, Calvin S. Brown, Horace Kephart, Lester V. Berrey, T. J. Farr, Bess Alice Owens, L. R. Dingus, Joseph Sargent Hall, and Charles Carpenter.

Allison, Vernon C. "On the Ozark Pronunciation of *It*," *American Speech*, Vol. IV (February, 1929), 205–206.

> "The pronoun *it* is pronounced *hit* only when used at the beginning of a clause, or when unusual emphasis is desired. I have yet to hear an Ozark hillman use the word in any other way." Dr. Allison points out several "curious inconsistencies" in my own discussion of this point.

Anonymous. "Sayings, Jokes and Songs Typical of Arkansas Wanted," *Arkansas Gazette*, Little Rock, Ark., May 3, 1942.

> An article listing 93 words and expressions, the result of a week's collecting by Pat Flynn, newspaperman. Flynn was working for the late Gene Howe, a Texas publisher who planned to write a book on the dialect and folklore of Arkansas.

Arnold, Charles. "The Missouri Ozarks as a Field for Regionalism." M.A. thesis, University of Missouri, 1925. Typescript in the University of Missouri library.

> This paper contains a brief discussion of the Ozark dialect (pp. 130–40), with some references to the literature.

Barker, Catherine S. *Yesterday Today, Life in the Ozarks.* Caldwell, Idaho, 1941.

> The author lived at Batesville, Ark., for eleven years, and was a case worker for the Federal Emergency Relief Administration in the nineteen thirties. She knows the country and the people. What she has to say about the dialect (pp. 126–32) is well worth reading.

303

Berrey, Lester V. "Southern Mountain Dialect," *American Speech,* Vol. XV (February, 1940), 45–54.

A general description of Southern Appalachian and Ozark speech, with the emphasis upon pronunciation and survivals. Berrey thinks that the Blue Ridge, the Great Smokies, the Cumberlands, and the Ozarks are pretty much alike, although "the dialect may vary slightly with the locality." He gives several examples of this variation, and ends with a bibliography of 37 titles.

Bess, Charles E. "Podunk in Southeast Missouri," *American Speech,* Vol. X (February, 1935), 80.

Writing from the Junior College of Flat River, Mo., Bess lists some popular place-names applied humorously to backwoods settlements, such as Possum Hollow, Hog Heaven, Rabbit-Skin Hill, Pull-Tight, Puckey-Huddle, Barely-Do, Bugtown, and Hardscrabble.

Bey, Constance, and others. "A Word-List from Missouri," *Publication of the American Dialect Society,* No. 2 (November, 1944), 53–62.

142 words and phrases contributed by thirteen Missourians and one Arkansawyer, members of an English class at the University of Missouri in 1941. Except for half-a-dozen items, some of which may be local creations or "family talk," the material is representative of the Ozark region.

Breckenridge, William Clark. "Books Containing Missouri Dialect," pp. 9-10 in *Books Containing American Local Dialects, a Series of Lists Compiled by the St. Louis Public Library,* St. Louis, 1914.

Breckenridge lists 26 books by 16 authors, with a short paragraph of criticism for each. He thinks the dialect reported by James Newton Baskett, John Monteith, and Harold Bell Wright is good, but denounces most of the others in very blunt language. In reviewing Rose Emmet Young's *Sally of Missouri,* he writes: "The author does not know anything about the dialect of this region, and if she did she would not know how to spell it. The dialect is neither consistent nor correct. The farmers, miners, and others [in Miss Young's book] do not speak the dialect of the Ozarks or anywhere else."

Brewster, Paul G. "More Indiana Sayings," *American Speech,* Vol. XVI (February, 1941), 21–25.

When Professor Brewster taught at the University of Missouri in 1938-41 he checked these Hoosier words and phrases with his students and "indicated by an asterisk each saying which appears to be current in Missouri." 94 of the 238 items are so indicated.

Carr, Joseph William. "A List of Words from Northwest Arkansas," *Dialect Notes,* Vol. II (1904), 416–22.

158 items from the vicinity of Fayetteville, Ark., where the author was a professor in the University of Arkansas. Carr acknowledges his indebtedness to Marion Hughes' *Three Years in Arkansaw* (Chicago, 1904) for

some of his quotations. A few of Carr's terms are new to me. The old-timers I have known often called big black ants *emmets*. But Carr says that *emmet* means an industrious person, and "is never used in the sense of *ant*."

———. "A List of Words from Northwest Arkansas, II," *Dialect Notes,* Vol. III (1905), 68–103.

A word list of 834 entries, plus three pages of valuable "Miscellaneous Notes" on pronunciation, peculiarities of grammar and syntax, folk-etymology, proper names, etc. An important paper.

———. "A List of Words from Northwest Arkansas, III," *Dialect Notes,* Vol. III (1906), 124–65.

1,237 words and phrases, some of which appeared in Carr's earlier papers. A very valuable contribution.

———, and Rupert Taylor. "A List of Words from Northwest Arkansas, IV," *Dialect Notes,* Vol. III (1907), 205–38.

In this paper the authors compare their Arkansas material with that reported in *Dialect Notes* by G. D. Chase, W. E. Mead, W. O. Rice, and D. S. Crumb. They find that 86 northwest Arkansas items are listed also from Cape Cod, 518 from central Connecticut, 337 from southern Illinois, and 418 from southeastern Missouri.

———. "A List of Words from Northwest Arkansas, V," *Dialect Notes,* Vol. III (1909), 392–406.

435 words and phrases, some of which appeared in Carr's previous lists. There are a few words not often heard in Arkansas, most of them contributed by John B. Davis of Chelsea, Okla. Less important perhaps than Carr's papers of 1904, 1905, and 1906, which totaled more than 2,200 items, this is nevertheless a substantial contribution to the study of Ozark speech.

Clemens, Nancy. "The Ozark Language Changes Little," Kansas City *Star,* Kansas City, Mo., August 21, 1938.

A very intelligent newspaper reporter, a native of Cedar County, Mo., discusses 40 old-time turns of speech.

Cralle, Walter C. "Social Change and Isolation in the Ozark Mountain Region of Missouri," *American Journal of Sociology,* Vol. XLI (January, 1936), 435–46.

This is an abstract of a Ph.D. dissertation, University of Minnesota, 1934. The author is a professor at the Southwest Missouri Teachers College, Springfield, Mo., and has considerable first-hand knowledge of the hillfolk. "To find the Ozark dialect," he writes, "one must go into the most isolated communities. Even here the rural teacher, the summer tourist, and the radio have made considerable inroads, especially upon the speech of the younger members of the population." What Dr. Cralle has to say about obsolete words and survivals is worthy of attention.

Criswell, E. H. "Experiment in State-Wide Dialect Collecting," *Publication of the American Dialect Society*, No. 9 (April, 1948), 65–73.

Dean Criswell, of the University of Tulsa, collecting dialect from every part of Oklahoma, enlisted 50 graduate students, school teachers and enthusiastic amateurs to help. The hillfolk in some of the eastern counties are pretty much like those just over the border in Missouri and Arkansas, so Criswell considers the Ozark speech as one of the Oklahoma dialects. Dean Criswell's project is, so far as I know, the first organized attempt to collect such material in this region. His paper is a lively account of the difficulties encountered and the progress made.

Crumb, D. S. "The Dialect of Southeastern Missouri," *Dialect Notes*, Vol. II (1903), 304–37.

A list of 929 words and phrases, collected during thirty years of residence. It is not clear in which counties Crumb worked, but he says (p. 304) that few Negro expressions are included in his list and that "there are very few Negroes in the part of Missouri where I have lived." An important and valuable contribution.

Cushing, Charles Phelps. "The Ozark Dialect," New York *Evening World*, May 28, 1928.

Cushing registers his dissatisfaction with the dialect in the fiction of Harold Bell Wright and Rose Wilder Lane. Also he is disturbed by the differences reported between the Ozark speech and that of the Southern Appalachians. "If the hill speech has been preserved by isolation, and keeps its close kinship to the tongue of the Elizabethans for that reason, why should it suffer a sea-change in crossing the Mississippi?" he asks.

Dale, Edward Everett. "The Speech of the Pioneers," *Arkansas Historical Quarterly*, Vol. VI (Summer, 1947), 117–31.

This piece runs as smoothly as a popular lecture, without any technical terms or learned footnotes, but contains a great amount of valuable information. Dale lists many old sayings about Indians, firearms, hunting, fishing, cooking, farming, courtship, family life, wisecracks, and salty proverbs.

Dorrance, Ward Allison. *We're from Missouri*. Richmond, Mo. 1938.

Two chapters (pp. 17–22 and 31–35) are devoted to the Missouri dialect. The author is a professor at the University of Missouri.

Gentry, Alice Baker. "Folk Expressions," *Arkansas Folklore* (Fayetteville, Ark.), Vol. II (May, 1952), 6.

Some 37 items from a list which Mrs. Gentry, who lives at Berryville, Ark., contributed to the archives of the Arkansas Folklore Society.

Harris, Alberta. "Southern Mountain Dialect," M. A. thesis, Louisiana State University, 1948. Typescript in the University Library, at Baton Rouge.

Having spent her girlhood in Springfield, Mo., where she graduated from Drury College, Miss Harris is now teaching in a Little Rock high school. Her chief interest is in pronunciation. She made some tape recordings near Rogers, Ark., and transcribed the material in the IPA symbols. In this thesis she compares the Ozark speech with that of the Appalachians and the hill country of East Texas.

Harris, Jesse W. "The Dialect of Appalachia in Southern Illinois," *American Speech,* Vol. XXI (April, 1946), 96–99.

Harris says that southern Illinois "belongs to the Ozarks, whose foothills extend across it from east to west. Most of the pioneer inhabitants came either directly from the Appalachian highlands or by way of Kentucky and inland Tennessee." The words and phrases he lists are nearly all heard today in southern Missouri and northern Arkansas.

Lane, Rose Wilder. "On the Ozark Dialect," Springfield, Mo., *Leader,* June 5, 7, 1928.

In these two communications Miss Lane comments upon a letter by Charles Phelps Cushing in the New York *Evening World,* May 28, 1928, which was reprinted in many Missouri newspapers. A resident of Mansfield, Mo., author of several Ozark novels, she points out some of the difficulties encountered by the writer who tries to use the Ozark speech in fiction.

Lincoln, Lewis A. "Ozark Anglo-Saxon," *Ozark Guide* (Eureka Springs, Ark.), Spring, 1946, pp. 323–25.

A rural school teacher in the Arkansas Ozarks, Lincoln discusses 14 "hillbilly" words which may seem strange to the outsider, but which are good English according to *Webster's Dictionary.*

Lyon, Marguerite. *Fresh from the Hills.* Indianapolis, 1945.

Chapter XIV, "Lick Your Calf Over" (pp. 131–37), is a discussion of the Ozark speech, with amusing comments on twenty local words and expressions. The author does a weekly column about the Ozarks for the Chicago *Tribune.* She has lived in the Ozarks for twenty years, and knows the dialect better than many persons who write solemn papers about it.

Masterson, James R. *Tall Tales of Arkansaw.* Boston, 1943.

In Chapter XIII (pp. 180–85) Masterson deals with the controversy over the pronunciation of the word *Arkansas.* See pp. 351–54 for several unexpurgated texts of the famous "Change the Name of Arkansas" speech attributed to Senator Cassius M. Johnson. Dr. Masterson is, so far as I know, the only man who has ever published this masterpiece of American humor without bowdlerizing it.

Mencken, H. L. *The American Language.* 4th ed. New York, 1936.

Mencken has long been interested in the dialect of Missouri and Arkansas. See pp. 308, 359n., 360, 428n., 450n., 462, 463, and 469 for references to the Ozark speech.

———. *The American Language: Supplement I.* New York, 1945.

See pp. 654–55 for a discussion of Ozark euphemisms and taboos. These items, says Mencken, "survive today only in the back-waters of American speech, *e.g.,* dialects of such regions as the Ozarks."

———. *The American Language: Supplement II.* New York, 1948.

For comments and quotations concerning the Ozark speech see pp. 105, 116, 119, 120, 126, 129, 132, 156, 173, 200, 332, 357, 358, 361n., 362n., 366, 378, 379, 380, 385, 387, 391, 482, 485, 592, 593n.

Morris, Robert L. "Readin', a Scene in the Arkansas Ozarks," *University Review* (University of Kansas City, Mo.), Winter, 1936, 125–34.

A one-act play in dialect. Dr. Morris is a professor of English at the University of Arkansas. Note his introductory remarks (p. 125) on the Ozark pronunciation.

———. "More Ozark Speech," *American Speech,* Vol. XXIII (October-December, 1948), 304–305.

Morris gives 25 samples of the spoken and written language of his students, remarking that "their vocabulary continues to show traces of local origin."

Morrison, Estelle Rees. "You-All Again," *American Speech,* Vol. IV (October, 1928), 54–55.

Miss Morrison says positively that she has heard *you-all* as a singular, in Missouri and elsewhere. Cf. her earlier paper (*American Speech,* Vol. II [December, 1926] 133) on *you-all* in the singular as a polite form.

Nelson, Joseph. *Backwoods Teacher.* Philadelphia, 1949.

Nelson is a native Arkansawyer who taught a rural school near the Missouri border in the early nineteen forties. This book contains much valuable information about the Ozark speech. See pp. 32, 46, 60, 61–64, 105–106, 109, 116, 124, 129, 132, 133–34, 137, 140, 162, 171, 185, 192–93, 200, 215, 242, and 284.

Oklahoma: A Guide to the Sooner State. Norman, 1941.

This is one of the official state guidebooks compiled by the Federal Writers' Program of the WPA in the nineteen thirties. See p. 121 for some remarks about the speech of eastern Oklahoma: "Hill folk are apt to say *et* for ate, and follow the cockney English custom of dropping or adding the aspirate. *You'ns, they'ns* and *nary-uns* are in general use, as are *I taken* and *I done.* The Elizabethan *quote* is often a substitute for echo, *sorry* means inferior, and *evenin'* is any time between noon and dusk." As Mencken says (*American Language: Supplement II,* 199–200): "In the speech of the lowly Okies there is little to distinguish it from that of the adjacent wilds, especially the Ozark regions of Missouri and Arkansas."

Perkins, T. W. "You-All Again," *American Speech,* Vol. VI (April, 1931), 304–305.

Perkins points out that Charles Morrow Wilson, "who prides himself on his birth and bringing up in the Arkansas hill country," makes one of his backwoods characters (*Acres of Sky* [New York, 1930], 157) use *you-all* as a singular.

308

Bibliography

Picinich, Donald George. *A Pronunciation Guide to Missouri Place-Names*. Columbia, Mo., 1951.

This is No. 3, Vol. LII of the *University of Missouri Bulletin*. It gives the pronunciation of more than 700 names, with IPA and simplified respelling in parallel columns. Useful in connection with the monumental place-name study carried out by Professor Robert L. Ramsay and his students, which required twenty years and covers every county in the state.

Randolph, Vance. "A Word-List from the Ozarks," *Dialect Notes*, Vol. V (1926), 397–405.

133 words and phrases from McDonald, Barry, Stone, and Taney counties, Mo.; Benton, Washington, Carroll, and Boone counties, Ark.

———. "More Words from the Ozarks," *Dialect Notes*, Vol. V (1927), 472–80.

A word list of 148 items.

———. "The Ozark Dialect in Fiction," *American Speech*, Vol. II (March, 1927), 283–89.

An examination of the dialect writing in fifteen Ozark novels, from 1844 to 1925.

———. "The Grammar of the Ozark Dialect," *American Speech*, Vol. III (October, 1927), 1–12.

A preliminary study, much of which is incorporated in Chapter III of this book.

———. "Verbal Modesty in the Ozarks," *Dialect Notes*, Vol. VI (1928), 57–65.

Much of this material was reprinted in *The Ozarks*, pp. 78–86, and many items appear in Chapter V of this book.

———. "Literary Words in the Ozarks," *American Speech*, Vol. IV (October, 1928), 56–57.

This paper lists 48 words not often used by illiterates in other sections of the country.

———. "A Possible Source of Some Ozark Neologisms," *American Speech*, Vol. IV (December, 1928), 116–17.

The role of the village half-wit or "joky feller" in producing local peculiarities of speech. Cf. Frank K. Sechrist (*Pedagogical Seminary*, Vol. XX [December, 1913], 422).

———. "Is There an Ozark Dialect?" *American Speech*, Vol. IV (February, 1929), 203–204.

———. "A Third Ozark Word-List," *American Speech*, Vol. V (October, 1929), 16–22.

Here are 101 words and phrases from southwest Missouri and northwest Arkansas.

———. "Recent Fiction and the Ozark Dialect," *American Speech*, Vol. VI (August, 1931), 425–29.

An examination of the dialect in eight Ozark novels, from 1927 to 1931.

———. *The Ozarks, an American Survival of Primitive Society*. New York, 1931.

Chapter IV (pp. 67–86) is devoted to the Ozark speech.

———. "A Fourth Ozark Word-List," *American Speech*, Vol. VIII (February, 1933), 47–53.

Contains 208 words and phrases.

———, and Nancy Clemens. "A Fifth Ozark Word-List," *American Speech*, Vol. XI (December, 1936), 314–18.

This includes 134 items from McDonald, Barry, Stone, and Taney counties, Mo.; Benton, Washington, Carroll, and Boone counties, Ark.

———, and Patti Sankee. "Dialectal Survivals in the Ozarks," *American Speech*, Vol. V (February, 1930), 198–208; Vol. V (April, 1930), 264–70; Vol. V (June, 1930), 424–30.

———, and Anna A. Ingleman. "Pronunciation in the Ozark Dialect," *American Speech*, Vol. III, (June, 1928), 401–408.

Rascoe, Burton. "A Bookman's Daybook," New York *Sun*, October 30, 1931.

Rascoe once lived in Seminole County, Okla., and recalls that the Oklahoma hills are full of Ozarkers and their descendants. His remarks about the dialect are interesting, particularly the reference to *you-uns* or *you-ens*. See also a letter headed "You-uns and You-all," signed "Missourian," New York *Sun*, November 5, 1931. Rascoe returns to the subject in his column in the *Sun*, November 21, 1931.

Rayburn, Otto Ernest. *Ozark Country*. New York, 1941.

Rayburn has lived in the Ozarks since 1920, and has written many newspaper and magazine articles about the hillfolk. This book is the fourth volume of the "American Folkways" series edited by Erskine Caldwell, and it is Rayburn's best work. See pp. 10, 16, 43–44, and 49 for references to the Ozark dialect.

———. "Heard in the Ozarks," *Ozark Guide* (Lonsdale, Ark.), Summer, 1945, p. 69.

17 samples of the sayings and proverbs which Rayburn has collected over a term of years. This material, with two additional items, is reprinted in *Ozark Guide* (Eureka Springs, Ark.), Autumn, 1950, p. 41.

Read, Allen Walker. "The Strategic Position of Missouri in Dialect Study," *The Missouri Alumnus*, Vol. XX (April, 1932), 231–32. Reprinted as "Folk-Speech in Missouri," *Arcadian Magazine*, June, 1932, p. 13–14.

Reviewed in *Missouri Historical Review,* Vol. XXVI (July, 1932), 426–27.

A brief survey of the literature dealing with dialect in Missouri, with a paragraph listing the persons who have published word lists and the like. There are several references to Mark Twain's writings, also to Monteith's novel *Parson Brooks* and Weeks' *Hound-Tuner of Callaway.* Read wonders what the "dialectologists" working on the *Dialect Atlas* will find when they get to Missouri.

———. "The Basis of Correctness in the Pronunciation of Place-Names," *American Speech,* Vol. VIII (February, 1933), 42–46.

Concerned largely with the controversy over the pronunciation of the name *Arkansas.* An important study, with rich documentation.

———. "Pronunciation of the Word 'Missouri'," *American Speech,* Vol. VIII (December, 1933), 22–36.

A fine paper with many references and quotations. Read ends by pointing out that the Missourians themselves have determined the pronunciation, rather than "so-called authorities" outside the state. The "defensible pronunciations" all have the *z* sound rather than the hissing *s.*

———. "Attitudes Toward Missouri Speech," *Missouri Historical Review,* Vol. XXIX (July, 1935), 259–71.

This is Read's best work on the subject, fully documented, with quotations from little known books and papers. He says that "the character of Missouri speech was determined by the particular mixture of the dialects brought from east of the Mississippi River. Of these, the Southern predominated." (p. 261.) Missouri has received more attention than most states in language study "because the Ozarks, which make a *speech-pocket,* contain such rich, rewarding material." (p. 264.) Read mentions, in his footnotes and annotations, all the publications on the Ozark dialect available at the time this article was written.

Rice, W. O. "The Pioneer Dialect of Southern Illinois," *Dialect Notes,* Vol. II (1902), 225–49.

A word list of more than 700 items from Union County, Ill., where Rice lived for forty years. Many of the peculiarities of speech noted in his paper are common today in southern Missouri and northwest Arkansas.

Starr, Fred. *From an Ozark Hillside.* Siloam Springs, Ark., 1938.

This book is made up of extracts from Starr's weekly column in the *Northwest Arkansas Times,* Fayetteville, Ark. One section (pp. 35–39) is entitled "Ozark Hillbilly Lingo." Starr lists 37 odd words, pronunciations, and expressions. He reports three nouns—*losel, moldwarp,* and *dorts* —which I have not heard in the Ozarks.

Strainchamps, Ethel Reed. "An Ozarker's Reaction to Formal Language," *American Speech,* Vol. XXIII (October-December, 1948), 262–65.

This author lived among the hillfolk of Polk and McDonald counties,

Mo., and later moved to the mining town of Joplin, Mo. She makes some penetrating comments about the differences between the speech of the rural areas and that of the Ozark towns. *You'ns* is common in the lower economic groups, she says, while *"y'all* is used only by the upper classes." Miss Strainchamps finds that "the hillbillies still talk much the same as they did when I was a child," and she was born in 1911. A brief but very valuable and stimulating paper.

———. "The Ozark Dialect Still Resists Change," St. Louis *Post-Dispatch,* St. Louis, Mo., April 30, 1952.

Reprinted in the *Arkansas Gazette,* Little Rock, Ark., May 4, 1952.

Taylor, Jay L. B. "Snake County Talk," *Dialect Notes,* Vol. V (1923), 197–225.

A list of 829 items from McDonald County, Mo., with a three-page introduction written in dialect. Mr. Taylor is a native of Nebraska, but lived near Pineville, Mo., for many years. This is the first word list ever published from southwest Missouri. It is a sound and important contribution to our knowledge of the Ozark speech.

———. "In Defense of His People," *Missouri Magazine* (Jefferson City, Mo.), Feb., 1938, pp. 9–11.

Mr. Taylor calls attention to numerous errors in my dialect papers. Cf. *American Speech,* Vol. III (June, 1928), 401–408; Vol. IV (October, 1928), 56–57; Vol. V (February, 1930), 198–208.

Thanet, Octave. "Folklore in Arkansas," *Journal of American Folklore,* Vol. V (1892), 121–25.

Octave Thanet was a popular novelist, whose real name was Alice French. She spent many winters in Lawrence County, Ark., and was fascinated by the "Arkansas dialect." Miss French noted archaic words and phrases, which were used by Shakespeare and other Elizabethans. She says that the Arkansawyers pronounce *been* "in the old way, as it is spelled." I have heard *been* rhymed with *seen,* but it is not a common pronunciation in the Ozarks nowadays.

Tozer, Geraldine. "The Ozark Dialect," M. A. thesis, University of Kansas, 1932. Typescript in the University library at Lawrence, Kansas.

The introduction to this thesis includes brief sections on Ozark grammar and pronunciation, with 30 quotations from Chaucer and many samples of the dialect as used by modern novelists and rhymesters. There is a glossary of 1293 items, mostly from books and from word lists in *Dialect Notes* and *American Speech.*

Warner, James H. "A Word List from Southeast Arkansas," *American Speech,* Vol. XIII (February, 1938), 3–7.

Sixty-five items collected at the Agricultural & Mechanical College, Monticello, Ark.

Bibliography

Weeks, Raymond L. "Notes from Missouri," *Dialect Notes*, Vol. I (1892), 235–42.

> This paper is divided into two parts: "Peculiar Words and Usages" and "Pronunciation and Grammatical Points." It represents "the rustic dialect in Jackson County, Mo.," but includes many items common to the Ozark region. Weeks was head of the Department of Romance Languages at the University of Missouri. Cf. his *The Hound-Tuner of Callaway* (New York, 1927), a collection of tales about the early days in Missouri. Note especially Professor Weeks' remarks about the dialect, pp. 208, 259.

Wentworth, Harold. *American Dialect Dictionary*. New York, 1944.

> Wentworth gives considerable attention to the Ozark region and quotes from many books about Missouri and Arkansas. He includes most of the items reported in *Dialect Notes* and *American Speech* by Raymond L. Weeks, D. S. Crumb, Joseph W. Carr, Rupert Taylor, Charles Morrow Wilson, Allen Walker Read, Nancy Clemens, and other workers in this field.

Whaley, Storm. *They Call It: A Guide to the Pronunciation of Arkansas Place Names*. Siloam Springs, Ark., 1951.

> Published by the Associated Press for the use of radio announcers, this book indicates by IPA symbols and simplified respelling the pronunciation of some 1500 names. The keys and parallel column arrangement are identical with those used in Donald George Picinich's *Pronunciation Guide to Missouri Place Names*.

Williams, Walter. "Missouri Dialect of High-Born Origin," *Missouri Magazine* (Jefferson City, Mo.), December, 1928, pp. 7, 25.

> "The Missouri dialect is the finest flowering of the English language," says Williams, president of the University of Missouri. Many Missouri expressions which seem odd to outsiders are survivals of older English, "the speech of Oxford and Cambridge and of Stratford-on-Avon." He gives 24 examples of archaic words and pronunciations. President Williams thinks that the Missouri dialect is full of seventeenth-century expressions because the early Missourians were fond of reading "a certain Old Book," by which he means the King James version of the Bible.

Williamson, Thames. "The Novelist's Use of Dialect," *The Writer*, January, 1935, 3–5, 28, 40.

> This article was written shortly after Williamson completed *The Woods Colt*, an Ozark novel heavily loaded with dialect. The author describes his difficulties with Ozark speech, and advises other novelists to employ dialect very sparingly.

Wilson, Charles Morrow. "Elizabethan America," *Atlantic Monthly*, Vol. CXLIV (August, 1929), 238–44.

> Wilson writes of the Appalachians as well as "the Ozark hills of southern Missouri, northwestern Arkansas, and the southeastern tip of Okla-

homa." The first two pages are devoted to the dialect, with particular attention to Elizabethan survivals.

———. "Beefsteak When I'm Hungry," *Virginia Quarterly Review,* Vol. VI (April, 1930), 240–50.

A fine popular article about the speech of the Great Smokies, the Blue Ridge, the Cumberlands, and the Ozarks. The so-called mountain dialect, says Wilson, "is probably the most sparklingly fascinating segment of current American speech."

———. "Ozark Dialect Dates Back to Chaucer," St. Louis *Post-Dispatch,* June 9, 1930.

"A majority of the usages prevalent among farming people of the Ozarks hark back to illustrious precedents," writes Wilson. He cites 112 words and phrases, many of which are certainly archaisms.

———. "Friendly Days in the Ozarks," *Travel Magazine,* March, 1933, pp. 18–21, 45.

"Hill speech," says Wilson, "is a survival and not a corruption of the language of other centuries." He lists about 50 dialect items (pp. 21, 45), most of them obsolete or archaic English words and expressions.

———. "Ozarkadia," *American Magazine,* January, 1934, pp. 58–60, 112.

Even in a popular magazine article about the Ozark region, Wilson seldom fails to discuss the dialect and its honorable antecedants, mentioning Chaucer, Hakluyt, Piers Plowman, Sir Philip Sidney, and the speech of Old England before the Battle of Hastings. In this story (p. 60) he devotes nearly a column to such matters.

———. *Backwoods America.* Chapel Hill, N. C., 1934.

This book deals in part with the Appalachians, but the emphasis throughout is upon the Arkansas hill country where the author was born and raised. Chapter VII (pp. 61–71) is entitled "Backwoods Language" and contains much material from Wilson's magazine and newspaper articles.

Wilson, George P. "The Value of Dialect," *Publication of the American Dialect Society,* No. 11 (April, 1949), 38–59.

Professor Wilson's paper does not deal specifically with the Ozark speech, but it contains many passages which should be read in connection with this book, particularly chapters IV and V.

Wilt, Napier. "Ozark Words Again," *American Speech,* Vol. XII (October, 1937), 234–35.

A brief criticism of the word list which Nancy Clemens and I published in *American Speech,* Vol. XI (December, 1936), 314–18.

Index

This index includes terms explained in the text and the names of persons quoted or referred to at some length there, but not all names and folk terms in the Preface and Chapters 1–8 have been listed, for to have made an all-inclusive index would have resulted in an unwieldy and impractical mass of material. Since the Word List and Bibliography are already arranged alphabetically, nothing from these sections has been indexed.

Index

UNIVERSITY OF OKLAHOMA PRESS

NORMAN